Praise for *Working the Blue Lines*

Jean-Michel Blais takes the reader through a lifetime of principled decision-making in both his professional and personal leadership experience....Blais uses the teachings of the great historical philosophers and ethicists to show the timelessness of empathy, integrity, honesty, accountability and fairness as we go through life's journey. A worthy read!

JPR Murray, Commissioner (Retired)
Royal Canadian Mounted Police

A must-read for those who want to improve their leadership skills...Unfortunately, I have met a few Marlos in my professional career, and this book is an excellent reference for handling these "delicate" situations. I also love the "Calls from the blue line" summarizing the important points of each chapter. Félicitations, Jean-Michel!

Brigadier General Martin Girard, Canadian Army (retired),
former Chief of Military Staff,
United Nations Stabilization Mission in Haiti

Experience is a treasure, especially the tough time which increases our willpower, gives us lessons and teaches us to know ourselves and know the world...These tremendous experiences constantly improved and developed Mr. Blais' leadership.

Leadership does not exclusively belong to those in positions of authority. It can be learned and developed intentionally through our day-to-day life....The key is to be a person with conscience, to live with passion and a growth mindset to draw lessons and sum up the experiences from the little things in life, while learning from others to overcome our human flaws.

Neil Xia, Former Chinese National Police Officer
and United Nations Peacekeeper

That which makes organizations perform well is not found merely in the policies or the playbooks, but rather from the inspiration and insight of those who are called to lead.

Noel C. March, former United States Marshal

How Jean-Michel connects his leadership experience with life, hockey, and law enforcement will give you an idea of the small things you could do each day to help others, through a career in law enforcement or in everyday life.

Will Black, former US law enforcement officer
and UN police peacekeeper

Cover design: Rebekah Wetmore
Author's photo courtesy of Dalhousie University
Editor: Andrew Wetmore

ISBN: 978-1-990187-32-2
First edition May, 2022

MOOSE HOUSE
PUBLICATIONS

2475 Perotte Road
Annapolis County, NS
B0S 1A0

moosehousepress.com
info@moosehousepress.com

We live and work in Mi'kma'ki, the ancestral and unceded territory of the Mi'kmaw people. This territory is covered by the "Treaties of Peace and Friendship" which Mi'kmaw and Wolastoqiyik (Maliseet) people first signed with the British Crown in 1725. The treaties did not deal with surrender of lands and resources but in fact recognized Mi'kmaq and Wolastoqiyik (Maliseet) title and established the rules for what was to be an ongoing relationship between nations. We are all Treaty people.

Preface

I wrote this book from mid-2020 to early 2022, during a period of disruption involving cascading international crises. We all lived the worldwide COVID-19 pandemic, resulting in the infection and death of so many people, the accompanying stress and despair that put individuals and whole communities on edge and created unparalleled economic fallout and political division. We witnessed the international groundswell of criticism towards policing and social unrest following the murder of George Floyd. We lived through an acrimonious American presidential election and a turbulent transition. We all watched with horror the Russian invasion of Ukraine.

We also saw more-localized emergencies such as the massive explosion in Beirut and a plague of a different kind, with billions of locusts affecting several east-African nations, threatening food sources in an area of the globe already dealing with developmental challenges.

Regardless of where we lived, the 2020-2022 period will be studied for many reasons, not least for how we humans struggled with these and so many other issues.

We also witnessed the challenges leaders of all stripes had to deal with, including politicians, businesspersons and first responders. Some leaders demonstrated visionary governance, dealing effectively with the complexity they faced. Others were unable to rise to the task, unwilling to overcome their egos or immobilized by the enormity of the job and responsibilities at hand. It's thanks to the successful leaders who guided and directed governments, businesses and communities through these challenging times—and through other past periods of uncertainty—that we've been able to learn and grow from them.

So, with that in mind, this book is, first and foremost, a work of gratitude to those people.

Life has a way of teaching us important lessons that almost always come from our interactions with others. Interactions with people let us form meaningful relationships, experience significant events and feel diverse emotions. This is the human condition, a part of which I was fortunate enough to live and contribute to as a police officer for over thirty years and as an ice hockey referee for over sixteen (and counting). But it's not been without its moments of stress, frustration and pain which, by their intensity and frequency, added even more to the relentless learning experience that is life.

That's why I'm grateful. I want to start this book by acknowledging the people I've met and seen in action who have demonstrated the best and, at times, even the worst in human nature. They've supplied me with a wealth of material from which to learn and write. I'm also grateful for the lessons that I obtained through readings provided by many authors, past and present. I've learned so much from their teachings that I've actively applied during my careers as a police officer and hockey official. Regardless of who they are and how they contributed, be it through positive or especially negative examples, in person, or in writing, I am grateful for their contributions.

The dichotomy of such lessons reflects the continual challenges of living in society and the recognition that, as the Polish social psychologist Henri Tajfel observed, humans are social and antisocial beings at the same time. People are social beings because they like to belong to groups. They're also antisocial beings because they don't like members of other groups. I fully suspect that I, too, have demonstrated comparable tendencies towards others; on occasion, even showing the best and the worst that I had to offer them.

This dual-edged reality reveals the notion that we enjoy life through the help and society of others. We also suffer in life because of the machinations, mean-spiritedness and sheer stupidity of some of the same people. How we decide to deal with the authentic and the impostors alike determines our successes and failures in life. For that reason, I'm grateful for the opportunity to have witnessed some incredible things, learned from some exceptional people and compiled those lessons for others to appreciate.

Leadership and complexity management are vast areas requiring a sober, mindful analysis and intentional application to fully understand, counter and even benefit from the challenges that abound in life. I'm cognizant of the contributions of former British police officer and present Temple University professor Jerry Ratcliffe through his numerous works, including his *Evidence Hierarchy*, in which he lists police chief memoirs at the lowest level of evidence for policy decision-making.[1] I can't say that I disagree with him; he places in that same category quotes from academia and infomercials.

My goal is not to provide policy advice. While I haven't written a doctoral thesis, I won't be selling any device to straighten and whiten teeth or absorb ten times its weight in water, either.

But there is significant value to gain from the lessons of others, especially from those who have actually led or attempted to lead in crises, and not just from those who only studied, reported on or critiqued the actions of others. I hope that you'll benefit from my (sometimes) hard-earned lessons while thinking about what truly is essential in your own life, all the while being grateful for the continual opportunities that present themselves to become a better leader. Do this with the knowledge that if you can lead others, you can improve life for them, yourself, your family, friends, neighbors and strangers, regardless of the challenges out there.

Do this to make the life you lead the best one possible, as precious as a work of art.

JMB

To my children:
Tori, Beca and Jean-Cédéric

Chief Davies,
on behalf of the entire
team at Forest Green, please
enjoy this read.

Jill Blais

Contents

Preface...3

Introduction..11

1: The lesson of randomness and complexity....................27

2: The lesson of scanning..66

3: The lesson of self-knowledge......................................100

4: The lesson of hubris...118

5: The lesson of character...137

6: The lesson of bias...168

7: The lesson of human nature..192

8: The lesson of conflict...221

9: The lesson of influence...250

10: The lesson of personal sustainability........................290

Select bibliography..339

Acknowledgements..343

About the author..345

Notes...347

JM Blais

Introduction

On the last day of grade six, my teacher distributed achievement awards: those beige felt patches with a one- or two-word description of an area of recognized work from the school year. That day he gave me four, for track & field, composition, citizenship and leadership. I guess they were intended for people to display on the sleeve of a jacket or a kitchen bulletin board.

Mine never made it that far, eventually being relegated to a box of keepsakes. But at that moment, I was pleased to be recognized in front of my classmates by my teacher. Before leaving school that day, I proudly showed them to the principal, Mr. St. John, where he stood at the front entrance bidding everyone a good summer.

John St. John was a tall, balding, gentle, yet imposing figure who spoke calmly and authoritatively. When he engaged people, everyone, including me, listened intently. He asked me which patch I thought was the most important.

Frankly, I didn't understand what citizenship or leadership were, and my track & field patch was more for playing games than anything else, as far as I was concerned. After a few moments of reflection, I meekly pointed to the composition patch; I had received some good marks for a few short stories I had enjoyed writing that year.

Mr. St. John smiled understandingly and gently took the leadership patch from my hand. He told me that, even if I didn't yet understand what leadership was, it would become the single, most important skill I would develop in my life.

I left the conversation still unaware of what leadership was, but I did understand that it was something pretty darn important.

As I continued my education through middle school, high school and eventually college, I began to understand what Mr. St. John had meant. Not only did I see the value of leadership from an intellectual perspective, but I also saw its relevance as I became more involved in organized sports, with student groups and especially in the workplace.

I started my work life as a paperboy, delivering copies of the Toronto Star. Then I became a grocery store clerk, a mobile disc jockey, a theatre cleaner, a bartender, a restaurant server in Montreal and finally a cab driver in Toronto for 16 months before I eventually became a police officer.

During this progression, I saw people in influential positions with significant responsibility succeed and fail as leaders. I even saw some people recognize, appreciate and reward negative traits as hallmarks of leadership.

As a police officer, I remember my feeling of utter disbelief when I learned that a group of young-adult students had picked Adolf Hitler as a leader worthy of study because he had achieved, in their minds, great things. These students were not rabid anti-Semites or closet Nazis, but simply did not understand that leadership required doing something positive instead of just doing anything.

Thanks to such intellectually humbling experiences, I slowly came to understand what leadership is, and mostly what it isn't. I also learned that leadership isn't management. They are separate, albeit related activities, but they aren't the same thing.

Management is having the authority, responsibility and accountability for systems, structures and processes. This implies that a manager's most important traits are technical knowledge and skills, which a person can learn, develop and master over time.

On the other hand, in the workplace and elsewhere, leadership is having the authority, responsibility and accountability for people. Leaders are primarily responsible for their subordinates' performance and well-being. The goal of leadership isn't getting the most out of people but getting the best out of them. And because leadership deals with people instead of things, a leader's essential traits are their character and the wisdom they demonstrate through action. Wisdom is acquired through experience; it can be and is developed over time, guided by people and events. However, character cannot be learned; it's formed through our individual choices, often in response to adversity.

These were important distinctions I tried to keep in mind as I climbed the ranks in policing.

I did recognize, though, the undeniable link between leadership and management. Management and leadership are complementary skill sets. Like a two-strand rope, when you combine them, their collective strength is greater than their individual force.

Because of this symbiotic relationship, both tend to be static in their approaches, especially when people regard leadership as a role, position or individual competency. But leadership must be dynamic, and even asymmetrical at times. Asymmetry refers to the quality of being irregular and uneven, and in this sense capable of adapting to any given situation.

As a result of the Severe Acute Respiratory Syndrome Coronavirus 2 (SARS-CoV-2 or COVID-19) pandemic and the increasing availability of technological solutions, the workplace is evolving from a traditional in-person, office-based environment to remote teams and individuals. The skill sets. for managers and leaders alike in such a new context have also adjusted, emphasizing organizational skills and abilities that facilitate connections at a distance between colleagues, partners, stakeholders and clients. Hence the constant dynamic adaptation of leadership to the times.

To succeed in any business, we require both management and leadership because leadership without management is chaos, while management without leadership results in a lack of direction and apathy. We have all seen great managers who are poor leaders. They may know management success but fail miserably in their leadership. We have also seen great leaders with no management skills. They may influence people but get nothing done.

What we want to avoid is "corporate personality disorder," in which good people are simultaneously crushed by poor leadership or poor management through bad planning, bad policies and even worse execution.[2] Leadership success, then, is continually facing and effectively dealing with the demands of reality, events and people.

Leadership has four basic features.

First, leadership involves influencing others. It requires us to inspire and encourage people to do something in the future, whether immediate or far-off. And we can only achieve that persuasion of others through leadership's second feature, trust.

Trust is the subjective conviction others hold that we're working in their best interests. People won't allow us to influence them if they don't feel physically and psychologically safe, believing what we say and especially what we do.

The third feature is that leadership, as influence through trust, is intended to achieve some higher good. Best expressed by the Latin expression ad meliora ("towards better things"), this feature distinguishes true leaders from the despots, the ideologues, the hucksters and the shills out there.

Finally, because we're dealing with people who can sometimes be irrational and unpredictable, leadership must not be a static exercise confined to a specific role, position or competency. Leadership must be dynamic in its application, approach and especially adaptation to the environment to which we apply it. The key to leadership is not to just interpret the world around us, but to actually change it.

In 2019, a few months after I retired as chief of police, I attended a police educator conference. The group included civilians and sworn police officers of all ranks, including senior managers, deputy chiefs and a few active chiefs. They shared a joint commitment to learning and continued professional development, primarily through e-learning and the application of newer technologies and techniques.

During one engaging presentation by a retired municipal chief on leadership, a serving chief from a small town stood up to ask a question. He wanted some guidance about leadership: was it science, or was it art? Essentially, he was looking to qualify leadership so he could understand and eventually measure it accurately. If it were science, we should be able to measure leadership's effects and, in his opinion, as we have often heard, what's measured can be improved.

Because leadership involves mobilizing people from one idea, point or situation to another, I always thought that leadership contained elements of both science and art. This was because even individuals who didn't have any recognized authority, such as colleagues, neighbors, teammates, siblings and even strangers could still demonstrate leadership of others using different techniques, some based on facts, others on creative persuasion.

It was then that I realized that it was neither. As much as various authors, including me, can lay claim to discovering the rules, habits, principles, laws and elements of leadership, there's no single unifying formula applicable in all situations. This is because of the diversity of people, personalities, and problems that we come across in our respective worlds.

Leadership certainly can't stand up to rigorous scientific examination like the laws of physics or thermodynamics. Science is intended to disconfirm ideas and notions as often as it confirms them. In this sense, science is exclusionary: it excludes things that don't make sense. But we can't really evaluate leadership through exclusion alone.

Conversely, leadership isn't uniquely an art form either, although some highly charismatic and artful types have achieved influential positions and results. It seemed that the answer to the chief's question lay somewhere in between science and art: leadership is a means of change, innovation and fusion.

I came to see leadership as part science and part art, a form of modern-day alchemy that relied not on any one feature but an entire suite of them. As modern alchemy, leadership is an act or series of acts of transformation, creation and combination.

When we hear the word alchemy, we think of magic, a bespectacled young sorcerer transforming base metals into gold. Alchemists were, in a way, the precursors to modern chemists. The word alchemy comes from the Old French word alquemie, itself derived from the Arabic word al-kimiya, meaning 'composed of two parts'. So perhaps if leadership is neither science nor art, it's a modern form of behavioral alchemy, the intention of which is to blend science and art to form a catalyst that can influence people.

Most importantly, leadership involves doing something to bring about change and create something good with others' help.

Climbing the ranks in policing and, to a lesser extent, in ice hockey officiating, afforded me the chance to further realize that leadership, in and of itself, is simply not enough to succeed in life, be it at work, in sports, or with a family. As we've seen, leadership cannot be a one-size-fits-all proposition, either.

The level of complexity that bedevils our society today results in leadership being only part of the equation, albeit an important one. The other part of that equation is embracing, contending with and managing complexity. It doesn't mean learning to master all technologies or the intricacies of the processes we encounter daily, but learning to understand how they guide and impact our actions and those of the people we interact with and try to influence. From those interactions, we learn how individuals behave and how we can work with them to achieve ordinary and not-so-ordinary things. And for me, nowhere in society is that more prevalent than in policing.

Policing is much more than the enforcement of laws, public service or community protection. Policing is dealing with problems and challenges that people themselves cannot, will not, or should not deal with. Whether it's stopping a speeder on a highway, responding to calls for help in unusual predicaments or intervening in a criminal matter, police are often the only people able and mandated to solve those problems. Police must often intervene in situations in which people experience the worst moments of their lives: mental-health crises, significant loss, accidents, and disasters of all kinds provoked by themselves, others or their immediate environment.

Police officers and police employees at all levels, including call-takers, dispatchers, analysts, communicators, administrative and front-counter staff, are problem-solving community contributors who focus on reactive and upstream proactive social solutions. Individually and collectively, police officers and employees respond to and solve problems in their communities that often have nothing to do with public safety. In many jurisdictions, police operate 24/7, unlike any other non-first-responder public or private-sector service. Quite often, and especially in many rural and isolated communities around the world, police are the only consistent representatives of state sovereignty or government services. No wonder they're called upon to deal with problems outside of their primary mission of law enforcement.

At worst, police are subject to intense media and community scrutiny, even reviled by some, as well as regularly experiencing fatigue, trauma and work-related dangers. At best, citizens and colleagues alike revere them, and they take pride in building relationships that help others solve problems, thereby enhancing public safety and welfare. Hence the recent recognition of community safety and well-being in policing as opposed to serving and protecting as policing's primary mission.

Police officers bring three unique attributes to any situation: specific legal authorities, dedicated training and specialized equipment. Those attributes change and evolve as the level of complexity shifts in our society, as new laws are adopted, as learning needs evolve, as social mores change and as technology progresses. Because of the increased complexity of life, policing, as a microcosm of that very life, has slowly morphed into an intellectual pursuit that involves continually absorbing new knowledge, and translating and operationalizing it to fit the moment's needs.

This often occurs on the fly. Unlike the military, which for the most part, in peacetime, operates in a stable training environment broken up by occasional bouts of intense operational deployment, policing exists in an almost-exclusively operational climate, broken up by periods of condensed, intense training. The opportunities to reset in such a working environment are few and far between.

Like many of their non-police counterparts in the public and private sectors, effective police leaders must be dynamic and asymmetric in their approaches, open to constant evaluation and adjustment, all the while swimming in complexity and frequent conflict. To this mix, we must add innovation. As innovation is applied creativity, leaders must also see and be open to using new ideas, not just participating in brainstorming or sterile notional creation. And that means problem-solving through better decision-making, especially under moments and times of stress and uncertainty.

I further realized that policing and refereeing hockey shared some common features. Both involve enforcing predetermined rules. Like police officers, on-ice hockey officials (referees and linespersons) have specific authorities, dedicated training and specialized equipment such as uniforms, protective gear and even whistles for communicating. Most importantly, hockey officials are on the ice during the game, not in some ivory-tower-like broadcast booth, safely commenting on the play. They have much to lose should they make a wrong decision, including their credibility and even health if they become injured during play, which in my case occurred more than a few times. That's because they have skin in the game, risking something during the process.

Police officers and hockey officials must also remain impartial: they must apply the rules fairly and equitably while actively resolving situations as they arise. In hockey, the term is "game management," which means ensuring that things don't get out of control and that both teams play the game out safely and fairly.

Linespersons have territorial responsibilities that, amongst other things, are focused on the blue lines, those lines that define the zones of the teams defending their respective goals. The two linespersons must ensure that no offensive player enters the defensive zone before the puck does, creating an offside situation and an automatic stoppage of play. If this occurs, play resumes through a faceoff, the dropping of the puck by a linesperson, outside the blue line, between two players, one from each team. The linesperson's work of enforcing offsides, having the correct positioning and making the right calls is, in hockey jargon, "working the blue line." This also calls up allusions to the Blue Line of policing.

In policing, the actual term is the "Thin Blue Line." Not unlike the positioning of a linesperson in hockey, it refers figuratively to the position of police in society as they attempt to ensure that people remain onside of the laws so that peace and order reign and society and individuals can evolve and prosper.

The term began as a reference to the famous "Thin Red Line" of the British 93rd Highland Regiment of Foot who, dressed in their red tunics, stood their ground against an intense Russian cavalry charge at the Battle of Balaclava in 1854 during the Crimean War. The term "Thin Blue Line" first appeared in 1911 in a poem by Nels Dickmann Anderson in his book *The Voice of the Infinite, and other poems*, referring to the United

States Army, whose uniforms were blue in the late 18th and 19th centuries. In the 1950s and 1960s, its use morphed into a reference to American police services because of their uniforms' predominant color.

The concept hasn't been without its share of controversy in light of the murder of George Floyd and other events that have shaken community trust in policing. But, regardless of how it's displayed and the interpretations people assign to it, the reference 'Blue Line' is still synonymous with police services across most of the Western world.

So, working the blue line refers to both policing and hockey officiating. From that perspective, this book intends to provide leaders of all stripes who deal with significant personal, social and workplace challenges the tools to deal with the complexity that abounds in our society. It also aims to help them manage their game as effectively as possible by making the right calls and decisions. The goal is to develop the skills necessary to influence others through trust to achieve some higher good, regardless of the objectives, game or situation. That higher good can help community members avoid crime as a victim, witness or perpetrator, keeping a team focused on a particular goal or assisting others in their lifelong objectives.

~

This is not a 'tell-all' book, where I expose the secrets entrusted in me as an agent of the 'states', first with the Royal Canadian Mounted Police (RCMP), then with the United Nations (UN), and finally with Halifax Regional Police (HRP), to feed some individual or collective curiosity. Rather, this is an attempt to chronicle and share a series of lessons recognized and reinforced through over three decades of policing in several different roles, regions and countries.

These lessons come from the sayings, teachings and primarily the actions of people of different backgrounds and nationalities who allowed me to look deeper into my own motivations, emotions and expectations while working with them as a police officer and a hockey referee. In turn, this strengthened my ability to act as a guide for deciphering other people's behavior, influencing it and, where required, even countering certain negative aspects of it. This skill has allowed me to deal effectively with the fallout of people's behavior and leverage its advantages. These lessons also emanate from my failures to lead, make the right decisions and influence others as I should have.

I hope these lessons help you, the reader, obtain success in life when dealing with people, resolving complex issues, navigating the treacherous waters of interpersonal relationships or advancing specific causes.

The fundamental task of a leader is to provide far-reaching, even audacious vision, and to work for the greater good of the group they are leading while enhancing, encouraging and advancing its unity.

To become an effective leader, we must master four fundamental competencies. They are:

1. advanced thinking skills and superior decision-making
2. intentional relationship building
3. targeted influencing
4. courageous execution

You need to be competent at all four to be able to exercise influence through trust and attain a higher good. They're also integral to complexity management.

But these fundamental competencies aren't enough to ensure success as an effective leader. Because of the complexity we face, we must adopt a systematic approach when dealing with the reality of our daily lives. The path to effectively mastering these fundamental competencies while managing the complexity of the challenges we face encompasses a four-step approach:

1. Knowing and understanding the environment in which we live

Our interpersonal interactions have been and will become even more influenced and determined by technology as it embeds itself further into our lives. In a few short decades, we've become an information-rich, attention- and reflection-poor society. The amount of time we have to reflect on the challenges we face has become less and less. Expectations to perform various functions and take stands on specific issues as they arise occur more frequently and with more intensity.

Bombarded by information, we need to separate what's relevant, local and helpful from what's irrelevant, far-off and merely curious or trivial. We do this by developing an appreciation for today's complexity, including technology's role in influencing our perceptions and how we process and react to information. Critical to this is the development of our spatial and temporal awareness. Combined, these skills allow us to scan our event horizons and act more strategically.

This step also includes the appreciation of life's randomness and the misleading role that prediction plays in it. Effective leadership and complexity management require preparation, not prediction. As human beings, we're not so good at predicting but really good at postdicting. So we need to recognize and adjust, as much as possible, to the hidden and open asymmetries (or irregularities) in life. Admittedly, this will be the most intellectually demanding part of this book because complexity is, well, complex.

2. Knowing and understanding yourself

Having the lay of the land helps us understand where we are. What's then required is to understand who we are. This is where the notions of developing a superior character and advanced decision-making skills are critical to navigating our life's landscape. We do this through understanding our own biases, particularly our cognitive and inherent biases, and how they influence our decision-making daily, from what we eat and whom we associate with, to how we invest our savings and time. Understanding how we developed our decision-making processes over the years allows us to avoid the mental traps that lead us astray. Critical to this is our openness to other ideas and seeking out a diversity of thought from others who have lived different lives from our own. It requires an approach to our relationships and thought processes that is not centered on us but on others.

Many obstacles will impede us as we develop the requisite awareness of our strengths and weaknesses on the road to developing what Niccolò Machiavelli (1469-1527) termed "nobility of character" in tandem with the development of advanced thinking skills. Chief amongst those obstacles will be hubris: the arrogance that comes from an increased self-confidence that, unchecked, leads us astray, playing on our envious nature and resulting in extreme narcissism. This same hubris causes blindness leading to vulnerability. This is where we require empathy—the opposite of envy—to allow us to apply the one quality that keeps hubris in check: humility. Personal humility lets us see situations clearly and develop higher levels of trust in those we influence. It's the hallmark of a superior character.

As human beings, we are driven by our emotions, which in turn are driven by our perceptions, interpretations of the words, actions and events that touch our lives. The basis of our interpretations are our preferences and biases; specifically, our cognitive biases. By understanding them, we can see life's reality through an unbiased, unclouded view, thereby beginning the process of understanding others.

3. Knowing and understanding others

By beginning with ourselves, we can then understand how people in general function in society. This is where human nature comes into the discussion, helping us decode and better understand others' actions and motivations, and eventually allowing us to influence them. As much as we think and would like people to act within specific parameters, the reality is that they (and we) just don't. Unexpected actions or inactions result from various reasons. Understanding the why behind their actions or inactions allows us to better deal with other people. It's also key to our ability to influence them. This is known as social intelligence, an awareness of people's personalities and motivations that leads to a better understanding of their behaviors.

As social beings, we have a drive to belong to various groupings: familial, social and professional. This drive manifests itself while we grow up and continues well into adulthood, with a strong and, in some cases, overwhelming desire to fit into groups, be they sports, work, community, social or political. We support our favorite sports team, political affiliations, workplaces, social groups, worldviews and ideologies. This also implies learning to work within the dynamics of those particular groupings. Maintaining our individuality in a group setting allows us to focus on the reality of the moment and the long-term goals we set for ourselves.

As both social and antisocial beings, we're at the same time drawn and repelled by conflict. We're eager to watch others as they deal with conflict and ready to use it when necessary to support our aims, but timid to counter violence and aggression others direct at us. This becomes even more difficult as we belong to various groups and fall under the spell of massed groupings in which individuals feed into and adopt the group's personality.

Related to this is the understanding of generational divides. Since at least Plato's time, elders have complained of the perceived laziness of youth. As societies become polarized along political and ideological divisions, such divides tend to accentuate the gulf between generations. Understanding the role that intergenerational divisions play and recognizing the anchors of different generations allows us to appreciate better the main issues and factors at work in individuals, groups and entire communities.

4. Using that knowledge and understanding to influence others

Once we're armed with a sense of the lay of the land, the requisite self-knowledge and the understanding of what motivates and drives us and others, we can start the process of using that information to influence others. Leadership implies a dynamic, evolving relationship between a leader and those they lead. That relationship is predicated upon varying levels of willingness to cooperate on the part of team members. Some members will be open and welcoming to your mentoring, coaching and sponsoring, choosing to profit from your counsel and follow your examples. But you'll invariably encounter the uncertain and the intransigent, those diverse personalities that, like road hazards, will occupy your route in life: the bad attitudes, the social vampires who drain people dry, the malignant narcissists, histrionics, sociopaths and psychopaths, and the just plain senseless people who are bent on making life difficult for all.

This list will also include people who will try to impose their views on you while you're working hard in the trenches to solve problems: politicians outraged by a complex issue and demanding a simple solution; contrarian journalists who write according to their ideological bent, blatantly disregarding facts to advance some cause; sedentary fans who may or may not have played the game screaming their reprobation at the officiating of a sporting event; intellectuals and academics alike who think their opinion always matters (especially when it's outside of their field of study); and self-styled social-media mavens who feel moral outrage at the slightest of perceived transgressions. Learning to respond effectively to these types of individuals and others is critical to influencing people.

The second part will be to understand what the psychologist Carl Jung (1875-1961) described as the "Shadow Self;" its role in how we act and influence others. The Shadow Self is that side of us that our ego and insecurities rule, that unresolved childhood pain drives. Many things, including alcohol, drugs, personality disorders, fatigue, hunger, stress, idleness and even the results of sports matches can stimulate the Shadow

Self's manifestation in us all.

Technology, through social media and the anonymity it affords, facilitates this manifestation. Social media is not all bad. It enables information exchange, communication over distance, entertainment, learning and curation of memories. Like any other technology, you must master it to get the best out of it. It also allows for negative characters to reside, thrive and troll.

~

At this point, allow me to introduce you to **Marlo**. A composite character, Marlo represents the Shadow Self in all of us whose actions will litter this book like an inconsiderate teenager tossing their favorite burger chain's garbage out the window of their car as they drive home from a late-night scoff. Marlo can be a woman, man, transgender, straight, queer, Black, White, Asian, Indigenous, living with disabilities, able-bodied, tattooed, pierced, bearded, bald, beautiful, ugly, short, tall, obese, athletic, intelligent, illiterate, educated, introverted, extroverted, socialist, liberal, conservative, unionized, management, pious or atheist.

Marlo is our ego, our irrationality, our narcissism and our hubris all wrapped into one. Marlo represents real-life, anonymized examples of people who have caused and continue to produce so much frustration, pain and damage in our lives. We can qualify them as troubled souls, an impossible person or, in some cases, even an idiotic individual. You most likely don't personally know the Marlos of this book, but you probably do know people like them, maybe even intimately.

Marlo is often the physical manifestation of Ruckert's Law, which holds that nothing is so insignificant that it cannot be blown out of proportion. They are prone to 'catastrophizing,' so their hysterics and desire for melodrama are their signature trait. For Marlo, no slight is too small, no look too benign and no word too soothing. It's all about them, and we are but pawns in their game of social life.

Their victories are often hollow and can even be Pyrrhic: a triumph that inflicts such a devastating toll on them that it is tantamount to defeat. Someone who wins a Pyrrhic victory has also paid a heavy price that negates any real sense of achievement or irreparably damages long-term progress and relationships. One would be inclined to say that, at times, Marlo is simply, positively stupid. And we'll see why that very well may be.

Throughout this book, we'll hear a lot from Marlo because they've provided me with some of the best lessons in life on how to do things, how not to do something and especially how not to treat people. You may even recognize certain traits of Marlo as they attempt to wreak havoc in others' lives, including your own. You may have allowed Marlo to get the better of your personality at one time or another, creating havoc in your and others' lives. I know I have.

We'll also look at what drives Marlo and what we can do to counter their nefarious character traits and actions. Most importantly, we'll learn from Marlo what to do and mostly what to not do.

~

Once we've understood these four fundamental approaches, we can proceed to the last chapter. It deals with the lesson of personal sustainability: how, as a leader, you must ensure that you have the necessary abilities, stamina and resources to accomplish the task of dynamically influencing others through trust to achieve some higher good. That means having a burning desire to develop the right physical, mental and spiritual stamina and other attributes that will allow you to be the best you can be so you can get the best out of others while managing the complex problems you'll encounter.

For me, the lesson of personal sustainability has been the bitterest and most rewarding in my life. I have lost many a friend through death and decisions because of their inability to take care of themselves. I have also had to come to terms with my limits, both physical and mental, and especially my own mortality.

Following my times in Haiti, I was diagnosed with a post-traumatic stress injury. In the years to come, I chose not to let the diagnosis limit my abilities nor define who I was.

Instead of remaining psychologically fragile or just being resilient and maintaining the status quo, I chose the arduous path of post-traumatic growth. As part of that path, I decided to disclose my diagnosis to my work colleagues and community as a whole. I even made a TEDx talk at a local university event about going from self-improvement to community improvement.

Such disclosure is fraught with risk; certain people elected to criticize my stance while others embraced and learned from it. But I also learned that their opinions of me as a person were really none of my business.

Most people are eager to improve their life circumstances, but they are unwilling to improve themselves in the process. If we don't improve ourselves to live our best life, we can't expect others to do the same. The key is to design and execute a plan that lets you build a life, a good life, that will last an entire lifetime, not just part of it, such as those 35 or so years during which you work at a 'job'.

That means loving life, living it passionately while taking it seriously. It also entails pursuing what is meaningful, not what is expedient or short-term.

At the end of each chapter, including this introduction, I've incorporated a one-page summary of key points under the heading, 'Calls from the Blue Line.' These are the salient points that will serve as reminders from each chapter. As a linesperson working the blue line, you have to make calls regarding offsides. For our study, it means encapsulating those essential points that will help keep you onside with this book's material.

My goal for you is to become a student in leadership and complexity management. This will allow you to develop skills that will add to your understanding of the environment in which you live and work, to understand yourself more, to know others better and to use that knowledge to counter behaviors that challenge your ability to influence others through trust to achieve some higher good. In essence, it means facing the reality of living, and thriving while doing so.

Let's start this journey through an understanding of the landscape in which we live and operate.

Calls from the blue line

- Understand the difference between management and leadership: management is about systems, structures and processes, while leadership is about people. The goal of leadership is not getting the most out of people but getting the best out of them.
- Leadership is the dynamic influence of others, through trust, to accomplish some higher good. A modern form of behavioral alchemy, leadership blends science and art to form a catalyst to influence people.
- To achieve leadership success, we need to embrace, contend with

and manage the complexity in our lives every day.

- Policing deals with challenges that people otherwise cannot, will not or should not deal with. Police officers should be problem-solving community contributors and not problem creators. Like police officers, hockey officials must remain impartial in applying the game rules, ensuring the game is played safely and fairly for all. The ability to demonstrate leadership and deal with the game's complexity is known as "game management."
- The most crucial task of any leader is to provide far-reaching, even audacious vision to work for a group's greater good and unity.
- The four fundamental leadership competencies are:

    1. advanced thinking skills and superior decision-making
    2. intentional relationship building
    3. targeted influencing
    4. courageous execution

- The four-step approach to becoming an effective leader is:

    1. knowing and understanding the environment in which you live
    2. knowing and understanding yourself
    3. knowing and understanding others
    4. using your knowledge of the environment, yourself and others to influence people

- Be ready to duel with the Marlos in your life by understanding who they are and what they do, and how to counter their harmful effects.

1: The lesson of randomness and complexity

[The new Prince] must therefore keep his mind ready to shift as the winds and tides of Fortune turn, and, as I have already said, he ought not to quit good courses if he can help it, but should know how to follow evil courses if he must.

-Niccolò Machiavelli (1469-1527)
The Prince
Chapter XVIII, on *How Princes Should Keep Faith*

Dearest Haiti

Just 681 miles to the southeast of Miami, Florida is Haiti, the western third of the island of Hispaniola, neighboring the Dominican Republic. It was Hispaniola that Christopher Columbus 'discovered' on December 5, 1492. Its indigenous population of Taino Arawak and Ciboney inhabitants was virtually wiped out in the 16th and 17th centuries by disease, forced working conditions and violence perpetrated by Spanish, then French colonizers.

The Treaty of Rijswijk (1697) formally ceded the western third of Hispaniola to the French, effectively paving the way for colonial rule and African slavery. It was a wealthy, lush colony providing France in the mid-18th century with almost a quarter of its imperial riches through its coffee, sugar, cacao and indigo, Haiti became known as the *Pearl of the Antilles.*

After twelve years of insurrection, Haiti became the world's first Black republic, obtaining its independence from Napoleon's France on January 1, 1804. Unfortunately, independence from France was not the panacea that its top general, Toussaint Louverture, or its first president, Jean-

Jacques Dessalines, had envisaged. History has not been kind to Haitians: first, onerous French reparations, then war with the neighboring Dominican Republic, followed by a 19-year occupation by American Marines starting in 1915, then a kleptocratic, despotic father-son team known as Papa and Baby Doc Duvalier. In the two centuries following its independence, Haiti has suffered immeasurably from political and economic instability and unrest; so much so that it is now the poorest country in the Western Hemisphere. Despite the obvious challenges that Haitians face daily, it has a strong and rich culture unique among Caribbean island countries. When people, both Haitians and non-Haitians alike, refer to the country, they use the endearing expression *Ayiti cherie.*[3]

To assist in Haiti's development, the United Nations, along with its member countries such as France, Canada and the United States, began various missions supporting the rule of law and economic development in the early 1990s, following the departure of the dictator Baby Doc Duvalier.

In 1995, I became part of that United Nations support when I was sent as a young Royal Canadian Mounted Police (RCMP) constable for a six-month mission in the central plateau town of Mirebalais. I then returned to Haiti for a one-year assignment in January 2008 as the Deputy Police Commissioner in charge of the UN police operational component. During that second mission, I had 1,700 police officers from 43 different countries under my command. The goal was to support the fledgling Haitian National Police (HNP or *Police nationale d'Haïti*) through monitoring, mentoring and operational support.

During the first weeks of my 2008 deployment, I attended a high-level overview of the potential threats facing Haiti and the UN's intended responses. The overview's summary identified four main categories of significant environmental threats: geological hazards such as earthquakes, tsunamis and landslides; hydro-meteorological hazards such as tropical storms, flooding and drought; biological hazards such as epidemics and disease outbreaks; and technological threats from environmental degradation.

Of all these hazards, the number one identified threat in terms of probability and impact was from earthquakes. The presentation detailed how three major active fault lines represented the most apparent seismic threats to Haiti.

Since the establishment of French colonial rule in 1670, each century had seen a major earthquake somewhere in the country. In 1751, an earthquake destroyed the newly established capital, Port-au-Prince,

while in 1842 and again in 1904, separate earthquakes along the Septen-
trional Fault in the north destroyed the city of Cap Haïtien, killing approximately 4,000 and 5,300 people, respectively.

As part of the evaluation, a 2004 risk assessment stated that the probability of an earthquake sometime in the 21st century was possible (between 1 percent and 10 percent probability in the following year or at
least one chance in the next 100 years) with a very high vulnerability
and an impact that could be catastrophic for both people and infrastructure.

That risk assessment would soon prove to be prophetic.

At 4:30 pm. on January 12, 2010, in the central Port-au-Prince neighborhood of Bourdon, the Special Representative of the Secretary-General
(SRSG) in charge of the United Nations Stabilisation Mission in Haiti (MI-
NUSTAH as it was known by its French acronym), the Tunisian national
Hédi Annabi, began chairing a meeting with a delegation of senior Chinese police leaders. The meeting was held on the UN headquarters'
fourth floor in a revamped seven-story hotel known as the Hotel Christopher, around a large rectangular mahogany table in the SRSG's conference room.

The hotel had a main, older wing and a newer outcropping built to accommodate the UN headquarters' staff overflow. During my time as the
Deputy Commissioner, I had attended many a meeting seated at that
same table, on which hard candies were placed in a blue metal pot in the
middle for participants to enjoy.

As per protocol, Mr. Annabi was seated at the head of the table. The
Chinese delegation, seated to his right, was four police executives at the
senior colonel and general ranks, an interpreter and a video photogra-
pher. Sitting to the SRSG's left were Mr. Annabi's deputy, the Brazilian
Luiz Carlos da Costa, RCMP Superintendent Douglas Coates [4] and the
SRSG's advisor, Frederick Woolridge.

Superintendent Coates had replaced me as the Deputy Police Commissioner in charge of UN police operations in Haiti in the spring of 2009,
following my departure from the Mission. When the UN Police head left
at the end of 2009, he had become the interim Police Commissioner.

The meeting was to discuss the eventual departure of the 8th Chinese
Formed Police Unit (FPU) from the Mission. An FPU is a company-sized
(120 member), self-sustained unit employed in various UN missions
worldwide for enhanced security, public order and public safety capac-
ity-building. MINUSTAH used several FPUs as part of its public order
support role of the Haitian National Police. The FPU's commander, Senior

Colonel Li Qin, was a highly-decorated police officer who had gained a solid reputation for his work dealing with drug trafficking along the Sino-Vietnamese border in the 1990s. He was soon to end his second tour of duty in Haiti as FPU commander, having previously commanded the 6th Chinese FPU.

As with most high-level meetings between Mission management and country contributors, preliminary remarks, light-hearted banter and an exchange of gifts preceded the official discussions. The interpreter, He Zhihong, also known by her western name of Catherine, sat behind the SRSG to his right. During this time, the Chinese police video photographer, Zhong Jianqin took numerous photos around the meeting table.

Soon after the meeting began, a 7.0 magnitude earthquake struck Haiti. Its epicenter was near the town of Léogâne, along the Presqu'Ile du Sud fault line, a mere 15 miles to the west of the Haitian capital. Port-au-Prince was home to an estimated 3.5 million people. It was this same fault line that would later be responsible for another earthquake on August 14, 2021 that resulted in the deaths of over 2000 people.

When the earthquake struck, the participants sought shelter under the massive meeting table. Senior Colonel Li intentionally covered his visiting commanding general under the table with his own body. Superintendent Coates, himself a seasoned UN mission veteran and a former member of the RCMP's Special Emergency Response Team (anti-terrorist SWAT team), did the same for Mr. Da Costa.

As the earthquake's intensity increased, the seven-story building quickly began to disintegrate. Its roof collapsed onto the top floor and then onto the floors below in a sequence of cascading destruction. A large, concrete support beam fell onto the meeting table on the fourth floor, crashing down and killing all the meeting participants who had sought protection under it.

The entire older wing of the building collapsed into itself, leaving the newer wing still standing. Within seconds, gone with the older wing were the Mission's senior civilian and police leadership. Also gone were some 250,000 Haitians and a significant number of UN personnel and international visitors throughout the greater Port-au-Prince area.[5]

The Deputy Force Commander, General Ricardo Toro-Tassara, a career military officer from Chile, was elsewhere in Port-au-Prince in a meeting with his commanders. General Toro, as he was affectionately known, had been in Mission since December 2008. During the Force Commander's absence over the holiday period, he oversaw the 9,000 international soldiers assigned to MINUSTAH.

Upon learning of Hotel Christopher's collapse, General Toro immediately headed there to assess the situation and take control of the recovery efforts. He did so with a personal dread as he knew that the Haitian Presidential Palace and another important Haitian landmark, the Hotel Montana, had also collapsed. It was in the Hotel Montana that his wife and daughter were staying during their extended holidays in Haiti.

Several hours later, General Toro learned that both his wife and daughter were missing and most likely dead in the collapse of the Hotel Montana along with over a hundred others, predominantly international visitors and hotel employees. Later that night, when he met with his senior staff and other members of the UN military force, an exasperated junior officer asked, "Where will I sleep tonight?" General Toro calmly replied, "My wife and my daughter have died today. I don't know how I'll even sleep tonight. Count your blessings and know that at least you'll be able to sleep *somewhere* this night."

In Canada, RCMP senior management started mobilizing a response to assist those Canadian police officers on the ground in Haiti and the general population. Two days after the earthquake, I touched ground in Haiti.

Upon my arrival with the Canadian Armed Forces Disaster Assistance Response Team (better known by its acronym, DART) aboard a CC-177 Globemaster of the Royal Canadian Air Force, I was greeted by the Canadian police contingent commander, Michel Martin, a 28-year veteran from the *Sûreté du Québec*, the provincial police service for the province of Québec. Martin would have the herculean task of leading and supporting the individual Canadian police officers in Haiti over the following year.

Martin drove me to what remained of the apartment building where I had stayed for the final six months of my 2008 mission. It was now a pile of broken concrete and twisted metal.

Visible among the debris was the crushed and deformed upper torso of Sergeant Mark Gallagher, an RCMP member who had just returned to Haiti after spending Christmas vacation in Canada. There was no way for us to wrest his body from the debris. It would be another three days before a recovery team lead by the French *Gendarmerie nationale* would be able to extract his body along with two of their own from the pile of rubble.

The next day, I found myself with Constable Julie Dupré, a Montréal City Police officer who was the executive officer to Superintendent Coates. She and I headed straight to Hotel Christopher. It was disheartening to see this once-busy building more than half-reduced to rubble with people wandering about, trying to listen for any survivors. In some places, canine search and rescue teams from Israel and Brazil were going over the ruins without finding any indication of survivors.

With a large excavator and additional search teams from China and Brazil, we began the arduous task of digging. In consultation with the Chinese delegation, I directed them to the spot in the debris field where we could expect to find the bodies of their compatriots and Superintendent Coates. It took 40 hours before we recovered Superintendent Coates, the SRSG, his deputy, the senior Chinese police officers, and others.

Amongst the rubble, I found a completely intact, high-end digital camera. It was the camera the official Chinese FPU video photographer had used during the meeting. We found his lifeless body not far from his camera.

I gave the camera to the head of the Chinese delegation that was assisting the recovery efforts. Several months later, they sent me a photo of the final moments of the meeting participants before the earthquake hit. Everyone in the room was smiling, unaware that an earthquake was about to claim their lives.[6]

Five days after the earthquake, the Danish national Jens Kristensen, a senior humanitarian affairs officer with the Mission, was rescued from the UN headquarters' debris. I must have climbed the debris field just above where he was trapped a dozen times.

I had known Jens during my deployment and had developed a good working relationship with him. He had been sitting at his desk on the third floor of the building when the earthquake struck.[7] Jens' office was just above that of the Police Commissioner, which was on the second floor.

Within feet of where he was found were the bodies of the Police Commissioner's two administrative assistants, the British national Ann Barnes and the Haitian national Pierrena Perrin Annilus. During my time in Haiti, I worked daily with Ann and Pierrena, developing friendships with them both, particularly with Ann. In the summer of 2008, she and her spouse had visited my family cottage in Canada.

On Friday, January 22, I saw Jens again at the ramp ceremony for the departure of Superintendent Coates and Sergeant Gallagher's bodies to Canada. I could not contain myself when I saw him at the ceremony. I gave him a big bear hug, much to the surprise of those who had gathered for what was a very somber event. Many years after our meeting, I read how Jens had heard the moans of both Ann and Pierrena immediately following the collapse of their building. It didn't take long for their groans to stop.

Locus not locusts

As humans, we attribute our success in life to those things we think we can influence and direct, including the outcomes of events. This is known as our *locus of control*, not to be confused with our *locus of concern*, things over which we have no control, influence or direction, yet retain our keen interest. Included in this latter group are such things as the weather, interest rates, inflation, traffic, our height, celebrity dating habits and other things that are, frankly, irrelevant to our lives. We also gravitate towards easy, often single-reason explanations for our success. However, a constellation of factors or a concatenation (the linking together of elements in a series or a chain) determines our success, including avoiding multiple errors and failures along the way.

Chief among the factors of our success is our good luck or others' bad luck. Did we show up to the race injury-free, rested and adequately fueled while our competition arrived fatigued, hungry and hurt? Could the match's outcome, the event or the decision have been different had other, more capable competitors shown up, better prepared or in better condition than us? We know and have seen that any given team can win on any given Sunday or any other given day of the week. It's that intersection of luck and timing that is one of the keys to success in life. However, we're inclined to ignore the role of chance and randomness, thinking that it's because of what we do, of what is part of our locus of control, that results in us succeeding. This is misleading.

Before the end of my 2008 mission in Haiti, I had filed a request to extend my stay for another year, until late January 2010. Unfortunately, I had had some conflict with the Mission leader's deputy, Mr. Luiz Carlos da Costa. He flatly refused my request for an extension.

When I left the Mission, I was full of rancor towards Mr. da Costa for his refusal. However, had he granted my mission extension request, I would most likely have been in Haiti during the earthquake, and in the meeting in Superintendent Coates' place. I suspect that it would have been Superintendent Coates' duty to recover *my* body.

I came to this awful supposition just as we recovered Mr. da Costa's body, mindful of the irony of seeing this man I had previously blamed for my departure from the Mission. I silently thanked him for his refusal as I saw his remains in the body bag.

Added to the intersection of our good fortune and others' bad luck is others' contribution to our success. Did someone provide us with indications about the best time to apply for something or the best place to go? More importantly, did we have a mentor, coach or sponsor who tutored us on the best approaches to training or preparing for the competition, the job interview or the appearance? Did we have people who so cared about us that they risked hurting our feelings and our relationship with them to set us straight? We must never discount the role others play in our success.

Another factor is whether we display good judgment. Without good judgment, many people have lost out greatly in life, both professionally and personally. By good judgment, I mean applying the broad range of life experiences and practical knowledge that allow us to develop informed opinions and the courage to act on them. This also implies recognizing similarities or correlations that others cannot see—or, in the case of ideologues and those blinded by their biases, refuse to see. Have we the ability to detach ourselves intellectually, cognitively and emotionally from an event or analysis to see a situation's reality? To have good judgment and solve problems, we must be ideological agnostics, striving to be as objective as possible.

We're also subject to the times. Did the choice of our product, our service or even ourselves as the chosen candidate result from the whims of the public, of those of a board of directors or of political elites who were in search of something new? We might have just shown up at the right place at the right moment when what we had to offer was so unique that it became a preferred option to the deciding person or group. During my policing career, I had fourteen transfers, seven physical relocations and six promotions. At least two of those promotions were dependent on the hiring panel's whims or the decider looking for someone different at the time, more than any other factor.

We all know the expression, "It's not what you know, it's who you know," as being part of success. But it is less about who *you* know and more about who knows *you* and especially what they know about your work that counts. The expression should more aptly read, "It's not what you know or who you know, *but who knows what about you.*"

In 2004, I was chosen to be a national disciplinary adjudicator in Ottawa because the unit's head had interviewed me when I was applying to become a commissioned officer several years previously. I must have impressed him, as he never forgot me and came looking to recruit me for his unit. Three years later, in 2007, I would replace him as the RCMP's chief disciplinary adjudicator, essentially the Force's judge advocate general.

A good portion of what people know and appreciate about us comes from our ability to navigate social interactions. This is the basis of our reputation: can we deal effectively, collaboratively and equitably with people? If we have a good reputation, people will be more inclined to want to deal with us. People tend to support those they know, like and—especially—trust.

Our success must also be based on our abilities: our ability to get things done, our ability to create something and meet the objectives set, and our ability to respond to the needs of others. In his masterwork, *The Prince*, Niccolò Machiavelli wrote of the quality of "fortunate astuteness"—a phrase that some have associated with cunning opportunism. But Machiavelli recognized that sometimes success was not based on merit or good fortune, but rather on combining the two. Hence, his amalgam of cleverness and good luck. For us, fortunate astuteness means our ability to roll with the times and benefit from the same while others are roiling with the moments and lost in their uncertainty. Machiavelli's forged his wisdom from his mistakes, bad fortune and suffering. *The Prince* was only published in 1532, five years after his death.

Finally, our success means that we commit fewer errors and suffer fewer failures than others. We do so by focusing on one thing at a time, by paying attention to the small stuff before it becomes the big stuff. We also recognize the limited value of anecdotes based on opinion instead of empirical evidence based on fact. We're alive to our biases and habits that preclude us from considering all the possibilities in a given situation or context. We ensure that our cognitive faculties operate at peak efficiency, having sufficient sleep and fuel, devoid of negative influences and inputs. And we promote a personal life based on consistent emotions, chief amongst them, satisfaction: satisfaction in what we have and what we do.

The challenge, though, is that we tend to overestimate those same abilities in ourselves. Because we've had success in the past, we think that it stemmed more from our proficiency than to the intersection of our good luck, the bad luck of others, our timing, the contributions of others, the times we live in, our good judgment and the scope of our reputation. It sometimes takes a series of events and factors to coincide to result in success, especially at a high level. Our recognition of this fact allows us to develop the necessary focus on those things that we can control and those we cannot. Hence, our locus of control begins with recognizing those things that we don't know or always understand.

Professor Marlo and the monochromatic animals, small and large

Professor Marlo was a university lecturer. One day, the professor sent me a message complaining about the officers under my command who had responded to a call of a woman who had stabbed two other women with a knife in the professor's neighborhood. Professor Marlo detailed how the responding officers had arrived on the scene with their service pistols and a patrol carbine drawn. As far as the professor was concerned, there could have been a shoot-out resulting in numerous injuries of innocent bystanders, including his young children, who were at home with a babysitter at the time. Professor Marlo was irate that such a possibility could have arisen because of the officers' actions. The officers had arrested the assailant with no shots fired, no further injury and no property damage.

Despite this successful conclusion, the professor was convinced that the officers could have done better. In his estimation, a safer approach would have been for the officers not to have displayed their firearms, opting for less lethal-looking methods such as deploying their telescopic batons, conducted energy weapons and even martial art skills to subdue the assailant. After all, Professor Marlo was a tenured professor in medieval studies. He must have known something about edged-weapons combat that the officers didn't.

My email exchange with Professor Marlo was informative. When I wrote a concise, detailed and authoritative explanation of the officers' actions, the Professor appeared to be impressed by my ability to put two words together and my academic credentials in the signature block. I immediately noticed the change in his attitude towards myself and the officers at that point.

When dealing with a Marlo of this type, it's preferable to punch holes in their apparent logic, even calling them out. Conversely, if Marlo is your boss or someone with sway over your career, sometimes all you can do is play their game, acknowledging how informed they think they are by stroking their ego, even if they're blatantly wrong.

In his book *Skin in the Game–Hidden Asymmetries in Daily Life* (2018), Nicolas Nassim Taleb dedicates an entire chapter to what he qualifies as the "Intellectual Yet Idiot" or IYI for short. In his view, IYIs are what the German philosopher Friedrich Nietzsche (1844-1900) referred to as *bildungsphilisters* or "educated philistines." Taleb warns his readers to "Beware the slightly erudite who thinks he is an erudite, as well as the barber who decides to perform brain surgery."[8]

Before this book, Taleb wrote *The Black Swan—The Impact of the Highly Improbable* (2007), in which he qualified a Black Swan (capitalized, no less) event as having three attributes: first, the event lies outside the realm of regular expectations; second, it has an extreme impact; and third, because of our biases, such an event makes us concoct after-the-fact explanations to justify its occurrence in the first place. Recent examples of 21st-century Black Swan events are the terrorist attacks of September 11, 2001, the 2008 financial system meltdown and Haiti's 2010 earthquake.[9]

According to Taleb, though, the COVID-19 pandemic was not a Black Swan event because it did not meet the first criteria, that being an event outside the realm of regular expectations. In his view, the recorded history of humankind has been full of pandemics. Just looking at our recent history, we can list some of the most severe pandemics of the past 100 years: the HIV/AIDS pandemic from 1991 to the present, which has been responsible for hundreds of thousands of deaths *every year*[10]; the 1968 flu pandemic which reportedly killed upwards of four million people; the 1956-1958 Asian flu pandemic which killed upwards of two million people; and the Spanish influenza pandemic from 1918 to 1920 which was estimated to have killed between 3 to 5 percent of the world's population at the time, some 50 million persons.

On a personal note, my older sister was stricken with polio as a child in the late 1950s. The long-term effects of post-polio syndrome (PPS or *poliomyelitis sequelae*) would eventually claim her life. During its peak in the 1940s and 1950s, polio paralyzed or killed half a million people, predominantly children, worldwide every year. It, too, was a pandemic.[11]

In August 2020, the World Health Organization (WHO) reported that wild poliovirus had been eradicated from the African continent, some 40 years after smallpox was declared eradicated from Africa and the world. Today, unfortunately, wild polio still exists at alarming rates in Pakistan and Afghanistan. As for smallpox, it was responsible for the death of some 300 million people in the 20th century alone and countless others in the centuries prior, including many indigenous peoples like the Taino Arawak and Ciboney, Haiti's first inhabitants. In 2010, cholera also struck Haiti, killing over 1,000 people. There have been seven identified cholera pandemics globally since 1817, and numerous recent epidemics and outbreaks resulting in the deaths of tens of millions of people, predominantly those living in poverty.

Since time immemorial, epidemics and pandemics have been part of human society, topping various risk registers for decades. They are recognized events, although we never know exactly when the next one will occur. Yes, they have a huge impact, and we tend to see them as evident in hindsight, but they are not Black Swan events. Instead, some have argued that the correct metaphor for such an event is a "Grey Rhinoceros."

American author Michele Wucker coined the term "Grey Rhino" to designate those events that are charging toward us, with highly probable consequences and substantial potential impact. Most importantly, we can see them coming with a certain degree of accuracy and foresight.

Today's world contains interconnected and interdependent complex systems such as the global economy, the environment, sovereign countries, technology, terrorism, organized crime and social movements. To effectively deal with the local and non-local effects these interconnected complex systems generate, we need to better appreciate the nature of the interdependent yet connected and adaptive systems that exist. We know and recognize that such complexity is often unpredictable, capable of producing significant, system-wide events. These events are forceful or robust in their adaptation and emergence while producing amazingly novel and evolving phenomena never seen previously.

The totality of a complex system behaves in ways that the actions of the system's individual components do not reveal. That also implies that complex systems don't have a discernible, one-dimensional cause-and-effect structure. A single car speeding in traffic does not mean that all cars do, or that traffic is flowing properly.

This is the challenge we have with today's ever-increasing complexity: it's understanding the importance of the interactions between the individual elements of a system more than the actual nature of those individual elements that counts. Just because something is complex doesn't mean that we shouldn't attempt to understand it.

One example is the issue of crime. Numerous studies have suggested that since 1992 crime has been trending downwards in Western societies, yet our perception is that society has become more, not less, dangerous. This may be partly because of the societal awareness and emphasis on terrorism. But there are other factors at play. A 2016 study from the United Kingdom demonstrated that 53 percent of all victims of crime resulted from online-facilitated crime, the first time that cybercrime surpassed traditional crime in the UK.[12] A 2020 private-sector report determined that 87 percent of all large UK companies had been victims of cybercrime the previous year.[13]

In November 2020, a year-long investigation coordinated by INTERPOL, "Operation First Light," involved searches in over 10,000 locations worldwide and led to the arrest of more than 21,000 persons, the freezing of 310 bank accounts and the seizure of over US $150 million. Law enforcement agencies from some 35 countries participated in the massive investigation, illustrating the transnational nature of the threat of telephone and internet-based fraud, which in many cases exploited the COVID-19 pandemic situation.

This raises the question of whether crime has effectively diminished or has merely morphed into something else, operating online as opposed to offline, penetrating directly into our homes, offices and meeting places without the perpetrators ever having to physically leave the safety of their computer chair in some other country.

In the early 2000s, I was in charge of a unique investigative entity known as the Integrated Child Exploitation (ICE) unit, based in Winnipeg, Manitoba. Its role was to investigate online child pornography.

The first such unit was established in Canada following the dismantling of an American child pornography website named "Landslide" in August 2000 in the context of a police operation baptized "Avalanche." The website, housed in Texas and started in 1997 by Thomas and Janice Reedy of Dallas, quickly grew. By 2000 it had become a multi-million-dollar enterprise with at least 250,000 paying subscribers. When the website was taken down, follow-up investigations occurred in Ireland, the United Kingdom, Germany and Switzerland.

Canadian law enforcement participated in an operation baptized "Snowball." In Manitoba alone, it identified 82 individuals who had accessed and downloaded child pornography from the Landslide website. As a result of this operation, the ICE unit was created as a permanent fixture of provincial law enforcement to investigate child pornography.

Sometime in 2003, ICE received a complaint of a large bank of computers set up in a unit in a residential apartment complex. Nothing else was in the apartment, not even dishes in the kitchen. ICE investigators attended the unoccupied residence with a search warrant but could not determine anything related to child pornography. Nothing was seized.

A few days after the search, all the computers had been dismantled and there was no further trace of the occupants. It was later determined that the computers were used to commit online crimes outside of Canada.

Since then, we've seen more and more crimes committed by individuals from outside Canada targeting Canadians. These crimes range from computer hacking and ransomware demands to fraud and identity theft.

This demonstrates how we can easily misinterpret the complexity of a situation by labeling it in simplistic terms such as crime diminishing instead of a crime morphing. This may be a symptom of a more significant issue: our inability to adapt to complexity.

Canadian author Thomas Homer-Dixon writes in his book *The Ingenuity Gap* (2000) that our inability to deal with ever-increasing complexity creates a widening gap, as we don't have the appropriate social and technical ingenuity to keep pace with the complexity of our times. This reflects the constant state of flux in life. He qualifies the world we live in as being one of "unknown unknowns." Not only are we blithely ignorant of the various elements of the complex systems surrounding us, but we are unthinkingly unaware of those things we don't know that form part of that complex system. Athenian philosopher Plato (~428-347 BC) fittingly called this our "double ignorance," the ignorance of our ignorance combined with the conceit of knowledge.

Regardless of the type of event, be it a Black Swan or a Gray Rhino, leaders need to prepare for frequent and infrequent high-impact events through a better understanding of complex systems and the gaps in our responses, including our applied ingenuity and innovation, which are often inadequate. The great division between our generational response and that of future generations will not be political or economic rivalries but between those capable of handling complex events and situations and those overwhelmed by them. Being able to handle complexity means becoming qualified and interested in acquiring the necessary skills to deal with complex events while developing the requisite discipline that lets you steel your mind against the constant distractions our society hurls your way.

Understanding complexity further requires a systematic examination of potential threats, opportunities and possible outcomes, including those scenarios and notions that lie outside the margins of our current thinking and planning exercises. Machiavelli wrote of the concept of "anxious foresight," the intelligent organization of what information we have available to prepare ourselves for future challenges.

To use a driving metaphor, the goal is to stop driving our leadership car by looking exclusively through the rearview mirrors and making decisions based on what once was, and instead, looking through the front windshield at what will be. On occasion, that also implies glancing in the rear view and side mirrors to look for those trends and past lessons that can be useful in the future. We do this while being mindful that trends and patterns identified in the rearview aren't necessarily causes of actions.

So, while looking forward, we must be cognizant of what's behind us. Regardless, we shouldn't change lanes without first doing a shoulder check.

This also means that because the world is such an interconnected place, we must recognize that something that occurs elsewhere may influence or impact us, regardless of where we are. In other words, what happens anywhere can and does matter wherever we are. This is related to the *Butterfly Effect*[14], which holds that a small change in one state or situation can result in large differences in a later state or a comparable situation in another far-off land. This is also related to the notion of bounded applicability, which holds that different and contradictory things work in other bounded spaces.

Preparation, then, must start with ourselves. Are we mindful, without becoming obsessed, of the threats that abound in our lives? Are we able to react to the complex nature of the daily events that shape our lives? Do we demonstrate the requisite courage to put our imagination into action? Do we fall into the IYI trap of believing that we know everything because we have a little knowledge about something?

Taleb writes that, as human beings, we are good at *postdiction*, easily justifying things after the fact. In psychology, this is a cognitive error known as the hindsight bias or retrospective coherence, as in the expression "hindsight is 20/20." After an event, we suddenly see indicators that make us believe we should have seen the event coming in the first place. The problem is that although hindsight may lead to insight, it rarely leads to foresight.

One of the immediate challenges we face in applying best practices is that they quickly become past practices when we have to deal with a complex, dynamic environment or situation. Often, we attempt to explain the past, ours or others', but do so unsuccessfully for lack of information and understanding. If we can't even explain the past, think how futile an exercise it is to predict the future.

Although we may be good at postdiction, we're absolutely, positively lousy at prediction. Predictions are essentially educated guesstimates about the future. We desperately want to believe in the existence of sages, prophets and gurus who can predict the future by identifying some previously unknown recognition pattern.

Danish physician Niels Bohr (1885-1962) aptly noted that prediction is a highly complicated exercise, especially when it concerns the future. Warren Buffett, himself nicknamed the "Oracle of Omaha," fittingly stated that stock market forecasters exist to make fortune-tellers look good.

How many times have the experts correctly predicted stock market crashes or bull markets, crime sprees, significant weather events, Stanley Cup champions or the Powerball Lottery's winning numbers? Not often enough, if at all. If they did, they (and we) would all be richer, safer, drier and possibly even happier.

The problem with prediction is one of *asymmetry*: a lack of balance, proportion, order, harmony, correspondence or evenness in people and events. Something is asymmetric when there is an imbalance or irregularity, such as when an item is unequally divided into two different-sized parts. Or an unintended event occurs despite regular, planned action. Things often don't pan out as we hoped they would. And this is partly because of the inherent irrationality of human beings.

One of the most relied-upon aspects in policing is a suspect's habits. People rarely do something just once, especially if that something brings them an immediate benefit such as money, valued goods or a particular rush or feeling. As a young investigator, I would regularly participate in surveillance of drug traffickers or thieves with the expectation they were on their way to commit another crime. We were often surprised that they didn't do as we thought they would, or as we had been told they would through source intelligence or judicially authorized wiretaps. That's the challenge with humans: as much as we try, our actions, reactions and emotions are most often asymmetrical.

Best practices may be appropriate when dealing with simple contexts and repeat situations. However, past best practices may no longer suffice to deal with more complex and asymmetrical problems or those that you've never seen before.

Consequently, it's helpful to distinguish between high-impact, highly improbable crises and high-impact, highly probable crises like those coming right at us. Remember: we're all subject to hindsight bias, which shows that we're better at postdicting than predicting. Any prediction about future conditions and events is fraught with uncertainty. We're only as good as our last prediction, which, if right, we remember; if wrong, we forget.

The key to dealing with future complexity isn't to be predictive but adaptive; in an ideal world, to paraphrase Machiavelli, to be ingeniously opportunistic. It also involves understanding, appreciating and prioritizing the potential risks that exist.

Over the years, I've come to know many individuals who have allowed a sense of supreme self-worth to overtake their humility because of their advanced education and some relative success in the public realm. One university lecturer who had actively sought my help became opportunistically critical of me when he became a local politician, for no other apparent reason than to position himself before his electorate.

Like most people, I, too, have fallen prey to this on occasion. It's an enticing and inebriating form of self-delusion that makes us think that we understand *all* things because we know *some* things. Like Professor Marlo, we're better to stick to our areas of expertise. And even then, always make some allowance for doubt by others in our opinions.

If we are to have strong opinions, then make sure they're lightly held.

Da, data, datum, d'oh!

Because of the panoply of technology and measuring tools available today in applications, platforms, benchmarks and surveys, one significant dichotomy that we live with is measurement, particularly the opportunities and challenges it engenders. More than at any other time in history, we can qualify and especially quantify much of the phenomena we see and experience. Every day we collect data around economies, our environment and societal perceptions. Individually, we may monitor our glucose levels, our bank transactions and our caloric consumption. Thanks to a plethora of smartwatches, we can even track our heartbeats, steps and swim strokes.

You probably recognize the following quote: "What gets measured gets managed." Wasn't it Peter Drucker (1909–2005), the Austrian-born American business guru, who said this? No, it wasn't. It was a truncated version of what the academic V. F. Ridgway wrote in his 1956 paper, *Dysfunctional Consequences of Performance Measurements*. The British business journalist Simon Caulkin succinctly summarized Ridgway's premise as "What gets measured gets managed—even when it's pointless to measure and manage it, and even if it harms the purpose of the organization to do so."[15]

British anthropologist Marilyn Strathern was even more biting when she wrote that "When a measure becomes a target, it ceases to be a good measure."[16] In other words, as individuals try to anticipate the effect of a particular policy or initiative, they consciously take actions in relation to the policy, rather than to the actual work they are doing.

I've always been concerned about the value of reported crime statistics because I knew they didn't accurately reflect the actual number of crimes committed or people affected. That was because some people, for various reasons, chose not to report all crimes. When I would see an increase in multiple crimes, I would question them. Take, for example, increases in drug seizures. Which is more indicative of an increase in crime: ten seizures of one pound of cocaine or one seizure of ten pounds of cocaine? The answer is nuanced as it depends on other factors like the number of individuals involved, charges laid, and related crimes solved. That's why I would always temper my comments about crime statistics with the caveat that we must be careful when measuring crime and societal feelings of safety.

Ridgway criticizes the measurement mantra popular in the 1950s by comparing what Soviet managers and their American counterparts were doing at the time. He understood the inherent problems with measurement: *not everything that counts can be counted, and not everything that can be counted counts.*[17] He recognized that people tend to value those things they can measure, such as the number of tools, appliances produced, or time spent on production.

Ridgway cautioned that not everything that matters can be measured and that not everything that can be measured actually matters. Canadian management professor Henry Mintzberg proposes that starting from the premise that we can't measure what truly matters provides us with the best chance to face the challenge of measurement realistically.

With an ever-increasing demand for accountability in our society, we've developed a constant desire to validate everything through data measurement, making things important simply because we can measure them. The problem is that if we can't put a numerical value on something, we tend to overlook it. With many tools at our disposal, we've become slavish to measurement through key performance indicators and instruments such as balanced scorecards. We tend towards reducing our concerns to numbers to attempt to compare and understand them uniformly.

Analyzing numbers without proper context becomes intellectually perilous; suffering from innumeracy—the inability to understand and use numbers in calculations—becomes dangerous and acts as an intellectual trap. And attempting to understand the world exclusively through numbers leads us to incorrect conclusions, even if we think we understand those numbers.

By measuring things that we really can't measure, such as public sentiments regarding safety or employee satisfaction, we get false results that measure what we want instead of what's truly important. Polls, online surveys and petitions reduce governance to plebiscites, often capturing convenient samples and not genuinely representative ones. Social media 'likes' replace relationships, fueling the rise of the "attention economy," and the world is perceived according to binary clicks: good versus evil, rich versus poor, us versus them, metrics versus merit. And in today's world full of statistics, innumeracy is just as damaging as illiteracy because people cannot make informed choices and decisions based on their (in)ability to understand the numbers.

We have a natural bias to see things in equilibrium. We continuously search for symmetry. We define physical beauty as how well-balanced a face is, such as that of the *Mona Lisa*, or the size, proportions and length of an individual's muscles to determine their fitness, strength and stamina. We appreciate architecture by the flow and balance of a building's lines, such as the Parthenon in Athens or Giza's pyramids. We regale in nature's awesomeness by the sheer magnitude of the spectrum of colors of a setting or rising sun, the waves crashing on the rocks by a lighthouse, the simplicity of the five arms—or rays—of a starfish, the spiral of a conch shell or the petals of a rose. These natural and human manifestations are structured around a number known as the Golden Ratio that architects and artists alike use to locate aesthetically pleasing areas to situate subjects and distribute weight in drawings and paintings.

Similarly, we have a natural inclination towards the constant, the static and the aesthetic instead of the unpredictable, the dynamic or the deformed, also known as the asymmetric. We assume that there exists a certain level of predictability and order in the world. What's local receives our attention; what's far away is viewed as simple statistics or noise. Having a strong distaste for inconsistencies or incongruence, we humans look for symmetry in life, preferring equal, even and stable features, distributions, patterns and values. We attempt to do this by creating processes and institutions that ensure stability over time, often using data to inform and justify our decisions. This includes things from interest and inflation rates to our weight and cholesterol levels.

The problem with measurement is that we're inclined to search for proof of the presence of those things we wish to confirm. A good example is in training. We quantify the evidence of training such as the number of courses taught, the number of people trained, the number of online accesses to an individual app. But we rarely measure the proficiency in the skills taught. This is in line with societal demands for accountability through numbers and our cultural reactions to risk and liability, reactions that result in risk-avoidance and efforts to circumvent failure rather than demonstrate success.

If we don't pinpoint what we aim to achieve, we end up measuring something, anything for measurement's sake. For decades, we've been obsessed with measuring our weight or girth size instead of our physical abilities, cardiovascular performance or overall fitness. In policing, we have over-relied on reported crime statistics to determine patrol and investigative efficacy. We've been obsessed with earnings per share in business and other metrics that don't tell the whole story about a company's health, such as intangible assets like research and development and unacknowledged costs such as pollution and environmental scarring. As seen in the various accounting scandals of Enron, Worldcom, Tyco, Freddie Mac, Lehman Brothers, Bernie Madoff and others, it's easy to manipulate and inflate measurements around earnings, assets and loans, often leading to disastrous results.

By focusing on incorrect or unimportant numbers rooted in agenda-driven beliefs and narratives, we end up measuring the wrong things. That's why we must use measurement to support evidence-based, not anecdote-based or bias-driven, decision-making. A better approach is to use measures, when appropriate, to understand, appreciate and profit from the risk that exists instead of being risk-averse. Easier said than done when we're measuring the wrong things.

Here's one way to summarize evidence-based decision making:

1. A datum is a single unit of measurement.
2. Datum and datum equal data.
3. Data and data equal information.
4. Information and experience equal understanding.
5. Understanding and analysis lead to knowledge.
6. Knowledge and appropriate action lead to success.

But what if the initial datum upon which the analysis relies is skewed? There can be unintended consequences. In 2008, when I was Deputy

Commissioner, part of my area of responsibility was overseeing how the UN police monitored and mentored their Haitian counterparts. The best way we could measure this was through the number of reports by the UN police officers submitted. Each officer was responsible for monitoring and mentoring a certain number of Haitian police officers. When I arrived in Mission in January that year, there were just over 1000 such reports completed per month on average. Some 400 UN police officers were monitoring over 4000 Haitian police; an average of 2.5 reports per month per UN police officer.

To increase the amount of monitoring, I brought in a new directive that ordered all mission extension approvals to be based partly on the total number of monitoring reports the UN police officers completed. As many of the officers enjoyed the financial benefits of working in Mission —compared to the limited base wages they received in their home countries—this was a new and robust incentive. As a result, we saw the number of mentoring reports skyrocket from 1090 in January to 19,350 in October, an almost twenty-fold increase in less than a year.

As a metric, this was an outstanding success. It implied that UN police officers were undertaking more mentoring and monitoring of their Haitian counterparts because they were submitting more reports. However, the truth was more nuanced than that.

By implementing this practice, I inadvertently created an approach almost exclusively predicated on the number of reports submitted. There was no emphasis on the quality of the individual interactions leading to the writing of the reports, which was the primary goal.

To demonstrate their worth and justification for an eventual mission extension, the monitoring officers would fill in the reports with little, if any, description. The expected and required mentoring and monitoring leading to the reports didn't occur, with the UN police officers submitting their reports in a rote manner. Although the numbers looked great, it was merely an exercise of garbage in-garbage out.

The lesson for me was to ensure that we measured what was required while considering what we couldn't easily capture by the measurement, such as the quality of the individual interactions between UN and Haitian police officers.

American engineer and statistician W. Edwards Deming (1900-1993), credited as being the father of the post-World War II Japanese economic miracle, listed *14 Points on Quality Management*[18], of which points 11a and 11b are:

> Eliminate work standards (quotas) on the factory floor. Substitute leadership.

and

> Eliminate management by objective. Eliminate management by numbers or numerical goals. Substitute leadership.

In the same publication, Deming also listed what he qualified as the *7 Deadly Diseases of Management*, of which point 5 is:

> Use of visible figures only for management, with little or no consideration of figures that are unknown or unknowable.

We can't afford to dismiss all measurement as being useless. But we must be wary of individuals who overflow their reports, arguments, articles, podcasts and the like with graphs, obtuse formulae and statistics in place of rational or logical arguments. As human beings, we're simultaneously impressed and intimidated by a flood of information, preferring to reconcile the two by accepting the data presented to us at face value instead of being empirically skeptical.

Let me emphasize the advantages of being data-driven over its opposite, which is anecdote- or bias-driven. We need to make decisions with the best information available, including a thorough analysis of the same. The problem with being solely data-driven is that we sometimes end up not measuring or appreciating what's truly important, such as the quality of our relationships with family members, clients, communities and the natural world. When we don't see the symmetry and stability we expect, instead seeing nonlinearity and volatility, we think something is amiss. That's when we try to adjust what we see to match our biases, which feed our worldview. We can't understand today's world without numbers, statistics and measurement, but we can't understand it through data alone.

VUCA, or nebulosity at the speed of opacity

The complexity of today's world and the crush of information is such that many institutions and individuals have attempted to encapsulate basic tenets into a unifying notion or acronym. Some don't succeed, while others do relatively well.

One of the better examples is VUCA: Volatility, Uncertainty, Complexity and Ambiguity. The United States Army War College first used the acronym in the late 1980s to describe the world following the Soviet Union's collapse. But it wasn't until the terrorist attacks of September 11, 2001, that its use became commonplace. VUCA also implies that events are multipolar and symptomatic of the complexity that exists.

Unquestionably, the COVID-19 pandemic has tested our threshold of tolerance for uncertainty, and our willingness to trust our leaders. Outlying views and conspiracies spread when people lose confidence in institutions and the leaders that run them. An example related to the COVID-19 pandemic is the rise of vaccination hesitancy and anti-vaccine sentiment. Poland and France are two of many countries in which vaccine hesitancy is strong. There, like elsewhere, it's more an indication of general distrust and dissatisfaction toward government than scientific skepticism.

Referring to the threat of terrorism stemming from Islamic radicalism facing the United Kingdom in the mid-2010s, Andrew Parker, then the director of MI-5 (Military Intelligence, Section 5), stated in a speech to the Royal United Services Institute (RUSI) in Whitehall, UK, on October 8, 2013, that: "Overall, I do not believe the terrorist threat is worse now than before. But it is more diffuse. More complicated. More unpredictable."[19]

Indeed, regarding the specific issue of radicalism leading to terrorist attacks, in the years following Mr. Parker's speech, the threat has continued to be more dispersed, intricate and volatile than at any other time in history. We see extremists of all stripes who attempt not to deploy weapons of mass destruction but weapons of *mass disruption*. Sometimes those weapons can be online threats such as ransomware or the storming of government seats of power such as the United States Capitol on January 6, 2021.

These threats are generally in three areas: public safety, community cohesion and terrorism. Fear through terrorism (domestic or international) is their weapon of choice to advance their disruptive aims. These terrorists are far-right extremists, including white supremacists, anti-government extremists, accelerationists (those expecting the eventual upheaval of society), and radical religious extremists. They also include far-left militants such as anarcho-socialists, Trotskyites and viral insurgents. Between the two are traditional organized crime members, cultists, computer hackers, professional protesters and lone-wolf malcontents who want to make a quick buck, cause some damage, gain some notoriety or settle some grudge (real or perceived). Today's technology has let extremists and terrorists become even more effective in influencing, recruiting and manipulating vulnerable people to their causes.[20]

But have critical events not always been diffuse, complicated, and unpredictable? If they weren't, our predecessors would have been able to solve the issues and problems they faced or dealt with more effectively.

As tempting as it may seem, we must avoid making value judgments regarding today's complexity relative to past events and situations when evaluating what we face. History is awash with decision-making failures: military, economic, diplomatic, political and personal. The same can be said of what the future will hold for us. But the past is also replete with decision-making successes. And to think that we, as the most recent version of humanity, have the monopoly on good decision-making is merely generational hubris.

Collectively, we look at the short-term and current events to determine our successes instead of the long-term over decades, if not generations. We commit the same error while looking at the past and comparing it to the present to understand the future. This results in a myopic, biased and clouded view of events and developments over time.

I live in Halifax, Nova Scotia, a beautiful city that has known its share of tragedies, more so than most Canadian agglomerations. Certain parts of Nova Scotia's shoreline have witnessed as many shipwrecks as any other shoreline in the world in the past three centuries.[21] At the height of World War I, on December 6, 1917, a munitions ship blew up in Halifax's harbor, killing 1,963 and injuring over 10,000 people out of a population of 65,000 people. From 1918 to 1920, like many areas across Canada and the world, Halifax was hit with the Spanish flu pandemic, resulting in 2,000 more deaths and countless sick. One can only imagine how diffuse, complicated, and unpredictable the times were for the leaders of the day.

The key, then, is to see things as clearly as possible. Recognize the nuances that exist in any problem and the trap of our own biases. Try to understand the context of the situation instead of just the numbers. Don't fall into the simplicity trap in which we try to encapsulate our findings into a couple of words or, even worse, into a simple, unifying idea to explain what's occurring. We can do so when looking for a description of what's happening, but not to understand it appropriately and thoroughly.

When we stop at one word, one thought, one idea or one emotion, we invariably focus our attention and energies on looking at the situation through a single lens shaped by our own biases and experiences, both negative and positive. And when our explanation of the problem proves to be wrong, we become confused and upset, wanting to blame other forces and causes instead of our own (mis)perceptions.

Sailing the righteous ship Theseus

Errors in perception can lead to what American author Tim Ferriss qualifies as *bigoteering*: the unwarranted labeling of an individual or their ideas to exploit stigmas accompanying such labels, thereby forcing them to spend time and energy trying to defend themselves and rehabilitate their reputation instead of explaining their views. One highly educated and respected social activist I worked with said, "You can't defend yourself against a charge of bias." That's what makes such bigoteering so effective: targeted individuals are forever on the defensive, not allowed to explain their ideas but incessantly forced to explain themselves against claims that are often baseless.

Bigoteering is a widespread technique individuals of all political stripes and life stations employ. One of its tools is virtue-signaling. Virtue-signaling is a habit of indicating one's perceived sense of morality and righteousness by expressing disgust of or favor for specific political ideas or cultural phenomena. It also can serve as a moniker to try to reduce the effect of a critique, through what is known as a 'straw-man argument': a fallacious assertion that distorts the initial critique in an effort to undermine its credibility. Social media encourages virtue-signaling, as people can quickly and often anonymously express their perceived sense of superiority.

From an historical perspective, evaluating past figures or groups' actions through the lens of today's values is known as *retrospective bigoteering*, just as those in the next century will do when they judge our actions today according to their values in 2100 and beyond.

We need to move from VUCA to a broader, more open approach to alleviate such misperceptions. Developing the Vision, Understanding, Clarity and Agility (also known by many commentators as VUCA 2.0) to deal with our problems is necessary to combat misperceptions. This involves an intellectual effort to appreciate better the variables involved. This further entails using evidence-based approaches to decision-making by creating methods that prevent errors from occurring (fail-safe strategies) and designing solutions in such a way that potential mistakes will not have a negative effect (safe-to-fail approaches). Initiatives must be based on sound, articulable rationales and regular, methodical assessments.

As leaders, we need to search for and see the bigger picture. This is the basis of situational awareness, the ability to understand the nuances that present themselves as part of any problem. Situational awareness helps us develop a road map to solving the problem. By doing so, we can provide our group, our work colleagues or our family members with a compelling vision of things beyond the immediate.

The goal here is to work for your group's greater good, maintaining unity while demonstrating visceral empathy towards all group members. Various qualities, such as diversity and inclusion, are part of our collective strength, but the reality is that group unity is what people seek. That unity takes the shape of an overall vision, mission, purpose and commonly held desire. This also requires creating a work culture of safety and caring.

We know that teams change with the arrival and exit of various members because of voluntary or involuntary departures, promotions, demotions, reassignments, retirements and the like. A group or work unit can see a wholesale change in membership in a short time, resulting in a different look, but it's the same team, nonetheless.

Imagine if you had a group whose membership, infrastructure and equipment changed entirely, not just once, but several times over a short period. As a unit, the team looks the same as before and operates within the same parameters. In a way, your team is like the *Ship of Theseus*,[22] where every single part of the ship has been replaced, raising the question whether the restored ship is still the same object as the original. Although not quite like a ship, a team does maintain consistency of purpose and mission and must evolve with the environment in which it operates. This means that we must also adjust and adapt training, rewards and individual advancement to meet the new environment's reality, just as new members join the team and influence its functioning.

Apps for appsolutely everything

Life is considerably more random and unpredictable than people wish to admit or that conventional economic models assume. We crave simplicity over complexity, certainty over ambiguity.

We respond to many factors and variables, such as material incentives, customs, traditions and group influence. We are rational and irrational at the same time because of our emotions, perceptions and motivations, which are heavily influenced through ritual, some irrational beliefs and the attachment to the familiar. Emotions are our reactions to everyday events, while our perceptions are how we make sense of those same events. Our motivations determine the level of desire we have to do something during our day, at work or home.

Together our perceptions, emotions and motivations drive us continually in all that we do, especially at work. And nothing has a more significant impact on these attributes than our biases. In essence, we are the way we are because of our individual biases forged through a lifetime of living. These biases have a direct effect on our decision-making abilities and outcomes.

The only recourse we have against poor decision-making is through resistance to the obvious and the convenient, through the use of empirical skepticism, continued fact validation, and infinite patience in the face of complexity while being humble enough to recognize the limits of our intellect. Skeptical thinking provides the means to present and understand a coherent argument and, even more importantly, to identify a false or deceptive claim.

With all of its benefits, technology has contributed to creating a more complex society. It delivers significant quantities of information at an astounding pace, quicker than we can process it. Since 2010, the number of people worldwide accessing the internet has exploded from 1.8 billion to over 4.1 billion. What has facilitated this seismic shift in numbers has been the smartphone.

Before Apple introduced the iPhone in 2007, the internet and real life were two separate realms. In the late 90s and early 2000s, if you wanted to go 'online,' you needed an internet connection through a desktop computer or a laptop. You had to be at home, or in a hotel room or a library or workplace with wired internet connections or, in a few instances, wireless connections if your computer had such ability.

After 2007, that changed as people could carry around their personal mobile access gateway to the internet, merging the boundaries between real life and the online world. Just look at how individuals, colleagues and families have since modified their interactions at work, school, the supper table and in life in general.

This entrenchment of technology in our daily lives has also resulted in a phenomenon that we have just started to deal with in the late 20th and early 21st centuries: cybercrime. Essentially, we have to deal with old crimes in new ways as ill-intentioned people can now access more than half the planet's population remotely. We've seen technology as an instrument to facilitate crime such as child exploitation and pornography, cyberbullying, extortion and fraud, while also itself being the target of crime through ransomware, malware and the control of the internet of things. The former is known as cyber-enabled crime while the latter is cyber-native crime.

The Deep and Dark webs facilitate much of this as they provide fertile ground to spread misinformation, lies, rumors, hate, spite and fear, in addition to trafficking illicit products. Although the first recognized death resulting from a cyber-attack occurred in a hospital in Dusseldorf, Germany, in September 2020,[23] some commentators are concerned that this may become disturbingly regular with the advent of self-driving cars and large-scale fragilized infrastructure. The May 7, 2021, cyber-attack on the Colonial Pipeline led to oil shortages, power outages and loss of other essential public services upon which people's lives depend.

There's even a word for such script written to facilitate this: killware.

As we're analog (non-computerized) beings, there is an inherent incongruity between our biology and today's digital technology. The COVID-19 pandemic has resulted in a period of accelerated technological change, affecting our businesses and our homes which, in many cases, now double as workspaces, gyms, bakeries, schools and daycare centers.

Technology is quickly becoming more entrenched into all facets of our daily lives as we adopt pandemic workarounds, becoming further dependent on technology for work, learning, entertainment and socializing. Our previous traditions and habits are quickly changing to accommodate the pandemic's constraints and technological circumventions, being forever modified as a consequence.

Because of self-isolation and physical distancing, we live more atomized lives; our previous social links have been fractured, resulting in less social cohesion and more loneliness. In this sense, the term 'social distancing' is much more accurate than just "physical distancing."

British novelist E.M. Forster (1879-1970) provided a prophetic glimpse into this world in his 1909 short story "The Machine Stops." Forster weaves a dystopian future where people spend their days alone in an underground hexagonal room, much like the cell of a bee, in which they eke out their lives in a perpetual search for "ideas," a euphemism for meaning. Everything is available to them at the touch of a button or the flick of a switch. Not touching people is a sign of good breeding. Instead, they communicate with others through a system uncannily comparable to the internet, in short bursts analogous to social media usage today. The story doesn't end well as the technology upon which humanity relies for everything fails, resulting in humankind's eventual demise.

Real-world reminders of Forster's dystopia include bachelor-sized apartment workspaces and cubicles, a digital economy involving the almost-immediate delivery of goods and services and touchless social norms. His central premise was that a balance must be struck between technology and human connection, as he qualifies man as the measure of things: "Man's feet are the measure for distance, his hands are the measure for ownership, his body is the measure for all that is lovable and desirable and strong." In essence, although we may fashion technology to assist us in evolving, over a century ago, Forster pleaded that it should be human beings and their needs and not technology that drives that evolution.

As an example of the blending of our analog lives with digital technologies, we see the dissipation of the previous separation between video games and spectator sports as they are slowly melding into one. People promote the use of artificial intelligence (AI) in sport to measure all facets of a game, including individual human performance and automated officiating, to avoid human errors on the field, pitch or ice. Companies promote implementing such technology as a means of more accurately enforcing rules and reducing corruption, and to eliminate human error and bias amongst officials, especially in terms of offsides and penalty selection. Such famous officiating gaffes as Diego Maradona's "Hand of God" goal in the 1986 World Cup quarterfinals and NHL referee Tim Peel's "hot-mic" admission that he wanted to call a penalty on a team in March 2021 would be eliminated once and for all, according to the proponents of AI. Preliminary testing using AI has begun in such areas as offsides and goals in hockey and soccer and is the norm when reviewing challenges to certain calls in tennis.

One research study even estimated that referees, umpires and other sports officials face a 98 percent probability of eventual computerization; essentially being replaced by AI.[24] The challenge to automated officiating will be to properly manage the all-too-human emotions of the coaches, players and fans during the game and specifically to determine how a computer process could separate on-field pugilists. Perhaps one day, a cybernetic organism consisting of living tissue over a robotic endoskeleton will intervene when human egos and tempers flare, imploring the penalized players to "Come with me if you want to play."

Trade shows, celebrations and music concerts are further examples of this transformation, going online or not going ahead at all. In some cases, live music concerts are integrated into gaming platforms, such as with the virtual concert by rapper Travis Scott in the online game Fortnite in April 2020, attracting more than 12 million gamers worldwide, including my teenage son and his cohort of boisterous friends. Virtual traveling and visiting now occur, taking the place of in-person tourism. A further, more intimate example is the rise of sex technology or 'sex tech,' which spans virtual reality pornography, Bluetooth-enabled sex toys, remote sex interfaces and even sex robots.

In all of these cases, no additional in-person participants are required, further driving the atomization of our lives.

The 21st century's challenge is not for us, as analog beings, to conform to digital technology's needs, but rather for digital technology to adapt as it infiltrates our analog world. There's an expectation that we can and should solve every problem using technology, mainly through mobile technology such as applications. We often find ourselves asking, "Isn't there an app for that?"

As with training, apps can teach us the rules about something, but it's experience that teaches us about the exceptions in life. And we acquire that experience through interactions with people, quite often in person.

This will be one of the challenges for virtual and augmented-reality assisted by AI as it seeks to penetrate the human psyche. Through such things as digital therapy sessions, such conditions as depression, anxiety and self-esteem will be self-addressed. These issues typically require the development of stable, trusting relationships between analog beings.

The basis of those relationships is morphing from in-person contact to in-voice contact and now to informational communication through emails, texts and postings. This can often lead to unintended consequences, misinterpretation and conflict. How many times have people misunderstood a text's nuances because of how the words were written or presented by an errant capital letter or a misunderstood acronym?

Counting crows, and shooting them, too

In an article from the print version of *The Economist* for November 4, 2017, entitled "How the world was trolled," the authors wrote about how the average American touches their smartphone more than 2,600 times a day. They then compared that figure to some of the other activities Americans collectively undertake *every minute* such as liking things on Facebook (some four million times) and passing gas (about three million times). But what is even more revealing is the unintended role that outrage plays in social media:

When putting these media ecosystems to political purposes, various tools are useful. Humor is one(...). The best tool, though, is outrage. This is because it feeds on itself; the outrage of others with whom one feels fellowship encourages one's own. This shared outrage reinforces the fellow feeling; a lack of appropriate outrage marks you out as not belonging. The reverse is also true. Going into the enemy camp and posting or tweeting things that cause them outrage—trolling, in other words—is a great way of getting attention.

This outrage manifests itself most often through social media virtue-signaling: demonstrating support or reprobation for a cause, thereby demonstrating one's apparent moral superiority, or using it as an argument to deflect criticism. If enough people get involved and histrionics (melodrama) is added, this leads to social media show trials. A poignant example of such virtue signaling and the inherent dangers of same occurred following the Wednesday, November 11, 2015, Remembrance Day ceremonies in Halifax, Nova Scotia.

In Canada, as elsewhere in the British Commonwealth, Remembrance Day ceremonies are important moments for communities of veterans, their families and supporters to gather for a brief period, what one musician qualified as a "pittance of time." It's a moment to remember those who lost their lives in past wars, military missions, training exercises and peacekeeping operations. In light of the various terrorist and mass-shooting events that had occurred the world over, police in Halifax provided armed oversight at many Remembrance Day venues that day, the largest in Halifax being beside city hall in a square known as Grand Parade.

A local television producer posted to his Facebook account a photo of two Halifax police tactical officers with their patrol carbines at the ready during the Remembrance Day ceremony earlier that day at Grand Parade.[25] His posting was highly critical of the two officers, claiming that their heavily armed presence and alleged loud talking were disconcerting to many in attendance. Local mainstream and contrarian media alike amplified the post, garnering many comments critical of police. The next day, the producer indicated his desire to lay a public complaint against the officers. On Friday, November 13, 2015, there were six separate terrorist attacks in Paris, France, including at the Bataclan nightclub and theatre, killing 129 and injuring over 300 people. Over the weekend, as the tide of public sentiment and revulsion against the Paris attacks was building, a wave of hostile and insulting comments on the producer's Facebook page forced him to delete his initial posting critical of the armed police presence. That Monday morning, he meekly advised that he no longer wished to lay a complaint.

In the summer of 2001, while I was the acting officer in charge of Portage la Prairie Detachment for the RCMP in Manitoba, we had a significant community problem with crows ripping apart garbage bags, eating away at the contents. They would make a mess on town streets and driveways, beside homes and apartment blocks. The crows would also disrupt people's picnics and grab food left in cars and homes where windows were left open with no screens available. Unsubstantiated rumors even had crows attempting to fly off with infants. Public outcry made its way to city hall, and the mayor approached me to see if we could control the problem by shooting and killing errant crows.

I advised the mayor that shooting at crows was fraught with many challenges, most notably the issue of public safety and stray bullets and the optics of a town shooting at crows to protect its garbage. I suggested that he obtain expert evidence from someone in the know.

The mayor contacted Dr. Lynn Miller, an ornithologist from the University of Manitoba, who came to a council meeting one evening. Dr. Miller spent an hour explaining to the mayor and the town councilors how crows are fascinating birds that enjoy tall, large trees and, like humans, welcome offspring every year while living in family units. They're also highly intelligent, understanding the mechanics and timing of garbage days. Instead of attempting to control the bird population, it was better to control the food sources by encouraging the usage of large garbage containers and picking up roadkill (such as deer, geese and muskrats) as soon as they were discovered. The key was to understand the problem, minimize the negative impact crows had and not attempt to eradicate an issue that was one of inconvenience instead of legitimate public health or safety.

In his book, *Factfulness*, Swedish physician and author Hans Rosling (1948-2017) summarized the situation succinctly: we need to worry about the right things; ignore the noise of an over-dramatic, sometimes histrionic world; and remain cool-headed so we can understand and support the local and global collaborations we need to reduce those real risks that truly exist. He cautioned against our biases, including those that affect our instincts around urgency and melodrama. By being less stressed about imaginary or ideologically driven problems, we can be more alert to the real issues of our lives and the world and how to solve them.

Back in Portage la Prairie, to the mayor's and the councilors' credit, they adopted Dr. Miller's advice, eventually providing sturdy garbage containers to every household that all but resolved the problem of the aerial garbage pickers. By taking the time to look at all facets of the problem, this mid-west Canadian town avoided international reprobation. Most importantly, they solved their issue through an evidence-based approach instead of through bias and conjecture.

Bespoke decision-making

The key to dealing effectively with complexity is to tailor our decision-making approach to fit the level of complexity we're facing. This means recognizing the context of the situation with which we're dealing. Just because something is complex doesn't mean that it's overwhelming. By mastering our initial reaction to a complicated problem—often panic— we can look for those patterns and relationships that will allow us to deal with the challenge at hand.

For example, are we dealing with a relatively simple, ordered situation or context such as a crime that has been committed where a suspect is already in custody and the investigation is ongoing? This is the realm of best practice where there are 'known knowns.' This is the technician's or expert's domain that recognizes repeating patterns and consistent events that we've encountered before. Here we can deal with the intricacies of a situation quite effectively.

Or perhaps we're dealing with an ordered yet complicated situation or context involving a rash of unique crimes with no identified suspects and significant public concern. This is the realm of good practice where there are 'known unknowns' requiring the involvement of experts who bring their know-how to bear to validate existing facts.

Going further, perhaps we're dealing with a complex unordered situation or context involving interrelated public safety and community health issues such as the COVID-19 pandemic or the opioid epidemic. This is the realm of emergent or adaptive practice where there are 'unknown unknowns,' competing demands, emergence and contradicting pressures. Emergence occurs when an entity, situation or event has properties that its constitutive parts don't have on their own, due to the diverse interactions between those parts. At this juncture, we need strong technical, political or scientific leadership. As the context becomes more complex, the requirement for creative and innovative solutions becomes more pressing.

Or perhaps we're dealing with a chaotic situation involving an active shooter dressed as a police officer and driving a mock police vehicle in the middle of the night, leaving a string of victims in his wake. Such an event occurred on the night of April 18-19, 2020, just to the north of Halifax, Nova Scotia, in what became Canada's worst mass shooting. The rampage left 22 people dead before police stopped the killer, shooting him dead. This is the realm of novel or unique practice where we deal with a massive totality of 'unknowables' to effect rapid response to bring the context back to something relatively manageable or 'just' complex. Here we are unthinkingly ignorant of those things we don't know or can even conceive of in the immediate. Black Swans operate at this level as well as at the next.

Finally, the most complex situation we can confront occurs when disorder and extreme turbulence reign, leaving us to ask ourselves, "Where are we?" as the usual contextual landmarks and responses are absent. Such rare events result from unusual, asymmetrical events such as a significant earthquake, massive storm or multi-pronged terrorist attack. One recent example occurred following the second landfall of Hurricane Katrina on August 29, 2005, resulting in some 1,800 deaths. The New Orleans Police Department had to deal with power outages, levee breaks and extensive flooding. Almost 200 officers (out of 1,000) left their posts to find and rescue their own family members, leaving an overwhelmed and ill-equipped organizational response. This is the realm in which total confusion rules and leaders must attempt to break down the situation into constituent, manageable parts to be able to deal with an overwhelming context.

The unfortunate reality is that many of our tools to deal successfully with problems are mainly useful in the simple and complicated realms, in what can be considered ordered responses. But the significant challenges that cause us so much pain and suffering are situated in the complex, chaotic and disordered realms where our tools are often insufficient or useless. Here we require equally complex, if not almost-chaotic, responses to the disorder that reigns. Regardless of their situation, leaders must recognize the context they're dealing with and adapt their actions and tools to counter the context.

The five scenarios I described above fall into the domains of the Cynefin Framework,[26] one of many tools available for leaders to adjust their decision-making processes according to the level of complexity they're facing. Such adjustments allow them to make more appropriate responses to those challenges. Of course, this isn't the only approach available to deal with complexity. Other decision-making and preparation tools include strategic foresight and reference-class forecasting that help us examine potential threats, opportunities and likely developments while learning from past situations and outcomes.

Regardless of the tools you use, a leader's overarching role is to ensure the organization knows how to perform and is still capable of performing during any one of these situations. This requires developing actionable contingency plans while providing consistent preparation, proper equipment and adaptable leadership. This also means that both the leadership and the organization are capable of at least thinking the unthinkable.

The French government conducted a unique initiative in this sense in December 2020 when it hosted the first-ever Defense Innovation Forum. During the event, a "Red Team" of ten science-fiction writers created a series of "scenarios of disruption" that could occur between 2030 and 2060. The exercise's goal was to provide the French Defense Ministry with a list of potential threats so the French army could prepare for them in the future. One of Red Team's members, Romain Lucazeau, recognized the limits of their work, stating, "Our ability to predict equals zero. That said, I'm convinced that a process in which I listen to people who tell me things I cannot imagine within the bounds of my work can help me prepare for the unexpected."

This reflects the essential element of dealing with randomness and complexity: preparing for the unexpected. We need to be mindful and alive to what is happening, not trapped in old categorizations and reactions or one-word renderings of the situations we face. It also requires understanding what constitutes the unexpected, those scenarios that are plausible, not so improbable as to be far-fetched. Examples would be to prepare for real-life situations such as active shooters and significant environmental, public health and financial events, all of which are within the realm of the plausible, but not alien invasions or zombie apocalypses which belong in films.

In addition to imagining future scenarios for planning purposes, we need to take six other measures involving fail-safe and safe-to-fail planning approaches that help us to face the unthinkable and prepare for the unexpected:

1. Ensure continual maintenance of system infrastructure to avoid breakdowns at the wrong times. This includes protecting intangible assets such as stored data, research and intellectual property from cyber threats and traditional hazards to their storage. This approach requires a preoccupation with failure and the understanding that what *can* go wrong *will* go wrong.
2. Undertaking integrated, forward-looking analyses while moving from a predictive to an adaptive mindset, encouraging an opportunistic approach to challenges. Included in this is understanding the future costs and contingent liabilities related to new accountability mechanisms and policies intended to deal with such broad challenges as climate change and technological evolution.
3. Striving for organization-wide continuous learning by nurturing a workplace thirst for knowledge, understanding and execution. This requires individuals to learn about the broader community dimensions at work, not merely those affecting their immediate area of employment and interest.
4. Enabling self-organization and social networking across the entire workforce to allow for emergent and innovative activity that different work units can independently initiate. As crisis management rests on a foundation of daily beliefs and repeated action, it's easier to continue habitual behavior during irregular times thanks to those ingrained beliefs and actions. Underpinning this habitual behavior is the intimate understanding and encouragement of linked operational capacity and relationship building.
5. Decentralizing decision-making so those who have the most on the line (usually local, front-line employees) can react with the requisite authority to deal with any situation immediately. The key is to reduce adverse effects as quickly as possible while continuing everyday work priorities, if feasible. Allowing information to flow freely between different units or groupings requires an organizational commitment to resilience in the face of the unexpected.
6. Promoting a variety of thinking styles to effectively deal with the diversity of challenges and complexity we face. This promotion includes a marked reluctance to simplify interpretations of events.

These measures promote an adaptive mindset for the organization, shifting the emphasis from a static to a dynamic approach and response. This methodology requires all employees to develop an adaptive mindset in which they willingly take on new challenges, persevere in the face of extreme uncertainty and focus on the process leading to an eventual result. It also means avoiding a focus based strictly on the outcome, while accepting failure and criticism as a way to learn.

Finally, the leader's overarching role involves developing future leaders in recognizing the level of complexity and the context they're operating in so they can deal with the situations they face correctly, effectively as they surface. This requires patience, taking time to reflect on any given situation while fully understanding, defining and communicating the long-term objectives. It also requires preparing not just for natural disasters and hostile acts but also for those inevitable situations that result from deceptively simple sequences of events caused by human frailties and capriciousness. This starts with openness on the part of a leader to encourage people to send them ideas, suggestions and information, and to act upon them. As a leader, you can't know everything, but you must recognize that, somewhere, someone knows something that you don't. You have to develop the internal structures and culture in your organization that encourage and allow for that something to come to you in real-time. This is because knowledge travels through different ways and different people in any organization. Those who lead have the responsibility to shape how and when that information flows.

As present and future leaders, we need to be actively mindful of the reality of our situation; reality is the difference between what truly is and not what we wish for. Through consistent, useful scanning, we can understand situational cues and indications as challenges slowly or quickly manifest themselves. This further requires spatial and temporal awareness, which we can only develop through profound observation and listening. That is the lesson of scanning. Only then can we begin to understand what makes people, including ourselves, tick.

Calls from the blue line

- We attribute our success in life to those things we think we can influence and direct, including the outcomes of various events. This is known as our *locus of control*. Understand the difference between our *locus of control* and our *locus of concern*.
- Success in life isn't determined through any single factor but through what is known as a concatenation (the linking together of elements in a series or a chain), including avoiding multiple errors and failures along the way.
- Don't be like Marlo—stick to your area of expertise. If you want to step outside it, know what you're talking about. Or, at the very least, recognize what you don't know.
- Take a lesson from Machiavelli: the key to dealing with complexity is not to be predictive but to be adaptive, to be ingeniously opportunistic. Understand that complexity can be tricky, so you need to up your game to understand it.
- We're good at postdiction because of the hindsight bias, but we're absolutely, positively lousy at prediction. Don't try to predict the unexpected; try to prepare for it.
- In today's world, numeracy—the ability to understand and use numbers and statistics—is just as important as literacy. You can't understand today's world without numbers, data and measurement, just as you can't understand it through those parameters alone.
- The key to dealing effectively with complexity is to tailor our decision-making approach to fit the level of complexity we're facing.
- The five domains of being are:
    1. The simple realm
    2. The complicated realm
    3. The complex realm
    4. The chaotic realm
    5. The disordered realm

- The leader's overarching role involves developing future leaders to recognize the level of complexity and the context they're operating in so they can immediately, correctly and effectively deal with the situations they face.
- As a leader, you must be mindful by actively seeking to understand your situation's reality; reality is the difference between what truly is and not what we wish for.

2: The lesson of scanning

...information consumes the attention of its recipients, hence a wealth of information creates a poverty of attention.
- Herbert Simon (1916–2001),
American economist and psychologist,
winner of the 1978 Nobel Prize

Crushing blows

In 2008, as the Deputy Police Commissioner in charge of Operations for the United Nations Mission in Haiti, I had a general staff of ten international police leaders to assist me. All French-speaking men, they came from various countries in Western and Central Africa, Canada, the United States, France and Turkey. A few spoke English. Some were Muslim, some Christian, others agnostic. The officer in charge of our investigative unit that supported the Haitian judicial police (crime scene investigators) came from the West African country of Senegal. His name was Aliou Thiam. In his country, he held the rank of Chief Superintendent of Police, a high rank in his national police service, the *Gendarmerie nationale du Sénégal*.

Early in my stint, I had adjudicated a conflict between Mariko and one of his immediate commanders, a Canadian police officer from Québec. After hearing both sides, I ruled in Mariko's favor and transferred the Canadian out of the investigative support unit. It would prove to be a correct decision, as Mariko became one of my most trusted advisors. Simultaneously, the Canadian's stay was clouded by allegations of sexual misconduct with Haitian women.

On the morning of Friday, November 7, 2008, I was scheduled to deliver a speech at the Nigerian police contingent medal ceremony. Every country's contingent of police officers and military members organized an official celebration during which a senior mission official placed the UN medal on the proud peacekeepers' chests. In addition to distributing the medals, I would normally deliver a speech vaunting the contingent's continued efforts in the mission.

Unfortunately, I never made it to the medal ceremony. Around 9:30 that morning, in the Port-au-Prince neighborhood of Bourdon, about a mile south-east of my office, a church-run institution, the Evangelical Promise School, collapsed. The school's first floor had suddenly buckled under the building, resulting in the second and third floors coming down on over 150 students and several teachers. Some 93 people, mostly children between the ages of 7 and 15, would be confirmed dead in the days to come.

Upon receiving reports of the collapse, I rushed over to the site. The scene was chaotic. As I had never been in the immediate area before, I had no idea what the school had looked like before its collapse. All I saw was a flattened white concrete structure on the side of a hill in a ravine surrounded by densely packed shanties. It was like being in a large sports stadium with thousands of onlookers who were yelling, crying and imploring people to do something, anything.

I was sure that many of the people watching had children who were trapped inside the debris. Dozens of impromptu rescuers were feverishly chipping away with whatever tools they had at a solid concrete layer.

Minutes after my arrival, while I was feverishly coordinating the UN police response via cell phone, the UN military Force Commander, Brazilian Major General Carlos Alberto dos Santos Cruz, arrived. Visibly shaken upon seeing the site, he immediately commandeered a pickaxe from one of the locals and began to strike at the debris repeatedly. Not able to breach the concrete shell, the general soon gave up. Exhausted, he looked at me in a disheartened manner and began to bark orders to his aides who had been taking photos of their commander in action.

I spent the next three days there as the UN incident commander, observing a constant stream of lifeless young bodies as they were extracted from the rubble. I must have handled about thirty of those bodies myself. Some had crushed heads and twisted limbs, while many others had no visible injuries, having died by asphyxiation from the sheer weight of the debris on their young chests. They were all wearing the uniform of their school. I saw no survivors.

The next day, two search and rescue teams arrived, from Norfolk, Virginia and the French Caribbean territory of Martinique, to begin searching for survivors in the debris. The searching was a dangerous undertaking. The rescuers had to crawl through small entrances and crevices to determine if there were any survivors amongst the bodies and then effect their rescue. They had some exceptionally sensitive equipment that could detect heat signatures and sounds like breathing and even heartbeats to assist them.

To do this work, the rescuers required absolute silence. That meant stopping all digging and evacuating all above-ground searchers from the debris field. To someone in the know, this was a logical course of action. But to the thousands of people watching in the fishbowl that was the ravine, all they saw were above-ground searchers abandoning their work on the site.

In Haiti, there is a creole word called *télédyol*, of which the suffix *dyol* means 'mouth' in Creole. This is the Haitian version of the telephone game, or how information spreads quickly by word-of-mouth, sometimes over long distances, resulting in cumulative errors of rumors and gossip amongst the facts. The *télédyol* had been working overtime in the ravine that day, including spreading numerous bogus reports that children trapped inside the collapsed school had been calling their families from their cell phones.

When we started to direct the diggers to leave the site's top to allow rescue teams to penetrate the debris field from below, those watching didn't and couldn't understand. Their frustration instantly became palpable. Despite our best efforts to explain to those leaving the debris field what was occurring below, the onlookers began to chant and scream their disapproval. And to organize themselves.

Within minutes, a group of some fifty men, many armed with chunks of concrete from the outlying debris field, approached the site looking to continue the digging. None of the men wanted to engage in dialogue; they only wanted to get on the site. I met them at the edge of the debris field, along with, Mariko, who had come to join me that day, and a 24-man public order team from the newly arrived India FPU. None of the public order members spoke English or French; only their two junior commissioned officers spoke any English. I had instructed the public order unit not to wear any firearms and be armed only with shields with no drawn batons.

We formed a buffer line on the edge of the debris field to keep the group away from the site. Mariko was on one end of the line while I was on the other, neither of us having any protective equipment. For 30 minutes, we blocked access to the site, slowly inching our way towards the group of highly agitated men, not knowing what to expect. Aside from the onlookers who were still chanting and yelling from the ravine, there was no other sound on top of the collapsed school. It was a tense, pro-tracted moment in time as we stood our ground before the agitated group of men wanting to breach our line.

As soon as I received word from the rescue teams that they had car-ried out their work for the moment, with great relief, I ordered the public order unit to stand down and signaled to the men to return to the debris field to continue digging. I then took a small group of them aside to ex-plain what we were attempting to do. Once they understood, I asked them to use the *télédyol* to explain to everyone, including the onlookers in the ravine, what they had to do in the future. We had no further prob-lems when we asked the diggers to evacuate the debris field later that day.

To add to the local community's extreme anguish, an implausible tragedy related to the collapse occurred later that evening. A local com-pany had brought in a telescopic mobile crane, one of those huge, yellow, multi-axle vehicles you can see on construction sites worldwide. The hope was to employ the telescopic arm to lift large debris pieces to assist in the recovery efforts at the collapsed school site.

However, the enormous telescopic mobile crane couldn't negotiate the tight streets and alleyways to get the area. It stayed at a distance until a final decision was made about its use. It had been parked for several hours on a major, sloped thoroughfare, Avenue John Brown, beside streetlamps and power lines, with the operator waiting inside the driver's cabin enjoying the air conditioning while the crane's motor was still running.

Around 9 pm., an electric transformer immediately to the right of the elevated cabin of the parked crane suddenly blew up. The explosion, which was contained to the transformer itself, startled the crane driver, who immediately jumped from the cabin in fear of his life and limb. In doing so, he accidentally released the brake of his vehicle, resulting in this multi-ton behemoth rolling down the sloped main thoroughfare and plowing into several cars before finally coming to a stop when it crashed into and leveled a building.

I attended the scene about 30 minutes afterward. It was only minutes away from my residence. The chaotic accident area was like something out of a film, with crushed cars strewn about, people yelling, ambu-lances, and victims everywhere. At least seven people died in the car-nage, with dozens injured.

By daybreak, the entire site had been cleaned up, with all the wrecked vehicles towed away and all the victims, both alive and dead, transported to the hospital or morgue. Both the driver and the telescopic mobile crane were nowhere to be found. No one had obtained the mobile crane's plate number; it was unknown if it even had one.

There was a ray of light in all this despair. During the night of the runaway crane accident, one of the teams' rescue attempts inside the debris involved extracting a young survivor who was found sandwiched between two dead victims. The rescuers had to cut one of the deceased victims in half to dislodge the survivor. It was horrific work involving difficult decisions while risking the lives of the rescuers.

Upon my arrival that next morning, I was briefed on the rescue. For cultural reasons, the on-site Haitian authorities didn't want to claim responsibility for authorizing such a difficult procedure. I advised the senior Haitian police official on site that I would accept that responsibility as the incident commander. There was no eventual fallout from the choice. The survivor eventually recovered.

A tsunami of information

Author Stephen Covey (1932–2012) wrote that in life there are three immutable constants: change, principles and choice. Principles and choices relate to our character, which we will touch upon in a later chapter. Change implies that life is in a constant state of flux, full of unexpected asymmetry and distortions. As much as we would like to see constancy in life, nothing remains static. At times, the changing societal landscape outpaces our abilities to adapt.

This is undoubtedly true for many of our institutions, including policing. Specific to public safety, one commentator observed that as a society, we share an 18th-century view of sovereignty, a 19th-century judicial system, and a 20th-century law enforcement model that must contend with 21st-century crime and social issues.

Nothing remains static: we grow up, we acquire experience, we work, we love, we accomplish many things, all the while aging which results (unless accident or illness intervenes) in our finality, death. During the entire time, our thoughts and actions must adapt to what happens around us.

To successfully navigate the seascape of our lives, we must not get stuck on one idea or approach when examining things, ideas or people.

All that we can hope to expect is the unexpected, so we must be prepared for it as much as possible, and make the most appropriate responses while maintaining a specific course and direction.

In addition to preparing for the unexpected, we have to plan to benefit from it. This planning means being continually oriented in our actions towards the reality of the situation and towards growth, correctly identifying the reality we live in and adjusting to the changes we face. Our reality what truly is and not what we wish for.

Leadership requires an advanced ability to recognize, interpret and analyze many different things: ourselves, others, potential challenges and opportunities, the environment, trends, timing and processes. This advanced ability to read and scan allows us to understand better the environment in which we live.

The key to success in this unpredictable, VUCA-filled world is through seeing things as they truly are, not through the lens of our hopes, fears, beliefs and biases. This is where character and integrity come in. It requires us to have the moral and intellectual courage to recognize and then meet reality's demands. The key is not to deny any situation's existence but to deny the finality of that situation.

This approach means seeing the reality out there instead of the impressions, the expectations or the assumptions that we think are there while appropriately responding to that reality. It's impossible to have an unbiased view of reality. Much conspires against us as we attempt to see the world we belong to, both our immediate one and the larger one that goes beyond our direct locus of control.

One of the biggest obstacles in discovering reality is the crush of information that confronts us daily. Some have qualified this information crush as being "infobesity" or "infoxication." Think of the multiple sources of information in your own life: work and personal emails, presentations, constant meetings and personal interactions, the endless flow of text and direct messages, written reports, telephone calls, social media feeds, and traditional media sources such as radio, television, magazines, newspapers and books that all gush forth information for you to consider and act upon. We live in the most-informed yet least-reflective society of all time because of the sheer volume of information we receive and have access to. The challenge is our inability to process all of that information that constantly bombards us.

Mass media flood us with bad news and provide standards of unattainable perfection that compete for our attention. If you want to quickly establish a barometer of the amount of information that assaults you, try to count the number of different passwords you have for everything you do at home, work and online. It can be simply overwhelming.

That information overload results in the shortening of our attention spans, limiting the time available to reflect appropriately on those matters critical in our lives, including those issues directly affecting our families and our communities. We often focus on the sound bites and the noise instead of the crucial matters and signals that affect us individually and collectively. We're forced to continually ascertain what truly matters in this age of perpetual distraction. We search for bite-sized morsels of information to swallow, preferably deconstructed and pre-digested, that allow us to save some time and intellectual energy.

The burden we then assume is that our opinions become influenced and pre-formed by others, individuals who may be better at explaining than understanding and better at criticizing than doing. Information isn't only there for us to seek, but seeks us out in a perpetual attempt to influ-ence us. This is social engineering.

As a social sciences discipline, social engineering comprises those efforts intended to influence particular attitudes and social behaviors on a large scale in targeted audiences. We can see this at work through government programs, media campaigns, general marketing promotions and even online criminal enterprises.

Today's social media influencers are perfect examples of social engineering at work. Through blogs, podcasts, posts, comments and videos, these individuals connect with a specific audience to persuade their many followers to consume products and accept ideas through entertaining recommendations and opinions. They also make significant money while doing so. Social media influencers work in almost every area of human interest, be it food, travel, music, fashion and style, sport, photography, gaming and politics.

Malevolent actors can also use social engineering to manipulate people to perform harmful actions, such as purchasing useless and overly expensive goods or divulging confidential information about themselves from which the malevolent actor can derive unwarranted economic benefit. Extremist groups, under cover of anonymity or even sometimes very openly, also use social media to convey messages, organize activities and attack foes.

Another social engineering goal such groups use is to form and manipulate public opinion by promoting information layered with some truth but fashioned to arrive at a particular conclusion. This is the first cousin of fake news, known as 'synthetic news,' and popular amongst some politicians and those wishing to advance their causes and careers.

Because we humans are sense-making and rule-making beings, we search for meaning in almost everything we do. We do so to understand events, actions and systems. If meaning is absent in the information we receive, we fill in the gaps to provide value, often with incorrect assumptions. Consequently, the noise we're assaulted with through the crush of information becomes a signal, then becomes a narrative. We feel we need to act quickly on the information not to lose an opportunity or deal with a challenge, leading us to jump to conclusions. Those narratives then shape our decisions. Our decisions, the same decisions that started out only as noise, then form the mental models that guide us in this world.

American actor Danny Kaye (1911-1987) partially summed this up when he spoke of a woman he did not appreciate in these terms, "Her favorite position is beside herself, and her favorite sport is jumping to conclusions." The lady is not alone.

Avoiding tactical hell

In early August 2017, a widespread landline and cellular telephone outage hit the four Atlantic Canadian provinces, New Brunswick, Nova Scotia, Prince Edward Island and Newfoundland & Labrador. The communications blackout affected one of three large mobile phone carriers. Flights were delayed and canceled while automatic teller machines suddenly became inoperative.

Halifax Regional Police is the largest municipal police service in Atlantic Canada. As a result of the outage, we couldn't make or receive cellular phone calls, and our computer-assisted dispatching was interrupted for a protracted period.

We started to dispatch those calls for service we did receive through cell phones and landlines that still worked. The older police officers on shift had no problems 'doing it old school,' and they easily adjusted. The younger employees were like fish out of water, unable to understand how to operate without being presented information through their mobile data terminals.

The outage lasted for about 24 hours; luckily, no major event occurred during that time. It was a unique opportunity to gauge how people react differently to changes in information flow.

To properly deal with the crush of information, separating the signals from the noise is critical in seeing the reality we face. To reconcile the often-conflicting information that overwhelms us, we tend to gravitate towards (over)simplification and specialization. We feel that we understand complex events and issues with greater coherence, precision and depth than we really do—something that psychologists have labelled "the illusion of explanatory depth"[27].

This overconfidence in our abilities to understand phenomena leads us to favor dualisms (good versus evil, right versus wrong, us versus them) and absolutes (unified theories of how and why things operate, ideological stances, including conspiracy theories). This approach colors and limits our perceptions of events and ideas, leading us to often incorrect conclusions.

Being for or against any particular idea makes us blind to information that does not conform to our perspective. Amongst many assumptions, it presupposes that people of one identifiable group, ethnicity, persuasion or profession are of one voice, one culture or one worldview. This is false and hampers our quest for understanding the reality of any given situation.

In his work *The Gulag Archipelago*, Russian novelist and political prisoner Alexander Solzhenitsyn (1918-2008) pointed to this temptation to see each other in stark terms, to believe that harm results from someone else who is different from us, and most likely wicked:

> If only there were evil people somewhere insidiously committing evil deeds, and it were necessary only to separate them from the rest of us and destroy them. But the line dividing good and evil cuts through the heart of every human being, and who is willing to destroy a piece of his own heart?

Solzhenitsyn's observation was that a better understanding of history starts with a broader understanding of human beings and their nature: we're all flawed and all part of the problem at the same time. The opposite, then, can also be asserted: we're all part of the solution.

In his masterpiece, *The Art of War*, strategist Sun-Tzu (544–496 BCE) wrote of the crucial importance of seeing events precisely as they are and not how we would like to see them. He noted that success in human interactions such as politics and war was based on "the art of deceit," which would lead to success with minimal bloodshed if adequately interpreted and executed.

He further recognized that one of our most significant human short-

comings is to be fixated on one thing, one idea, one principle, one experience or one emotion. This fixation creates a permanent filter, lens or bias
through which humans see things in their lives. This results in us not
seeing the reality of a situation; at worst, even losing contact with reality.

Such a skewed view regularly occurs in people with personality disorders and under the influence of drugs, alcohol or another's manipulation.
They lose touch with reality and become unable or unwilling to see it,
even if it's right in front of them.

The key to maintaining our sense of reality, leading to an effective
overall strategy in life, is to adapt our thoughts to what's happening
around us at any given time. This broad strategy demands that we have
an interest in what goes on. Personal interest implies having skin in the
game—having direct exposure to what's happening and what results.
Furthermore, it means that we have something to lose if we don't adjust
our approach. The lessons we garner from the negative and positive consequences of our decisions allow us to understand the reality we're facing intimately. Provided we're open to seeing them.

For Sun-Tzu, the art of war revolved around winning with minimum
bloodshed and minimum violence. For us, Sun-Tzu's reference to war can
be a modern metaphor for the daily struggles we all go through in life, including the larger societal struggles such as poverty, ignorance and prejudice.

To adjust our perspective and actions, we must avoid being stuck on
one idea, notion or ideology. Ideologies are simplified ideas, often dis-
guised as science, philosophy, or religious dogma. The goal of ideology is
to explain the world's complexity, offering straightforward, cause-and-effect solutions to the various problems we face, avoiding the complexity
of existence and required explanation.

Ideologies can become substitutes for the version of truth ideologues
perpetuate. They may claim to have the answers to society's problems,
even if they have yet to even deal with their own personal problems.
Their *modus operandi* is to engage in interactions where they present
themselves in the dominant role, denigrating or ridiculing others by using selective evidence and impressing those already sharing the same
opinion of the validity of their simplistic worldview. The goal of the ideologue's interaction with others is to convince their audience that *not*
thinking is the right path when addressing a particular issue. Anyone
who doesn't share the ideologue's conviction and zeal about the issue is
not only misguided but immoral and shouldn't be listened to.

As the saying goes, only fools and fanatics are sure of everything.

When we become fixated on a single aspect of a problem, we can only see and interpret the issue or event through a form of tunnel vision created by our own biases and experiences. This inhibits our ability to see things as they truly are because things, events and actions are almost always multi-faceted, with various nuances and hues that can go undetected if we refuse to look for them. We avert this sad state of affairs by avoiding dualisms and absolutes. We need to see life in more fluid terms.

The author of several books on the art of power and strategy, Robert Greene, qualifies our constant reactions through single-dimensional thinking as "tactical hell." To Greene, when we lose sight of our long-term goals, it's because we're asserting our ego to prove ourselves right rather than seeking the truth. To avoid this, we need to raise our perspective high enough to always engage in strategic thinking.

Ideally, we need to develop further a mindset that he qualifies as being "grand strategy." We do that by understanding what exactly our values and priorities are in our life, constantly reminding ourselves of what truly matters. Referencing Sun-Tzu, Greene asserts that, just as in warfare, in life strategists will always prevail over tacticians. An example of such an approach is remembering that our goal is not to win arguments but to win, period. But first, you have to know what constitutes victory.

To know where you are and where you are going, you need to have a crystal-clear view of your direction. You can attain this by listing your values and priorities through some form of personal or professional balanced scorecard, strategy map, mission statement or similar document.

If you don't have such a document, you need to put pen to paper (or finger to keyboard) to craft one. Include in this list:

- what your mission in life is (what is it you wish to do with your life)
- your vision (how will you achieve this mission through a series of action statements)
- the essential values and fundamental qualities you want to live and project, each and every day.

You can break up the action statements according to those areas you want to develop, such as

- understanding complexity
- management experience
- leadership experience

- personal development.

The key is to have something written down that reflects who you are and what you want to achieve in life; essentially the direction you want to go in.

This list will act as your lighthouse when the fog of tactical hell surrounds you, when you are lost searching for direction and desperately need that elevation of perspective.

By putting down on paper those things we value and desire in our life, we develop that crystal-clear view of what direction we want to move in. This direction fuels our overall strategy and allows us to determine what actions we want to partake in and those we wish to avoid. In turn, it'll enable us to set practical goals for us, our family and work team, guiding them forward in their achievements.

The key is to respond with intelligent action based on an overall, predetermined strategy, leading to sound tactics. That means not falling into the trap of doing things impulsively, such as buying that car because it looks good at the moment, leaving that partner because you're ticked off or consuming something just to make you feel temporarily better.

Part of this process involves asking ourselves the right questions. Questioning forces us to have a defined strategy to determine our goals and always drive towards them.

Develop the habit of regularly asking what you are doing, and why you are doing it. By creating a type of internal inquisitor function in our head, we can develop skepticism that questions our actions' worthiness instead of acting blindly or automatically.

When I was in college, I was fortunate enough to have an older acquaintance who consistently offered me practical advice. On one occasion, he spoke of his brother who had "laser-sharp focus" when he approached any goal. Before he honed into a specific objective, he always scanned his environment to determine where he was and where he was going, adjusting his actions as required. This approach is the epitome of having a master strategy.

We need to understand two things: the inherent conflict of ideas and life's complexity. We can begin developing the requisite overall strategy to deal with life's challenges while we forge forward with our plans to understand these two issues.

Adjusted to today's circumstances and in light of those objectives, Sun-Tzu's approach involves three main components:

- adopting a strategic mindset

- understanding complexity
- embracing conflict as a means of solving problems.

All three parts require being pro-active and fully engaging our thought processes to deal with the complexity and conflict we face and develop the strategy we require.

One unique example of a consistently defined overall strategy was that employed by Andrew Marshall (1922–2019), the Pentagon's longest-serving military strategist, from 1973 to 2015. He was known to take a longer view of events, usually in spans of ten years, realizing that a more protracted, broader approach was required to influence world events.

As a student of history, Marshall spent several hours daily reading anthropology, economics and behavioral studies to understand people and events better. He realized that the Cold War's arms race was considerably more than just about weapons; it was about demonstrating what the nuclear superpowers could do to one another outside the military realm. Although he was surprised by the rapidity of the fall of the Soviet Union, he recognized the eventual rise of Chinese influence on the world's stage long before many others did.

A solitary, taciturn personality, Marshall shunned computers and the Internet, preferring to have emails read to him. Although he was a master strategist, he didn't consider himself a futurist, a term he disliked. He recognized that humans' non-rationality, especially in conflict and war, made prediction impossible.[28] Marshall was in a unique position to contribute to the strategy of the day, himself thinking more in strategic terms than immediate tactical ones.

Today's society emphasizes our present existence's apparent deficiencies while vaunting how the future will be better. Yes, some take a different tack, pining about the past and prophesying about how bad the future will be because of environmental degradation, political upheaval and even humankind's eventual demise. Their fears are abundantly reflected in various films and books.

But for the most part, our society encourages the conviction that life is getting better. This allows us to want to progress and do things, because we wouldn't be encouraged to act without the motivation of a better future.

But to see our future, we must focus our minds on what we desire and what we value in the present, much like Marshall, by embracing a master strategy.

Invisible gorillas and the economy of perception

What we aim our vision at determines what we see. That's because of our vision's physiological limits, leading to what's known as inattentional blindness. In effect, we look, but we do not see.

Vision is psychophysiologically expensive, taking up vast amounts of neurological effort. The fovea centralis is a small pit in the macula's center of the retina in our eyes. This is the area of the eye that provides for the clearest vision and we use it for such essential things as facial recognition.

The challenge is that we have only so much energy for noticing things. We use our limited high-resolution visual capacities for skimming and scanning for those events, people, words and things that allow us to progress while spotting potential threats and obstacles to that same progress.

Generally, there are three things our vision cannot keep from noticing: food, attractive people and threats. We tend to ignore everything else. That's why when we look for the salt in a cupboard while thinking of the recipe we're preparing, we cannot see it, despite it being right in front of us. And when we look back, things are different than what we really noticed at the time.

An example of vision's neurological costs is the study and subsequent video clip made by American psychologist Daniel Simons and his associates at the University of Illinois at Urbana-Champaign. The video, known as *The Invisible Gorilla*,[29] shows two groups of three people, each in a hallway beside a bank of elevators. Each group is wearing different-colored t-shirts, passing one another a basketball. Participants in the study were asked to watch the video and count the total number of passes of the basketball by one of the two groups, ignoring the second group's passing of their basketball.

Right in the middle of the action, a person dressed in a gorilla suit walks through the unperturbed players, stops and looks at the camera, thumps their chest and walks off the set. The gorilla is present in the video for about nine seconds. According to the study, about 50 percent of all people who watched the video didn't notice the gorilla. I was one of those people. After the researchers told us of the gorilla's presence and we viewed the video a second time, we were shocked that we'd missed it.

In a subsequent study, it was determined that, on average, those who missed recognizing the presence of the gorilla spent a full second looking at it during the initial video sequence. Despite our physically seeing the gorilla, its presence didn't register in our conscience.

We can draw two lessons from this study. The first is that looking isn't the same thing as seeing; we must focus our attention on seeing to become aware of what we are looking at. Second, we recognize when we've noticed something unexpected, but we aren't aware of the times we've missed something unexpected. This is because we deal with the complexity of the world around us by effectively filtering most of it out, concentrating minutely on our private concerns, especially those things that interest, motivate and threaten us. We are cognitively blind to everything else.

As a tool, vision helps us get what we want and desire. If we wish to see beauty, we'll see beauty. If we want to see injustice, we'll see injustice. If we wish to see mediocrity, we'll see mediocrity. There's enough of all three in our world. The cost of using this tool, though, is blindness to everything else.

Social ecosystems and the depth of diversity

Each person is fundamentally unique. This uniqueness is influenced by our particularized DNA, resulting in our differing physical abilities and attributes. Our distinctiveness is also dependent on how our brains are hard-wired, impacting our cognitive, social and intellectual skills. Finally, our life experiences sculpt our views, our preferences and responses to the various stimuli we encounter.

In the natural world, ecosystems with little or no diversity are usually desolate, barren and unproductive. As humans, we also operate in a social ecosystem. The healthiest and most sustaining cultures have encouraged and benefited from the greatest internal diversity amongst individuals, resulting in significant advances in the sciences and the arts.

Think of classical Athens (480-323 BC) where modern democracy was born; the Chinese Song Dynasty (960-1279 AD) during which banknotes, gun powder and compasses were first discovered and widely used; the Italian Renaissance (1400-1700 AD), which marked the transition from the Middle Ages to Modernity; or the Roaring 20s in the Western World, a decade of social, artistic, cultural and industrial dynamism. Thanks to the social ecosystems' embraced diversity, these cultural epochs greatly influenced subsequent periods and societies.

Much has been written these past few years about the importance of diversity. What with the various hashtag-expressed cultural phenomena and movements such as #BlackLivesMatter, #BlueLivesMatter, #MeToo, #ACAB, #OKBoomer and so many others, we're bombarded with competing expressions of ideology, culture and concerns. Diversity is one of many competing notions, but an important one, nonetheless. Unfortunately, we tend to view diversity through the limited lens of race, gender or sexual orientation. Diversity is so much more than that. If diversity were an iceberg, most of the traits that make up people would be concealed underwater.

During a trip in the Yarmouth area of southwest Nova Scotia in the summer of 2020, my wife and I stayed at a bed and breakfast belonging to a kind and talkative host who was a retired high-school physics teacher. She told us the story of Tim Doucette, a local man from the nearby hamlet of Quinan, an amateur astronomer who created the Deep Sky Eye Observatory even though he is legally blind.[30]

I called up Tim to talk about his life. He told me that he was born blind with congenital cataracts. As an infant, he began a series of operations resulting in the lens of his eyes eventually being removed by age 16. He describes his eventual condition in these terms: while the eyes of an average seeing person are like a 10-megapixel camera, his eyes only have the resolution of a one-megapixel camera. During the day, he only has 10 percent vision. However, if an object becomes magnified, he can see it relatively well. But that 10 percent daytime vision also remains constant at night, allowing him to see differently—and in some instances better—than a person with average vision.

During an outdoor evening get-together with some fellow members of the Royal Astronomical Society of Canada in the mid-2000s, someone took out a telescope and invited Tim to view a nebula. Tim astounded the group by describing the beautiful colors, brightness, and hues of the nebula and other celestial objects he saw through the telescope; brightness and detail that a person with normal vision wouldn't be able to see with that type of telescope.

At 16, as his final childhood operation resulted in his ocular lenses being removed, Tim couldn't see well in the day. However, at night, his eyes became exceptionally sensitive to light, especially to ultraviolet light.

Tim's condition allowed him to see a spectrum of colors that the average seeing person cannot. When he saw a bug zapper or blacklight emitting ultraviolet light at a distance, it would fill up his visual field. He was even able to see the ultraviolet light that flowers emit to attract pollen-collecting insects. That evening, he was able to see the ultraviolet light emitted by the nebula in all its splendor.

Tim's story is a unique example of the biological diversity in one small, albeit important, part of our physical existence: our vision. As vision is psychophysiologically expensive, we require a great deal of neurological effort to see most things. Hence, we only see what we focus on. In Tim's case, he sees what he is physically able to focus on: ultraviolet light from things that the average seeing person cannot.

Adversity or diversity

From the age of six, I grew up in north-end Toronto. I went to high school in a highly multicultural area that had three predominant groups: Black, Chinese-Jamaican and European White immigrants. Multi-generational Canadians (of which I was part) were in the minority. Multiculturalism and pluralism were the norms for me and my high-school experience.

In 2001, as a newly-minted senior officer in the RCMP, I attended an intermediate-level course on diversity for federal government employees. When I arrived, it took about 20 minutes before I realized that the five-day course was about diversity and not *adversity* as I had initially thought. I remember thinking why the term 'diversity' was such a strange concept as I had grown up in a truly diverse neighborhood and had friends of all stripes, backgrounds, religions and cultures.

I wondered why the word diversity was employed as opposed to multiculturalism. That was because diversity was so much more than just ethnic or cultural representation.

Many years later, when I was police chief, the civilian in charge of our informatics unit, himself of Sikh faith, was temporarily seconded to a municipal hiring panel to select a new informatics technician for the municipality. The board had a standard set of questions to ask, including the now-ubiquitous one about the value of diversity in the workplace. They asked the candidate, a White 30-something male, about his experience in diversity. He calmly responded that he had worked on diverse digital and technological platforms in his several years of experience in information technology, listing off an impressive series of them.

Realizing that he had misunderstood the question, the panel chair rephrased the question, asking the candidate to talk about how he would demonstrate respect for people's diversity. Motioning his understanding with a nod of his head, the candidate described how he treated each digital platform he dealt with equally. He specified that by attempting to master each platform's basic rudiments and even learning a bit about how the coding worked, he was able to offer better service to the people he worked with who all had differing needs. He did this by asking for advice from different people.

Obviously, for him, diversity meant something other than what the panel had initially intended.

In the months to follow, subsequent hiring panels used a modified question that would allow people in this specific area to properly articulate their understanding of people's diversity as it related to technology.

In July 2018, I received a high-level visit from three senior officers of the Singapore Police Force (SPF). Serving a population of just under six million people, SPF has a total complement of 15,000 police officers, employees and national service conscripts. We had broad discussions about their challenges and opportunities. It was surprising how SPF had similar issues to us in North America, such as community concerns, especially around police legitimacy and community policing.

When I asked them about their organization's demographics and diversity, they indicated Singapore was a multicultural society with 75 percent of the population being ethnic Chinese, 15 percent being Malays and 7 percent being ethnic Indians. The remainder, around 3 percent, were Caucasian. They had trouble recruiting from the Malay, Indian and Caucasian communities, mentioning that their lone Caucasian officer had recently left to join the Hong Kong Police Force. His departure was not much of a concern for them considering the relative size of the Caucasian community in Singapore; hiring in this demographic simply wasn't a priority for them.

Trust, distrust and mistrust

Diversity deals with the intersection of people's individual characteristics, varied experiences and thought processes because of who they are and what they've lived. Their makeup—skin color, age, gender, cultural background, education, sexual orientation, spoken languages, level of neurological and physical abilities, temperament, impairment or prolonged exposure to a variety of cultural reference points—contributes to the person they are. These attributes shape their perspectives, ideologies and how they interpret their world.

It can significantly impact parts of a person's life and how they live it. Included in this would be how they view themselves individually and collectively, including their notion of hierarchy and equality, their approaches to formality and informality, their communication style, their familial links and social structures and even their concept and use of time.

Below the waterline of the iceberg of diversity would be the less discernible traits than gender, race, age and physical abilities: values, character, political leanings, individual experiences, sexual identity and orientation, languages, accents, family status, learning and communication styles, mental abilities, education and talents. Together, all these traits determine the overall personality of an individual.

Our individual identity can and does change according to the moment, the context and the experiences we acquire in life. Although some traits such as skin color and DNA are immutable, many of our features can change, especially as we age, acquire more experience and react to the varied stimuli in our lives. If there are sufficient stimuli and experiences in a person's life, the result is an amalgam of different perspectives and an enhanced socio-intellectual background.

What diversity provides through such differences amongst people is a certain suspicion and wariness that a person can only overcome through engagement with others. To a certain degree and initially, diversity undermines the trust necessary to collaboration, which is not immediately bad. We can qualify this as *distrust*: an initial lack of confidence resulting in doubt and even suspicion when people first interact. Compare that to *mistrust*, which implies having evidence to justify a lack of trust, such as prior negative experiences.

Initial distrust is a positive feature in relationships, as it forces us to convince others with substantive justification to support our views, leading to better decision-making. Provided, of course, that we and they are open to changing our perceptions.

Imagine two people of clearly different backgrounds sitting in a café for a business meeting for the first time. They look different because they are of different races, and one has piercings and the other a tribal facial mark or tattoo. They're of different genders, wear different clothes and headgear, even smell different because of the soap they use, the perfume they apply and the food they regularly eat. One is drinking Turkish coffee while the other is having a sports drink. They can communicate through a common language, although each speaks it with a different accent. They're different in so many ways.

Although they have a common goal (to advance a joint business opportunity), they partake in small talk to assess each other's intentions and abilities. Their minds race in the background of their conversation as they ask themselves: *Does this person have the same goals, values and interests as me? Are they competent enough to do this deal? Can I even trust this person?*

They can react in one of three ways:

1. They can reject those differences, basing their relationship on their personal perceptions of the other, resulting in limited collaboration.
2. They can show basic respect for those differences, resulting in some collaboration
3. They can accept and even embrace the other's differences, overcoming the initial distrust and opening the way to a constructive beginning to the relationship.

In the third scenario, after spending time with one another, they find commonalities. They may both have children, studied the same courses, appreciate the same books or have traveled to the same destinations.

Because of the points in common, no matter what they are, they slowly replace their initial distrust with trust as they recognize their ability to work together. They start to embrace their differences as positive contributions to their business dealings.

This can only come about through some form of social engagement. But what's essential to developing this relationship is the initial lack of trust they shared, which resulted in them remaining cautious and scrutinizing information, leading to better individual decision-making. It forced them to look beyond the differences to find commonality and judge the other person's actions, not appearances. And that's a good thing.

What diversity and its initial distrust engender is better decision-making. Having diverse people in groups has been linked to enhanced innovation (applied imagination), greater collective productivity, and, in settings such as teams of surgeons and airline pilots, fewer mistakes, which leads to better, safer and more productive outcomes. That diversity must represent different disciplines, perspectives and expertise garnered through disparate experiences.

When everyone in a group shares many, if not all, the same characteristics, the desire for unity and group cohesion results in people wanting to accommodate others to avoid rocking the boat. American psychologist Irving L. Janis (1918–1990) referred to the in-group pressures of conformity and friendship as groupthink that results in the systemic errors in collective decisions such as mental efficiency deterioration and reality testing, and defective moral judgment.[31]

Janis defined groupthink as an approach by group members to minimize conflict to reach consensus without critically testing, analyzing or evaluating ideas; essentially, by throwing any empirical skepticism or evidence-based decision-making out the window simply to maintain group cohesion.

Groupthink results in narrow-mindedness and poor decision-making. Amongst its symptoms are polite conversation, superficial congeniality and limited psychological safety. Groupthink results in the absence of the frankness in discussions that is critical to better decision-making.

One antidote to groupthink is to assign a specific role of Devil's Advocate to a group member.

Started under Pope Sixtus V (1521-1590, pope from 1585-1590), the canonization process used by the Roman Catholic Church leading to the papal confirmation of a saint involved one critical participant known as the 'Promoter of the Faith' or the Devil's Advocate. This canon lawyer's role was to argue *against* a candidate's canonization, taking a skeptical view of the candidate's character and apparent miraculous deeds. In 1983, under Pope John Paul II (1920-2005, pope from 1978-2005), the role was modified to be a 'Promoter of Justice'. A canon lawyer is in charge of examining the accuracy of the inquiry into the saintliness of a candidate.

For any decision-making group, the advantage of having a Devil's Advocate is to avoid the mistakes attributable to groupthink by ensuring that at least one voice speaks out to challenge the group's collective decision. If everyone agrees with a particular decision or course of action, we need to find someone who can make the case against it. The goal is to stress-test the decision-making process and to confirm that it led to the best decision possible.

I would do this as much as feasible during my time as police chief. Whenever I saw everyone agreeing to a conclusion during my senior management team meetings, I would go back and ask why the decision wasn't the right one. Often we would modify the final decision because of some rationale provided to oppose the initial decision. During my time as an investigator, especially during major investigations, I'd actively seek opinions that ran counter to what we were focused on to encourage the Devil's Advocate role in the investigative team.

Another antidote to groupthink is using a thinking tool known as the 'premortem.'[32] By working backward from a project's imagined failure, a team can determine what potentially could lead to its failure. The main benefit of the premortem is that it legitimizes and encourages doubt in group decision-making. As previously explained, diversity, through initial distrust, also acts as an antidote to groupthink.

Diversity, then, is much more than the quality of one's ethnicity. I've known 5-foot-4-inch Black female officers and six-foot-tall White male police officers who think exactly alike, sharing the same values and perceptions. Conversely, I've worked with 6-foot-5-inch hulking men whose cultural awareness and experiences were different from the norm of most police officers, male, female or transgender, thanks in large part to their varied life experiences. Among their unique experiences were extensive international travel, personal exposure to other religious and ethnic constructs, unusual interests and hobbies, and intense bouts of personal hardship and adversity. These men had grown up seeing the hues and different colors of the human experience. That made them better police officers, better people and better decision-makers.

Thanks to their varied experiences, their contributions were invaluable in helping the group arrive at better collective decisions, frequently allowing them to provide insight and see opportunities that others in the group would typically miss.

And that is the advantage of diversity: diversity of experiences allows for a diversity of thought, resulting in better decision-making.

Diversity, in and of itself, isn't enough to ensure the best decision-making possible. To allow for the diversity of thought to come out in people, there's a visceral need for psychological safety to encourage those of different opinions to express differing viewpoints that the others can hear and respect. Psychological safety is defined as the shared belief that a team or organization is safe for interpersonal risk-taking, especially when speaking up within an organization, without fear or sanction.[33] And that's where inclusion comes in.

On guard against idiocy

During a summer course I took in college in the 1980s on politics in third-world countries, the professor spoke about the importance of workforce diversification, including women and people of color. In his opinion, there were three reasons why a diverse and inclusive workforce is essential.

First came the compelling economic argument that if a company were to hire only individuals of one gender or race, it would be unnecessarily restricting the available labor pool's size, driving up labor costs. If the company were open to hiring from all known groups, costs would drop as there would be a larger labor market from which to draw potential employees. In this sense, inclusion widens the pathway to larger talent pools.

Second, the company would want to represent its client or community base, allowing it to draw market intelligence from the community it serves and the employees who belong to that community.

Third, and most importantly, the workplace should also promote diversity of thought, leading to better decision-making and better company outcomes. Diversity of thought goes beyond the color of one's skin to a whole gamut of cultural, geographical and social experiences, including physical abilities and neurodiversity. It allows for a broader perspective and a more strategic view in the workplace.

My professor was right on all accounts.

To think strategically, understand complexity and embrace conflict, we need to scan our event horizon, not just in front of us but also behind, above and inside us. This applies to the present and especially to the past. The study of history, other cultures and other countries is of tanta-mount importance to us developing an appreciation of the immense diversity in life.

An Arab proverb says that we have a different personality for every language we speak beyond our native tongue. One of the best ways to cultivate diversity is through learning another language; it can be a modern or ancient language, American Sign Language, computer coding, advanced mathematics or any form of communication that is new to us.

Once we have a better view through the diversity of thought, we can make better decisions. This is another of the gifts of the variety of opinions and experiences in this world.

Modernity, cultural influences and the excess of information have resulted in a form of cognitive myopia: our event horizons and our personal spaces shrink as we live for short-term stimuli and instant gratification, just as others in the crowd do. This manifests itself in the political realm where competing perspectives approach their event horizons diametrically: while the progressive left encourages hope for a better future, however illusive, the conservative right is transfixed on the potential sense of loss, becoming nostalgic. This results in both sides not seeing reality and their inability to deal effectively with the other groups' collective complexity.

History and learning about cultural diversity teach us to broaden our horizons and shift our perspectives. Knowing where we are and where we come from counts significantly when analyzing any situation. History is the ultimate guidepost, directing us in how others managed change in the past and providing us with the lessons they learned (and didn't learn) from their errors and triumphs. "History," writes columnist Bagehot in the July 20, 2019 issue of *The Economist* article entitled *The end of history*, "can be a safeguard against outright idiocy."

Collective safeguards

During 13 days in October, 1962 the world was riveted by the events occurring just off the United States' southern coast in the Caribbean Sea. That period, known as the Cuban Missile Crisis, involved a diplomatic and military confrontation between the US and the Soviet Union. The confrontation was precipitated by the deployment of Russian ballistic missiles in Cuba following a comparable US ballistic missile deployment in Russia's neighbor and America's ally, Turkey.

The Crisis' tension apex arrived on October 27, 1962, when US warships located a Soviet submarine, the "B-59", a Foxtrot-class diesel-electric submarine, in international waters just off the coast of Cuba in an area that the US Navy had declared blockaded.

The B-59 had been traveling for nearly four weeks from its base on the Kola Peninsula near Murmansk in Russia's far northwest region. Its destination was the Caribbean Sea to support "Operation Anadyr," the delivery of Soviet arms to Cuba. The flagship of a flotilla of four submarines, the B-59 had T-5 ten-kiloton, nuclear-tipped torpedoes with the destructive power of the bomb dropped on Hiroshima some 17 years prior.

During its trip, mostly submerged, the B-59 had minimal communication with Moscow, as it needed to surface to enter into radio contact. The submarine's crew was unaware of the growing tensions in the area from mid-October on.

On October 27, a squadron of the US Navy—the aircraft carrier *USS Randolph* and its escort of 11 destroyers—located the B-59 and began to depth-charge around the submerged boat to force it to surface.

Because of the depth-charging, the captain of the B-59, Valentin Grigorievich Savitsky, believed that his country was at war with the United States. Accordingly, he ordered the loading of a T-5 torpedo to target the *USS Randolf*. Before launching the counter-attack with this new weapon, the B-59's political officer, Ivan Semyonovich Laslennikov, and Captain Vasili Alexandrovich Arkhipov, the 36-year-old overall commander of the submarine flotilla onboard the B-59, had to agree with Captain Savitsky on this course of action.

Contrary to his two colleagues, Captain Arkhipov refused to grant permission for the torpedo's firing, arguing that the pattern of depth charges was a deliberate message to the B-59 to surface and wasn't intended to destroy it. He encouraged the captain of the B-59 to surface to seek validated orders from Moscow and to gauge the American reaction.

With the boat's batteries running low and its air conditioning failing, Captain Savitsky acquiesced, and the B-59 surfaced. One of the American destroyers met it, but no boarding occurred.

Upon receiving updated orders, the B-59 set course back to Murmansk. In the days to follow, the Cuban Missile Crisis was resolved as the Soviet Union eventually withdrew the weapons it had placed in Cuba and that were en route.[34]

By refusing to fire a nuclear-tipped torpedo at the *USS Randolf*, Captain Arkhipov averted a likely third world war. His diversity of opinion and leadership in a time of considerable pressure and complexity allowed for cooler heads to prevail and better decision-making, avoiding the possible thermonuclear destruction of the planet.

Described as a humble and shy man, Captain Arkhipov was an avid reader who kept himself current in world events. By accessing his education, knowledge, training and empirical skepticism in a time of unbearable stress and uncertainty, he was able to keep his sights on the bigger picture, avoiding tactical hell by being strategic in his approach.

Captain Arkhipov eventually rose to the rank of vice admiral in 1975, retiring in the 1980s. He died in 1998 at the age of 72 from complications due to radiation poisoning he'd suffered early in his naval career as the executive officer onboard the ill-fated K-19 submarine, which, in July 1961, had experienced a near-fatal nuclear meltdown that irradiated the entire crew, killing 22 submariners. In 2017, Vice Admiral Arkhipov was posthumously awarded the first "Future of Life Award" by the Boston-based *Future of Life Institute,* which recognizes exceptional measures performed despite personal risk and without obvious reward to safeguard the collective future of humanity.

Personal threat assessments

Our personal threat assessment is part of what drives our consumption of social and traditional media: potential threats attract our attention— the weather, the rush-hour traffic, crime, the stock market, gas prices, our horoscope, and as we have seen during the pandemic, the number of new daily cases, hospitalizations, deaths and vaccinations. Some have even postulated that the COVID-19 pandemic has dominated news coverage more than any other topic since World War II.[35] Hans Rosling aptly described the situation in his book, *Factfulness*: "Fears that once kept our ancestors alive, today help keep journalists employed."

Unlike traditional media, though, social media platforms allow individuals to collectively express concern for various causes, sometimes resulting in public clamor akin to a mob rule.

By itself, social media doesn't cause division or factionalism (mob rule) as much as it amplifies it, resulting in a landscape that's a fertile space for public reprobation and shaming. Because of its construction, with followers, likes, images and limits like 280-character posts, there's little room for rational discussion. Social media confirms people's viewpoints, particularly their social and political ones, rather than challenging them. Because of the anonymity and few psycho-social risks involved in particular social media platforms, cruelty can rule the day.

We've all seen what amounts to social media show-trials, where keyboard warriors of all stripes participate in a form of virtual blood sport through relatively risk-free reputation destruction, revenge-posting and self-righteousness. To fulfill our collective desire to find a scapegoat, there has developed a virtual finger-pointing culture instead of actual problem-solving. Even those who would apparently benefit from popular trends have denounced this perverse consequence of social media.[36]

Many people form their worldview through what they take in online.

This is akin to an individual forming an overall opinion of another based on a photo of the former's hand, not nearly enough of an image from which to produce a most basic impression of another's looks, let alone their personality.

In such situations, the most common type of individual is the self-righteous passive-aggressive: an individual who exploits virtue for image enhancement, personal gain and increased social status. This is achieved through subtle or not-so-subtle put-downs of others in a conscious effort to elevate themselves, asserting their moral authority or virtue.

Passive-aggressives express their hostilities indirectly by denigrating others and pushing their buttons without actually appearing to do so. Persistent passive aggression was previously considered a personality disorder under the *Diagnostic and Statistical Manual of Mental Disorders* (DSM-IV), the American Psychiatric Association's publication to classify mental disorders by providing a common language and standard criteria. DSM-5, published in 2013, is the latest version. Persistent passive aggression is no longer considered a personality disorder. That doesn't make it any less present or toxic.

Your virtue should not be something that you advertise, nor should you loudly announce it, as if to say: "Look at me and how virtuous I am because I believe in X or Y while Marlo over here does not!"

Social media provides fertile terrain for individuals to be passive-aggressive. Some of the more prevalent passive-aggressive social-media techniques individuals employ include sub-posts, vaguebooking, humblebrags and overzealous grammar checking. Regardless of the approach we use, social media allows for the virtual manifestation of those behaviors we already employ on a daily in-person basis.

It's entirely up to us to choose what to focus on in an era of constant distractions. This means distinguishing between the noise and the signals that genuinely matter to us and have a bearing on our lives. Because of the critical mass of information, constant expectations and time constraints thrust upon leaders today, there's a lack of regular reflective practice allowing for strategic consideration and expression.

Marcus Tullius Cicero (106-43 BC) has long been considered Rome's greatest orator. Cicero coined the expression *summum bonum*, or "highest good." According to the Stoics, a group of Hellenistic-influenced philosophers of which Cicero was the first and most influential Roman representative, the highest good was the pursuit of wisdom and virtue as exemplified in the traits of good judgment, courage, temperance and justice. Virtue is not holiness, nor is it moral superiority; it's ethical and civic excellence in our daily lives.

This notion has endured the test of time. Leaders in all cultures and at all levels over the centuries have repeatedly demonstrated it. And it's this principle that should motivate all our actions, offline and online.

In applying the Stoic definition, if we are virtuous, we contribute to our community's moral and civic fabric through such acts as volunteering, encouraging and mentoring youth, donating blood, charity work and donations. In essence, we help build social cohesion and not social division, serving the greater community's needs. It presupposes human beings acting compassionately, being willing to sacrifice for the common good, striving to become what's known in Latin as *homo communis*.

Marlo on ice

Marlo had officiated hockey since the age of 15, attaining relatively high levels of officiating in his early 20s. As time went on, Marlo's interest in officiating at higher levels waned as his work and family life took up more of his time and energies. By the time Marlo was 45, he was no longer interested in advancing hockey or developing younger officials; he was only interested in making money. Because of an apparent back injury, Marlo left his job to go on long-term disability. But he somehow managed to continue officiating hockey despite the injury.

Marlo optimized his schedule and availability to officiate according to the highest-paying and easiest games, while working as many games as possible throughout the year. He would officiate in several leagues and associations, doing minor and adult hockey, seven days a week. Eventually, Marlo officiated upwards of 40 games a week, quitting his full-time work to concentrate full-time on refereeing, making around $25 a game.

As the Canada Revenue Agency (CRA) considered hockey officials to be volunteers, it assessed no income tax on these earnings. The vast majority of officials are low-income earners such as students and retirees, who only officiate around ten games a week for a limited period during the year and significant expenses that offset much of their earnings. Very few individuals would or could officiate full-time, as Marlo was doing.

The quality of Marlo's officiating slowly deteriorated. Marlo was no longer aware of his surroundings on the ice or the time left in games. If a player fell behind him, Marlo assumed that it was because of another player's actions and would call a penalty, known in the game as making a "phantom call."

When angry coaches and parents confronted him after games, Marlo became overly dismissive, using abusive language to shut people down. During games, Marlo skated slower and slower, appearing uninterested in the game. Over time, parents, coaches and other officials became resentful of Marlo's on-ice and off-ice attitude.

When there was less hockey in the summer months, Marlo took part in his true passion, competitive sport fishing. He participated in numerous tournaments, traveling with his boat throughout eastern North America, searching for any competition. Not only was fishing an enjoyable pastime for Marlo, but it also quickly became quite profitable as he began to win some impressive money, which he never declared to the authorities.

With all the tax-free cash Marlo was making, he bought himself a new, high-end fishing boat and a pick-up truck to haul it. Marlo became increasingly comfortable in his life, taking old friends, neighbors and even family for granted. Life was good for Marlo as all he really did was officiate hockey and fish.

But Marlo had become blind to the effects of his attitude and excesses on others. His spouse left him. He became estranged from his adult children.

Eventually, someone contacted CRA, which proceeded with an audit of his finances. He lost the boat and the pick-up, having to sell both to pay a sizable income-tax assessment for years of avoiding income taxes.

It was Marlo's lack of scanning and willful blindness that resulted in his downfall. Eventually, Marlo gave up officiating hockey altogether and was forced to fish from docks as he no longer had a boat, and no one wanted him to fish from theirs.

We can easily find ourselves in Marlo's skates, becoming fixated on the lure of money, power or prestige. To avoid losing perspective in life, we need to ensure a few things.

First, we must not fall prey to blind ambition, avoiding envy (wanting what others have), greed (getting more of what others want), and avarice (accumulating and hoarding more of what we have).

Second, we must avoid becoming blind to what goes on around us, such as the challenges those in our immediate family and entourage are going through. This requires being open to seeing what others are living and the difficulties they face.

Finally, we must realize that being in a position of authority or responsibility, such as a referee or a leader, isn't about us and our issues;

it's about others and their issues.

In all three cases, we need to see with our eyes, our minds and our hearts. That is the role of empathy.

Skate like the Great One, not like Marlo

Two critical abilities leaders require to be successful are spatial and temporal awareness.

Spatial awareness is our ability to construct an organized understanding of the environment around us while recognizing where we are in that environment. There are two levels to this: the mental representation or cognitive map we maintain of the actual physical environment surrounding us and the social cognitive map we maintain of the interactions in which we engage. For leaders, this means knowing where we're situated within any given context and where we're going.

As we've seen, spatial awareness is critical for developing tactics and especially strategy. At the most basic level, it implies having a proficient internal compass—not only a moral compass but a bodily compass that orients our physical direction through a rudimentary understanding of cardinal directions and the use of our body. It also implies navigating social situations, relying on knowledge of both social and physical environments.[37]

In many cases, spatial awareness is a critical component of our personal safety and well-being. Examples are avoiding walking into a closed glass door, finding oneself alone in less-safe neighborhoods or getting lost on a hiking trail.

Halifax Regional Municipality was created in 1996 from the fusion of four municipal jurisdictions: the cities of Halifax, Bedford and Dartmouth, and the area surrounding them known as Halifax County. The municipality occupies over roughly 2,000 square miles, comparable in size to Rhode Island's total landmass. With a population of only 445,000, there are many uninhabited wooded and water areas with numerous hiking paths. Strangely enough, because of the proliferation and ease of GPS technology, there has been an increase in the number of individuals reported lost in the municipality's vast area over the years.

So dependent are hikers on their technology that they become lost once their battery runs out, not having the requisite spatial awareness to get back to their starting point. At this juncture, authorities try to locate the lost hikers and extract them from the area. But those individuals who don't rely on technology and are adept at orienteering, understanding their positioning by using a map, compass or land markings, very rarely get lost.

Leaders shouldn't overlook the importance of spatial awareness as they determine where they want to go and how they want to get there. As Wayne Gretzky, arguably the greatest professional hockey player ever, stated: "I skate to where the puck is going to be, not where it has been."

But you have to know where on the ice you are and where the puck is to accomplish this. This means having a strong sense of direction and good overall physical health while being alive to the environment through proper, continuous scanning.

Lionel Messi, the Argentinian master footballer, exemplifies the critical importance of scanning. Individuals dedicated to assisting athletes to attain peak physical and mental ability, known as sports scientists, have long recognized the important role of scanning which is defined as looking around to take visual snapshots of play while analyzing where the object of the play will go next. It has been postulated that the most successful footballers scan the pitch about 50 times *per minute*. An interesting research article qualified scanning in football (soccer) as "(...) an active head movement where a player's face is temporarily directed away from the ball to gather information in preparation for subsequently engaging with the ball."[38]

The second critical skill is temporal awareness.

Temporal awareness involves developing an internal time structure that monitors our movement and actions over time. Physical manifestations of this are hand-eye and foot-eye coordination. These are fundamental skills elite baseball players, world-class soccer players, racing car drivers, fighter pilots and air traffic controllers consistently demonstrate, regardless of their gender or physical strength.

Strong temporal awareness allows for an advanced ability to understand sequences and timestamps while dealing with multiple time constraints. In effect, it gives you an understanding of the timing and sequencing of past, present and future activities for yourself and others. This includes the intersection between these various activities. Temporal awareness is also essential to harnessing time practically throughout your entire life, going beyond simple time management.

Different cultures view time differently. Some cultures view time more linearly, segmenting it, compartmentalizing it and viewing it as a commodity; either use it or lose it. Punctuality is seen as being respectful and efficient. Other cultures have a cyclical sense of time, in which time is not a commodity, nor can it be compartmentalized. It's just there and will always be there. Punctuality is not prized; relationships are, so keeping track of time isn't necessarily a priority.

In her unique essay, *The Time Value of Life,* American educator Tisa Silver Canady postulates that since time is more valuable than money, we must learn to manage it just as well, if not better than our finances. As our life's value depends on what we do with our time, the key is to stop squandering present time and "invest" in future time, ensuring that we're careful in making that investment.

This means being mindful of how we spend our time, in what activities, with whom and how much we have at our disposal. This includes respecting deadlines, being on time for various appointments and events, and ensuring regular maintenance crucial for human functioning such as workouts, leisure, relationships and sleep.

Once we recognize and understand the environment we're operating in and have a handle on our physical location and timing, we can develop the first key leadership competency: advanced thinking skills and superior decision-making.

This competency requires several different aptitudes, not least to cultivate what can be called 'omni-directional thinking.' This is the opposite of tunnel vision, in which our focus is overly centered and narrow-minded. Resulting from limited information selection and excessive filtration through our individual biases, tunnel vision leads us down wrong decision-making paths. We must avoid it at all costs. Hence the importance of looking at our event horizon using omni-directional thinking.

In hockey, when the play is deep in the defending zone, the referee must not single-mindedly focus their vision on the puck. Instead, they must keep their head on a swivel, constantly looking around to ensure that no penalties occur, monitoring the game's general flow and looking out for threats to themselves, such as erratic slap shots, body checks and getting caught up in the play.

They also have to be alive to any potential threats to the play on the ice. Throughout the years, I've seen unusual things arise that compromise the safety and fairness of the game, such as a second puck coming out of nowhere, a rink door suddenly opening or a fan sitting in an overhanging seating area accidentally dropping a cell phone onto the ice.

By not becoming overly focused on one aspect of the game and maintaining omni-directional thinking, the referee can manage most issues that compromise play. This, too, is part of game management.

We obtain the second aptitude required for this leadership competency through reflective thinking as opposed to intuitional thinking. Whenever possible, we don't bow to institutional or social pressures and time constraints—self-imposed or other—to arrive at a decision. This also implies the practical application of the philosophy of empirical skepticism, emphasizing the role of empirical evidence in the formation of ideas rather than the simple application of intuition or rote tradition.

By scanning our environment and adequately questioning what we see, we arrive at better environmental scan inputs. Critical to this is the management of meta-data or significant quantities of information.

The final aptitude we need to achieve advanced thinking skills and superior decision-making is focus, specifically being highly concentrated on the matter at hand and not easily distracted in a world of information overload and diversions. This implies a delicate balance, as we want to ensure our omni-directional scanning without falling into the trap of tunnel vision. Maintaining a laser-sharp focus while scanning, analyzing and deciding is determinant in developing advanced thinking skills and superior decision-making. As we have already seen, an essential part of this is understanding and embracing the complexity and ambiguity that exists in our outer world.

Now that we know where to look and how to look, we need next to look at our inner world, the world that determines our emotions, motivations, and perceptions. We do this by understanding who we are and by recognizing the creature with whom we share our internal space.

This is the lesson of self-knowledge.

Calls from the blue line

- Leadership requires an advanced ability to recognize, interpret and analyze many different things: ourselves, others, potential challenges and opportunities, the environment, trends, timing and processes.
- Only fools and fanatics are sure of everything. We become foolish or fanatical when we're riveted on a single aspect of a problem,

seeing and interpreting an event through a form of tunnel vision created by our own biases and experiences.

- Having the moral and intellectual courage to recognize and meet the demands of reality means having the requisite character and integrity. The key is never to deny a situation's existence but to deny its finality.

- The key to maintaining our sense of reality, leading to an effective overall strategy in life, is to adapt our thoughts to what's happening around us at any given time.

- Construct a lighthouse that guides you when the fog or waves of tactical hell surround you; build a written list of your mission, vision, values and priorities. This list should include those values and qualities you want to live by and project to others each and every day.

- Create an internal inquisitor that always asks questions about what and why you do something, forcing you to maintain a defined strategy to determine your goals.

- Diversity is more than just skin deep—look at an individual's entirety to determine how deep it goes. Group diversity, primarily through diversity of thought, leads to better decision-making. Lack of thought diversity leads to groupthink and poor decision-making.

- Be like a hockey referee during the heat of the game: keep your head on a swivel, scanning in all directions, on the lookout for infractions, threats and opportunities.

- Don't be like Marlo: don't lose perspective by becoming overly focused on one aspect of success. Scan and understand what others are going through and don't forget that it's not all about you. We're not the only ones in this game of life.

3: The lesson of self-knowledge

The child is in me still...and sometimes not so still.
-Mr. (Fred) Rogers (1928-2003)

Locked-up memories

In the late morning of January 17, 2010, following the recovery of the re-mains of Superintendent Coates and Sergeant Gallagher, I communicated by satellite phone with the RCMP's Ottawa National Operations Center's duty officer. He advised that Superintendent Coates' family had asked us to recover an electronic safe containing important personal effects be-longing to Doug. The electronic safe was somewhere in his residence.

With Constable Julie Dupré and three Canadian Forces search and res-cue (SAR) specialists, we headed to Superintendent Coates' residence be-side the devastated Hotel Montana, in Delmas 60. In a sadly ironic twist, Superintendent Coates resided in the same building as the Deputy Force Commander, General Ricardo Toro-Tassara, whose wife and daughter had perished in the collapse of the Hotel Montana.

We arrived at the split-level home, which was separated into three separate apartments. The building was intact but was severely damaged, with huge fissures and cracks in the stucco-covered cinder-block walls, one of which was precariously tilted inwards. It looked like the entire structure would collapse at any moment. The stench of death was every-where as it had been over 90 hours since the earthquake, and unrecov-ered bodies in the Hotel Montana and surrounding neighborhood were rotting under the heat of the Caribbean sun.

Although we had the keys to Superintendent Coates' apartment, the door wouldn't open as it had been compressed due to the pressures on the door frame. We forced the back door open, and Constable Dupré and one of the SAR specialists went into the residence. Inside, they heard cracking noises from the unstable structure.

They quickly recovered Superintendent Coates' barrack box and some personal effects. They also found the locked electronic safe bolted to a wall in the bedroom closet, but didn't dare try to dislodge it from its moorings for fear of causing the building's collapse.

The barrack box contained a small notebook computer and some personal effects, but not the items the family was hoping for, including various USB thumb drives and a laptop computer containing Superintendent Coates' extensive writings. I contacted Superintendent Coates' family and asked if they knew the combination to the electronic safe. They did not. I asked if the family used a regular sequence of numbers for passwords and codes. Again, the family replied in the negative.

I finally asked them for Superintendent Coates' regimental and commissioned officer numbers. In the RCMP, each police officer is assigned a unique regimental number that also doubles as their badge number. In Superintendent Coates' case, as he was a commissioned officer, he also had a unique commissioned officer number. I thought that, had I been in his position, I would have used one of my two identifying numbers as a safe combination, just in case something happened to me.

Armed with both numbers, Constable Dupré and the SAR specialist went back inside. They tried the regimental number without success. But when they tried the commissioned officer number, the safe swung open. Inside were Superintendent Coates' laptop and personal cell phone.

I immediately advised his grateful family of our success. It was a bittersweet moment for us all; as for a change, we had some good luck, thanks to Doug, who was, like most of us, a creature of habit.

Lie, just don't believe yourself

Our personality manifests itself in various ways, including how we act when alone and regularly interact with others. Traits, behaviors and actions we repeat form our habits, established through a lifetime of small, sometimes imperceptible, personal experiments and adjustments of how to do things, which routes to take and which activities to practice.

To understand the randomness and complexity of the world we live in and adequately scan the environment that affects us, we need to know how we as individuals operate both separately and as part of the greater collective. That collective takes the form of our various personal environments, such as home, extended family, friends, social and work settings.

One of the most enduring aspects of our habits and how we interact with others is telling non-truths. Lying is part of the human condition and something that we humans are very well versed in from a young age. Just ask any four-year-old.

Humans learn early to lie as a form of protection. We're the only animals in the world capable of lying to ourselves and believing our own lies.

We lie for several reasons. First, to obtain protection from painful consequences such as shame, embarrassment, conflict or violence. The second reason is to protect and advance our interests to get what we want, be it material possessions or attention. Third, to conserve the few resources we may have, such as time, effort or money, we may lie to avoid expending them. The fourth reason is to protect our self-opinion by shoring up what others think of us and the perceived respect they accord to us; self-opinion being the sum of stories we have about ourselves and our past. Finally, we return the favor, lying to protect others' feelings and their self-opinions.

Lying as self-deception can take four primary forms:

1. We become information resistant, so we seek out only that information that confirms our beliefs.
2. We obfuscate or cloud an issue by hiding, concealing or modifying the truth, again to conform to and verify our self-opinion and perceptions.
3. We lie to ourselves, the classic case of self-deception.
4. We avoid the truth because we perceive it to be too painful to accept.

Regardless of how we delude ourselves or self-deceive, we end up with the same result: we don't accept the truth and the reality we face. We lie mostly to hide inadequacies and protect our and others' feelings. But we also lie and deceive others to gain unjust rewards. Just like when we tell the truth, we lie through our communication with others, be it in writing, talking or even through nonverbal methods such as body language.

But how good are we at communicating? Being an effective communicator, whether as a police officer, a referee, a lawyer, a teacher or a Walmart greeter, involves proficiency in reading the totality of the context we find ourselves in, correctly interpreting the emotional aspects of human behavior, learning to take nothing personally and having a laser-sharp focus on our goal at the moment.

In the game of hockey, communicating is the single, most important skill a referee or linesperson can possess. Hockey officials communicate in real-time on the ice in four different ways:

1. With their whistles, which they use to signal a stoppage of play or gain the attention of the players.
2. With their visual signals when indicating penalties, a goal or non-goal, a net being off its moorings or potential offsides and icings.
3. With their voice to direct players to move the puck, vacate a zone on the ice or identify a penalized player.
4. With their eyes as they look to their partner for help to cover their blue line or see if there's an icing.

In all these situations, referees communicate for very specific purposes and in real-time. Although people can't read our minds, they can understand our communications if we're clear and succinct in our delivery. Added to this is the importance of the officials being in good enough physical shape to keep up with the play and even blow the whistle or intervene at the right moment while maintaining a professional posture and being in the right place.

In sports in general, and in hockey in particular, crisp, clear signals by officials let the players, coaches, fans and other officials know what's going on, be it a penalty, a non-goal or an offside. Failure to communicate effectively can lead to misunderstandings by players, coaches and fans. It can also result in the game being played in an unfair or unsafe manner. Knowing how we communicate and constantly improving on our abilities in this area are critical to exercising leadership.

In the months after becoming police chief, I asked our corporate communications manager to critique my communications style. She had significant experience and was a consummate professional but was a tad hesitant, becoming more so when I asked her to be as brutally honest as possible. I was looking for those habits, ticks, phrases and pauses that impeded my ability to communicate effectively. I needed to have an unbiased opinion of my delivery because I knew that I couldn't assess the reality of how I communicated, being too close and concerned about my own self-delusion. The one thing I didn't want was to protect my self-opinion.

She eventually provided me with a two-page list of my strengths and areas for improvement garnered from her own observations and those of her team. The areas for improvement included reducing the use of sensationalized terms, the importance of treating each media outlet equally, and providing full and concise sound bites, all great suggestions for improvement. But what I genuinely appreciated from the list were her observations of the nervous ticks I was not aware of: my tendency to shake my knees when seated and flex my pectoral muscles while being interviewed for TV. I accepted the list with great appreciation, much to our manager's relief, who wasn't sure how I would receive the directness of her observations. I even had the document laminated to ensure that I kept it as a constant reminder of the truth about how I communicated.

My goal in actively seeking this information was to temper my self-opinion with self-awareness, promoting better self-control, thereby avoiding grandiosity's pitfalls. Wanting to feel unique and significant —'special' in today's terms——can lead to grandiosity. Grandiosity is a distortion of our self-opinion, occurring when we have some degree of perceived power or responsibility, or a unique skill set. It leads us to develop an excessive sense of self-importance, self-absorption and a high need for admiration, along with a keen sensitivity to criticism.

Self-deception and self-illusion, perpetually lying to oneself, facilitate these traits. If we don't hold grandiosity in check, it can lead to disastrous consequences for ourselves and others. We're unable to see the reality of any situation and especially the unintended consequences of our actions. If we're to lie to ourselves, the key then is not to believe our own lies.

Sticks, stones and names all hurt when you're seven

Each of us has been affected by events and our personal interpretation of them from our past. To a significant extent, key childhood experiences and influences forge our personalities. In our adult lives, we're prone to imitate the very values, biases, thoughts and actions our parents or caregivers inculcated in us, some positive and others negative. To varying degrees, we spend our lives trying to live up to our mother or father's expectations, even trying to make up for their mistakes. Many of us spend our lives trying to avoid repeating our parents' errors.

We're also subject to the impact of childhood wounds and injuries:

slights, mistreatment, unmet expectations, loss, negligence, abuse and trauma. Perhaps we had a relatively stable life, devoid of significant painful events, but had a mother or father who was too distant, critical, aloof or involved in their own childhood-inspired adult problems to think anything of ours. Or perhaps we were one of many children relegated to a constant competition for parental attention, nurturing, love or food around the dinner table. Conversely, because of death, divorce, imprisonment or violence of some sort, perhaps we didn't have a parent, were relegated to being a ward of the state or an extended family, or were shuffled from one foster home to another as an underage couch surfer.

These painful life moments and actions remain indelibly etched in our minds like wounds that never heal, barely forming a scar, leaving only a lasting ache. They shape our thoughts, providing emotional fuel for our adult biases, decisions and actions that often operate below our consciousness.

As we age and become adults, these unhealed wounds can also manifest themselves as anxieties, depressive streaks and obsessive worrying. These manifestations may expose themselves at the wrong times, having a significant effect on our lives and how we interact with others. We may have exaggerated or inappropriate reactions to various events, engaging in impetuous, damaging and unsafe activities. We may commit ourselves to long-term toxic relationships or avoid healthy, positive ones in misguided attempts to put right what once went wrong. Our social judgment becomes twisted and we end up trusting those people whom we should not trust and not trusting those whom we should.

Our unhealed childhood wounds influence how we react to criticism through avoiding, withdrawing, attacking others or attacking ourselves. Because of those wounds, we're unable to accept criticism of our actions. It's just never our fault.

The reality is that our adult selves are not responsible for the internal emotional turmoil resulting from these wounds. It's the seven-year-old still living inside of us, the one who was hurt by mom, dad, Uncle Bob, our older brother, grade 2 teacher, family doctor, local clergy or any person we looked up to as having any authority, credibility, love or power over us. 'Us' being the cute, adorable, innocent kid who was abused, neglected, pushed around or, conversely, wasn't recognized, appreciated, or loved enough.

Austrian neurologist Sigmund Freud (1856-1939), the founder of psychoanalysis, wrote about how our childhood wounds can morph into noxious, volatile attitudes and responses in our adulthood. For many reasons, we feel that, while growing up, we never had enough or were forced into undeserving circumstances. As a result we feel slighted and carry a permanent chip on our shoulders, becoming chronically antagonistic, quarrelsome or argumentative; also, we may be drawn to people, views, and activities that allow for the release of such toxicity.

In his 1916 essay "Some Character-Types Met within Psycho-Analytic Work," Freud provided a character study of what he labeled as "The Exceptions," those who suffered from what he qualified as a childhood narcissistic injury. The injury results in a lifelong fixation by the individual who feels that they were subsequently entitled to special privileges as ongoing compensation. He wrote, "We all demand reparation for our early wounds to our narcissism, our self-love." These injuries hold significant sway over our worldview, our comprehensive conception or apprehension of the world. We lose a proper, broader perspective, trying to fit our interpretation of the world and the people in it according to emotional silos as seen through a particular lens, be it insecurity, anxiety, inferiority or oppression. We then counter an incident that confirms our lens view with a pre-determined reaction, such as an aggressive response or an outburst of grievance in an effort not to repeat being injured the way we were as a child.

During moments of fear and overwhelming stress, we revert to our child-like reactions, reliving the anxiety and vulnerabilities of a seven-year-old. Sometimes it has nothing to do with us, but with our own children through whom we live vicariously, to avoid them living the same childhood injuries as we did. In both contexts, the results end up being disappointing, if not downright disheartening.

Marlo misses out on history

Marlo is a hockey parent, a *crazy* hockey parent. He drives his daughter everywhere for her hockey, watching every practice and every game intently. Marlo cheers louder than anyone else during games, and is the first to blame officiating and coaching for anything and everything that goes wrong for his daughter and her team.

Marlo's daughter is just 11. In her short hockey career, she has played at the highest level of her age group on good teams that have frequently done well. Marlo takes no guff and believes that his daughter is destined for greatness, most likely as a starter for an NCAA team on a full-ride scholarship. Who knows, she might just play for Team Canada in the Olympics one day.

One evening in early 2016, Marlo's daughter was playing out of town. As usual, Marlo was in the crowd, cheering on her team. But that night was unusual because her team didn't win. They lost, and they lost badly.

To Marlo, there was only one reason: it was because of the poor officiating. And Marlo just had to let those officials, especially the 17-year-old referee, know how poorly they had officiated the game. As the referee and even younger linespersons were leaving the ice, Marlo, who had been impatiently awaiting them at the rink door, launched into a deafening tirade about what a lousy job they had done and how they deserved to be verbally and even physically chastised. As the scared officials quickly headed to their dressing room, the arena's security guards had to restrain Marlo. Police were eventually called. Although no criminal charges were laid, Marlo ended up being barred from entering two of the area's arenas for the remainder of the season.

Marlo's daughter and her team rebounded from the embarrassment of the rare loss and her father's actions. In fact, her team made it to the provincial championship final. As luck would have it, the final was held in the other area's arena, the second arena from which Marlo had been barred. And poor Marlo, who had put so much time, money and effort into his daughter's career and season up to this point, couldn't attend the championship game in person.

On a cold Saturday afternoon in March 2016, the championship game took place. Typically, a hockey game at this level would last between 60 and 90 minutes. Little did anyone, including Marlo, suspect that this game would last over four hours and be called after the seventh overtime period because the 10- and 11-year-old girls and the crew of three officials had reached their physical and psychological limits. Towards the end of the game, some players collapsed on the bench because of fatigue, prompting provincial hockey officials to become genuinely concerned about their welfare.

In a Solomon-like fashion, the teams were declared co-champions for the season. The game, played over ten 15-minute periods resulting in a 1-1 tie, was believed to have been the longest hockey game ever played in Nova Scotia and one of Canada's longest minor hockey games. History had been made that afternoon.

Marlo had to wait outside and receive reports about the game and his daughter's performance via text messages the entire time. I know Marlo was outside because I sat and watched him for 30 of those minutes, to make sure he respected the ban. Like his daughter's team, Marlo also made history. He set a record for the longest wait outside an arena by a hockey parent. Ever.

Dealing with individuals who have no self-awareness, like Marlo, involves putting skin in their game to force them to understand what they're doing incorrectly. But before we can do that, we need to change our approach to dealing with such people. The key is to become an active spectator, learning and applying what American author Catherine A. Sanderson describes in her book *Why We Act—Turning Bystanders into Moral Rebels* (2020) as "bystander intervention techniques."

We do this by first believing in the change we want, recognizing the cost of our silence to ourselves and others. The next step is to learn skills and strategies to intervene succinctly, at the right moment and with the right amount of 'oomph' without going overboard. As with any skills, we need to practice them to be comfortable using them. It can be something as simple and non-threatening as saying, "Whoa! Would you like it if someone did that to you?" or, "Calm down, take it easy. I'm sure you have more important things to worry about."

Of course, depending on the person, the reaction may not be what we expect.

We also don't need to take on all the Marlos in the world at once. We can do it one small step at a time. Even through *not* doing something, we can achieve the same result: by not laughing at an offensive joke or not encouraging insulting behavior, as just two examples.

Perhaps the most useful thing we can do for ourselves and those we care about is to foster empathy in all that we do: genuinely trying to understand what others live and go through. We can go one step further by demonstrating compassion and actually doing something to assist someone in need.

Putting skin in a Marlo's game involves having them poignantly realize the pain they are inflicting in others. My wife did this once in brilliant fashion, putting skin into the game of a loud-mouth hockey father who was criticizing the officiating during his son's game. The father's mistake was that the referee he was loudly criticizing was our fifteen-year-old son. And he was doing it right in front of my wife. After a particularly acerbic sequence of insults hurled in my son's direction, my wife asked the father if his son was playing in the game. He responded yes, even indicating his son's jersey number. My wife then asked the father how he would like it if she were to critique and heckle his son every time he touched the puck. Shocked at hearing this, the father bristled, "Why would you do that?" to which my wife calmly replied, "Because that's exactly what you are doing to my son—the referee!" He didn't say another word for the rest of the game.

Denounce bad behavior from the outset. Report bullying if it's in the workplace. Decry actions that mistreat others. Sometimes simply taking a picture of another with our smartphone while they're doing their deed is enough to convince them to act otherwise. The key is not to condone what a Marlo is doing, regardless of the source of the pain that inspires them to act the way they do.

Only The Shadow knows

Unresolved childhood pain contributes to the development of our ego and individual insecurities. Collectively, they rule that darker side of our personality, known as the "Shadow Self." Carl Jung described the Shadow Self as the sum of our negative, darker qualities that we attempt to deny and repress:

> Unfortunately, there is no doubt about the fact that man is, as a whole, less good than he imagines himself or wants to be. Everyone carries a shadow, and the less it is embodied in the individual's conscious self, the blacker and denser it is.

Jung wrote that the "little weaknesses and foibles" contributing to this state can collectively create a mass from which "emerges a raging monster." The Shadow Self forms part of our unconscious mind, driven by our insecurities and childhood injuries, forming repressed ideas, instincts, impulses, weaknesses, desires, perversions and fears, all of which, if exposed, would be too embarrassing, distressing or humiliating to face.

That's why we hide them so well. We actively display a mask or outer persona to the world, a façade that demonstrates the type of person we would like to be and how we wish to be perceived by the people around us, effectively hiding this side of our personality. We can augment that mask through many forms of wardrobe, our particular lifestyle, station in life, words and attitudes. Lying is one of the tools we use to hide the Shadow Self from others and even from ourselves.

Literature is brimming with examples of the Shadow Self: Shakespeare's tragedies of *Hamlet* and *Macbeth,* Victor Hugo's *The Hunchback of Notre Dame*, Robert Louis Stevenson's *The Strange Case of Dr. Jekyll and Mr. Hyde,* Joseph Conrad's *Heart of Darkness,* and Gaston Leroux's *The Phantom of the Opera* to name but a few of the many better-known works. Television and film have expanded this repertoire, giving life to these stories and producing new ones, even morphing old ones into updated masterpieces such as Francis Ford Coppola's *Apocalypse Now*, a modern adaptation of *Heart of Darkness*. The entire *Star Wars* franchise is based on the battle between "The Force" and the "Dark Side," representing the dichotomy of good and evil in all of us.

In the art world, Norwegian painter Edvard Munch (1863-1944) embodied the Shadow Self through his work *The Scream*, of which four versions still exist out of the more than fifty Munch painted. It is considered one of the most famous images in art history, only after da Vinci's *Mona Lisa.*

No wonder these works have become so popular: as humans, we're drawn to what is outwardly forbidden, frowned upon or even embarrassing. This fascination plays out in our lives on the internet, with the proliferation of pornographic, gambling and extramarital-affair websites, three of the most popular, widespread and most-often-visited types of sites.

The Shadow Self can manifest itself in different ways and to varying degrees. Many things, including alcohol, drugs, personality disorders, temporary illness and pain, fatigue, hunger, stress, idleness and even sports matches can trigger the manifestation of the Shadow Self. We may encounter individuals who demonstrate extreme traits revealing their Shadow Self's depth: bullies, martyrs, passive-aggressive virtue signalers, ideologues, rigid traditionalists and self-righteous snobs. Each individual demonstrates clear, forceful traits that distinguish their affect from the usual ways of acting in social settings. This distinction from others shows just how special they are to themselves, temporarily calming the storm, caused by the Shadow Self, that rages in their interior.

However, some people find other, more productive ways to soothe this tempest, not channeling their energies negatively towards others. Norwegian playwright and theatre director Henrik Johan Ibsen (1828-1906) described this struggle through his professional activities:

> Our whole being is nothing but a fight against the dark forces within ourselves. To live is to war with trolls in heart and soul. To write is to sit in judgment on oneself.

For centuries, music critics have opined that Wolfgang Amadeus Mozart (1756-1791) explored his darker side in several of his works, most notably his *Requiem,* which was unfinished upon his death. For many individuals, myself included, participating in sports and physical workouts, including powerlifting and bodybuilding, are a means of tapping into the Shadow Self's energy in a positive way.

In *Satires*, the Roman poet Juvenal (first century AD) wrote:

> No deed that sets an example of evil brings joy to the doer of it. The first punishment is this: that no guilty man is acquitted at the bar of his own conscience.

To live a fulsome life based on reality, we'll all invariably and at some moment have to face, deal with and sit in judgment of those aspects of our personality that we find to be difficult and even disturbing. This includes facing our greatest fears.

Before we can even get to this point, though, we must realize that as individuals, we each have substantial, if not complete, responsibility for our reactions to the events and circumstances that befall us in our personal life. Known as the "responsibility assumption," this doctrine is paramount to initiating and guiding any change in our lives. From this assumption, we develop agency, the independent ability or power to act out our will.

In an era that deluges us with information, we starve for introspection, that ability to look deep into ourselves to figure out how we tick. To deal with our personality's darker side, we begin with introspection to first recognize our Shadow Self for what it is, what Scottish psychoanalyst W.R.D. Fairbairn (1889-1964) labeled the "Internal Saboteur." We do so by observing ourselves and our actions, looking for contradictions in our behavior, unjustified emotional outbursts, vigorous denial, absurd assumptions, obsessions, overidealization and the projection of our fears, faults and shortcomings on others.

Look around to see how others engage with you. Are they open, genuinely happy and caring, or are they guarded in what they say to you? Recognize their actions as reactions to your behaviors. Do what's called the "Mom test": would your mother be pleased or embarrassed to read about your exploits on the front page of the local newspaper? Or use the updated version of this test, the "Viral test": imagine a video of your actions that just went viral on some social media platform. How would others perceive your actions? In an ideal world, we would watch intently viral videos of other people acting out as we've behaved, asking ourselves, "What would I do in such a situation?"

The key is to shed some objective light on our actions so we can determine how we truly act and what animates such action. In a work setting, a 360-degree assessment allows us to anonymously learn from our entourage the effects we can have on them, helping us understand what we do and possibly even our motivations. Far from being a perfect representation of who we are, such an evaluation at least allows us to step back and receive some honest feedback.

For such feedback to be useful, we have to be open to it and willing to use it to improve. I was fortunate enough to have such feedback once, back in 2000, just before becoming a commissioned officer. It was the most important professional feedback I ever received, coming at the right moment in my career before I became a police executive.

In the absence of such feedback, approaching someone we know and trust to ask for their unvarnished opinion can also help. But this is predicated on the type of relationship we have with the individual, their level of comfort in speaking the truth, and our willingness to listen, really listen, to that truth. Sometimes, we're fortunate enough to have someone who cares about us and is willing to help.

When I was a seventeen-year-old grocery store clerk, my manager sat me down to tell me why he wasn't going to approve further training for me. The training would have allowed me to work at the check-out, providing more work shifts and more money for college. He was honest, telling me that I wasn't yet mature enough to handle the cash. But he did one more thing. He told me that if I demonstrated my maturity over the following three months, he'd reconsider his position. He detailed exactly what I needed to do to improve myself.

Initially slighted, I took his suggestion to heart and worked hard to be as responsible and mature as possible. Eventually, he changed course, and I was trained to operate the cash register, allowing me to obtain more shifts. It was thanks to his honesty and his willingness to embrace the potential conflict that I became better. The lesson served me well beyond that early job.

Stabilizers, underminers and obstinators

Remember that our goal is not to repress or eliminate the Shadow Self, but to recognize its presence and influence in our daily lives. Once we're armed with that knowledge, we can diminish its potential destructive power. Following this action, we can then tap into and channel its abundant energy for different, more constructive purposes.

This requires embracing the Shadow Self through exploration, seeking to control, channel and integrate it into our conscious personality. For example, if we aren't overly confident, we use the Shadow Self's energy to assert ourselves. If we're too ambitious, we use the Shadow Self to define and drive our direction. If we're needy and vulnerable, we use the Shadow Self to display greater empathy, attempting to develop as much independence as possible. If we're overly aggressive, we use the Shadow Self to advance prosocial causes and efforts. We approach the fears that animate the Shadow Self to determine their degree of baselessness and deconstruct them.

The key is to be as blatantly honest as we can about what drives our conscious and subconscious emotions so we can understand what we are continually trying to protect inside. We then focus and channel the energy available to the Shadow Self into something rational and beneficial to ourselves, creating an 'inner stabilizer' instead of an 'inner underminer.'

This inner stabilizer allows us to determine what's best for ourselves, directly affecting how we treat those most important to us: our family, friends and work colleagues. The creation of the inner stabilizer implies being responsible for everything in our life, especially how we interpret and act upon events. The ultimate goal of exercising this agency over our lives is to have the courage to see the reality that exists instead of falling into the trap of believing our bias-tainted version of reality.

Refusing to give in to the inner underminer, we focus and prioritize what advances our goals, not in an ego-centric manner, but by contributing to others and learning from our errors, misinterpretations and assumptions. This also means that we try our utmost to generate the best actions we can create. It's not perfection but excellence in all that we do: bringing life to the expression:

How we do anything is how we do everything.

This is the key to self-knowledge and its eventual goal of self-mastery. Self-knowledge comes through introspection by determining what is truly important to us. We do this by understanding not what we say but for what we're willing to risk. By looking at how we do things and, mainly, *why* we do something, we're better positioned to understand who we are.

Look around to determine what you have. Take stock of your skills, education, experiences and emotions. Only after that should you take inventory of your possessions, which are mere reflections, trappings and indulgences of your preferences in life.

This evaluation can't and shouldn't be done just once, or during moments of duress or when we feel particularly self-defeating. It should be a repeated exercise that we carry out at different times in our lives. Preferably, we should carry it out after a significant event or life experience by doing something comparable to what the military and first responders call an 'after-action report': a deep dive into an event to determine what went right, what could have been done better and what should be done next time a similar event occurs.

This process should be a regular, ongoing means of improving our decision-making. And the interesting part is that you can use it to analyze events, mistakes and even successes by others in far-off locales.

Taking stock of our qualities and emotions, we must continually evaluate them. Such an evaluation should be running in our minds' conscious background. Much like antivirus software, we're forever scanning our actions and thoughts to understand those important life-affirming aspects while containing and purging those malignant, self-harming views and motivations that sabotage our lives and can damage the lives of others. This frees up space for positive attributes and behaviors such as gratitude and humility to surface more continually, while allowing us to master our thoughts and actions.

Italian painter, inventor and engineer Leonardo da Vinci (1452-1519) is widely considered one of the most diversely-talented individuals who ever lived. He was a polymath, an individual whose knowledge base spans a wide range of subjects and interests. Da Vinci's leitmotif, or guiding life principle, was *ostinato rigore* ("obstinate rigor"). It implied relentless improvement and a work ethic that resulted in numerous works of art and copious inventions and conceptualizations, including flying machines, solar power, the parachute and the automobile.

Da Vinci wrote: *Uno non può possedere capacità più grande o più piccola della padronanza di se stesso* ("One cannot possess skills greater or lesser than the mastery of oneself"). This mastery of oneself requires understanding ourselves, taking stock of our strengths and weaknesses, channeling our negative traits into something productive and engaging our daily thoughts towards our life purpose. Da Vinci recognized the challenges we have with our skewed worldviews and how they impeded our ability to see the reality in life. He wrote that "the greatest deception men suffer is from their own opinions."

Hence the critical importance of avoiding self-deception through critical thinking. Not cynical, envious, self-defeating thinking, but an open, questioning approach to broaden our perspectives on life. By being intellectually honest, we can improve how we travel through our lives and deal with the invariable challenges and complexity.

Without ongoing self-knowledge garnered through self-awareness and self-evaluation, we become subject to our non-truths and deceptions.

Shine a light on ourselves

By occasionally shining a direct light on ourselves to determine how and why we do things, we can begin the process of self-mastery. United States Supreme Court associate justice Louis D. Brandeis (1856-1941) wrote in a 1913 article in *Harper's Weekly*, "Sunlight is said to be the best of disinfectants." Although he was referencing the advent of electric lights as "the most efficient policeman," many jurists and observers have reprised his famous quote as a plea for transparency in all areas.

In matters related to self-mastery, that means transparency of the self: shining the light of reality on what makes us tick and holding ourselves accountable when we fail to live up to our expectations and aspirations.

We often deceive ourselves into *thinking* that we think, when in fact we don't. What often passes for thinking is a re-hashing of the same words, ideas, criticisms, biases and fears we reveal to ourselves every day, many of which we obtain and reinforce through the deluge of information and opinion we receive. A good leader is acutely aware of the interplay between the Shadow Self and the light of reality, using the latter to expose the former.

Self-transparency through true thinking is hard, arduous work. It involves having an honest conversation inside our minds. Any dialogic interaction requires an eloquent and concise speaker as well as a thoughtful, deep listener. For self-transparency, we need to let the speaker say what's on their mind and listen intently to what comes out. This dialogue works best in moments of quiet reflection; the challenge is to be quiet enough to let the other half speak.

The best leaders are those who can make a realistic appraisal of themselves, including their strengths, weakness, influences and preferences. Besides being lifelong learners of external information and skills, they nurture a devotion to inner truth and reality. By acting this way, they avoid self-deception, being as transparent and honest with themselves as possible. This means understanding what they do on a regular and irregular basis, the consequences related to their actions, and why they act in such ways.

We can never know or understand enough about ourselves. Constant and honest self-evaluation is an effective remedy, if not an outright antidote, to unknowing and unwitting self-deception. This starts with self-awareness and self-transparency, collectively the keys to seeing the reality of life. Through self-knowledge, we can avoid the cousin of self-deception: hubris, arrogance born of overconfidence and self-importance, which have caused the downfall of even the most competent individuals.

Calls from the blue line

- Humans learn early to lie as a form of protection. We're the only animals in the world capable of lying to ourselves and believing our own lies.
- Since we are going to lie to ourselves, the key is not to believe ourselves.
- Just like a hockey referee who must communicate while keeping up with the play, strive to be the best communicator possible in all areas of your life, adjusting as required.
- As we age and become adults, our unhealed childhood wounds can manifest themselves as anxieties, depressive streaks and obsessive worrying, which often expose themselves at the least-convenient times and can have a significant effect on our lives and how we interact with others.
- Unresolved childhood pain contributes to the development of our ego and individual insecurities. Collectively, they rule that darker side of our personality known as the "Shadow Self."

- Our worldview is our unique, comprehensive conception or apprehension of the world, resulting from a specific perspective that we have developed over the years since childhood.
- The Marlos of the world display bad behavior because they're allowed to do so. Remember what Irish philosopher Edmund Burke (1729-1797) said: "The only thing necessary for the triumph of evil is for good men to do nothing." Putting skin in Marlo's game is one of the best ways to counter their actions.
- Self-knowledge comes through introspection, determining what truly is important to us. We do this by understanding not what we say but what we're willing to risk. By looking at how we do things and, mainly, *why* we do them, we're better positioned to understand who we indeed are.
- Be like Leonardo da Vinci: make self-mastery the single, most important habit in your life.

4: The lesson of hubris

When anyone asks me how I can best describe my experiences of nearly forty years at sea I merely say uneventful. Of course, there have been winter gales and storms and fog and the like, but in all my experience, I have never been in any accident of any sort worth speaking about. I have seen but one vessel in distress in all my years at sea, a brig, the crew of which was taken off in a small boat in charge of my third officer. I never saw a wreck and never have been wrecked nor was I ever in any predicament that threatened to end in disaster of any sort.

- Captain Edward John Smith, RMS *Titanic*, in 1907
while he was captain of the RMS *Adriatic*;
quoted in a *New York Times* article on
April 16, 1912, the day after
the sinking of the *Titanic*.

The worst kind

My direct boss in Haiti in 2008-2009, the United Nations Police Commissioner, had a unique personality. He was a 60-year-old Guinean career police officer who had reached the rank of Major General in his country, a land which was almost as poor as Haiti. He had been deployed with the UN for several years before becoming the Police Commissioner for MINUSTAH in 2007.

The Commissioner was an exceptional orator. In my entire career, I had never met anyone so eloquent in French or any other language. He was able to take any subject and expound upon it with fervor and eloquence, able to weave a parable out of nothing, spellbinding listeners for minutes, and on occasion, for hours.

One of his favorite talks to new UN mission arrivals was about the sexual exploitation of local girls and women. He implored newly arrived male peacekeepers to place their libido in a zip-lock bag and throw it in the freezer for the duration of their mission. One thing for which the Commissioner was consistent was that he never was at a loss for words.

Following my arrival in Haiti as the Deputy Police Commissioner in January 2008, I spent time touring border points between the Dominican Republic and Haiti with the Commissioner. During my first week of work, we went to the town of Malpasse, opposite the Dominican provincial capital of Jimani, about 35 miles to the east of the Haitian capital of Port-au-Prince. It was one of two official border crossings between the countries; many other unofficial points dotted the landscape along the 220-mile frontier.

During a break in our visit, as we were watching the flow of goods and people between the two countries, the Commissioner gave me his opinion of the UN police officers (commonly known as UNPOLs) under his command. He told me in French that *Les UNPOLs sont la pire espèce,* "UN-POLs are the worst kind (of people)." He then provided a litany of the poor character traits he had observed, including laziness, greed, ambition and envy, among the men and women under his command, ending his tirade with a warning for me not to trust them at all.

This was a shocking wake-up call for me. I had never heard a senior police leader talk about his subordinates in such a way. Was he correct in his evaluation? How could he view them with such disdain? How could he hope to develop the requisite trust to influence these people to accomplish a common goal? I also wondered what his people would say about him if they knew his low opinion of them.

I learned very quickly that this exceptional communicator had numerous detractors at all levels in his organization and elsewhere in the UN hierarchy, for many reasons, but not least because of his contempt for people, frequent indecision and general arrogance. The following year would prove to be one of the most challenging postings for me as a police executive because of this man's actions and inactions. But it would also prove to be the most intense learning experience I've ever had.

In April 2008, the Commissioner went home to Guinea for a four-week vacation. During that period, we experienced two weeks of violent riots related to escalating food prices and political uncertainty. The riots were predominantly in the capital, Port-au-Prince, and the southern city of Les Cayes. Dozens died from the rioters' actions and a few at the hands of local police, while many more were injured. Meanwhile, businesses and government buildings sustained significant damage.[39]

The news of the riots went around the world. Not once did the Commissioner reach out to contact me for an update despite my repeated emails to him.

Before going to Haiti, I knew that the Commissioner had a difficult personality; this had been part of the lure for me. I had been warned that he was narcissistic, risk-averse and quick to blame others for his indecision. The Commissioner suffered from an exaggerated sense of pride and self-confidence, resulting in what is known as **hubris**. Associated with a lack of humility, hubris denotes overconfident arrogance and pride in one's actions and behavior.

Following an escape of several inmates from a poorly constructed and maintained jail in the north of Haiti, the Commissioner laid the blame squarely on my shoulders, indicating to his superior, Mr. da Costa, that he had previously instructed me to reinforce site security.

The only problem was that the Commissioner never gave such an order. Even if he had, I had neither the resources nor the mandate to effect such change. He simply wanted to deflect any criticism from Mr. da Costa onto me.

I refused the criticism. This led to my falling out of favor with Mr. da Costa, who eventually refused my mission extension request.

Knowing ahead of time what to expect from the Commissioner, I felt the experience in the face of such overwhelming hubris was worthwhile, especially since I knew that it was only for a year. I wanted to learn, and I viewed this opportunity as a form of apprenticeship, a chance to transform my mind and modify my character.

Becoming a good leader involves not only learning from the best but also learning from the worst. It involves choosing places of work and opportunities that offer the greatest possibilities for learning. This can mean selecting an apprenticeship that is both challenging and even uncomfortable. In this sense, I knew that the year wouldn't be one of passive but active learning, filled with moments of frustration.

The best leaders tend to reinforce what we already know, whereas the worst leaders teach us what *not* to do. Such people and their actions or inactions show us that sometimes we can get closer to the truth through negative occurrences than positive ones. They also demonstrate that we can actually improve something by taking something away, as opposed to adding something, such as another layer of accountability or oversight. This is one aspect of what is known as the *via negativa*.

The notion of *via negativa* originally developed within the Christian tradition, meaning a way of speaking about God's attributes, or lack thereof, to learn more about Him. However, I use the expression as the author Nassim Nicholas Taleb refers to it:

> The principle that we know what is wrong with more clarity than what is right, and that knowledge grows by subtraction. Also, it is easier to know that something is wrong than to find the fix. Actions that remove are more robust than those that add because addition may have unseen, complicated feedback loops.[40]

In Chinese, the expression *wu wei* means "inexertion," "inaction," or "effortless action." Considered to be the height of wisdom, it implies reacting to something by not doing anything. In his writings, Taleb further expounds upon the notion of falsification advocated by Sir Karl Raimund Popper (1902–1994), the Austrian-born British philosopher of natural and social sciences. Falsification advocates the search for observable exceptions to any given or postulated rule. As such, disconfirmation is more rigorous than confirmation as we can sometimes learn more from the elimination of knowledge than from its accumulation.

Applying falsification to life in general, it's sometimes better to know what to avoid than to learn what to gravitate towards. Examples abound: preventing the ingestion of those substances that are noxious, such as tobacco, junk food and drugs that impair; avoiding wasting time doing things that add nothing to our life, such as mindlessly surfing the internet and social media or watching TV; avoiding toxic relationships that cripple.

Even in hockey, *via negativa* manifests itself through what are known as "non-calls", when a linesperson doesn't call an icing because the players are not skating hard enough to get to the puck. Regardless of the domain, the key is to learn about what not to do to increase our knowledge base, focusing on the most important things we should do and learn from.

Knowledge has been described as the absence of ignorance. One of my favorite cartoonists is Bill Watterson, the creator of the cartoon strip *Calvin and Hobbes*. In one of his most memorable panels, the main character, Calvin, a rambunctious and overly imaginative six-year-old boy, laments that he wasn't dumb but simply had a "command of thoroughly useless information."

The key is to avoid the thoroughly useless information that constitutes the noise and the trivia of our lives, keeping us ignorant of what's truly occurring in life. Noise funnels directly to us via social media, the internet, television and water-cooler innuendo. Trivia is the excess, useless tidbits of information that only add to mental fatigue, confusion and helplessness if given attention.

We are what we focus on, and if we choose to feed our soul with mindless chatter and predigested judgments, then what comes out will reflect that lack of sense. In a word, ignorance.

We all have an inner voice that talks to us continuously. It allows us to determine what to do, say and feel next. Researchers have determined that every minute we speak between 300 and 1000 words in our heads.[41] And almost 90 percent of all daily communication occurs using the same 500 words and ideas, including that mindless chatter and predigested judgments. As a good portion of our communication is nonverbal, that leaves much room for miscommunication. And misinterpretation.

Learning from the very worst kind

In 1949, in what would become a classic experiment reproduced hundreds of times with similar results, the American psychologist Bertram R. Forer (1914-2000) administered a personality test to 39 students in his introductory psychology class. It was the students themselves who had asked that he administer the multi-part test to them.

As the first part of the test, Forer gave the students a Diagnostic Interest Blank (DIB) sheet to complete, detailing the interests, hobbies, job duties, secret hopes and ambitions of their ideal person. Forer then advised the students that he'd review each DIB and provide every student with an individualized personality sketch or write-up reflective of their DIB. Each sketch contained the student's name and 13 statements intended to summarize the student's individual personality.

Forer then asked the students to rate how well his personalized sketch applied to them individually. On average, the students rated their personalized sketch's accuracy as 4.3 out of 5.0 on a scale of 0 (inferior) to 5 (excellent). This indicated that the students felt Forer had correctly summarized their personalities in the sketch.

Only after the ratings were all returned did Forer reveal to the students that they had all received the exact same personality sketch. The statements came mainly from a newsstand astrology book. He advised his students that he had carried out the experiment as:

(...) an object lesson to demonstrate the tendency to be overly impressed by vague statements and to endow the diagnostician with an unwarrantedly high degree of insight. Similarities between the demonstration and the activities of charlatans were pointed out.

Forer then published his findings in his aptly-entitled paper "The Fallacy of Personal Validation: A Classroom Demonstration of Gullibility."[42] In the years to come, the experiment results became known as the Forer Effect, a common psychological phenomenon. The Effect recognizes that individuals give high accuracy ratings to descriptions of their personality that, although tailored to them, are so vague and broad as to apply to an extensive range of individuals. In 1956, American psychologist Paul Meehl (1920-2003) relabeled the term the Barnum Effect in honor of the American showman P.T. Barnum (1810-1891), who was alleged to have said, "There's a sucker born every minute."[43]

The value of this test, beyond exhibiting the basis of the techniques used by supposed psychics such as palm, tarot and crystal-ball readers, is that it demonstrates the so-called "acceptance phenomenon," the general tendency of humans to accept any personality feedback, bogus or not, at face value. It further reflects a related and more general cognitive bias known as subjective validation or the personal validation effect, whereby two unrelated or even random events are perceived to be related because a belief, expectation, hypothesis or authority figure (such as a professor) demands such a relationship. This sets the stage for our view that we're individually more special than we truly are, based on our self-esteem and narcissism, which form our self-opinion.

As a personality trait, in limited quantity, controlled and held in check by humility, narcissism is an essential component of our self-esteem and self-confidence. The problem is when that narcissism goes unchecked, it becomes unbridled grandiosity, leading to arrogance in our thoughts and actions. This can then result in hubris, that noxious mixture of vanity and overconfidence.

Along with grandiose narcissism and entitlement, hubris is driven by the ego and powered by our pride. French author Victor Hugo (1802-1885) qualified our pride as our internal "fortress of evil."

Ego, driven by excessive pride or even shamelessness, is tyrannical and despotic, interpreting all information in terms of self-preservation. Perhaps the most notable example of ego is found in the Abrahamic (Christianity, Judaism, and Islam) religions' description of the angel Lucifer's spiritual descent into Satan. Literature is also rife with examples such as Mary Shelley's *Frankenstein*, in which Dr. Frankenstein's hubris results in his bitter regret for creating life through technological means; and Kit Marlowe's *Doctor Faustus* in which arrogance and pride lead the title character to sign a deal with the devil.

History is also replete with examples of hubris. The destruction of the 7th Cavalry Regiment at the Battle of the Greasy Grass, more commonly known as the Battle of the Little Bighorn, in southeastern Montana on June 25-26, 1876, is a notable example of military hubris Lieutenant-Colonel George Custer committed. Not only did Custer die along with 268 of his soldiers, but so did his two brothers, a nephew and a brother-in-law.

Such examples demonstrate the notion that hubris breeds vulnerability. With an inflated view of their abilities, hubristic individuals, groups and organizations make assumptions around their abilities to deal with various situations. Just as with Custer, such assumptions can be deadly wrong.

Our ego is built by those emotions that turn us inward, building walls to separate us from others, impeding us from seeing the reality beyond those walls. Our ego creates a chasm between how it wants us to identify ourselves, using protective cloaks and self-serving fictions, biases and opinions to mask our true self.

We end up dwelling on our anger, fueled by our insecurities and often-fictional perceptions of unfairness. We view the world through our own narrow emotional lenses of anxiety, insecurity, depression, persecution and victimization. We develop an ego-driven script that determines how we're to assess and respond in any situation.

Because of the ego's iron grip on our personality, we require an approach that deliberately circumvents the ego in order to see the reality of life.

Our present-day society reinforces the development of hubris. The social support systems that previously existed have slowly eroded. Organized religion, great social movements rooted in shared beliefs and social cohesion through mutual assistance encouraged a certain subservience of the personality to something more significant than oneself.

Admittedly, that same subservience, unfortunately, encouraged lemming-like followings, resulting in abuses of all kinds in religious, political and cult movements. Partly as a reaction to such violations, the institutions and practices that inspired such negative behaviors have slowly lost their appeal and influence, being replaced by an overwhelming reverence of the self instead of any god, social philosophy or community ideal.

As we are unable to channel our personal needs and visions of grandiosity through the traditional social supports, various fault lines have emerged. Religious, political and social divides continue to expand, driven by higher levels of individualism and grandiosity of the self, in some cases forming a cult of the personality. Politics, in particular, has adopted much of the fervor and zeal previously reserved for religion, resulting in righteous, moralistic, unforgiving and dogmatic adherence by members of the populist right and the woke left alike.

In the past, we've seen this development through the collective adulation and blind devotion towards various historical figures and their movements, such as Maximilien de Robespierre (1758-1794) during the 'Reign of Terror' of the French Revolution, Hitler (1889-1945) and Nazism leading to World War II, Josef Stalin (1878-1953) and forced collectivization, Mao Zedong (1893-1976) during the 'Great Leap Forward' (1958-1961) and the 'Cultural Revolution' (1966-1976) in China, as well as Pol Pot (1925-1998) and the Cambodian genocide (1975-1979).

On a smaller scale are the examples of Jim Jones (1931-1978) and David Koresh (1959-1993), respectively responsible for the collective suicide of 918 commune members in Jonestown, Guyana in 1978 and 82 Branch Davidian members in Waco, Texas in 1993. Even in business, leaders such as Dhirubhai Ambani (1932-2002), the successful Indian business tycoon of Reliance Industries; the Chinese magnate Jack Ma, the founder of Alibaba; the "Oracle of Omaha" Warren Buffett; and Elon Musk, the founder of SpaceX and Tesla have achieved cult-figure status.

These examples demonstrate the willingness of people to assume the roles of guru, messiah or supreme leader, and the willingness of other people to accept them in these roles.

I've seen senior police executives also fall into this trap of hubris. One prominent municipal chief I knew decided to impress those in attendance at his first-ever town-hall meeting by lowering himself into a darkened amphitheater on the end of a rope as if he were descending from Heaven, with strobe lights and pounding electronic dance music. He only impressed those in attendance of the extent of his self-opinion.

One retired RCMP commissioner and an active small-town police chief co-presented on a panel before a 2012 international gathering of police executives, including me. They spoke for 40 minutes about the importance of developing leaders. The only problem was that the small-town police chief was Canada's longest-serving senior police executive, having held his position for twenty years. His co-presenter, the retired RCMP commissioner, had openly touted his desire to be the Force's longest-serving commissioner, effectively sending the message to those aspiring senior leaders waiting in the wings that their time would never come. After only six years in his position, he reached the end of his rope, long before he had anticipated. Neither individual spoke from a place of credibility on the subject of developing leaders, but only of hubristic self-delusion.

The final individual who presented at that same conference was a celebrated California sheriff. During his presentation, he spoke of the importance of having "noble thoughts" and acting as "a model of temperance and strength at the same time." His apparently noble thoughts led to an FBI investigation resulting in charges and a subsequent conviction for felony obstruction. He was sentenced to three years in federal prison.

Stolen ideas, dignity, money and valor

Our inability to deal with today's life absent traditional supports contributes to people feeling lost, without any direction. This exacerbates existing pathologies such as depression, anxiety, and addictions, and increasing hubristic tendencies powered by our ego.

Although a small word, ego represents a huge impediment to our seeing the reality of life around us. It prevents us from seeing our blind spots, our most deficient qualities and character flaws. It impedes our ability to see the reality of any given situation and its effect on others. Absent sufficient information, our ego leads us to fill in the gaps, making assumptions about people's motivations and actions, effectively blocking us from understanding others. An inability to productively and politely disagree results, leading to incivility. A further cost of this blindness is the loss of credibility with others.

How do we get around the trap of our ego? First, we must maintain a realistic attitude and appreciation of our particular abilities, energies and limits. We must also assume that those we interact with are just as competent as we are, if not more.

We begin by understanding that we are neither gods nor icons, but simple human beings, replete with flaws and foibles, not superior to anyone else. From this starting point, we can better appreciate our limits and capacities through a trio of qualities:

1. curiosity
2. empathy
3. humility

Curiosity allows us to be open to the differences that are present in any situation. It involves seeking feedback from a trusted source to understand our blind spots and improve upon them. This requires openness and the ability to set aside our defensive posturing. We're looking to become better; when we think there's nothing left to improve, we're blind to our reality.

Empathy, especially visceral empathy, drives connection with others. In this sense, it's the opposite of sympathy and envy, which drive disconnection. It allows us to see and comprehend what someone else is going through, forcing us to change our perspective and attitude to deal with their situation. It also allows us to see the humanity in others. When I was a teenager taking my Bronze Medallion swimming lessons to become a lifeguard, I remember being taught an important concept. It was the motto of the Royal Life Saving Society: *Quemcunque miserum videris hominem scias.* This translates into *Whomsoever you see in distress, recognize in them a fellow human being.*

As American social worker and author Brené Brown states, empathy is feeling *with* people, not *for* people. It involves four things:

1. the ability to recognize the other person's perspective
2. being non-judgmental when learning another's situation
3. recognizing emotions in others
4. communicating our recognition of their emotions and feelings

It further requires connecting with something deep inside us that's comparable to what the other person is going through. Rarely can any response or any words assuage someone's pain, frustration or sadness; but connecting with that person just might.

Leadership involves a dynamic relationship between those who lead and those they lead. By being attuned to the effect we have on others, both conscious and unconscious, and by recognizing what they're going through, we can begin the vital process of seeing their situation's reality and influencing our, and eventually, their actions. This starts with being connected to them.

In determining what's important to people, we must look at what matters to them: what they pay money for, risk things for, invest their time and energies in, and value through their actions, not just or only through their words. When it comes to the ego, it's always deeds before words.

The key is to resist our ego's pull, the biggest impediment to developing what can be qualified as an exemplary or superior character. Our ego is composed of narcissism, hubris, a sense of entitlement and other personality conditions and negative traits, many of which require and generate substantial amounts of energy. By harnessing that energy to pursue larger, significant projects and challenges that contribute to others, we can tame it, mitigating its adverse effects while building something of substance.

The struggle against our ego is incessant and requires attention to what we say and, more particularly, to what we do. This means accessing and using our inner stabilizer to maintain a constant interior dialogue with reality, asking if we correctly see the truth of each situation while acting appropriately, scaling down our grandiose designs and behaviors.

One of the best ways to overcome the pull of the ego is through humility. When we fail to demonstrate humility, we lose our empathy, generosity, spirit and place in this world. Humility is one of the cornerstones of a superior character; it is often viewed as the parent of all other virtues. For some of us, the path to humility is through humiliation: being stripped of the ego's deceptions and defenses as a result of a recognized failure. This means living failures and viewing them as opportunities to right the course, thereby developing further humility.

Humility implies testing our assumptions for weaknesses and being unpretentious about the extent of our expertise or lack thereof, searching continually to invalidate our knowledge instead of just confirming it. In the hundreds of numerous investigations I undertook or participated in during my career, I always attempted to validate facts instead of cultivating them. The difference was to look at the evidence and validate its presence and pertinence to the investigation instead of merely finding proof of any evidence or creating links where none existed. My goal was always to give life to the aphorism, "The absence of evidence is not the same thing as the evidence of absence."

This means making allowances for our ignorance. Since my time as the officer-in-charge of Major Crimes Services in Manitoba, in 2003, regardless of where I worked, I always had a glass plaque on my desk in full view with the following quote from Sherlock Holmes in Arthur Conan Doyle's novel *A Scandal in Bohemia* (1891):

It is a capital mistake to theorize before one has facts; insensibly, one begins to twist facts to suit theories instead of theories to suit facts.

I'm looking at that very plaque as I write these words.

It's not uncommon for a leader to have visual reminders of what to do and what to avoid. During a February 12, 2015, speech at Georgetown University, former FBI Director James B. Comey described how he kept a copy of then-Attorney General Robert Kennedy's 1963 approval of FBI Director J. Edgar Hoover's request to wiretap Dr. Martin Luther King. It was a single page containing only five sentences of grounds in support of the wiretap. The grounds were without fact or substance, based on the blatant assertion that there was "communist influence in the racial situation."

Director Comey always kept the document as a reminder of his own mistakes and the importance of learning from them. Its direction would serve him well in the later years as the country's top police officer during a particularly challenging time in US presidential history.

Such humility makes allowance for our errors and how they have affected our choices and outcomes over the years. The key is not to dwell incessantly on them as sources of embarrassment, but to understand that, as humans, we're prone to such mistakes and must remain ever vigilant not to repeat them.

Regardless of our status as a manager or a leader, we have authority over processes or people; maybe even both. Having authority means that we must make decisions. People may appeal some of those decisions, whether it's to our common sense, our supervisor or an appeal entity. When such an appeal happens and our initial decision is overturned, we cannot allow our ego to block us from learning from it. Every error we commit is an opportunity to learn. If we see errors in that light, we can circumvent the ego's defensive posture.

As mentioned, one of the best ways to learn is from the mistakes of others. Of course, the advantage is that others make the mistake and pay the price for the error while we benefit from the lesson. Here's a brief selection of people who were ruled by their ego and betrayed by their hubris, offering us lessons on how *not* to live or act:

- Jan Hendrik Schön, a German physicist who, in the early 2000s, briefly rose to prominence after a series of breakthroughs with semiconductors that were subsequently discovered to be fraudulent, but not before he had won several prizes for his 'achievements'. The prizes were later withdrawn.

- Jian Gomeshi, a Canadian musician and talk-show host accused of sexual misconduct and bullying tactics by numerous individuals, women and men alike. He was charged criminally and acquitted of three separate charges in 2016. A fourth complaint resulted in the withdrawal of charges when he apologized to the complainant in court. His employer, the Canadian Broadcasting Corporation (CBC), fired him in 2014.

- Elizabeth Holmes, the former Stanford University dropout and self-made billionaire CEO of Theranos, a now-defunct company known for its fraudulent claims to have revolutionized blood testing using surprisingly small blood samples, such as from a fingerprick. This unverified technique allowed her company to raise more than $700 million in equity markets. At its height in 2015, the company had a market value of $9 billion. Theranos no longer exists, and Holmes has been found guilty on four counts of defrauding investors. It's alleged that she used a contrived baritone voice in phone interviews to add to her credibility.

- Franck Gervais, a man who masqueraded as a decorated Canadian Army sergeant during November 11, 2014, Remembrance Day ceremonies at the National War Memorial in Ottawa, Canada. He was interviewed on television by the CBC, at which point members of the Canadian Armed Forces and veterans' groups recognized that Gervais' uniform and the rack of medals he was wearing weren't correctly assembled. He was subsequently charged criminally and plead guilty to unlawfully wearing a military uniform and medals. Before his conviction, it was revealed that he had also worn the same uniform during his wedding ceremony, earlier in 2014. More than anything else, his was a crime of stolen valor.

These four people provide poignant examples of what ego and hubris can produce if left unchecked: the loss of trust by people replaced by a sense of betrayal, resulting in significant, if not irreparable, damage to one's career and reputation.

Striking a balance with humility

Contrary to popular convention, the 16th-century father of modern political science, Niccolò Machiavelli, never wrote, "The ends justify the means" in his classic, *The Prince*. Rather, his view was to do whatever was necessary to get a job done without going overboard. He specifically listed those virtues (*virtù*, in Italian) that he viewed as being singularly important:

- mercy
- good faith
- integrity
- humanity
- religion

For Machiavelli, *virtù* meant to be as effective as possible by being as relentless as the circumstances required, but not more.

Beware those individuals who espouse the notion that the ends justify the means. These people often see themselves as morally superior, and present as sanctimonious and divisive while having a dangerous tendency to put the ends before the means. They also tend to become ideological and tribal, forgetting how to talk or deal with those of opposing views, becoming self-righteous in the process.

Certain professions are more susceptible to this tendency. Some journalists claim to be objective when they do investigative journalism. Some politicians attempt to search for and speak the truth when dealing with social issues. In some instances, the problem is that both are more interested in promoting themselves and their beliefs based on their own biases rather than finding and fixing a problem. In wanting to make a difference and promote lasting, progressive change, they condemn what they view as systemic evils, promoting and encouraging their own version of justice.

We can't address a problem unless we've identified precisely what that problem is, not according to our desired outcomes or biases, but according to the situation's reality. Hubris clouds our faculties, impeding this search for truth and reality.

In addition to humility, what's required to deal with hubris are altruistic thinking and actions. We do this by putting others' needs first: giving quietly or anonymously, investing in others intentionally and continuously questioning our motives when dealing with them. Humility allows us to think and act in this manner.

We can use humility to motivate and guide us in two important but related areas of our lives:

- By valuing learning over money or the importance of acquiring experience over worldly goods.
- By developing a childlike curiosity and recognition that there's significantly more we don't know than we do know.

This latter point involves gravitating towards unusual situations that promote learning, even if they involve discomfort. We continuously seek to understand others and ourselves, regularly reflecting on what we do and why we do it, learning from our successes, but mostly from our mistakes. This means welcoming mistakes, ours and others', as opportunities to learn.

Humility also helps us battle those emotions that stop us from learning and advancing: boredom, panic, frustration, insecurity, fear and envy. We do this by seeking and maintaining a higher sense of purpose and direction beyond ourselves—towards our family, community, faith and the environment—something that we can view as a life's work. To complete this humility-centered approach, we must cultivate a work ethic based on excellence, not for anyone other than ourselves, which will allow us to achieve our higher sense of purpose.

American agricultural scientist George Washington Carver (1864-1943) summarized well the role of humility when he stated, "How far you go in life depends on your being tender with the young, compassionate with the aged, sympathetic with the striving and tolerant of the weak and strong. Because someday in your life, you will have been all of these."

A final word about humility: although it is an effective antidote to hubris, like any medication, it can be over-prescribed. As we age, we limit ourselves physically and mentally as part of our self-preservation mode. We've also internalized much of what we've heard and been told by others, particularly their criticism of us, fueling our self-doubt. We may even question our abilities, refuse certain positions or think of some new task as too challenging to overcome or not deserving of our attention.

Yes, humility must be used to temper our hubris, but it must not limit our actions and objectives. As with any tool, use humility with circumspection at the right times and for proper purposes.

It's a matter of striking the right balance.

Marlo can only follow a leader

Marlo was a 25-year police veteran who, by his own assertion, had solved numerous crimes, uncovered serious corruption within his service, and was worthy of being a senior officer without the need to undergo the requisite tests or processes. But events and especially senior managers had conspired against him to the point where he was relegated to working in a small analytical unit in what he considered a meaningless job. In Marlo's estimation, he was "a leader in a follower's position."

Marlo viewed himself as so competent and skilled an investigator that only he could see the truth in anything and everything, even when he wasn't involved in the event. During major incidents such as a shooting of a police officer, Marlo would immediately start his own investigation by going to social media to contact the alleged shooter's family and friends; this, despite Marlo not being assigned to the investigation or remotely involved in its response. When a journalist did an exposé on a murder investigation, Marlo, who never had anything to do with the investigation, openly offered his ill-informed take on the investigation, creating nothing but confusion.

Marlo's self-view was at odds with what he had actually done over the years. Marlo had spent an entire career alienating friends and work colleagues. Wherever he went, Marlo spread vitriol, hate and frustration, always insisting that he knew all the answers and was the most competent one around. When things went wrong, which happened a lot with Marlo, it was still always someone else's fault.

Marlo initiated several lawsuits against neighbors, his employer and even his extended family members, knowing that some would be dismissed while others would lead to a negotiated settlement in which people would pay to get rid of a vexatious or unfounded claim. Marlo even alleged criminal activity by his superiors but had nothing to substantiate his accusations.

Marlo finally retired. Bitter, he still claimed that he had been the target of various organizational and individual machinations. A deep narcissist, Marlo was unwilling to see the lies that he had constructed about himself and others as being far from the truth. For Marlo, humility was simply an empty word meant for suckers and not for him. The damage he wreaked upon others was considerable, but the damage Marlo caused himself was even more substantial.

Dealing with the hubris and narcissism of a Marlo requires understanding that we can't fix them; we can only contend with and contain their self-opinion. By acknowledging that self-opinion, we can lower their defensive posturing, then attempt to influence them by teaching them what behaviors they need to conform to their worldview.

The key is not to act like them but learn from them.

The intolerance of the (self-)righteous

Hubris is made of a series of traits that contribute to its physical manifestations, including vanity, narcissism, overconfidence and self-aggrandizement. Hubris can manifest itself in any forum or media, but the most accessible platforms today are on social media.

The most evident quality hubris appears as is self-righteousness. Also known as sanctimoniousness, sententiousness or holier-than-thou-ness, self-righteousness is a feeling or display of smug moral superiority over others. This sense of moral superiority derives from overconfidence in one's beliefs, actions or affiliations that results in presenting as more virtuous than others. Self-righteous types are convinced that their opinions are not only right, but noble, and feel obligated to share them with others.

The challenge with self-righteousness is that when people see their path as a noble one, they fall into the trap of special dispensation for moral lapses. In this age of arrogance, this includes being intolerant of the opinions and behaviors of others. In this sense, self-righteousness is pure prejudice, the same kind that fuels xenophobia and racism.

Also situated in this trap is the cognitive distortion known as noble cause corruption. In policing, noble cause corruption is an ends-based culture that prompts investigators to become blind to the totality of facts, including contradictory evidence. It leads to inappropriate and unprofessional behavior and the perception that anything they do is legitimate, since they are pursuing a vital public service.[44] It results in breaches of police ethics and even wrongful convictions.

This isn't unique to police officers; it can and does manifest itself in prosecutors, lawyers of all stripes, journalists and academics, to name but a few other professions in which many people think only their worldview is the right one.

In hockey and business terms, it means doing anything that advances the team's chances of winning, even if it ends up sacrificing team chemistry by having an exceptionally talented but uncontrollable team captain or office manager. They may obtain results in the short term but circumvent established protocols and have moral lapses resulting in significant risk to the team or organization in the long term.

The remedy to such behavior is not to think we're always right but understand that we could be wrong in our assessment of anything, as English Nobel laureate Rudyard Kipling wrote in his famous poem *If* (1895):

> If you can trust yourself when all men doubt you,
> But make allowance for their doubting too.

The second part of that remedy is to not think so highly of our opinions that we always need to share them. If, as the saying goes, discretion is the better part of valor, then we should reserve our opinions to those times when their advancement can actually make a difference; not to calm some personal storm brewing within, but to constructively deal with a mistake, injustice or defect outside ourselves.

Humans, like diamonds, are unique. Although we're all made from the same material, we're uniquely diverse. And uniquely flawed. Not always in some critical manner, but through an accumulation of imperfections developed collectively and individually over time. Collectively, ignorance frequently overshadows our knowledge. Individually, irrationality sometimes surpasses our wisdom while our shortcomings eclipse our strengths. And our hubris far too often exceeds our humility.

An unknown author wrote, "It is better to be motivated by the soul's hunger than by the ego's greed." Because of the significant changes in our society these past 50 years, including substantial leaps in technology, the avenues to express the ego's greed and resulting hubris have grown exponentially; hence, the need to develop a shield of personality traits that can withstand such forces.

This is the calling of character, that which emanates directly from our soul.

Calls from the blue line

- Becoming a good leader involves not only learning from the best but also learning from the worst. The best leaders tend to reinforce what we already know, whereas the worst leaders teach us what *not* to do.
- Although a small word, ego represents a huge impediment to our seeing the reality in life. It prevents us from seeing our blind spots, deficient qualities and character flaws. It impedes our ability to see the reality of any situation and our effect on others.
- How do we get around the trap of our ego? We maintain a realistic attitude about and appreciation of our abilities, energies and limits. We recognize our flaws, realizing that we are not gods, nor icons, but simple humans. We leave our egos in the dressing room when we play the game of life.
- Dealing with our ego and hubristic tendencies means cultivating our curiosity, empathy and humility. What's required to deal with hubris is altruistic, selfless thinking and actions.
- Dealing with a hubristic Marlo means recognizing that we can't "fix" them. But we must deal with them while learning from them what *not* to do.
- In policing, noble cause corruption is an ends-based culture that prompts investigators to become blind to the totality of facts, including contradictory evidence. It leads to inappropriate and unprofessional behavior. It can affect anyone, though, not just the police.
- In hockey, avoid drafting, recruiting or hiring a player or coach who only believes in winning. Especially for team sports, winning is rarely everything it's made out to be. Development of players and officials so they can go to the next level should be the most important consideration. This also applies to non-sports activities and business.
- We don't always need to share our opinion. We should reserve our opinions to those times when their offering can actually make a difference: not to calm some personal storm brewing within, but to constructively deal with a mistake, injustice or flaw outside ourselves.

5: The lesson of character

There is no honor like knowledge.
There is no belief like modesty and patience.
There is no attainment like humility.
There is no power like forbearance.
And there is no support more reliable than consultation.
-Hazrat Ali (600-661), First Imam
of the Shia Ismaili Muslims

A promise made and kept

On January 15, 2010, following the devastating earthquake in Haiti, I was on the ground in Port-au-Prince with Superintendent Doug Coates' executive officer, Constable Julie Dupré, participating in the recovery efforts at what was left of Hotel Christopher, the United Nations mission headquarters. That evening, a senior French gendarme, Colonel Pascal Messager of the Department of Crisis Management of the *Gendarmerie nationale*, advised me that he had a recovery team with him. Their mission was to recover the bodies of two French gendarmes who had died in the same collapsed building as Sergeant Mark Gallagher.

In very diplomatic prose, Colonel Messager stated that it would be a "point of national honor" for his team to recover Sergeant Gallagher's remains as well. I thanked him and wished him and his team Godspeed in their work.

In the early afternoon of the following day, we recovered Doug's remains and placed his body bag in the back of what was both my (when I was in mission) and his UN-marked sports utility vehicle. Constable Dupré and I took a break from our work.

It had been 40 hours since we had first arrived on scene, without any supplies, and with very spotty communications through a satellite telephone. We were tired, thirsty, run-down and quite dejected as we had hoped to find someone, anyone, alive.

We sat down on a curb at the corner of Avenue John Brown and the roadway leading to what was left of Hotel Christopher. We looked around and saw people in pretty much the same state as us: dejected and in shock.

Out of nowhere came a French gendarme whom neither of us recognized. He introduced himself as Warrant Officer Hervé Dumarski. He said he knew why we were there, and he expressed his condolences on the loss of our compatriots. We thanked him and returned the same on the loss of his countrymen.

He had two packages in his hands, which he gave to us. They were French Navy MREs (meals-ready-to-eat). Once he left, we dug into the MREs. They were sublime in their contents: a croissant, foie gras, a delicious stew, chocolates, and, of course, some wine. We ate and drank ravenously.[45]

About half-way through our meal, we saw a Haitian family of four seated on the ground across the street: a mother and her three children. They were even more spent and dejected than us.

Both Julie and I stopped eating. We looked at one another, and without a word, crossed the street to give the remainder of our meals to them. At that moment, we realized that, for us, despite our temporary circumstances, our comfortable homes and lives awaited us back in Canada. In contrast, this Haitian family had probably lost the few possessions they had.

It was a humbling experience that strengthened our resolve to return to our work and bring the fallen back home to their families.

After that brief meeting with Colonel Messager, I never saw him again. But I committed to one day thanking him for keeping his word and recovering Mark Gallagher's body.

I eventually made good on my commitment, when in July 2012, the general in charge of the *Gendarmerie nationale's* international program came to Halifax to attend the Royal Nova Scotia International Tattoo. I arranged for the RCMP commissioner, who was also at the Tattoo, to host a celebratory supper.

During the event, the commissioner gave the general a plaque as an official gift of appreciation and recognition to the *Gendarmerie nationale* and a separate gift intended for Colonel Messager.

Values as the fingerprints of character

Leadership requires many skills and traits. Of all those attributes, character is the single, most important one.

But character is not as much a skill as a choice, or series of choices. It is the intersection of our thoughts, feelings and actions resulting from the sum of our choices over time.

We all have frequent opportunities to make choices, both big and small. They determine how and if we overcome life's challenges and adversities. Those choices help fashion our lives and define who we are.

The result is the formation of our character. The consistently observed pattern of right decisions throughout one's life is what we can qualify as a superior character.

A superior character is the compilation of character traits that act as a shield against ego and hubris and, on occasion, a sword to ward off the negative aspects of others' egos. In terms of leadership, a superior character requires choosing to be a leader, learning what it takes to be a leader and continually doing the right things to become that leader.

In their seminal work, *Character Strengths and Virtues* (2004), Drs. Chris Peterson and Martin Seligman provide a framework that details 24 individual character strengths evident in the most widely influential traditions of thought in human history. These character strengths exist in all cultures and all individuals to varying degrees:

- Courage – bravery, perseverance, integrity, enthusiasm
- Humanity – love, kindness, social intelligence
- Transcendence – appreciation of beauty and excellence, gratitude, optimism, humor, purpose
- Temperance – self-control, prudence, humility, forgiveness
- Justice – leadership, fairness, teamwork
- Wisdom & knowledge – perspective, love of learning, open-mindfulness, curiosity, creativity

This framework provides a template for understanding and further developing those qualities we need to build a superior character, implying that we already have some of those attributes in place.

But just how is our character formed? It starts with our genetics: our primal predisposition to certain moods, inclinations and individual mental states (e.g., depression or hyperactivity), including a propensity towards certain activities (e.g., sports, music, art) or, conversely, physical limitations that inhibit such manifestations. This genetic predisposition can even include food preferences and allergies, and in some cases, a predisposition to addictions (as may result from Fetal Alcohol Syndrome or other chemical dependencies during pregnancy).

Next comes our childhood attachments, those relationships we developed and experiences we lived as children that taught us how to handle or regulate stress. Of those attachments, the most important is the depth of our relationships with our parents or caregivers, particularly our mother or female proxy. We may or may not have developed the requisite adaptive skills during our early years, resulting in various anxieties or continually searching for love and support. This may continue well into adulthood.

The third factor in our development of character as we grow older is our habits, how we learned to handle conflict while developing and maintaining interpersonal relationships. This is where we develop empathy towards others and learn to deal with conflict quickly or effectively, even becoming a bully on occasion. This is also where we begin to learn to deal with adversity, either persevering through it or resigning ourselves to accepting the inevitable setbacks in life.

Finally, once we are of age to become aware of our character flaws, we attempt to cover them. We do this by developing small, noticeable biases intended to create an entire wardrobe of outward appearances and masks leading to a double or even triple life. We present a façade to the whole world that may appear to be consistent, mature and rational, but underneath we're subject to our shifting emotional landscape.

We can gauge our relative strength of character through how well we regularly handle adversity. It's easy to operate when life goes along swimmingly, but it's different when things go wrong. If we tackle it appropriately, adversity leads to perseverance and helps us develop an advanced or superior character, spawning confidence and success.

The basis of those choices and decisions that result in a superior character is our values, or, as Peterson and Seligman indicated, our character strengths. To use a policing metaphor, values are like the fingerprints of our character and soul, particular to each person. Just as no two people have the same fingerprint pattern recognition features, no two people have the same values regarding their presence and intensity. They may share some common values, but the concentration and the behavioral manifestation of those values vary.

It is the choices that we make, not the words we say, that demonstrate our values: *acta non verba* ("Deeds, not words"). This is especially evident if we have something to lose, such as money, a meaningful relationship, health or even our life. This is the essence of having skin in the game.

By observing others and how they operate, and noting what drives their character, we can better appreciate who they are and what they stand, no matter what they say they represent according to the façade they're wearing.

Beyond our character strengths, there are actions that can also lead to a superior character. Our willingness and ability to work with others is one of those actions. This presupposes a heightened empathy level in our relationships and agency over our envy and covetousness; not wanting what others have but appreciating what we do have.

Amongst the other essential facets of a superior character are the desire and ability to solve problems, not create them. Our ability to keep promises and be dependable while paying attention to detail are further aspects. These attributes require having a relatively stable temperament, keeping an even keel and remaining steadfast and robust during adversity.

Dealing effectively with adversity also implies being resilient, adaptable and even opportunistic while being patient with people's differences. Those differences are often less about their physical traits (race, gender and other physical characteristics) than about how they communicate, act and work.

As humans, we have an innate drive to satisfy our curiosity. This allows us to understand our natural and social worlds, leading us to learn and evolve throughout our lives. Being a life-long learner facilitates superior character formation, presupposing the ability to grow from learning opportunities such as setbacks while having goals and a defined purpose in our life.

Underpinning all of these behaviors is the character strength of self-regulation, the ability to delay gratification in a world of immediacy. As the ancient Greek tragedian Sophocles (495-406 B.C.) wrote, one must wait until the evening to appreciate the splendor of the day.

This isn't intended to be an exhaustive list but a preliminary one to which you can add others according to your experiences, direction and needs. These new experiences will also have a cumulative effect on your character development as you grow older and progress through your work life, meeting, interacting with and being influenced by people of diverse backgrounds.

The most poignant lesson

From 2002-2004, as a newly-commissioned RCMP officer, I was asked to volunteer (i.e., voluntold) as an aide-de-camp for the provincial Lieutenant-Governor in Manitoba. In Canada, each province has an individual designated by the province's Premier to represent the Governor-General (who, in turn, represents the Queen, Canada's head of state), in provincial legislative governance and protocol areas. These individuals are usually men and women who have contributed significantly to their province's economic, cultural or community life through decades of service.

Unpaid, volunteer aides-de-camp assist the Lieutenant-Governor, overseeing official visits (such as to a school, cultural event or university convocation) by making the necessary arrangements at the venue and escorting the Lieutenant-Governor during the event. The aides-de-camp come from various police services, the three branches of the Canadian military, and the civilian sector.

It was and still is a prestigious role as far as volunteer positions go. At the time in Manitoba, aides-de-camp also acted as drivers for the Lieutenant-Governor, taking them safely to and from the various venues. As a Mountie, I carried out this role in the evening and weekends on my own time, sometimes accompanied by my wife, and I was always in some form of uniform, often in the iconic red serge.

In September 2002, I accompanied the Lieutenant-Governor and his wife to Winnipeg's Health Sciences Centre 2002 Laureate of Excellence Dinner. The evening's honoree was Martin Johnson, founder of the Manitoba Firefighters Burn Fund, a province-wide organization that supports burn care, treatment, rehabilitation and research.[46]

As a young firefighter in 1978, Johnson had helped save a two-year-old girl's life in a tragic house blaze. Ninety percent of the child's body was severely burned. She would survive her ordeal, attending burn camp, school, university; finding a job; and leading as normal a life as possible. She became his inspiration to start the Firefighters Burn Fund. That evening, she was seated at the dinner beside my wife and me.

Growing up, I had several friends who had portions of their bodies burnt to varying degrees, but I had never had the opportunity to spend time with a person whose body was almost entirely covered in burns.

She was a confident, 26-year-old woman without hair, fingers, or toes. Despite those impediments, she competently moved about the reception room and enjoyed dinner with us all, being talkative and engaging.

Aside from the elegant dress she wore, the only features that allowed us to identify her gender were her voice and name. We could not determine her race or any other distinguishing features of her physical appearance aside from the color of her eyes.

With remarkable candor and courage, she told those seated with her about her life growing up, attending burn camps where other children looked somewhat like her, going to school and doing her best to fit in. We didn't listen to any of the official speeches going on in the background that evening, so enthralled were we with this incredible woman who willingly shared her life, her struggles and her path to becoming the person she was.

In a short two-hour period, she had managed to touch us all, inspiring us to understand what character development was: the growth of intrinsic values, despite and because of life's challenges.

She was the single, most inspirational person I've ever met. When things in my life and career would become difficult, and at the darkest of times, I would go back to that dinner and relive the conversation we had, realizing how lucky I was in my life. It was a humbling moment from which I was able always to draw strength and inspiration. It also helped form my own character, even at the tender age of 40.

The eyeless striped Cyclops

In 2005, upon my transfer to RCMP national headquarters in Ottawa and at the insistence of a work colleague, I became a hockey referee. It would become one of the most important decisions I made in my life as it became more than a simple pastime, morphing into a perpetual learning seminar as I'd see some unusual reactions to what was simply a game, really just a child's game. I also learned that hockey without officials is only shinny, street hockey or plain old recess.

I've always found it sadly fascinating how some hockey parents would very quickly, and often aggressively, come up to me to complain about another referee's or my own on-ice decisions during their child's game. Some people couldn't wait to talk to me as I'd get off the ice. On two separate occasions, parents, one a mother and the other a father, took to filming me and my fellow officials (both of them adolescents) as we got off the ice after a game, telling us that they'd put the video up on social media to let everyone know just how bad we were.

On still another occasion, an irate mother charged into our dressing room full of men, both young and old, in various stages of undress, as some had just finished their refereeing assignments for the day and were showering while others were preparing to go onto the ice. Fortunately, my daughter, a referee herself, was outside and quickly hauled the incensed woman out of the change room, chiding her for the intrusion.

As for the less-invasive but still grumbling parents who would accost me about a referee's decision, after listening to them and their extensive, insightful analysis of the incident, I'd ask them why they didn't officiate hockey themselves. After all, they claimed to have such a profound knowledge of the game. Invariably, they would say they were too busy, not in good enough shape, not a good enough skater, were too old or couldn't handle the conflict and stress that regularly occurred on and off the ice. I would reply that they had no right to complain if they weren't willing to contribute to the game by assuming responsibility for it either as a coach, hockey association volunteer or official.

Armchair quarterbacking implies nothing to lose and no skin in the game. Hence, limited value to their opinion.

Hockey Canada is the official sports body that oversees all minor hockey in Canada. In the United States, USA Hockey fulfills a comparable mandate. In both countries, all officials, whether they are returning or brand new, must recertify through an annual clinic or seminar and pass an exam. On average, Hockey Canada has about 35,000 officials registered in their program at the minor hockey level. The United States has around 26,000. For years, Hockey Canada has stated that the attrition rate has been very high in hockey, claiming that upwards of 10,000 officials quit hockey every year, many of them between the ages of 12 and 15.

In 2019, Hockey Eastern Ontario, the branch responsible for all minor hockey in the greater Ottawa region, conducted an analysis of attrition rates amongst officials. They determined that for individuals under 18, 33 percent quit within their first year while 55 percent leave officiating during their second year and an astonishing 70 percent leave during their third year. Hockey officials may leave the game for various reasons, including going off to college; finding a more consistent, better-paying job; developing other interests; or the most prominent cause of all: dismayed by the abuse.

Unfortunately, this situation isn't only found in hockey. It's typical of most, if not all youth sports.

To counter this high attrition level, Hockey Eastern Ontario has developed a new program entitled the "Green Armband Initiative" in which all officials under the age of 18 wear a green armband in addition to the usual red if they are a referee, or none if a linesperson. All infractions such as abuse of officials that are directed towards an underage official are automatically doubled. The hope is to curtail the amount of abuse young officials receive, hoping to stem the tide of attrition from the game.

The idea came from a successful program with baseball and softball underage umpires in Canada which was initially adapted for hockey in Montréal.

In March 2020, the National Association of Sports Officials (NASO) compiled the results of a 2017 survey of 17,487 sports officials which included 162 questions and 6,000,000 data points. The National Officiating Survey involved officials from virtually every sport practiced in the United States by youth and adults. The results around sportsmanship were particularly telling, as 57 percent of the respondents stated that sportsmanship is getting worse while only 15 percent stated it was getting better. More than 50 percent of all officials have felt unsafe or feared for their safety because of administrator, coach, player or spectator behavior, including conduct by other members of the officiating community.[47]

But abuse doesn't just affect the officials. A unique review of parental behavior studies during hockey games detailed negative or derogatory comments ranging from 5 to 37 percent of the total observed and recorded behavior. Another study determined that negative parental behaviors at sports events are often the cause of inhibited performance, competitive stress and subsequent dropout among young athletes.[48]

The reviewers cited several motives behind the negative parental behavior, including the lure of the prestige and earning possibilities of professional sport, the perceived status parents garnered from their children's on-ice achievements, the stress to obtain a "return on investment" for the money, time and effort they spend, and the vicarious experience that a parent obtains seeing their child do what they once did or could never do.

While on the ice, it was rare to hear the individual comments and jeers coming from the fans because my attention would be focused on the game and the players. Aside from the sounds of the on-ice play, everything else was usually just background noise, along with the arena's ventilation system and the sound system's music between plays, if there was any.

On the rare occasion when the rink configuration allowed me to hear comments that went beyond booing and were insulting and derogatory, I would respond by directly pointing at the individual and telling them to be quiet, or kicking them out of the rink immediately. When I wasn't working on the ice, I'd be seated amongst the crowd, preparing coaching reports for the on-ice officials that I'd deliver after the game. During games, I would irregularly hear complaints about the officiating, listen to people singing *Three Blind Mice*, and even hear such imaginative comments as "Hey Ref! If you had an eye, you'd be a cyclops!"

I always found the best hockey parents to be those mothers and fathers who were there for their kids but didn't get in their way. They encourage their budding athletes to play, have fun and develop at their own pace, not according to some unrealistic standard. I would be impressed by the parents who would volunteer as a coach, especially at the beginning levels, and how they would encourage the children to play the game and have fun doing so.

Working the blue line as a linesperson with a players' bench at my back, I would listen intently to the coaches' encouragement (and sometimes disparagement). I often made it a point to speak to the coaches after the game and congratulate them on how they treated the players. This type of coaching not only encouraged the kids; it did wonders for us officials as well.

Self-identifying problem children

We live in a time that has promoted individualism and overconfidence, such traits becoming symptomatic of the infection of excessive self-admiration. A telltale feature of an individual's values, especially those influenced by their ego, narcissism, and in certain instances, the Shadow Self, is how they respond to interpersonal friction and conflict.

Friction is one step below conflict, when an individual attempts to determine just how far others are willing to go before they actively confront another's words or actions. Again, from hockey, on more than one occasion, when a coach was aggressively questioning my calls, in an (unsuccessful) attempt to intimidate me, they would say something to the tune of "Do you know who I am?" Sometimes, it would even be a former NHL player turned minor hockey coach, usually not one who had enjoyed a long and stellar professional career.

The rhetorical "Do you know who I am?" is intended to intimidate a person into thinking that the questioner is someone of importance whose opinion, rank, station or abilities in life far outweighs our own. I've heard this used by off-duty police officers stopped for speeding, lawyers unhappy about customer service at a business, academics trying to win an argument during a social event and journalists attempting to gain access to a venue they had no right to attend.

But not everyone acts this way.

One of the best examples of this opposite tack I ever witnessed was from a Calgary Police Service senior officer. I knew and worked with this inspector on a national executive committee on police discipline for three years. One late afternoon, she and I were talking on the phone about some committee work. While I was in my office in Halifax, she was driving in Calgary using the hands-free option in her unmarked police car. Suddenly, and uncharacteristically, she cursed and advised me that she had to stop the car and would call me back when she had a chance. About 45 minutes later, she called back to tell me what had transpired.

According to the inspector, as she left a local highway to take a secondary road during our conversation, she didn't lower her speed fast enough to match the posted limit. She swore when she saw a patrol vehicle from her police service, which had been approaching from the opposite direction, slow down, turn on its emergency lights and make a quick U-turn. She knew that she had been caught for speeding. She immediately pulled over, ended our call and waited for the police officer.

He was a newer officer who didn't recognize her as she was dressed in plain clothes. When he learned that she was a senior officer, he meekly advised her that all was well and for her to go on her way, to which she replied, "Do you know who I am?"

She explained to the young officer that she oversaw discipline for the police service and that she was not above the law nor exempt from discipline. She instructed the officer to issue her a ticket, which he reluctantly did. The question was intended to clarify her responsibilities toward the officer and not the opposite, intimidating him to gain an advantage. Her reaction spoke volumes of her values and especially her character.

As a police officer, I have been stopped by law enforcement officers on six occasions in three Canadian provinces and one US state. I received speeding tickets three times and warnings three other times. I never had to order anyone to give me a ticket, but I never had to ask anyone if they knew who I was because I never invited my ego or my badge to any of the discussions.

Tortoise or hare: which one is the first-rounder?

In 2018, during a town-hall discussion on senior police leadership development as part of a police training conference I attended, a deputy chief for a large Canadian municipal service candidly asked, "How do you teach someone to grow a spine?" The group had been commiserating about new middle and senior managers who could not or would not make hard decisions.

I, too, had seen individuals who were promoted into various leadership and adjudicative positions who were afraid, even terrified, to decide on anything, spending days, weeks or months mulling over all facets of a decision. The reality is that they weren't accustomed to making tough decisions and had never developed both the requisite courage and regularity to make determinations of fact and then act on those findings. Consequently, they spent a significant portion of their career either mitigating risk or transferring it somewhere else, most likely to another person.

This isn't confined to policing. I have seen many individuals who were unable or unwilling to decide, including those paid handsomely to make decisions and having a duty to act, including arbitrators and, on rare occasions, even judges.

Indecision in middle and senior managers has more to do with recruiting, hiring and promoting those individuals. We don't always select people based on their character. To level the playing field and ensure that everyone has a qualifiable and quantifiable chance in a selection process, we examine their technical skills and achievements, assuming everyone can go to the next level.

The Canadian educator Laurence Johnston Peter (1919-1990) wrote in his book *The Peter Principle*:

> In a hierarchy every employee tends to rise to [their] level of incompetence (...) [I]n time every post tends to be occupied by an employee who is incompetent to carry out its duties (...) Work is accomplished by those employees who have not yet reached their level of incompetence.

The corollary to this is the *Dilbert Principle*, named after the popular comic strip, which states that companies tend to promote incompetent employees to management positions simply to get them out of the workflow, those positions that are critical to productivity, unlike the position into which the incompetent employee has been promoted. Unfortunately, I've seen this principle in action a few times.

The assumption in many workplaces is that an employee who does good work deserves to be promoted to the next level simply because of the work accomplished. Indeed, if someone does an exceptional job in a particular file or situation, the assumed reward is often a promotion. The challenge with such assumptions is that although an individual may excel at the technical aspects of the work they perform or manage, they may not have the requisite people skills or cooperative emphasis that leadership inevitably demands at the next level. Hence, a promotion may result in a competent executant being transformed into an incompetent supervisor or manager.

As the employee in search of a promotion or the next job, the way to circumvent both the *Peter* and *Dilbert* principles is to determine our hierarchy of priorities in life. This hierarchy should center around our health as well as intimate and family relationships. The order of priorities should then guide us in our choice of positions.

We must avoid the challenges associated with promotions by only accepting those positions for work that genuinely interest, inspire and develop us instead of merely promoting us. Finally, we must understand that the higher we climb, the greater demands there will be on our time, often resulting in overwork and dissatisfaction. The key here is to recognize and avoid our level of incompetence and disinterest in any job.

Remember the story of the tortoise and the hare: slow and steady versus fast and erratic? Which one would you hire or draft in the first round of your fantasy football pool?

If you're looking for speed, then the hare is what you want, obviously. If you're looking for consistency, then maybe the tortoise is better. Of the two, which one has a better character? One would be inclined to say the tortoise does. But what if you wanted to form a group of individual sprinters or wide receivers. Would you still hire the tortoise as a teammate? The answer is no. You would want the hare because she runs like the wind, and if you could just get her to change her approach to be more consistent, you'd be in a better position.

Unfortunately, the tortoise cannot change how fast he runs, no matter how consistent he is. But if the hare cannot modify her choices around running consistency, you're better off without her.

The same thing applies to character. Select, hire and promote for character, first and foremost. That means hiring individuals who have a demonstrated track record of improving themselves through education and varying experiences. Hire as well for the contributions they've provided in the past. We want employees to deliver asymmetrical returns: productivity beyond their representation level in a workgroup.

If the new employee is one of ten workers, do they produce 10 percent of the collective outputs or more? You want someone who delivers more. You can always train someone up to do the job. Skills can be developed and learned, but character comes from deep within and cannot be imposed or trained.

British physicist Derek John de Solla Price (1922-1983) developed a theory about his peers in academia who dominated the publications within any particular subject. He found that value creation was asymmetric: a minority of people were responsible for producing at least half of all contributions.

Specifically, *Price's Law* stipulates that 50 percent of the work is achieved by the square root of the total number of people participating in the work. Practically speaking, if 25 people are working in a particular unit (e.g., salespeople, writers, musicians), five of those people (the square root of 25) are probably responsible for at least 50 percent of the sales, books written or songs published.

This is related to the *Pareto Principle,* developed by the Italian economist Vilfredo Pareto (1848-1923). In 1896, he observed that 20 percent of Italy's residents held some 80 percent of the wealth. He then expanded his view to posit that 80 percent of consequences come from 20 percent of the causes. Also known as the '80/20 Rule', we've heard this used to describe how 20 percent of all individuals (be it problem employees, virus super-spreaders, criminals, or penalized hockey players) represent 80 percent of all the issues we deal with (labor problems, infections and outbreaks, crimes or hockey penalties).

These principles serve as a general reminder that the relationship between inputs and outputs is often not balanced, symmetrical or proportionate.

Developing nobility of character requires that we have the intrinsic motivation to do better. Think of the people you may have studied in history and how they demonstrated superior or noble character, influencing others towards a common good. This is what we seek when we recruit individuals to join our ranks, regardless of the organization, group or team. Once we hire or recruit them, we must give them the requisite authority and support to exercise their responsibilities to allow that nobility of character to manifest itself and contribute beyond their representation level in the group.

Where true loyalty lies

Character is a framework of interconnected dimensions that influence our decision-making, evaluations, behaviors, and ultimately, our actions. Those dimensions include good judgment, the courage of convictions and courage of action, passion and drive, collaboration, self-control, accountability, empathy and appreciation. By elevating these dimensions, we can develop not only a good character but a superior one.

However, a person can demonstrate all these dimensions without necessarily having a superior character. What's required is to go simply beyond the rote or ordinary, everyday manifestations of these dimensions that people are obliged to do by law, traditions and societal norms.

Like everyone, I've been impressed and influenced by various historical figures at different times in my life. I present to you three individuals whose contributions were determinant in our world at different levels while being instrumental in mine:

- In grade 4, I remember the first history book I ever read. It was about Dr. George Washington Carver. Despite the challenges of being born a slave, he persevered and became the most prominent African-American scientist of the early 20th century. Thanks to his work in soil depletion, poor farmers in North America learned to improve their soil and well-being by planting other crops, most notably peanuts and sweet potatoes, for sale and personal consumption.
- As a teenager, my older brother took me on a battlefield tour of the Gettysburg National Military Park. He led me to Little Round Top to tell me about the heroic actions there by Colonel Joshua Lawrence Chamberlain (1828-1914) of the 20th Maine Volunteer Infantry Regiment. After the war, Chamberlain became the 32nd Governor of Maine and President of Bowdoin College, his *alma mater*. Fluent in 10 languages, he'd also been a professor of rhetoric. He was said to have been influenced by his college professor's wife, Harriet Beecher Stowe (1811-1896), author of *Uncle Tom's Cabin*. He was the last known Civil War veteran to die of his war wounds.
- Following my transfer in the RCMP to Halifax, Nova Scotia in 2010, I learned of Viola Desmond's story (1914-1965). In 1946, almost ten years before Rosa Parks refused to relinquish her seat

in the "colored section" of a bus to a white passenger, Ms. Desmond refused to leave a whites-only area of a Nova Scotian movie theater. She was subsequently convicted of a minor tax violation for the one-cent difference between the cost of the seat she occupied and the one she had initially paid for based on her skin color. She was posthumously pardoned for the infraction, and in her honor as a social activist, in 2018, she became the first Canadian woman to appear on a Canadian banknote.

These individuals demonstrated some of the qualities that best exemplify nobility of character: abnegation (selflessness, self-denial or the giving of oneself); knowledge that's shared for the betterment of others; inspiration for others in challenging times; principle-centered action; and recognition of others' contributions, motivations, perceptions and emotions.

Where is loyalty in all this? Is it one of the dimensions of a superior character? The answer depends on what, not who, we're loyal to. Loyalty to a person isn't a dimension of a superior character. If we tie our loyalty to a single person or group of persons, we link our character to those individuals' flaws, biases and errors. Loyalty must be to a value or notion. In policing, that loyalty isn't to a chief of police, a sheriff, a police commissioner or a director of public safety. It must be to the rule of law, but not to making others obey all laws. I'd always be astounded to hear how people wanted police to enforce the law, any law, simply because it was a law, without considering the social determinants of crime such as poverty, lack of education and social ignorance. As a society, we can't solve a problem through arrests and tickets.

In hockey officiating, loyalty isn't to the referee-in-chief or the local minor hockey association's president but to the game itself. That loyalty is intended to ensure that the game of hockey is played fairly and safely. This applies to any sport. By being values-based instead of person-based, the loyalty of a superior character implies that we're accountable to the why of what we do. It further means that we're responsible to ourselves for the results of our actions, including learning from our mistakes. One of the best ways to learn from mistakes is to learn from those committed by others.

Marlo's loyalty

It was a cold December day in Ottawa in 2007. Christmas was right around the corner. It had snowed the night before, and the roads were still slippery, a mix of slush and brine. I just got off my bus and pulled out of the park-and-ride with my minivan. Traffic was bumper to bumper, moving very slowly.

Tired after a long day, I wasn't paying as much attention to the driving conditions as I should have. Suddenly, I realized I was approaching the car in front of me too quickly. My bumper touched the other vehicle's bumper. Actually, it more like *kissed* it.

Regardless, I got out of my car, as did Marlo from his. We looked at the two bumpers and decided that there was no damage. We got back into our cars, and I drove home.

About an hour later, I received a call from an Ottawa police constable who asked that I come down to the local station as Marlo claimed we'd been in an accident and wanted to confirm my identity. I went to the station, met the constable and Marlo, a young man who presented himself quite well.

We all went outside to look further at his bumper. Again, there was no apparent damage. It was dark, the lighting was poor, and Marlo's car was covered in a layer of dirt, hindering any close-up view of the bumper. One thing was sure: it didn't appear damaged in any way.

Marlo and I climbed into my minivan and exchanged personal details and insurance information. I asked Marlo what he did for a living. Marlo told me he was studying police foundations at a local community college and wanted to be a police officer. I asked Marlo why he wanted to become a cop. Marlo replied that he felt it necessary that people obey the law, and he wanted to make sure that people respected the law, even for minor infractions. He was often disappointed that so few people respected the law as he regularly saw people driving through a stop sign or a red light. This was the driving force behind his desire to be a police officer.

I told Marlo I would take photos of his car's bumper and provide my version of the facts for his file should he ever find any damage once the car was clean. The next day I completed my text and submitted it via email to Marlo. I wrote my notes in the form of a police report, using the appropriate terminology and formatting.

Shortly into the new year, I received a phone call from Marlo. He told me he'd shown my text to one of his professors, who said that a police officer must have written it considering the format and language. Marlo wanted to know if I was a police officer.

I told him that, indeed, I was and that I was the director of disciplinary adjudications for the RCMP, essentially the judge advocate general for the Force. Marlo wanted to know why I hadn't told him that beforehand. I told Marlo that my profession wasn't relevant to the matter.

He then asked me why I'd become a police officer. I told Marlo that I wanted to help people, not because I wanted them to respect the law or my authority in any way. I said to him that policing was about solving people's problems, not creating ones for them. I concluded the conversation by telling Marlo that my loyalty was to the rule of law, not making people obey the law, an important nuance that I hoped he would understand if he ever became a police officer. I never knew if he did.

I've seen many a person complain about minor traffic offenses such as speeding (even only a few miles over the limit) or rolling stops (also known in various parts of the world as the "California Roll," the "Montréal Stop" or the "Jakarta Slide"). Regardless of the jurisdiction, traffic infractions are the most common quality-of-life complaint police services field.

But how much do such violations actually affect the quality of people's lives? Just as the saying goes, "If a tree falls in a forest and no one is around to hear it, does it make a sound?" When it comes to traffic infractions, if a car rolls through a stop sign and no one is around to see it, does it constitute an infraction?

I'm not saying that people should disobey minor traffic rules; too many accidents and deaths have occurred because of excess speed and rolling stops through crosswalks resulting in a person being hit and dying. What's important to remember is that discretion is key when dealing with minor offenses of any type. The operative word here is 'minor.' Just as we cannot arrest our way out of any social problem, we cannot ticket our way out of one either.

Marlo mistakenly viewed the role of police as ensuring absolute rule compliance. He was suffering from a misaligned sense of duty and loyalty that bordered on obsessive compulsion; essentially, everyone had to conform to his expectations. The reality is that in society, such expectations are untenable. People will cut corners to get things done.

In some cases, those corners are street corners, resulting in jay-walking. Sometimes people will be hit and die as a result of their injuries when they're hit. In almost all cases, an individual safely crosses the street. The key to not acting like Marlo is to accept that not every transgression can or should be sanctioned. People deserve second and sometimes, even third chances. Simply indicating their misconduct without sanctioning is often the best way to proceed.

Most importantly, loyalty to a notion that transcends us is best, but it must be a notion that's flexible and adaptable, not rigid like the enforcement of all laws. What we do in life must be for the betterment of others, not merely for ticking a box or applying everything literally.

Best. Boss. Ever.

Two Gallup studies, conducted over 25 years in the late 1980s and early 2000s of more than one million employees and eighty thousand supervisors, determined that managers are the key to employee satisfaction. The studies determined that people leave a job because of their managers more than for any other factor. Hence, the saying, "People don't leave bad jobs, they leave bad bosses."[49]

As I climbed the ranks of policing, I determined that one of my guiding principles when accepting or seeking a new job was who my direct supervisor would be. One of the reasons why I asked to go to Haiti in 2008 was that my supervisor at the time, although one of the most technically proficient individuals I'd ever worked with, was incapable of inspiring and encouraging many of her direct reports, me included. She created a culture of mistrust, and I could see very quickly that she had no time to listen to or support my and others' efforts.

So I left her, not my job, which I had enjoyed immensely. When I came back from my United Nations mission in February 2009, she retired, and her replacement was someone with whom I enjoyed working.

On the opposite end of the spectrum, I ended up meeting my best boss ever when I was transferred to Halifax from the RCMP's national headquarters in July 2010. Oonagh Enright held the rank of chief superintendent and was the Chief Human Resource Officer for the RCMP's Atlantic Region, which covered all four of Canada's Atlantic provinces for the RCMP.

What made Oonagh so special? A horse lover, Oonagh had been a member of the famed RCMP Musical Ride. She had a master's degree in mathematics, was bilingual in English and French, and admittedly was a tad nerdy. Oonagh was a reflective thinker and took her time to analyze a situation before rendering any critical decision. She spoke truth to power and was not afraid to provide her direct reports and her supervisors alike with honesty, which she did respectfully, always succeeding in allowing people to maintain their dignity. She gave support through words, actions and the occasional hug while challenging all of her direct supports to think using logic and evidence as their goalposts.

When things went south, or if I made a mistake, she calmly reflected and corrected me as required. She, and not her ego, was invested in her direct reports and the organization's success. That made her the best person I ever worked with and for.

We're still friends to this day. I've visited her small horse ranch in rural Nova Scotia, which she lovingly maintains with her wife and daughter.

If you wish to be like Oonagh and be the best boss, the best supervisor, the best leader you can be, make sure that you do what others expect you not to do: play with them, eat with them, dance with them, laugh with them, cry with them, be with them, learn with and from them, and, occasionally, even hug them. It also means sometime saying goodbye to them as they seek opportunities elsewhere.

I always advised people I worked with, regardless of the organization, that they could rely on my unconditional support when they left to pursue other opportunities. For me, the departure of an individual to a better paying or more prestigious position was a sign that we succeeded in providing development opportunities for them to advance.

During my time in HRP, five senior officers left to assume new positions as chief of a small-town police service, a senior executive with the provincial Sheriff, a senior director with provincial corrections, a senior officer with the RCMP and even as the executive director of the Canadian Association of Chiefs of Police. I was proud to bid them all good luck as they left us, knowing that they would continue to contribute to the community in ways other than with HRP.

When I first became chief of police, I needed to qualify with HRP's firearm. They offered me a private training session, which I promptly refused. I asked to be part of a regular training group of police officers who had to qualify annually with their firearm.

For the following six years, I participated in annual firearms qualifications and regular block training with constables and non-commissioned officers alike. During one scenario involving immersive reality training, I had to confront an armed individual who was shielding himself with a hostage. Upon obtaining appropriate cover, I had to call for backup. Somewhat excited by the level of reality of the training scenario, I called instead for reinforcements, to which the trainer accompanying me asked dryly, "Would you like an airstrike with that as well?" It was a good lesson in communicating during stress.

Participating like any other employee in training allowed me to spend time with frontline members and learn from them. It also allowed those who wanted to convince me to adopt a new technique, approach or piece of equipment to do so. Thanks to these interactions, I eventually approved new tactical flashlights, toques and protective body armor carriers.

The challenge we have in our interconnected world is that it's watching us. Watching to see us trip up, make an error or create a fool of ourselves. The key is to establish a baseline of calmness and sobriety and stick to it privately and publicly. One of the significant advantages I obtained from officiating hockey was that I'd referee the children of my coworkers, industry colleagues and community members with whom I interacted regularly. They'd see me in a different environment than work, allowing me to develop even more trust with them because of the competency I displayed and how I reacted when I made mistakes. It means being humble in life. When dealing with those we lead, humility goes a long way.

A good part of humility is acknowledging what we don't know. By doing so, we're always open to new learning. This is a lifelong process that requires commitment and constancy.

Be open to continuous learning, preferably with and from others. It decreases mistrust while increasing the satisfaction that people look for at work. People will want to stay because they enjoy the job. They'll enjoy the job because they'll enjoy working with you.

A bear in the belfry

Humility is best developed through experience. When something unexpected occurs, we learn an important lesson about our frailties, hubris or lack of preparation. It can be a significant irregular incident, an everyday event or a one-off occurrence. And, in retrospect, it can even be humorous.

As a young constable, I had volunteered to personify the RCMP's mascot, known as Safety Bear, during public events such as parades, blood drives and community get-togethers. It was a great way to promote police-community relations, especially with children.

The mascot's costume was a relatively heavy ensemble, comprised of brown, puffy, padded pants attached to suspenders; an oversized, padded red jacket or serge; and a smiling bear's head with the iconic Stetson hat on top. To qualify to act as Safety Bear, I had to take a full-day course on wearing the costume, caring for it, and the best techniques and approaches for interacting with people, especially children.

Safety Bear doesn't talk, so an assistant accompanies it to direct and answer any questions that Safety Bear cannot respond to through hand signs and non-verbal communication. As we didn't always have public events to use the costume, we were allowed use the outfit to attend birthday parties of police officers' children during our personal time to develop our skills with it.

During one party, I was in costume having a good time with the children when suddenly, something from inside the Safety Bear head fell in front of my face, covering it entirely. It was a dryer sheet that the previous wearer had placed in the head to absorb the odor from their sweat. In those days, the head portion of the costume didn't have an integrated fan, and I had failed to check the head cavity before I put it on.

The dryer sheet was an extra-large one; consequently, I was having trouble breathing and started panicking as I couldn't remove it.

The kids thought that Safety Bear was even more animated than usual as its movements became more pronounced, with flailing arms and erratic jumping up and down. It wasn't until Safety Bear used the universal sign of choking distress by clutching its throat with both hands that the assistant, also a first-aid trained police officer and father of the birthday girl, recognized that something was wrong. He hauled Safety Bear off to another room and ripped off its head to free the sweaty, flustered and panicked person that I was underneath.

Another occurrence was during surveillance of a known drug-runner in a small town in rural Québec. Because of the Catholic Church's primacy in French-Canadian communities, the local church steeple was always the highest building point in a community. Steeples made for perfect spots from which to observe the movements of vehicles.

On a warm September evening, a bit after 7:15 pm, with the local parish priest's permission, I climbed the ladder to the bell chamber of the belfry from which I had an unobstructed view of the town in all four directions. I knew the color, make and model of the target vehicle and the relative area from which it would appear. Armed with a pair of binoculars and a fully-charged radio, I was in constant communication with our surveillance units on the ground who would follow the car once I indicated its direction.

According to our intelligence, the drug-runner was expected to leave his cache around 7:30 pm. A few minutes before that time, I spotted the vehicle in motion and advised my colleagues of its direction. As I observed the car stopping at an intersection, I heard a mechanical noise beneath me in the lower belfry. The automated bell ringer mechanism started the process of swaying the 2500-pound bell back and forth.

As soon as the clapper struck the bell, its vibration shook me to my core. It also forced me to cover my ears to protect them from the noise. At that very moment, the target vehicle unexpectedly turned left at the intersection.

I radioed my colleagues, but every time I transmitted my message, all they heard was the bell's ringing, my voice completely drowned out by it. By the time the bell had stopped ringing, I had lost sight of the vehicle.

When I finally reached my colleagues, they were laughing uncontrollably on the airways at what had transpired. Not only were my ears ringing, but my ego was stinging.

These two unexpected and humorous lessons in humility guided me well in the years to come. Most importantly, I learned to not take myself so seriously.

Character formation

We can't examine or treat character as a simple skill. Character is the sum of personal preferences and choices that we demonstrate over an entire lifetime. You can't learn character in a weekend retreat or measure it through an exam or quantified testing.

We've all seen exceptionally talented people who have accomplished great things as members of a team or by themselves, but who can't lead others. Regardless of one's accomplishments in life in any area, personal or professional success doesn't always translate into good leadership. One can be an engineer, a scientist, a concert pianist, a professional singer or even a former astronaut who speaks six different languages; these qualifications are no guarantee to having a superior character, one that inspires trust and influence, allowing for good leadership. One can even have accomplished all of the above.

Julie Payette, Canada's 29th Governor-General, became the subject of an investigation by the Privy Council Office (the secretariat of the federal cabinet) in July 2020 for allegedly creating a toxic work environment through verbal abuse couched as "rigorously high standards." Her great background and experience still didn't guarantee that she would be a good leader.

According to those who worked for her, the Governor-General allegedly used aggressive conduct and public humiliation when dealing with staff. On January 21, 2021, immediately following the investigation report's issuance to the Privy Council Office, Canada's first female astronaut resigned from the $300,000-a-year position.

I also saw this lack of character in various senior-most police leaders over the years, as their hubris tainted how they treated their work colleagues and subordinates with disrespect through angry outbursts, extreme sways in personality or complete self-isolation during social interactions. Although highly capable in technical skills such as communication, finances, change management and crisis response, they failed to have the requisite character. They confirmed the vital lesson of hiring an individual based on their character, not solely on technical skills.

Every domain of human activity has individuals who have succeeded immensely at one level but couldn't translate that success to the next level, where leadership was the key attribute. We see it in fields as diverse as policing and professional sport, where hall-of-famers become head coaches of a franchise, only to meet abject failure because they can't influence their coaching staff and players.

The lesson is clear: select individuals for the skills that are easiest to change and the positive habits that are most anchored in their attitudes. We can easily teach someone the technical skills they need to do their job, but we can't teach character. Hire for character, give them the requisite authority and then support them as they work.

Supporting means ensuring that you never overrule your direct subordinates in front of their direct reports. That also means not passing judgment of their decisions in front of their employees (avoid what occurs in the TV show *Undercover Boss*). Don't hold any mass meetings with different levels of employees *unless* it's to discuss your priorities and how to carry them out. Avoid town-halls for town-halls' sake. Don't mediate or provide alternate dispute resolution between your subordinates and their direct reports. Have a third-party do that.

And finally, don't give any direction or feedback to your subordinate's direct reports unless you are complimenting them. The key is not to undermine the work that your direct reports are accomplishing. Let them lead their people, manage their processes and exercise their authority. This means recognizing that everyone has only one boss, which makes possible the unity of command.

Humility is the remedy

Humility is not timidity. Nor is it temerity. We take an approach to ensure that our minds are open to other perspectives while questioning our own beliefs and actions. Humility is the great equalizer that forces us to maintain some sense of perspective. Now considered by many organizations to be a core competency in the search and development of leaders, strangely enough, it's no longer viewed as a public virtue in this age of arrogance.

Humility demands several behaviors. The first is the courage to search for and see the reality we face daily. By meeting our reality's demands, we demonstrate integrity in our life, continually orienting ourselves towards truth. When people offer us their opinion or their experience in good faith, we readily accept it. At the very least, we listen to it. We do so even if it's to feed their ego.

I saw a new chief join a police service and refuse to meet with his predecessor, preferring to learn by himself the numerous files and personnel issues. The new chief ended up facing significant problems during the first year of his mandate. He could easily have avoided or mitigated those challenges had he been open and available to spending time with his predecessor, who was more than willing to meet and brief him.

The second behavior is to admit our mistakes, using them as an opportunity to learn and letting them generate curiosity instead of shame. This includes the willingness to be open to improvement by accepting criticism and differing views that conflict with our own.

Always question why we believe in something. It's often simply because we've internalized another person's opinion, which subsequently manifests itself as a feeling we've adopted. Distinguish between what we feel is right through gut instinct and what we think or know to be right based on fact. We do this through questioning fueled by curiosity and openness. This implies being realistic about the extent and especially the limits of our knowledge.

If we don't know enough about something, it's okay not to provide an opinion. That means sometimes saying, "I just don't know."

When I first became chief of police, a local radio talk show host interviewed me. He'd read some of my published papers and asked me for an opinion on a local criminal matter. To my communications director's relief, I replied that I didn't know enough about the case yet, but that I'd find out and get back to him. The talk show host was impressed by my humility instead of slamming me for being a know-nothing.

Curiosity involves an openness to new information and actively seeking out that information, embracing ideas that don't fit our worldview or that we rarely have, if ever, been exposed to.

Immediately after becoming chief of police, I instituted bi-monthly meetings called "Police Executive Development", or PED for short. PED meetings lasted an hour and brought together the senior management teams of HRP and my former employer, the RCMP in Halifax District. The goal was to expose all senior police leaders to different speakers who would not normally have access to police leaders.

I invited experts and community leaders to talk to us about homelessness; the challenges faced by transgendered people and members of the LGBTQ2+ community; mental health, Indigenous and Black community concerns; left-wing thinking and even law enforcement professionals who were against cannabis prohibition. In many cases, this was the first time that these groups had ever had the chance to address police employees.

Yes, at times, there was some eye rolling in the audience; but for the most part, we left each meeting more aware of the nuances of the subject than before. And that made us better.

The third behavior acknowledges and actively seeks contributions and lessons from others to help us recognize and overcome our shortcomings. One useful tool is a 360-degree feedback document, which I mentioned previously, in which we obtain honest, anonymous assessments and evaluations of our work and behaviors. If you haven't had a chance to receive such a document, ask for one; and then study it for improvement areas.

The fourth action is recognizing and celebrating others' contributions, avoiding a sense of moral superiority to validate our own sense of self and stature. In a review of the British military strategist Captain B.H. Liddell Hart's (1895-1970) book on nuclear strategy in the *Saturday Review of Literature*, John F. Kennedy stated, "Avoid self-righteousness like the devil—nothing is so self-blinding."

How do we encourage humility in ourselves? First, we start by recognizing the value of learning over money, by choosing employment that expands our knowledge base even if it pays less than a job with rote tasks, limited responsibilities and a bigger paycheck. We allow ourselves to enter into uncomfortable situations through tasks that push our limits.

When it comes to learning and knowledge, we revert to our childlike sense of curiosity, allowing our mind to acknowledge that we don't know everything but that we can learn something in every situation. When we make mistakes, we greet them as opportunities to learn, making mental and even physical notes to remind ourselves to not repeat them later in life.

We also seek to understand how things operate and why we and others act the way we do, becoming a student of human nature. We recognize and stifle those emotions that hinder our advancement: anxiety, boredom, frustration, panic, insecurity and fear.

Humility also implies acknowledging that every person has value and deserves to be treated with respect. This is the basis of inclusion: having the cultural humility to look at another for who they are in order to treat them fairly and with dignity. Sometimes that personal dignity is all they have.

We look for opportunities to witness, in person, high achievers at work, be it by attending a concert, a play, a sporting event, an art vernissage, a court trial or a press conference. This allows us to observe the mastery of particular skills and recognize others' abilities, gauging our potential in comparable situations.

One of the best lessons I learned in giving evidence in court was from a 14-year-old boy testifying in a criminal matter. His candor, eloquence and precision all contributed to him being a highly credible witness. Before he was released from the witness dock, the judge took the time to thank him and point out to those in attendance that he was an example of how a witness should depose themselves.

Included in these opportunities is to be in nature, to witness its splendor and enormity, to recognize what's possible, all the while realizing how we're a part of this planet. The goal is to cultivate a higher sense of purpose, a direction beyond just ourselves, understanding that we're all part of an incredible experience called life.

Our overarching goal is to transform ourselves from a person ruled by impatience, scattered ideas and absent self-restraint to a disciplined and focused individual having a character built to lead and a mind to deal with complexity. We cannot do this unless we master ourselves and our weaknesses. And that requires humility.

Carpe diem or *carpe vino*

The second leadership competency required to succeed is intentional relationship building. We achieve this by making character the primary feature of anyone we choose to work for, hire, or play or engage with in an intimate relationship. We learn from observing others and questioning ourselves, understanding the nuances of our own character traits, particularly those recurring, negative patterns that have impeded our success in the past. We avoid causes and cults based on envy and dualisms that advocate for eliminating certain established activities by others in a misguided effort to perfect our society.

To best determine a person's real character, watch how they react during times of crisis or extreme stress. Crisis reveals character while adversity shapes it. Such revelations also occur during times of duress when a person is tired, uncomfortable, hungry or impaired through alcohol or drugs. Here the Latin adage *in vino veritas* ("In wine there is truth") has particular application.

We can also observe how a person handles power and responsibility. Power, itself, does not change people but rather reveals their true nature in the same way inebriation does, except in a slower manner.

Notice how a person interacts outside the work environment, especially during activities involving any form of competition. See how they respond when they win and especially when they lose. These observations apply not only to others but to us as well.

When I lived in Ottawa in the late 2000s, I regularly officiated men's Friday-night hockey games at a local arena from 9 pm until midnight. It was always the same four teams playing two separate games. On one Friday night, things didn't go so well, with players disputing my calls and tempers flaring. A player, one of the pick-up league's organizers, a man slightly older than myself, started being abusive to my officiating partner and me. I ended up kicking him out of the game.

The following Monday morning, I took my car to the local dealership for service. As I was picking it up, an employee came up to the manager who was processing my payment, proudly indicating that I was one of the referees for his Friday-night hockey league. It was the abusive player-organizer from the previous Friday night.

I looked at him with amazement at his bluster. In front of his supervisor, I calmly asked him how he'd react if I were to loudly question his competence and call him all sorts of names, using offensive adjectives and profanities at that moment in his place of work. Taken aback, he replied that he wouldn't like that at all. I then told him that was precisely what he did to me on Friday night. He had been abusive to me at my place of work. During that game, his real character had revealed itself.

He meekly walked away. I never had any problems with him in future games.

Overcoming negative, chronic traits that hold us back must become our mission as we seek to become a better leader. Included in this is developing self-control to escape the continual, perpetual cycle of pain avoidance and the dogged pursuit of pleasure.

In our world today, we have a vast array of pleasures at our disposal, often at our fingertips through a keyboard and immersive reality: shopping, gambling, sex, stimulants, games and entertainment of all sorts. As we experience more pleasures, their marginal utility—the incremental pleasure we derive from them—actually decreases over time if we partake of them too much. Hence, the best way to enjoy such pleasures is by limiting them, seeking opportunities to promote the intensity of experience instead of pursuing constant sensory overstimulation.

The goal of intentional relationship building cannot be acquiring fame, attention, goods, money or success through others. If we espouse a higher goal and sense of direction while developing relationships that support our purpose, those other things will most likely come to us eventually.

However, we don't have to be strategic in absolutely everything. The uncertainty that life provides us often ensures the most pleasurable experiences and moments through serendipity, again because it's limited and not overly available, presenting these opportunities when we least expect them.

To intentionally build relationships, we must also avoid the feeling of individual helplessness and lack of meaning that characterize cynicism. We can choose to follow Aristotle and scrutinize our life through self-examination, or we can fall into the pit of ignorance and denial, fueling contempt of ourselves and others.

Such hatred of society will not only repel those we need to develop relationships with but will also attract those we most need to avoid: the malcontents and malignant personalities, the co-dependents and the abusive. We must develop the requisite knowledge and skills to recognize those character traits that are most toxic, that we should avoid or even confront as required.

Such self-examination involves not being a slave to the negative character traits and habits that we've developed over the years and that have continually held us back. We must determine our character weaknesses, identify and develop their complementary strengths, and gravitate towards those qualities we wish to live regularly.

If we're a perfectionist micromanager, we need to channel this energy into work instead of controlling people. If we're sarcastic and passive-aggressive, we need to be quieter, listening intently to others to understand better what makes them tick and not outwardly judging them. If we have a revolutionary or rebellious nature, we must channel it into imaginative and innovative ways to improve things instead of always fighting the establishment.

The key is to take those traits of our character that have been less-than-productive for us and use the energy we typically spend on them to change how we do things in a more positive and influential manner.

This approach starts with our worldview and the corresponding attitude we project. Be empirically skeptical, but don't be cynical, nihilist or escapist—attack issues, not people. Become a lighthouse, a constant, dependable source of illumination and guidance for everyone around us instead of an opinionated weathervane, twisting and turning with every social wind.

This starts by recognizing, understanding and resisting those biases that color our worldview, impeding us from seeing the reality of life and people. That's the lesson of bias. Not everything and everyone in the world is bad. But not everything and everyone is good, either.

Calls from the blue line

- Leadership incorporates many skills and traits. Of all the attributes, character is the most important.
- Character is the intersection of our thoughts, feelings and actions resulting from the sum of our choices over time. It results from our genetics, our childhood attachments, our lifelong habits, and even our attempts to cover up our character flaws.
- Character is a framework of interconnected dimensions that influence our decision-making, evaluations, behaviors, and ulti-

mately, our actions. Those dimensions include good judgment, the courage of convictions and courage of action, passion and drive, collaboration, self-control, accountability, empathy and appreciation.

- We should use humility, a cornerstone of character, to test our assumptions for weaknesses, searching continually to invalidate our knowledge instead of confirming it.
- We can gauge our relative strength of character through how well we regularly handle adversity, best defined as a state or instance of serious or continued difficulty or misfortune. Remember, crisis reveals character but adversity shapes it.
- By observing others and how they act, primarily what drives their character, we can better appreciate who they are and what they stand for instead of what they say they represent according to the façade they're wearing.
- Select, hire and promote for character, first and foremost. Select individuals having the easiest skills to change and the positive habits that are most anchored in their attitudes.
- Just as policing is about solving people's problems and not creating more for them, officiating hockey is about allowing people to play the game safely and fairly, not about calling every single potential penalty. Learn from Marlo: rules are meant to facilitate play, not control every aspect of it.
- Be empirically skeptical; don't be cynical, nihilist, or escapist. Attack issues, not people.

6: The lesson of bias

We do not see things as they are. We see things as we are.
-Cuban-French writer Anaïs Nin (1903-1977)
in *Seduction of the Minotaur*

Deep and dark, light and fair

I remember (or, as we will see later, I reconstruct) a grade 2 art project in which we had to use plaster on a piece of wood to create an outline of something or someone. Once we were done, the teacher asked us to make a quick presentation on what we had learned about our plaster creation.

I used the plaster to outline the continent of South America, including some of the Caribbean islands. I asked people about the area, countries, peoples and languages while reading as much as my second-grade mind could allow and understand. I also came across the names of several Caribbean countries, one of which was Haiti. When I asked my teacher about Haiti, she admitted not knowing much about it, other than it was a dark, hot and scary place. This description would color my view of Haiti for decades to come. When I arrived on my first UN mission in Haiti in July 1995, I immediately noticed many things: the level of the misery of its people as well as the land, sea and air pollution from plastics and burning coal. I also saw social differences and practices. Haiti was unlike any other place I had been in my life. I had spent time the Caribbean three times in tourist locations separate from the locals, and once living there, spending a summer in Aruba on an exchange program with the YMCA when I was 16. But Haiti was different. When I ended up in Mirebalais, about 30 miles to the northeast of Port-au-Prince, I met and talked to people, getting to know a different side of Haitians and their country. Despite the misery, its people were genuinely exuberant and had unique traditions and social rules around religious beliefs, social cohesion and death. I quickly learned that Haiti was not the dark, hot, scary place my second-grade teacher warned me about.

Before my deployment, along with several other RCMP officers, I went through preparatory training covering topics such as language, traditions and Haitian law. One of the instructors, a Canadian of Haitian origin, spoke about how we had to suspend our biases about everything we knew and held dear.

Easier said than done for many of us, including me. In Mirebalais, I lived with two other Canadians in a 400 square-foot three-room bungalow.

In the following weeks and months, I was able to witness and experience many things. Most enlightening was how the internationals working for the United Nations and various non-governmental organizations (NGOs) operated so very differently in Haiti from in their own home countries.

I saw individuals who maintained their moral compasses, focused on the good they were there to do with the limited resources at their disposal. In contrast, I saw a few others who, free from their home society's moral and ethical constraints, became, in some respects, the brutes Joseph Conrad depicted in his novella *Heart of Darkness*. Conrad's characters witnessed a world of depravity and evil exhibited by men of previous good nature, uninhibited by social mores to keep their darker sides in check. The company agent Kurtz's final words aptly summarized the evil he saw from within: "The horror! The horror!"

In particular, individuals who were typically pious in their home environments usually went one of three ways: they dedicated their stay to advancing the goals of their faith through aid and charity for all; they became judgmental of the local beliefs and viewed Haitians as being inferior in their attitudes; or they used their economic superiority and status to bring harm to the locals through theft, sexual exploitation and just plain disregard.

Seeing their hypocrisy and attempting to counter it was one of the greatest frustrations I've had in my life.

To be clear, this wasn't just from White, Christian North Americans or Europeans but also Muslims from the Levant and southeast Asia. Such behavior also manifested itself among some of the diasporic Haitians returning to work in their forefathers' country.

To this day, I still wonder how people can lose their moral compasses. Equally challenging, I wonder how people could manage to maintain their moral compasses absent those restrictions that initially built them and in the presence of those who had lost theirs.

Prisoners of biology

Our brain physiology provides us with time-saving tools. These tools are mental shortcuts that allow us to identify causal links, permitting us to quickly perceive things or spot trends and act in a given manner. An overly simplistic example is that if A is larger than B, and B is larger than C, it makes sense that A is larger than C.

Such simple illustrations do not usually pose problems for us. The challenge, though, is that sometimes such analyses aren't correct. We become prisoners of that same biology, a hard-wiring known as cognitive biases.

American psychologists Herbert Simon (1916–2001) and James G. March (1928-2018) presented a theory stating that we tend to *satisfice* (an amalgam formed by the words satisfy and suffice) rather than optimize our interactions as humans. Traditional economic theory, influenced by the Scottish economist and philosopher Adam Smith (1723-1790), holds that we're rational decision-makers (known by the Latin term *homo economicus*) as we attempt to optimize or maximize our outcomes, identified as the "payoff function."

Contrary to economic theory, though, Simon and March postulated that by satisficing, instead of attempting to optimize our outcomes, we search for choices only to the point where we find an appropriate solution, instead of continuing to look for the perfectly optimal outcome. We do this through mental shortcuts, employing what are known as heuristics or rules of thumb to make decisions. The solutions they produce may not be optimal but are sufficient when dealing with limited time frames, deadlines, or a lack of information or motivation.

Heuristics is the formal name for mental shortcuts that provide aid or direction in dealing with a particular problem, situation or decision. Typically, these shortcuts work out well; they allow us to determine the safest moment to cross the street, the best available everyday items to purchase and when to engage in conversation with a stranger. They assist us on an on-going, often minute-by-minute basis to resolve issues and problems and make decisions. Without them, we'd be forever stuck in analysis paralysis because of the sheer volume of information we encounter daily.

Through social media and technology in general, we're forced to form quick opinions and make rapid decisions based on the information thrust in our direction. This is one crucial area where heuristics helps us when sifting through this tsunami of information.

The challenge with heuristics, though, is that they sometimes lead us astray. Our cognitive limitations lead to illusions and errors in perception, judgment, and hence, decision-making. Our search for meaning or trends in various situations can conjure misinterpretations that don't exist. Rooted in our biology, cognitive biases result in systemic errors, subject to forces and influencers from deep within our psyche that drive our behavior.

Cognitive biases fall into four main areas, depending on how we perceive information:

Determining what we should remember: As humans, we prefer generalities over specifics and will store more exact information based on its recency than its frequency. As such, we're systematically overconfident, overestimating or overweighting in our assumptions.

Examples of this category of cognitive biases are the negativity bias, where we always see threats, or its opposite, the positivity bias, where we see the world through rose-colored glasses. The negativity bias results in us continually seeing hazards where none exist or, on the other hand, reminiscing about how life used to be so much better, cheaper, simpler and happier than today. This is because the emotional fallout of a bad result tends to exceed the emotional benefits of a good one, contributing to our complaining and worrying. We focus energy on those things that threaten us because our reactions are essential to survival. An example is what stock market watchers refer to as investors continually climbing a wall of worry. Conversely, with the positivity bias, which may be even more harmful to us: we may believe that everyone acts in good faith or that life is only full of opportunities, devoid of any threats or ill-natured people.

The need to act quickly: We focus on the immediate and relatable issues that are before us, tending to complete those things in which we have already invested significant time, money and energy. This category of cognitive errors results in us making poor decisions based on previous commitments, lack of time or over-investment of effort.

Examples within this category are the sunk-cost bias, *Occam's Razor* (preferring the more straightforward or simple explanation to any complex problem) and the loss-aversion bias. These cognitive biases result in us over-committing to something, such as an unhealthy relationship or shares in a company, the values of which have diminished significantly, while fully expecting the value to rebound to or beyond its prior heights. Many people overstay in an unhealthy relationship with the constant hope things will get better or be as they were before. Stock market history is full of examples of stocks that have soared in price although the company is devoid of value, and will eventually crash to become worthless while people still hold on to the securities. No wonder people climb that wall of worry.

Managing the crush of information: Things that have been primed in our memory get our attention. We confuse intensity with frequency and are drawn to those details that confirm our own existing beliefs. This decision-making error occurs once we form an opinion, and then seek out information that supports our views while ignoring facts that challenge them. We often mistake the salient or unexpected for the statistical or the norm. Events that are catastrophic in a far-off country are just another statistic for us to digest in the safety of our homes. We give more attention to something that occurs close to us and treat it as representative of the world at large because of its proximity, even if it's a one-off event.

Examples of this category are the confirmation bias, the framing effect bias, the availability heuristic and the post-purchase rationalization. When we look to buy a new car, the manufacturer's suggested retail price (MSRP) sticker effectively anchors the price point and establishes a starting point for price negotiations. Once we purchase a new car, we suddenly see more of the same model on the road than before; after we wash our car, it appears to drive more smoothly and 'cleaner' than before.

Thanks to the confirmation bias, victims of paranoia and self-styled politics can find a narrative that impeccably suits all the facts they come across. People can fall prey to the shared delusions of narrative fallacies and grievances, resulting in increased nationalism and the entrenchment of various identities through public references to past oppression, real and imagined.

Dealing with limited meaning: When presented with a little information, we fill in characteristics from stereotypes, generalities and prior personal experience to complete the picture. We use diagnostic labels of people and things to organize and simplify, relying on first impressions or one-word descriptions that others provide. We also simplify probabilities and numbers to make them easier to think about and manage. The error is that we base our decisions on those events, information and experiences we are familiar with or have had positive experiences with in the past.

Examples of this category are the halo effect, the group-attribution bias and the in-group bias. These cognitive biases can result in us choosing personal, business and intimate relationships with others based on previous positive experiences with an individual who looks like them (or even us), shares common links (from the same place, school or group affiliations), or is just pleasing to look at. I've seen complainants viewed as being more credible by investigators and members of the public simply because they're physically attractive.

Conversely, we may refuse to hire someone or engage in a relationship with a person who simply looks like a person who has harmed us before, displays a subtle or pronounced difference, or is not part of our in-group. The group could be as restrictive as someone from the same neighborhood, same ethnic group, same linguistic group or same financial position as us. In the latter sense, classism is a blatant example, with material characteristics and apparent worth of an individual often serving as the great divider in our society.

These four categories of cognitive biases have been graphically represented in the *2016 Cognitive Bias Codex*[50], which came about as a diagrammatic poster remix of the information presented in the September 2016 blog by Buster Benson entitled *Cognitive bias cheat sheet*. In his blog, Benson referenced Wikipedia's list of 175 cognitive biases. The *2016 Codex* contains 189. It's expected to grow as we develop a further understanding of our cognitive biases.

The reality about cognitive biases is that we don't see everything because vision is psychophysiologically expensive and takes up a lot of our ability to notice things visually. The cognitive errors and illusions we fall prey to don't occur in the eyes but in our brains. They become systemic misrepresentations and falsifications.[51]

Our desire for immediate action can also be flawed. It's usually predicated on our first choice advanced by intuition and habit, not on a fulsome analysis of any context. Modern TV has popularized the notion of a cop's gut instinct. Early in my career, I learned that I was more often wrong than right when I made suppositions based on my intuition. Better to validate facts than cultivate instinct.

Worrying wall climbs

Slightly more conscious than cognitive biases, implicit (or inherent) biases are the product of learned associations and social conditioning, usually resulting in stereotyping people, groups and things. They tend to be more malleable than cognitive biases as they develop through experience and education. With sufficient, sustained effort, we can identify, explain, and reprogram them.

Beyond these are our explicit biases followed by manifest biases. Cognitive illusions and errors are more stubborn than visual illusions. Tunnel vision, for instance, is more a failure of cognitive recognition than of visual appreciation. It's the product of various perceptive distortions that impede our analytical accuracy, affecting what we recognize and our interpretation of what we think we see. So, if we are subject to our motivations, perceptions and emotions, sometimes we get things wrong because we base our view of a problem or situation on an understanding that is flawed from the outset.

Much of what we do is based on our individual beliefs, preferences and biases instead of actual evidence and facts. That's because we only recognize what we understand. And we only understand what we're able to see. If we're interested in a particular item, sport or activity, we'll often look for those very things as we go about our day, avoiding recognizing other matters as they simply aren't important enough for us to notice.

Our rapid decision-making errors caused by these cognitive and implicit biases are further reinforced by our memory, which often doesn't provide accurate reconstructions of a lived event. What people tend to misunderstand about memory is that it's more often about reconstruction than recollection. Reconstruction is focused on the meaning we attribute to the remembered experience and the confidence we have in its remembrance.

Our view of an incident, a person or an encounter can quickly morph over time, tinted by numerous factors: previous and subsequent experiences (good or bad), the reactions of others at the time of the event or the recounting, the personal interpretation of interactions as seen through an old family photograph, parental storytelling of an event or our understanding of how we would have reacted or felt in such a situation using today's views as a barometer. Even our olfactory senses can skew the reconstitution of a particular event, as they can elicit strong memories from another event, creating confusion in its recollection. Our search for meaning can and does invoke illusions because of our personal preferences, biases and desires to see things as we wish to see them.

Each time we recall a memory, it takes on a slightly different hue. Not unlike scaffolding, we tend to layer memory upon memory, even merging disparate memories into a single reminiscence. We are incapable of extracting a perfect record of a particular memory and playing it back the same way every time, in part because of the recollection's decay over time based on the number of times it's recalled, and the time passed since the actual event. We only extract the memory based on the version of the last time we accessed it.

We can circumvent this through the use of notes made immediately following the event. In policing, the officer's notebook acts as an aide-memoire to assist them in the recollection of events should they be required to fill out a later report, account for their actions or testify in court. Most people rarely make such notes, with the exceptions of those who keep diaries or produce memoirs.

The term "flashbulb memory" designates those vivid, detailed memories of very surprising, consequential and emotionally arousing events.[52] Such memories are preserved or etched in our minds like a photograph when a flash goes off. The memory usually includes where we were, what we were doing, who advised us of the news and how we felt upon learning it. Each generation has numerous flashbulb memories, such as the assassination of President Kennedy, the Apollo 11 lunar landing, the winning goal in the 1972 Canada-Russia Summit Series (for Canadians), the American "Miracle on Ice" victory over the Russians in the 1980 Olympic ice hockey semi-final game, and the terrorist attacks of September 11, 2001. A defining question we ask one another is, "Do you remember where you were when that event occurred?"

When we add emotion to a memory, we develop nostalgia, which further cements our confidence in the memory's recollection. Although our remembrance of the event may be distorted and inaccurate, we nonetheless ardently cling to our flashbulb memory with the greatest of certainty. In this sense, nostalgia acts as a permanent beacon for people of all persuasions amongst the world's uncertainties, allowing us to have a source of reassurance and reaffirmation of our place in it. As American

175

columnist Franklin Pearce Adams (1881-1960) wrote, "Nothing is more responsible for the good old days than a bad memory." Unfortunately, that also means that there's no way to know we're in the good old days until we've actually left them. That's the power of memories.

Just like the story of the chained elephant whose childhood memory of the impossibility of breaking free from its chains was more potent than the real possibility of finally liberating itself from its adult bonds,[53] humans often remain attached to previous experiences and their interpretations of them. This manifests itself in the selection of memories we choose to harbor and perpetuate through recounting and narration. As the French author Raphaël Enthoven wrote in the preface of his 2020 novel *Le Temps Gagné* ("The Time Saved"), "This story is entirely imagined, because I lived it from the beginning to the end."

Short-circuiting shortcuts

Another layer of decision-making traps we're prone to are logical fallacies. Unlike cognitive or implicit biases, logical fallacies stem from errors in a logical argument instead of thought-processing errors. Examples of logical fallacies are the straw man, red herring and *argumentum ad hominem* fallacies, which redirect arguments by introducing ideas, notions or personal qualities about the subject discussed or one's opponent during a debate to change the focus of the discussion to intimidate the other person. The goal of logical fallacies is to shift or deflect the discussion's direction, not to lead to a rational exploration of the matter being discussed.

Related to logical fallacies is the concept of non-consequential thinking. This results from the speed and ease of access to the information we obtain today through traditional and social media, search engines and apps, giving people the illusion that they're informed and, more importantly, that they have thought deeply about an issue or situation. As the saying goes, if we read it on the internet in three separate places, it must be true, especially when an author or journalist presents us with seemingly endless numbers and graphs that cloud our ability to understand the facts or logical arguments. This is akin to being spoon-fed predigested information and analysis, replete with the emphases and biases of the author of the article, document or statement. We adopt the premises advanced by the commentator or author: hook, line and sinker.

Think of these all as potential decision-making traps into which we all can fall. Our challenge is to recognize the risk by being alive to these decision-making traps and their role in our lives. Recognizing that we're continually subject to decision-making errors and traps is the first step to seeing any situation's reality.

Sometimes, despite this knowledge, we don't worry about the pitfalls out there as we're intent on presenting a particular view of a topic, situation, person or entity.

Living in bling-filled glass houses

Canada has a national public broadcaster known as the Canadian Broadcasting Corporation (CBC). It's financed through public money and some advertising revenues while providing cross-country television and international radio coverage in French, English and some indigenous languages. It's not traditional public broadcasting like PBS (Public Broadcasting Service) or NPR (National Public Radio) in the United States but does have a specific mandate to provide Canadian content.

Like many Canadians, I have an intimate link to the CBC and its French-language broadcaster, *Radio-Canada*, listening to various programs, music and news over the years which continues to this day. I mainly listened to their programming during long drives across Canada, including work transfers and travel to my father's home for the holidays long before the advent of multiple radio stations, satellite radio and downloaded podcasts. When I was in Haiti on my first mission in 1995, I eagerly listened to short-wave broadcasts of Radio-Canada International to get news from home. For me, the CBC is an important part of Canadian culture.

As a cab driver in Toronto in the mid-80s, I drove home many a CBC employee after their evening shift from the CBC's national broadcast center on Jarvis Street. During the drives, I quietly listened to them talk about the events of the day. Often, the passengers openly commented on how misdirected those in government and the private sector were. They would detail how those in power weren't as enlightened as CBC employees, thanks to their role as members of the Fourth and even Fifth estates.[54]

It surprised me to hear them talk with such disregard for others' actions and views, especially those in influential positions of public responsibility. But as a young, recent college graduate in political science and economics, I just thought they were better informed than I was and were deserving of their opinions.

Little did I know that I would be dealing with the CBC in the years to come, with some interactions positive while others less so. Over the years, I learned that journalists, like anyone else, were subject to their own biases, some using their platform to advance their worldviews. On occasion, I would also see institutional bias at work—one organization's desire to cast doubt on another.

In July 2016, the CBC published a report on policing in Canada, determining that only one police service out of 22 of the largest urban centers was fully representative of the cultural communities it served: Halifax Regional Police. The article found that, while many police services had higher rates of diversity in its ranks, only HRP had a higher percentage of non-white officers than are present in the general population it serves.[55] As the chief of HRP, several media outlets asked me to comment on the study. I immediately acknowledged that Halifax was more homogeneous than other Canadian cities such as Toronto, Winnipeg and Vancouver. Consequently, it was easier for HRP to represent the communities it served because of the limited number of non-White residents.

In the article, one community activist who was interviewed didn't dispute the numbers but stated that HRP didn't have enough officers of African descent. The numbers did not bear him out, but he had other legitimate concerns about police-community interactions.

In my final year as chief of police, the journalist who penned the report would often attempt to pigeon-hole me by asking whether or not I believed systemic racism existed in policing and society in general. Every time he asked the question, I would ask him to define what he meant. Was he referring to truly systemic programs such as Apartheid or the segregationist Jim Crow laws in the late 19th and early 20th centuries in the United States, or the Nuremberg laws of Nazi Germany? Canada had also seen comparable laws in place that were slowly amended during the early 20th century.

The journalist would simply refuse to provide a definition, insisting that I respond to his question. I would decline to answer.

In January 2019, a second, unrelated news report was published by the same CBC newsroom detailing the results of an analysis of five years of expenses on 'police swag', obtained through a freedom of information request. Swag are those promotional items and merchandise branded with the organization's logo, given away to the public and some employees: pens, pencils, stickers, temporary tattoos, mugs, water bottles and small plush comfort bears for young victims of crime. The journalist found that in 2018 alone, HRP spent more on branded merchandise than in the previous four years combined.[56] The total five-year amount was in the area of $100,000. More than anything else, the article intended to denigrate our purchase of challenge coins.

The reason for the spike in spending in 2018 was that we had ordered 3,000 challenge coins that to present as awards and tokens of appreciation to police employees, various stakeholders, and partners in following years. Challenge coins had become more and more popular over the years and many organizations, including non-police groups, used them as a means of thanking others and creating a form of solidarity. I even occasionally gave coins to hockey players and coaches who displayed remarkable on-ice leadership during games I officiated.

In a subsequent article, a local self-styled contrarian journalist cited our purchase of the challenge coins as an example of the further militarization of our organization and police in general. Interestingly, he never commented on a later article in the mainstream press about the adoption of challenge coins by local bartenders and the potential militarization of local drinking establishments of which he seemed quite familiar.

As the CBC is a crown corporation (an entity established, regulated and financed by the Canadian government), it must respond to freedom of information requests, just as police services do. Once retired, I made two such requests, one for the demographic composition of the CBC's workforce in Nova Scotia and the other for money spent on swag during the same five-year period. The results were telling.

As of June 2019, the CBC in Nova Scotia had 144 total employees, 10 of whom were visible minorities (i.e., non-white). That meant that only 6.9 percent of their workforce were visible minorities, well below the 11.6 percent of the local population reported in their July 2016 article for Halifax. I recognize that although the CBC is headquartered in Halifax, its role is to provide service to all of Nova Scotia, where the level of visible minorities is lower than compared to Halifax.

During my tenure as chief of police, especially during the later years, I would be in the CBC Halifax building about once a month as I had regular interviews with a French-language talk show host. I'd intentionally look around to see the diversity that was present in the large open-concept workspace. The most non-White employees I ever counted during any given visit were three, two women of African descent and another of East Asian descent.

I did the same thing when I would go into the CBC's main television competitor's studio, where I would only ever see a single person of color. In my numerous times over the years in the studios of Halifax's lone independent talk radio station, I never saw a single person of color. What could account for such low numbers in local journalism? Could it be systemic racism? I think the answer is considerably more nuanced than that.

Regarding the access to information request for the swag, the CBC provided me with a DVD containing all the itemized purchases but with the individual dollar amounts redacted. However, it gave the aggregate amount spent on promotional giveaways and resale items during the five years: a total of $58,561.23.

Amongst the things listed were smartphone cases and wallets, umbrellas, buttons, flashlights, aprons, sunglasses, hand clappers, memo holders and travel mugs. But most items purchased were clothing. I noticed many a CBC employee wearing CBC-branded clothes, both at work and off work, which is expected. When compared during the same five-year period, HRP had spent around $100,000 for an organization of over 750 employees and volunteers (or about $135 per employee/volunteer) while the CBC had spent just over $58,000 for 144 employees (or about $406 per employee).

These are but two examples where I suspected institutional bias in a media outlet's reporting. But bias is a highly personal trait that manifests itself in all of us, including those we're trying to inform and help.

Marlo attends my presentation, and it doesn't end well

In March 2016, a local Canadian federal department head asked me to present on mental health and wellness to employees from different government sectors. Because of my public disclosure of having been diagnosed with a Post-Traumatic Stress Injury (PTSI), my TEDx talk on the subject, and the work that I had done as police chief in promoting discussions around mental health in the workplace, several organizations asked me to share my experiences and insight. I wasn't remunerated for this, as it was a favor to another level of government.

During my two-hour presentation, I noticed Marlo, seated in the middle of the room, reading a newspaper, checking emails on her smartphone, acting thoroughly disengaged. Not once did she look up at me, acknowledge what I said, nod in agreement or even demonstrate disapproval. After my presentation, as I was in the elevator going downstairs to walk back to my office, I noticed Marlo shadowing me, waiting for a moment when I was alone to talk. So, as I was walking to the exit, I stopped, turned and addressed her.

Marlo was quite direct about her evaluation of my presentation; she wanted to tell me how she couldn't hear or understand half my presentation because I hadn't spoken loud enough. She also said that my cultural references were outdated because she was born in the 90s, and I referred to people, events and things long before her birth and not culturally pertinent. Marlo then went on a litany of accusations about my political views, stating that she didn't appreciate my presentation or my work in general.

I asked her why she was so intent on sharing her impressions with me, but she refused to answer. I left the interaction puzzled about how Marlo could be so forthright without being honest as to the real intentions behind her concerns.

I subsequently learned that Marlo was a civilian employee working for the Canadian Armed Forces. She had an exceedingly high opinion of herself and very pronounced views about those in authority. On a particular social media platform, she qualified herself as "an awesome HR assistant," having important responsibilities over people who had little notion of what they were doing. It was evident that she had biases about policing, authority and me.

I could only gather that this was her chance to shine in her mind by confronting what she viewed as an authority figure she wanted to stand up to, something she couldn't do in her workplace.

Life is full of individuals who feel the need to communicate what they think for no other reason than to say something. Their discourse is unfiltered, and they simply need to get what they want to say off their chest.

At one time or another, we've all been in such a position ourselves. The key is to ensure that we have a particular justification for doing so: standing up to a bully, helping someone avoid a potentially dangerous situation or giving some constructive or positive feedback to another in a respectful way. The problem occurs when we have a Marlo who is ruled by their biases, so blindly self-centered that they can't help themselves. With social media and the anonymity it affords, we see this more and more often.

With such a Marlo, we can adopt several different tacks. Firstly, we can simply ignore them and their comments, accepting such individuals as part of the road of life, just like potholes that we drive around and avoid. Or we can take a more aggressive tack, telling Marlo where they can go or what they can do with their comments. In such a case, quoting Shakespeare may be the most appropriate method: "I do desire we may be better strangers." Finally, if we regularly interact with Marlo, perhaps the best way to deal with them is to resolve to make use of them and their attitude rather than attempt to change them. They're part of the social ecology and we might as well leverage whatever skills they have to our advantage.

Who knows, maybe one day we'll find ourselves listening to Marlo giving a presentation, and we may wish to offer them some pointers, too.

Authentically integrative

When dealing with workplace dynamics, as individuals and organizations, we need to create environments where we can manage our individual biases through intrinsic and extrinsic motivation. An essential component of this approach is through training.

Thinking specifically of diversity and inclusion, management of biases requires us to have previous experience in different cultural and social contexts that we can obtain most easily through travel, study and living abroad. American humorist Mark Twain (1835-1910) aptly described the benefits of life's voyages when he wrote in his book *The Innocents Abroad / Roughing It*:

> Travel is fatal to prejudice, bigotry, and narrow-mindedness and many of our people need it sorely on these accounts. Broad, wholesome, charitable views of men and things cannot be acquired by vegetating in one little corner of the earth all one's lifetime.

We can supplement such charitable views through additional, local encounters, experiencing a rural or urban lifestyle or developing personal, professional and intimate relationships with people of different religions, ethnicity, linguistic and socio-economic backgrounds. The advantage of such experiences and training is to lower our ethnocentricity levels through what can be qualified as cultural humility, reducing our distrust of others' ideas and contributions, with the goal of better decision-making and relationship building.

We can best develop this cultural humility, or cultural competency, through a deep understanding of our own cultural norms, an acceptance of the validity of the differences of other cultures, an openness and willingness to interact with those cultures, developing skills that will let us operate effectively in a world containing cultural differences and distinctions, and the empathy to appreciate what others experience. It doesn't require guilt, regret or blaming; it requires acceptance of ourselves and others.

One example of such training is the Canadian Association of Chiefs of Police (CACP) Executive Global Studies program. Since 2003, this unique professional development program has allowed police executives (civilian employees and sworn officers) and individuals from related public safety and criminal justice agencies to acquire research and leadership development experience at the international level. The program involves six months of intense study and collaboration, applying a research-driven and problem-based learning model augmented through on-site visits to law enforcement agencies and private entities worldwide.

In 2018, the CACP Board of Directors, of which I was a member, challenged the study cohort to examine the question of equity, inclusion and fundamental respect in diverse police organizations throughout the world. The cohort presented a comprehensive report[57] drawing on field studies in 17 countries, ranging from environments where inclusion and diversity mattered much to those societies where assimilation was the only apparent workforce diversity approach. In the latter instances, conformity overrides inclusion.

As could be expected, the cohort found an entire spectrum of organizational environments, ranging from "predatory" environments, characterized by workplace hunters and their prey; to exclusionary settings where individuals either belonged to a core group or did not; to structurally inclusive landscapes where individuals had yet to fully adopt the notions of inclusion which were already in place; to the highest and most widely shared aspiration, an "authentically inclusive" workplace where genuine, widespread and on-going efforts were in place to value and promote inclusion, respect and individual contribution. The cohort found no example of this ideal workplace in all its travels, but many of the organizations visited were diligently working towards such a state.

The value proposition of developing an authentically inclusive environment is that it promotes diversity of thought by encouraging the more profound character, talent and capacity traits of all employees to manifest themselves. Once this wellspring of potential is tapped, the thinking goes, organizations benefit from better decision-making, higher morale and greater trust at all levels. They become workplaces where competing ideas are held in creative tension, resulting in the best ideas and approaches being adopted. This is known as integrative thinking, and it's imperative when dealing with complexity.

Developed by Canadian professor Roger Martin, the notion of integrative thinking is defined as:

> The ability to face constructively the tension of opposing ideas and, instead of choosing one at the expense of the other, generate a creative resolution of the tension in the form of a new idea that contains elements of the opposing ideas but is superior to each.[58]

This thinking discipline involves taking a broader view of what's salient and pertinent while being open to multidirectional and nonlinear relationships, basically the complexity we face. This further requires avoiding the over-simplification of our thinking processes and the accompanying errors in our logic caused by our cognitive errors, logical fallacies and non-consequential thinking. The key is to be aware, open and alive to circumstances that we typically wouldn't consider because of our biology.

Diversity of thought allows for such thinking, which avoids mirroring our faults and biases.

Man, were we wrong

In May 2009, I attended the United Nations Senior Mission Leaders Course in Vienna, Austria. Participants came from around the world: women and men of different ethnicities from various diplomatic corps, national military branches, police services and international non-governmental agencies (NGOs).

The course's goal was to prepare the participants, all of whom had prior international work experience, to become future executive leaders in UN missions worldwide. Over the two weeks, high-level practitioners gave a series of presentations and led exercises. One of the presenters was the former US Ambassador to Angola, Mr. Donald Steinberg, who worked as a senior executive with an NGO dedicated to preventing and denouncing deadly conflict.

Mr. Steinberg was a 60-year-old White man who presented his material without audio-visual aides or fanfare, opting to have a simple conversation with the course participants. He was quiet, unassuming and not very dynamic, even frumpy in his appearance, preferring to sit during his entire 80-minute time allotment on gender issues. Like many of the other class participants that day, when he was first introduced, I questioned what this man could tell us about how and why we should promote gender equity in UN missions.

He began by giving a brief overview of his experience and appreciation of gender issues. He asserted that the single best investment in post-conflict peacebuilding is girls' education, as it results in later or less pregnancy and more community expertise and innovation. He then provided a litany of examples as to why this was, paraphrasing an African proverb, "When you educate a boy, you educate a person. When you educate a girl, you educate a community."

We quickly became captivated by this man's message, realizing that his wealth of experience and passion about the subject of girls' and women's rights were as extensive as his ideas were practical and achievable. During the final debriefing and evaluation of our course, all the participants were glowing in their assessment of Mr. Steinberg's presentation, acknowledging our collective bias about this man at the outset.

Luckily, we were able to get over our early distrust and benefit from his wisdom. He'd provided us with two equally important lessons that day: one on understanding gender issues and another on overcoming our own biases.

The bias ladder

Overcoming one's biases requires first acknowledging their existence, not through guilt or shaming, but through individual introspection and consistent questioning. To acknowledge their presence, we need to understand how our biases manifest themselves.

Every person, by their preferences, inclinations and feelings, has biases. To use a simple illustration, if we have a particular fondness for a specific pizza topping, or, more specifically, if we can't stand a certain garnish, we have a bias.

Our biases for and against things, ideas and people are determinant in almost all the decisions we make every day. Biases involve making a judgment regarding something or someone, assigning value to them and engaging in what is known as stratification: the separation and classification of something or someone into different groups. Driven by our desires and preferences, we prioritize and hierarchize things and people to decide what importance we give them.

You can place biases in a hierarchy according to how they express themselves.

At the top of the hierarchy are the most visible, our **manifest biases**, including our political, group and financial adherence. Amongst these would be any outward opinions, trappings or accouterments promoting these perspectives, including any external sense of moral superiority. Bumper and window stickers are unique visible displays of these overt biases as individuals outwardly exhibit their different affiliations: preferred political ideology, party or leader; favorite sports teams; educational achievements; sexual and religious identification; and even family structure. These indications are the outward definitions we wish to project. The type or location of tattoos, hairstyle, piercings or jewelry, and how we dress, including the brands we wear, are also physical manifestations of individual preferences, hence, biases, indicating our values, interests and in-group membership adherence.

This level also demonstrates the intensity and degree of labeling others we engage with, such as political, in-group, racial and class stereotyping, resulting in racism and classism. This is how we lead our days, openly manifesting our choices through various prejudices, both for and against people, ideas and things, be it towards or against political movements, people in certain positions of authority or belonging to different groups. It can also result in certain groups' demonization: cops as power-hungry, referees as blind, lawyers as unethical, politicians as corrupt, journalists as liars, public relations practitioners as spin doctors and academics (especially economists) as shills.

The next level in the hierarchy is our **explicit biases**. We knowingly and willingly demonstrate our preferences and repulsion to activities and life approaches, including food choices (e.g., vegan, vegetarian or omnivore), some group affiliations such as local or neighborhood associations, and self-righteousness. This level is the home of xenophobia, causing us to avoid people who are different and prefer those who are familiar. This determines our relationships and daily choices of how and with whom we live and associate.

The third level is our **implicit biases**. No longer overt and conscious, these preferences and reactions to various stimuli operate in our sub-conscious. Resulting from multiple life experiences and cultural biases handed down from our parents, siblings and immediate entourage, they include numerous phobias and preferences (e.g., of the dark, of animals, of people because of what they look like, what they represent or whom they resemble). This is the level of the gut feeling, intuition or blind spots in our thinking.

This level pre-determines how we perceive certain stimuli and people, encouraging, discouraging or persuading us in how we interact with others because of how they look, what they represent and especially how we feel around them. This also leads us to reject or accept potential friends or partners because they may simply look, act, sound or smell like someone we may have met in the past who hurt, betrayed or, conversely, nurtured us.

Our implicit biases can also lead to a sub-category known as design biases, where we create things and processes such as seat belts or protective equipment of which one size is expected to fit all, as we assume that specificity of design isn't required. This may lead to gender bias as it's assumed that the end-users are often only of a specific gender or a particular size. As an example, in the case of pulse oximeters, those devices used by medical practitioners to measure a patient's blood-oxygen level, there may be an overestimation of blood oxygen levels in people who are not Caucasian.

Recognizing the challenges around implicit biases, organizations have attempted to deal with the pernicious effects of this level of discrimination through training. The goal is to change attitudes, hence outcomes, not just people's minds.

The New York Police Department (NYPD) is the largest and one of the world's oldest municipal departments, with approximately 36,000 officers and 19,000 civilian employees. As a police service, they are only eclipsed in size by some country's national police services, including France's *Gendarmerie nationale* and *Police nationale,* which have 100,000 and 150,000 employees, respectively. In 2018, the NYPD began training its officers and employees on implicit bias, using a psychological theory seminar that described how unconscious stereotypes could lead people to make incorrect snap judgments. In policing, these inaccurate snap judgments can have life-altering and severe consequences for both police employees and members of the public.

Equally important, NYPD began studying the effects of the training on its employees.[59] NYPD researchers found that although its members expressed more awareness of the concept of implicit bias and a greater willingness to manage it, there was no meaningful change in the actual actions of employees. NYPD believes that the training's goal was to allow its employees to self-reflect and begin to understand the effects of implicit bias on their actions and decisions. It's doubtful that such training can lead to permanent change, absent any further reinforcement.

In 2017, I took the same training, finding it to be of some value in recognizing the presence of inherent biases. I'm not sure that the training alone was enough to change attitudes and outcomes, just as NYPD had determined. The challenge of changing attitudes and outcomes illustrates how ingrained our implicit biases are. Several organizations are carrying out more research in this area.

The final or base level of our biases is **cognitive biases**. These shortcuts or heuristics allow us to process information and make continual decisions, both large and small. These are the tools that enable us to screen things and better deal with the deluge of information in our world. As we've seen, they can be fraught with errors.

As the hierarchy shows, the more overt a bias, the easier it is for us to recognize it. As such, it should be easier to modify it. The more subconscious a bias, the more difficult it is for us to acknowledge its presence and counter its adverse effects.

Locked doors and fresh batteries

An example of an interesting bias in collective decision-making occurred when I was chief of police. A rash of thefts from and of cars happened in a rural residential neighborhood in my own sub-division. Thieves had hit one street in the area in question over two hours one night. Out of thirty homes visited, all of them on large, separated lots, 14 vehicles had items stolen from inside them, and three cars had been stolen. The thieves smashed no windows and used no lockout tool such as a Slim Jim.

With today's anti-theft technology, stealing a car should be exceedingly difficult. In 2012, during a presentation I attended, a noted Canadian criminologist even described car theft as a "sunset crime" because of advances in anti-theft technology.

Difficult, that is, unless the owner leaves or the fob in an unlocked vehicle. And that is precisely what had occurred on the street. People had left their cars and their homes unlocked, allowing individuals to steal whatever loose change, wallets and other items were left inside. If the keys were in the cars or the immediate front entrance to the unlocked house, the thieves simply stole the cars.[60]

To my knowledge, the only place in Canada where everyone is expected to leave their car doors unlocked is in Churchill, Manitoba, on the south shore of Hudson's Bay. They do so to offer an escape for pedestrians who might encounter a polar bear, not because they're lazy or overly trusting.

At a meeting of municipal directors in the weeks following the rash of thefts, I was making a point of the importance of locking our cars and homes to avoid such crimes of opportunity. After I finished my intervention, the fire chief, a most amiable and competent individual with whom I had a good working and personal relationship, looked at me quizzically. He candidly stated that he never locked his car or home doors as he had never had any problems in his life. He even left the keys in his car's ignition so that his daughter would have no problems finding the keys when she was going to early-morning college classes.

I immediately responded that not locking car and home doors is akin to not having working smoke detectors in a home.

Dumbfounded, he asked, "But why wouldn't anyone have working smoke detectors in their home? It's a matter of life and death. So much could be lost!"

I replied that the issue of locking doors could be just as important.

But my friend only viewed the situation from his perspective, based on his never having lost anything because of not locking his doors.

Think about the most poignant lessons you have learned in life: were they because of something you gained or because of something you lost? This isn't strictly reserved for personal items; you can apply it to lost opportunities to develop new relationships, live new experiences or make better decisions.

Correct decisions

Good decision-making requires three components. The decision must:

1. be based on validated facts, not cultivated ideas.
2. be free of logical fallacies and withstand those errors in our thinking that skew results.
3. resist the pull of cognitive biases, which may never be eliminated but can be reduced as much as possible.

A good decision provides the optimal result, being the best alternative of all potential or available choices.

These are steps that we all can intellectually carry out to ensure the best decisions possible. Of course, this involves giving ourselves the necessary time to decide, which isn't always a given.

The next challenge is dealing with the emotional tugs and yanks from deep within us, influenced by our social environment while growing up and becoming an adult. Although our biases can make decision-making challenging, the collection of forces that drive our behavior can be even more daunting, fuelling our irrationality. This is the lesson of human nature.

Calls from the blue line

*   Heuristics are cognitive shortcuts that allow us to recognize something and quickly decide on a course of action. The problem is that these mental shortcuts or biases can lead us down the garden path of errors.
*   Memory is more often about reconstruction than it is about recollection. That reconstruction is focused on the meaning we attribute to the remembered experience and the confidence we have in its remembrance, leaving much room for mistakes.
*   The value proposition of developing an authentically inclusive work environment is that it promotes diversity of thought by encouraging

all employees' more profound character, talent and capacity traits to manifest themselves.

- Our challenge is to recognize our cognitive errors by being alive to the decision-making traps such as cognitive biases, logical fallacies and non-consequential thinking, as well as their role in our lives.

- As absolutely everyone has their own biases, we must take what they do and say with a grain of salt. When Marlo has the uncontrollable need to let us know what they think, we can choose to ignore them, tell them off or use them somehow to our advantage. Or we can wait to return the favor.

- When a bias manifests itself, we judge something or someone, assign value to them and engage in what is known as stratification: the separation and classification of something or someone into different groups, prioritizing them and hierarchizing them.

- Overcoming one's biases requires first acknowledging their existence, not through guilt or shaming, but through individual introspection and consistent questioning.

- Be aware of the hierarchy of biases: manifest, explicit, implicit and cognitive. Understand how and when they express themselves. We can then avoid the errors associated with them.

7: The lesson of human nature

To become indignant at people's conduct is as foolish as to be angry with a stone because it rolls into your path. And with many people the wisest thing you can do is to resolve to make use of those whom you cannot alter.

-Arthur Schopenhauer (1788-1860),
German philosopher

Mutual funds we ain't

As we have seen, humans are great at postdiction ("See, I told you so!"), but lousy at prediction ("Well, I couldn't have seen that coming!"). And the primary reason behind our inability to foretell the future is our and others' irrationality. Under the influence of our hubris and our biases, we turn a blind eye to objective information, clinging to views, hopes and expectations, even if they are irrational.

In one investigation of an accidental death we conducted, the victim's family asked us to consider using the services of a self-described clairvoyant. This wasn't an unusual request. I had been involved in highly-charged missing-person and homicide investigations in the past where family members asked for 'outside' help. In many cases, and understandably so, loved ones looking for some resolution to their grief were willing to seek alternative means that would never be considered under typical circumstances.

Keen to assuage some of their concerns and offer them a degree of comfort, our investigators listened to what the mystic had to say. As expected, it didn't produce any leads, only fuelling conjecture and speculation. But we'd done as the family asked.

Years later, during a review of the investigation, we were criticized for having used the services of the self-styled psychic. One journalist even asked me if we would ever use psychics again. I told him that perhaps we would, but only during internal social events.

As human beings, we can be rational, irrational (either not rational, unfounded or nonsensical), or non-rational (contrary to reason, lacking an appropriate or sufficient reason), sometimes all at once. We also tend to be relatively consistent in these states, including being irrational more often than we think. Human beings are not mutual funds, which generally have the following caveat posted in their advertisements: "Mutual funds are not guaranteed, values change frequently and past performance may not be repeated."

Unlike mutual funds, though, with human beings, *past performance is indicative of future performance*. We can usually bank on our consistency in this regard. People rarely, if ever, do something just once, especially if that something is forbidden or prohibited by a rule. As a drug investigator, I was always surprised when individuals I arrested for trafficking would swear that it was their first time ever selling drugs, despite our having surveilled them several times previously engaging in drug trafficking.

People who have shown a proclivity to be regularly irrational in the past or in one particular area of their life will be unreasonable in the same manner in the future. This is because we're creatures of habit. And those various habits collectively form what's known as human nature. And human nature, as the wellspring of our personality, begets behavior.

Acquire social intelligence, an awareness of people's personalities and motivations, and we can begin to tap into that wellspring of knowledge to understand people's actions and influence them eventually. This requires being observant and nonjudgmental, going beyond our own particular issues to focus intensely on those of others. The key to this focus is empathy. Once we're focused on another and their motivations, we can read their behavior at the moment and, over an extended period, discern the reasons, expectations and emotions behind their actions.

One of the best indicators of that wellspring is habit.

Think of the difficulty we have dealing with change in our daily routine or, conversely, how we revert to old habits because they're comforting or simply because we don't know how to do things otherwise. We drive home from work or certain events using the same route every day. We regularly eat the same food. We work-out using the same routine. And we solve problems using the same approaches.

I drive a six-speed 2016 Honda Civic. It's a very good car; in fact, the model has been one of the world's best-selling vehicles for decades. But I almost didn't buy it.

In the 2016 model year, the Honda Motor Company decided to incorporate a small innovation in its vehicle lineup, replacing the radio volume knob with a sliding touchscreen control feature. I couldn't fathom adjusting the volume using the sliding touchscreen or the steering column's slider, a secondary control. I wasn't alone in my lack of appreciation of this novelty. People were accustomed to the volume knob and weren't willing to sacrifice it. The customer pushback was so significant that Honda reversed course and returned the traditional volume knob the following model year.

It was less about the actual knob than it was about the habit of adjusting the volume with a knob. I ended up buying the car, eventually appreciating the slider on the steering column, but shunning the sliding touchscreen to this day.

Another more widespread example of habit's sticking power is Canada's metric system acceptance and use. In 1971, the government of the day formed the Metric Commission. Its role was to implement metric measurements throughout the entire Canadian economy and civil society to conform to what was occurring elsewhere in Europe and Asia. People opposed metrication, as it was known, for many reasons and on many fronts in Canada, not least because of the difference in gasoline prices with the United States. The sale of gas in liters further complicated the conversion of price between the two countries, leading Canadians to feel they were being cheated and paying a higher price for fuel *because* of metrication. The Metric Commission was eventually abolished in 1985, but not before Canada had officially adopted the metric system.

Today, Canadians typically use a mix of metric and imperial measurements in their daily lives. They discuss the weather in degrees Celsius, purchase gasoline in liters, wine in milliliters and liters, and observe speed limits set in kilometers per hour. But they usually revert to imperial measurements when the temperature goes above 30° Celsius (90° Fahrenheit or so), when assessing fuel consumption through miles per gallon, describing their personal measurements in feet, inches and pounds, and purchasing their meat and produce in pounds, but not ounces, although they do so when ordering their glasses of wine in a restaurant. Canadian football is still played on a 110-yard field (with the 55-yard line as the center field line, or *centre* field), and golfers still expect courses to be measured in yards, not meters. During the COVID pandemic, Canadians respected physical distancing using both systems, staying six feet or two meters apart, depending on what business or government institution insisted upon it. To make things simple and in line with cultural norms, many Canadians simply preferred to respect appropriate physical distancing using a hockey stick's length, a gap they're more familiar with.

These examples demonstrate the grip that habit has in our daily actions, often transcending years, decades and even generations.

Falling in love with our digital reflection

Human nature stems from our nervous system's configuration, individual biology and emotional processing. This has developed for us through evolution over the course of millions of years as a species.

There are many aspects and sub-aspects to human nature that have developed socially through the centuries as well, influencing and influenced by laws, traditions and mores, as well as cultural and religious norms: food and drink choices to discourage the ingestion of potentially noxious substances, be it beef, pork or alcohol; the wearing of particular articles of clothing to protect one's head from the sun or to promote modesty; or the use of commandments, laws or traditions to dictate how people ought to act amongst themselves. These mores attempt to counter the self-harming aspects of our human nature.

Cross-culturally, they can also result in social contradictions and even conflict because of the world's diverse customs and usages. Some examples of social contradictions are: offering a beef hamburger to a Hindu; a pro-lifer contemplating an abortion, or, conversely, the woman who can't exercise agency over her body to obtain an abortion; Christians celebrating a same-sex union; or the communist living in a democracy. Such conflicts have always existed and continue to abound in human society. Although we're all part of the human race, our notions of what's right or acceptable are different depending on where we live and from whence we come. We can't expect someone from Moscow or Tokyo to have the same sense of fair play, ethics or modesty as someone from Paris, Jakarta or Port-au-Prince.

In *The Laws of Human Nature* (2018), American author Robert Greene writes that although humans are tribe-based, we're also self-absorbed and locked in our own individual worlds, living in the moment instead of in the long-term. We also have a deep need to believe in something, often a belief or notional system promoted by individuals having moral or political sway within the tribe.

Our tribe-based approach means that we continuously identify group insiders and outsiders and those views that challenge our tribe's belief patterns. We also quickly identify those changes that are disruptive to the continued functioning of the tribe. We do this as an evolutionary response to threats to our physical and social integrity, our families and our tribe from carriers of disease or people perceived to be envious of and intent on taking our possessions. This is the fuel for xenophobia that leads to other forms of prejudice.

Just like any individual, a tribe or group can display narcissism. Collective narcissism can manifest itself through the often-harmless immodesty of the flag-wrapped, face-painted fans at a sports event such as the Olympics or the World Cup. It can also be seen at the local arena for a hockey, ringette or sledge-hockey game.

This collective narcissism can further manifest itself through chauvinism, the communal belief that one group is superior to or dominant over another. The dominant-thinking group views itself as being virtuous and strong, while considering the other group to be unfit and weak. Derived from the supposed reaction of a fanatical follower of Napoleon Bonaparte (1769-1821), the legendary and likely mythical French soldier named Nicolas Chauvin, the term chauvinism now most often attaches to an attitude of superiority towards members of the opposite sex, specifically by men towards women, akin to misogyny and sexism.

Included in this collective narcissism is the high individual opinion we have of ourselves, leading us to believe that we're more righteous, more intelligent and simply better than others, even if some of those people belong to our own in-group. Group distinction, the darker side of our drive to bond as human beings, is the sentiment that results in a conscious separation between 'us' and 'them,' the classification and stratification of people into groups. By elevating ourselves, we automatically lower others. Hence, classism is more rampant than any other form of prejudice, resulting in perpetuated divisions based on socioeconomic status, perceived or actual.

Caste and indentured servitude still exist today, especially in traditionally hierarchical societies. In less stratified societies, such divisions also exist, even within the same ethnic or geographical groupings. In more extreme cases, classism still contributes to human trafficking, slavery and genocide. Inasmuch as it relates to socioeconomic status, classism may be the basis of most prejudice we see today.

Envy is another human evolutionary response to scarcity and survival, driving us to attain things, want power and dominate over others to allay our fears, often at others' expense. Envy comes from the Latin word *invidia*, itself a derivative of the verb *invidēre*, "to look askance at, regard with ill will, cast the evil eye on." In Roman mythology, *Invidia* was the goddess of envy and jealousy.

Envy can manifest itself in two ways: actively and passively. The active manner is often more insidious and destructive than the passive form. It leads some of us to go beyond the simple longing of passive covetousness, in which we're desirous of what others have to the point that we actively do things that undermine or harm the envied in our lives, and eventually ourselves.

Social media reinforces envy and covetousness by providing a continual glimpse into the lives of our friends, acquaintances, pseudo-friends and even celebrities. That glimpse, just like a glance over a neighbor's fence, can elicit strong feelings and responses on our part. One study determined that the presence of low-sum (less than $150,000) lottery winners in certain neighborhoods could lead to bankruptcy among non-winning neighbors. Researchers in Canada and the United States found that the neighbors of lottery winners had a higher probability of bankruptcy because of increased conspicuous consumption, financial risk-taking and excessive borrowing.[61] In essence, because they were trying to "keep up with the (winning) Joneses."[62] Our digital world has even created a hashtag to represent this, #FOMO, or "fear of missing out."

This habit of continually comparing ourselves to others promotes envy and worries of loss of status, resulting in social angst and authority ranking, directly influencing our relationship with social classification. As an antidote, we're better to compare ourselves to who we were yesterday instead of who someone else is today.

A considerable amount of consumption in our society is driven by envy, resulting in social competition and the insatiable drive to acquire things and seek status. This push also results in a drive to defend our possessions, physical integrity, relationships and self-opinion. American cosmologist Carl Sagan (1934-1996) postulated that people would go to extremes to protect their self-opinion, even claiming to have been abducted by aliens. Sagan saw this as a mid-20th century version of religious apparitions that existed for centuries prior, in many cases, to shield the victims of sexual abuse. Some would claim to have been 'visited' by a spiritual or demonic figure. These claims would protect the guilty of such crimes—often a family member—while protecting the victims from retribution and providing them with some degree of celebrity and compassion without their having to disclose the violation.

What drives much of our behavior is the desire to have control over our circumstances. This, too, has developed through human evolution, as we've continuously needed to master certain aspects of our environment to ensure consistent sources of food, warmth and shelter. We've equally developed a visceral need to feel a causal link between what we do and what we get. This leads us to develop the need to influence people and events in our immediate environment, which lessens our sense of vulnerability and lets us to see life as being more predictable than random. We do this by developing work skills and ethics that enable us to become indispensable to others and secure employment, giving us a sense of control over our future. Finally, this process allows us to seek and maintain a certain status level compared to others in our immediate circle.

We often seek social status through attention-grabbing activities and voiced opinions. Social media platforms provide a digital soapbox from which we can do this. LinkedIn allows us to proudly display our work achievements or exhibit our skills and accomplishments; on occasion, allowing us to vent before a mostly sympathetic audience. Twitter allows us to communicate information and promote our views. It also lets us shout down others who don't have the same views as us or demonstrate how important our opinion is simply because we have one that can be transmitted instantly to a broad audience. In extreme cases, it also facilitates virtual public shaming through show trials in the court of public opinion. On Facebook and Instagram we show others how cute our pets are, how ardent our love for our spouse is, and how great our vacation was. On those platforms we also share our losses and vent our frustrations.

Above all, social media enables us to demonstrate our moral superiority, which is a form of status-seeking. An often-seen theme of such moral usurpation is, "I keep insulting my (fill in the blank: coworkers, spouse, family members, friends), but I swear they deserve it." Reflecting some of the emotions that dominate posts, some social media platforms could very well be renamed *Bitter*, *Fakelook*, and *Instaregret*.

This pernicious cycle of social status-seeking results in a type of anxiety that permeates our online existence. Feeling that we can't conform to society's ideals of success in general and having this validated through social media, we become anxious. We feel unworthy because we haven't convinced people in the virtual world of our perceived worth. We then resign ourselves to being envious of those who have the outward trappings of success, while viewing ourselves with a certain tinge of awkwardness, if not outright embarrassment.

In his 1997 book, *Emotions, the Social Bond, and Human Reality*, American sociologist Thomas Scheff labeled shame, in its role as the opposite of pride, to be *the* social emotion, later qualifying it as the "master emotion of everyday life."[63] Pride, in the authentic or justified and not hubristic sense, is the positive or pleasurable emotion we experience thanks to recognized accomplishment. Shame is its cynical, painful opposite. Together, they drive us to act within socially acceptable ways, working as a pair of emotional guardrails. Both are rooted in the processes of how we internalize, perceive or imagine how others view us, contributing to social competition and status-seeking while providing a path for a personal sense of dignity. Of the two, it's shame that has a greater influencing role on us, as we will do more to avoid pain than to seek pleasure.

This social competition is further exacerbated through economic inequality. People need to feel valued and capable, able to contribute to their own situation to feel self-actualized. American psychologist William James (1842-1910) qualified this when he wrote, "The deepest principle of human nature is the craving to be appreciated."

Inequality and the excesses it brings contribute to anxieties already present in those with less. Social status then becomes an integral part of their identity, fueling evaluations of themselves and others through their level of perceived economic position and in-group condition. What results is a form of public stance or defense that attempts to shore up a person's confidence in the face of those anxieties. This can result in enhanced, exaggerated self-promotion and increasingly egocentric activities, fueled by unhealthy narcissism that at its base is insecure.

Unhealthy narcissism manifests itself particularly amongst younger people, especially males, through muscle cars, stone faces and sunglasses, fast driving, hypertrophied muscles, menacing facial and neck tattoos, oversexualized attitudes, and—the most dangerous manifestation of all—possession of a handgun. Young men who illegally possess and carry a firearm do so as a response to the perceived need for respect, willing to risk their lives to maintain their apparent self-worth. These activities are examples of responses to the drive to preserve the social self by being vigilant to threats that may challenge social esteem and status.

Being rank, recognition and status-conscious, we develop strong and ambivalent feelings towards others, especially those in leadership and authority roles. This ambivalence towards those in authority stems from an unconscious association to our parental figures and those having power in or sway over our lives. On the one hand, we recognize the need for leaders and authority; we're lost without them. But we tend to fear and despise those above us, afraid they will misuse their privileged position to accumulate more power and enrich themselves at our expense. We secretly envy the perceived power they yield, as well as the apparent recognition, privileges and benefits they enjoy.

Of MISE and men

Of all the individual groups I officiated during adult hockey tournaments, the three most challenging to referee were police officers, teachers and churchgoers. It didn't matter whether they were men or women, when it came to respecting the rules of the game and especially the authority of a referee, as soon as they donned their skates, members of these three groups were, for the most part, belligerent, ignorant and the total opposite of what they projected in their work and social lives. Their examples demonstrate the ambivalent and polarizing views they held towards authority figures; in some cases authority they, themselves, exercise in their work lives.

Think about how you feel when a police car is following you while you're driving. You see it in your rear view mirror and a low-level sense of foreboding and dread may descend over you. Although you go the speed limit and haven't committed any infraction, you're concerned about being pulled over, about the police officer abusing their authority, writing a ticket, arresting or even hurting you. This is a feeling that many people—myself included—can feel in such a situation. These feelings reflect our ambivalence toward authority.

Because our envy rarely manifests itself openly or directly, we continuously seek narratives or story lines to justify our feelings around it and other sentiments that can be perceived to be negative. With envy and covetousness, we develop a secret desire to negatively affect, wound or steal from the envied person to right some perceived inequity. This personal desire alleviates our envy and sense of inferiority by providing a temporary outlet to address the inequalities, even if only in our minds and for the moments that we dwell on them, sometimes even obsessing about them over extended periods from days to years.

National intelligence services have long known about the powerful motivating effect of envy and covetousness in individuals, playing upon the painful emotions resulting from the embarrassment of accepting one's perceived inferiority. To develop confidential human sources such as moles, double agents and fifth columnists, intelligence services have targeted four human weaknesses based on envy: money, ideology, sex and ego, collectively known in the industry as MISE (pronounced "mice"). Intelligence officers working abroad target unsuspecting individuals and attempt to ascertain their level of dissatisfaction and discontent with their present circumstances by collecting sensitive information that may help to compromise them.

In the late 2000s, during an official event that required me to interact with a delegation of senior Russian Interior Ministry officers, I met an embassy staff member I later learned was an intelligence officer. When I told him that I had worked in Haiti with Russian police officers, he claimed to be interested in that country's situation. Given that interest, I thought nothing of his invitation to go to lunch in the days following the event.

During our lunch-time discussion, he gently inquired into my financial situation, political opinions, relationship with my wife and general satisfaction at work. I found certain lines of his questioning somewhat intrusive but intriguing, because he appeared to be generally interested in me, my work and my personal life. I subsequently learned the real intent and structure of the Russian's questions. His inquiries focused on my perceived feelings of inadequacy, fueled by envy and covetousness. It was a subtle attempt to survey my level of discontent and determine if I could eventually be bought.

Childhood trauma and disappointment combine with social anxieties and envy to make for a potent cocktail in the form of rage, feeding the Jungian Shadow Self. On a trip to France in 2015, I discovered a political tract on a streetlamp. It was a small rectangular sticker in red, white and black with the following text (translated from the French): "In the face of misery and exploitation – ORGANIZE YOUR ANGER – Join the Young Communists."

I gently peeled it off. Our French hosts were a tad perplexed when I decided not to rip up the sticker but keep it instead.

Elias Canetti (1905-1994) was a Bulgarian-born, Austrian-raised British citizen who won the Nobel Prize for literature in 1981. In his 1960 anti-totalitarian work entitled *Masse und Macht* ("Crowds and Power"), he wrote:

> One of the most striking traits of the inner life of a crowd is the feeling of being persecuted, a peculiar angry sensitiveness and ir-

ritability directed against those it has once and forever nominated as enemies.

The Young Communists poster now graces the door to my basement home office as a constant reminder of how powerful and perilous envy in a group setting can be. I also found it a poignant example of the disaffection that the youth of the past, the present and the future can and will continue to have when fueled by individual trauma and feelings of inferiority.

Understanding how we interact with groups of any size is essential as we try to understand human nature, particularly our response to those interactions. We're drawn to groups because they have specific effects on us as individuals. As social beings, we have a desire to be part of a group. As members of any group, we also need to perform and showcase our abilities and competencies to other members. But we must also be alive to the emotional and social contagion of those groups. As mentioned earlier, groupthink can and does occur, and, especially in larger groups, can result in what we can call 'hypercertainty' leading to intellectual blindness. This state occurs when a group determines its view to be the only right one, not allowing doubt or opposable ideas to affect its decision-making.

Because of the sheer number of people in groups and the various forms they take, unless there's a concerted attempt to direct reasoning, people in group settings don't engage in nuanced thinking or in-depth analysis of issues. The larger the group, the more difficult this becomes. People gravitate towards the emotional and being swept up by the excitement and the promise presented by the group dynamic at the time. This dynamic is often characterized by overreaction as opposed to calm, reflective study and assessment.

Group thinking also tends to be simplistic, because of the challenges in communicating complex ideas to many people. Each group member has different intellectual abilities, understandings and knowledge of the issues presented. Decision-making in a group setting is often based on exaggerated opinions and fears or uncontrollable excitement, sentiments that an individual or authority who simplifies matters for easy intellectual digestion can easily exploit.

We must be mindful of the sway that groups, large and small, have on us and our decisions as individuals. In those groups where individual voices can be heard, such as at our work, in our families and particular community settings, we must encourage divergent opinions, gently steering group discussions in a rational, productive and collaborative manner. This must begin with the detachment of our emotions from those of the group. This is where a strategic approach over a tactical one is vital. Focusing on calm and patient reflection allows group members to arrive at the best decisions possible, absent the constraints or sway of emotions and impulsiveness.

Envy, empathy and finding echoes of another in oneself

Regarding the more passive form of envy, in the late 19th century, Friedrich Nietzsche coined the term *schadenfreude* (German for "harm-joy")– to describe finding joy or feeling smug about someone else's misfortune. It's a dark feeling we all experience. Extreme versions of *schadenfreude* would probably count as evil or sadism, going well beyond the passive version. Whether seeing and regaling in another team receiving a penalty, watching a work colleague stumble in a promotional competition or witnessing a bully getting their comeuppance, we delight in their misfortune. Celebrity magazines sold at supermarket check-outs are exceptional at providing us with regular doses of *schadenfreude* as we get to see inside the perceived lives of those celebrities we think we know intimately and of whom we're secretly envious.

This emotional response is not the sole purview of any particular ethnic group, but has permeated all human societies. The Japanese have a saying: "The misfortune of others tastes like honey." The French speak of *joie maligne*, a diabolical delight in other people's suffering. In Danish, it is *skadefryd* (malice or glee), in Mandarin, *xìng-zāi-lè-huò* (to take joy in calamity and delight in disaster), while in Russian, it's *zloradstvo* (malevolence or gloating).

The ancient Romans used the term *malevolentia*, giving us the words malevolent and maliciousness. Earlier still, the Greeks described *epichairekakia* (literally *epi*, "over," *chairo*, "rejoice," and *kakia*, "disgrace"), leading Olde English in the 1500s to briefly adopt the word *epicaricacy*, meaning rejoicing or deriving pleasure from the misfortune of others.

To deal with our envious nature and urges, we must be alive to the envy in ourselves and others. We must transform our compulsive desire to compare ourselves and our station in life to others into something less harmful and more positive.

One way to do this is to compare ourselves to those with less. By seeing those with less financially, physically, intellectually or emotionally, we can begin to appreciate what we have. Another way is to admire the excellence in others with whom we associate daily. Seeing their success as a benchmark and goal to aspire to affords us positive encouragement. A third way is through empathy, which is the opposite of envy. By focusing on others, suspending judgment and truly understanding their situation —how hard they worked or how much they sacrificed—we can truly comprehend how they arrived at their unique place in this world.

The final way is through gratitude, which is likely the best antidote to envy and narcissism, both individual and collective. By appreciating what we have and what we are, we can be satisfied with our life without being envious of others.

Passive envy mostly manifests itself through backhanded put-downs, and in insults through passive-aggressive behavior. As the term indicates, such action aims to express negative feelings such as anger, frustration, annoyance and envy indirectly instead of directly. This allows the passive-aggressor the opportunity to vent those feelings of frustration while masking the envy underlying them.

When passive-aggressive actions are limited to comments, we can afford to ignore them, tolerating them as an inevitably unfortunate part of social interactions. This implies that, as we obtain more responsibility and promotions in work or community spheres, we must be prepared to feel the effects of envy from those we care about most: friends, colleagues and family. This becomes all the more challenging when the envy is no longer passive but active.

As the first line of defense, we must learn to recognize and decipher active envy. We do this by learning the signs of envy that humans express, being cognizant of who in our immediate circle is more predisposed to it and understanding what can trigger it. By being mindful of passive envy, we can develop anticipatory mechanisms that will allow us to avoid the pitfalls of active envy. This defensive approach applies to others' envy and understanding when we, ourselves, act out of envy, both passively and actively.

Envy, our own and others', is best dealt with through its opposite— empathy. And the requirement for empathy is greater today than at any other time in history. Empathy is the ability to gain a deep understanding of another's feelings or problems. Unlike sympathy, which manifests itself through sentiments of pity and commiseration, empathy allows us to understand what another is going through, recognizing their challenges while being willing and able to offer some form of support and help.

That support may be simply listening to the individual as they vent their frustrations, helping in some concrete way or even assuming some of their burdens. The ancient Greek philosopher and polymath Aristotle (384-322 B.C.) surmised that the level of empathy we can feel towards another's misfortune is directly proportional to how easy or difficult it is for us to imagine ourselves, under similar circumstances, making a comparable mistake or being in a similar situation.

But empathy alone doesn't counteract the negative feelings that *schadenfreude* presents. What's required is to feel genuinely good about another's success in life, known in the Buddhist and Hindu traditions as *mudită*, the vicarious pleasure one derives from other people's well-being. In German, the closest word would be *mitfreude*, meaning deriving pleasure from seeing others succeed. In practical terms, this means allowing others to taste success by letting their best ideas percolate and encouraging actions on their part.

However, empathy is not enough to obtain *mitfreude*. What's required is compassion: a visceral desire to assuage another's pain willingly. To act in such a way, we must first be able to deal with our own issues effectively. Second, we must have the abilities and resources to deal with the other person's issues.

We do this by having the abundance mindset and the explicit recognition that we have enough to deal with our own life's challenges. We don't need excessive riches or even a steady income. We just need to feel comfortable with what we have.

In his book *Enough: True Measures of Money, Business and Life* (2010), American investor and business magnate John C. Bogle wrote that enough is always one dollar more than we need. This is the opposite of the paucity mindset, the first cousin to the victim mindset. Empathy, compassion and the abundance mindset are thus all manifestations of our better side.

Accurate self-awareness comes from our ability to understand both our better and Shadow sides, such as when we derive joy from someone's plight or failings. The key is to understand and come to terms with our Shadow Self while tapping into the energy that would be spent attempting to repress it. We do this through channeling that energy to more productive ends, such as deep introspection and courageous execution, leading to improving ourselves, others and our lot in life.

The human brain is hard-wired to be a sense-making machine. As social animals, we create rules to allow us to operate in social groups. Those rules stem from the sorting of things and people into various categories: little and big, young and old, quiet and loud, familiar and unfamiliar, beautiful and ugly, good and bad. Once we have sorted the things and people in our lives according to these categories, we assign them a value. Little things are manageable, big things intimidating; young things cute, old things venerable; quiet things safe, loud things rattling; familiar things comforting while strange things are threatening. We focus on those things that can potentially cause us grief and pain, as they are essential for our survival. We also focus on those things that allow us to thrive.

These are examples of how cognitive and inherent biases are used and maintained if not adequately understood and countered.

The challenge for us as human beings is to watch and understand others, all the while trying not to judge them in comparison to ourselves, sidestepping our envious urges and delight in their failures, replacing our feelings with visceral empathy and satisfaction in their success. The key is not to assign a value to them or ourselves, but to recognize what they are by embracing the social landscape they and others form around us.

Although we may wish to interpret them, their actions and words aren't designed with us or our individual situations specifically in mind. We need to view people and their actions as being facts of nature that exist and can't be changed simply because we want them to.

In this sense, it's never about us. The social ecology will ensure that there will always be idiots, egomaniacs, narcissists, caregivers, rescuers and saints. This requires us to avoid the tendency to focus on social stratification while embracing all the opportunities and challenges that come with that social ecology: uncertainty, frustration and inevitably conflict.

Stupid is as Marlo does

Marlo was a well-educated, good-looking, multilingual lawyer. He had studied at a prestigious European law school before doing his master's degree at one of Canada's best universities. Young, sociable, articulate, handsome and an impeccable dresser, Marlo had a certain charm about him that exuded confidence and erudition.

When people first met Marlo, they were immediately smitten by his suave manners and approach, as well as his apparently high intellect. Marlo enjoyed hobnobbing with people of rank and stature. Marlo always had an opinion about everything, especially about himself and his outstanding contributions to the organization he worked for.

The reality, though, was that Marlo was a poor performer who would spend inordinate amounts of time and effort going down rabbit holes. Responsible for disciplinary prosecutions of police officers, Marlo would charge a defendant police officer with the most serious infractions conceivable, seeking to end the careers of individuals who didn't deserve such treatment. Instead of being the morally-upright individual that the position demanded, Marlo's personality was severely slanted, spilling over into his judgment when dealing with everyone.

You see, Marlo was a narcissist. And a manipulator. And a sociopath. He lived and breathed the "Dark Triad" of personality disorders that served up the soul's fast food to almost everyone with whom he interacted.

When Marlo would send an email, which often contained a long passage about himself and his supposed contributions, he would expect and demand a reply in the following minutes, or hours at most, especially from his immediate supervisor. When things went wrong, Marlo would blame everyone else for his failings, often using his position of power to overcome opposition despite evidence to the contrary. Whatever Marlo wanted, he usually got, providing he yelled loud and long enough. One of Marlo's favorite tools was using harassment complaints to force his supervisors into giving him higher work appraisals or, at the very least, leaving him alone and unaccountable.

Quickly, colleagues learned to avoid Marlo at all costs, feigning ailments to forestall working with him or asking for transfers to other units to ensure they wouldn't be subject to Marlo's constant blame and toxic accusations. After ten years in the organization, Marlo had gone through six different supervisors, laying harassment complaints against every single one of them because they didn't give the superior, ego-boosting evaluations he felt he deserved.

When I became Marlo's supervisor, I was just another one of his intended targets. It wasn't a surprise, as I'd been warned before I assumed the role. Rather than meekly accepting his harassment complaint about a sub-par work evaluation, I submitted a counter-complaint, in proper legal fashion, for bullying from below.

Tired of the constant battles and never receiving credit for the "exceptional" work he'd done over the years, Marlo eventually left the organization, looking for adulating fans to impress and victims to intimidate elsewhere in another organization on another continent.

When dealing with this type of Marlo, our goal is to counter their negative side by limiting the damage they can cause. By being consistently firm with them in our expectations and reactions, we create the necessary boundaries in which they can operate. The key is for them to realize that they can't manipulate or cajole us into doing their bidding.

By laying a foundation that inhibits their negative side, we can slowly direct them into more constructive pursuits. We make sure that all agreements made with this Marlo are clear and specific. We use a team approach; we shouldn't have to do this by ourselves. We deal with their issues on our own schedule, not according to theirs.

Most importantly, we protect ourselves when dealing with such individuals. We are careful about what we share with them and set and maintain boundaries so we don't become a martyr, their martyr.

One of the lowest points

Sociopathy, per the Mayo Clinic, is the mental condition in which a person consistently shows no regard for right and wrong and ignores the rights and feelings of others. Sociopathy is termed an antisocial personality disorder, but 'antisocial' is often a misnomer, as these people tend to be actually quite sociable, using their advanced social skills to charm and manipulate people to obtain what they want. An asocial individual, who shies away from social activities, is very different from an antisocial person.

As antisocials, sociopaths are hard-wired to antagonize, manipulate or treat others harshly and with callous indifference and superficiality in the pursuit of their own goals.

Some of the standard features of sociopaths are their glibness, superficial charm, grandiose sense of self, and lack of remorse, shame or guilt. Most telling of all is their lack of empathy and inability to form close social attachments. Many are daredevils, not afraid of defying death, ignoring their loved ones' repeated pleadings to stop their dangerous activities.

Others can be qualified as 'lovable rogues.' Their trademark is that of fearlessness, as they are not afraid of social conventions or consequences. No surprise, then, when *Newsweek* reported on a 2020 study out of Brazil that sociopaths were more likely to refuse to wear a mask and conform to other COVID-19 measures to protect others.[64] Since they don't care about others, risky behavior is second nature to them.

In the hierarchy of antisocial behavior, one step above sociopaths is the psychopath, who's essentially an extreme sociopath. Examples abound: "The Dapper Don," John Gotti Jr., the Canadian mass-murderer Paul Bernardo, and his equally murdering ex-wife, Karla Homolka.

Not all sociopaths are psychopaths, though, as some can form attachments to others in ways that psychopaths can't because they have some limited degree of compassion. Psychopaths can't distinguish between conventional rules (e.g., laws in society or rules in sports that are authority-dependent) and moral rules (e.g., social conventions or mores such as not hitting someone who wears glasses or holding a door for an older person, that are authority-independent). Psychopaths are morally blind; they cannot understand ethical demands applying to them, but they definitely see them applying to others.

As a police officer, I've dealt with a few psychopaths during investigations for various crimes. However, one of the most blatant examples I ever came across was, sadly enough, a former police officer.

In the early morning of December 29, 2009, 51-year-old Ottawa Police Service Constable Ireneusz 'Eric' Czapnik was stabbed to death while parked in his police cruiser just outside the Emergency Department of the Ottawa Civic Hospital in Canada's national capital. He was brutally and mercilessly killed by an individual who, just over a month earlier, had been ordered to resign from the RCMP for a second time. I was one of the co-prosecutors in that second disciplinary matter.[65]

Following his murder, I, along with several hundred RCMP members attended Constable Czapnik's funeral on January 7, 2010, at the Ottawa Civic Centre. This was one of the lowest points of my policing career. The shame other members of the RCMP and I felt that day (and continue to feel) because of the actions of this former-colleague-turned-murderer is indescribable.

Members of both the Ottawa Police Service and Constable Czapnik's family were gracious and understanding during and following the service. Not once did a member of the Ottawa Police Service say anything disparaging to us; instead, they, thanked us for our presence. His widow, Anna Korutowska, displayed grace, poise and benevolence during the entire period leading up to and after the funeral service.

During this nadir in my career, I saw the worst and the best of human nature: the worst portion of one's Shadow Self and another's magnanimity, its polar opposite.

Lies, damn lies and statistics

Police officers' on-duty deaths, although relatively few compared to U.S. statistics, are common in Canada. Police officers die on-duty because of heart attacks following overexertion and in vehicle accidents. Some die because of homicide.[66] And far too many die because of suicide.

Statistics are rare regarding the exact number of active and recently retired police officers who die by suicide every year in Canada. Still, it has been estimated that the number can vary between 20 to 30. Compare this to the number of people who die in interactions with police in Canada.

Inspired by *The Washington Post's* police shooting database[67], Canada's national broadcaster, the CBC, did their own research and established what they labeled the "Deadly Force database."[68] Unlike the *Post*, the CBC included all deaths resulting from, during and following interactions with police. It's intended to keep track of deaths resulting from direct and causal interaction with a law enforcement officer where some form of force was used. It doesn't include in-custody deaths, self-inflicted wounds resulting from suicide, attempts to evade police or accidental police-related deaths such as traffic accidents. Despite this, the CBC's scope was considerably larger than the *Post's*, which only captured data around the fatal discharge of a firearm by American police.

The CBC's basic conclusion was that "Black and Indigenous people are disproportionately represented amongst the victims compared to their share of the overall population. The data also finds that most of those killed in police encounters suffer from mental illness or substance abuse." The CBC determined that 68 percent of people who died in police encounters were suffering from some form of mental illness, addiction or both.

When I was the chief of Halifax Regional Police, I asked our dispatch center to provide me with statistics on calls for service they received during periods of six months in 2015 and one week in 2018. On average, Halifax Regional Police receives more than 100,000 calls for service a year.

According to the analysis in both those years, only 12.5 percent of all calls for service involved responding to any form of criminality. The remainder involved diverse requests for service, including numerous mental health calls. Like many other North American jurisdictions, our three main policing issues revolved around mental health, substance abuse and at-risk youth. So, the finding that 68 percent of people who died in police encounters were suffering from some form of mental health or addiction was not surprising.

According to Canada's 2016 Population Census, 1,198,540 people of sub-Saharan African descent live in Canada, representing 3.5 percent of the total population. The same Census also lists 1,673,780 people of First Nations, Métis and Inuit heritage living in Canada, representing 4.9 percent of the Canadian population.

The initial CBC report contained information from 2000-2017, indicating that Canadian police officers had fatal encounters with 461 people, an average of just over 27 people a year. During these 18 years, of the 461 people who died during police interactions, 43 or 9.3 percent, were Black. Of those 43 people, 33 were armed with a weapon. An analysis of the cases of the ten unarmed Black people who died indicated that three resulted from a struggle with police, who initially deployed conducted-energy weapons. Police were cleared of wrongdoing in these cases. Four deaths were the result of natural causes such as cardiac arrest and cocaine-ingestion. No charges were laid in those cases either. Two resulted from a physical altercation in which the police officer punched or beat the person while subduing them. In one of those cases, the officer was charged with manslaughter but later acquitted.

The last case was a result of an accidental firearm discharge. The police investigative oversight body of Ontario, the Serious Investigation Unit (SIU), determined that, contrary to the CBC's report of the individual being shot in the back, the individual was shot in the chest during the scuffle. The SIU determined that there were no grounds for criminal charges against the officer involved.

CBC's research also found that 69 people, or about 15 percent of those who had died in police interactions, were Indigenous. Of those 69 people, 57 were armed while 12 were not. Of those 12 unarmed people, four died because of an overdose of some drug before the altercation. The police had not applied force against them. Five died after the use of a conducted energy weapon, pepper spray or physical aggression to effect an arrest. Three died after being shot: one was shot after ramming a police vehicle; one after placing the police officer in a headlock during a struggle in which the use of the telescopic baton and pepper spray had no effect; and the final one after several individuals had swarmed the lone police officer during a traffic stop. All the officers were cleared of wrongdoing in these last cases. The report's information didn't indicate how many individuals died from what's known as "suicide by cop."[69]

Statistics Canada, which is responsible for compiling statistics for the federal government, including organizing and carrying out a national Census every five years, reports that in the 2017/2018 fiscal year (April 1 to March 31), Canadian police received 12.8 million calls for service. This figure doesn't include police proactive interactions such as traffic stops, check stops, event security, school visits and community engagement activities. If we were to increase that number to, say, 15 million total police interactions per year (because of the additional police-initiated work), we'd see that death results in only 0.00007 percent of all interactions between police and individuals. The CBC reports that the number of fatal encounters per one million population had varied from 2000 to 2020 from less than 0.5 percent to just over 1.0 per million inhabitants.[70]

To add some perspective to this, 10 Canadians die every year because of lightning strikes. On average, there are 1,000 job-related deaths per year in Canada, although some reports indicate the actual number to be ten times that amount and include commuting fatalities, deaths from occupational diseases and unreported deaths.[71] In 2020, almost 16,000 Canadians died because of COVID-19. It's estimated that between 30,000 and 60,000 Canadians die annually from medical errors alone.[72]

This isn't intended to absolve police officers from those few incidences in which police actions are responsible for a person's death. Errors occur and people must be held to account. But the CBC's numbers and analysis imply that race was the main factor in the use of force by police, which is disingenuous. Even more telling is that, according to the statistics, almost as many active and recently retired police officers die by suicide every year in Canada as individuals who die in interactions with police.

The statistics around those few cases where unarmed individuals die from an interaction with police and the number of police officers who die by suicide paint a grim picture. Police need to continue to strive for no deaths, no harm, no bias and no mistrust of individuals who interact with them, along with no death and no harm amongst the officers themselves. At the same time, traditional media should be accountable for the bias and mistrust they breed through such reporting. The situation in the United States differs for many reasons, not least because of the significant differences in population (10 times that of Canada's), the historical and social contexts of that population and the omnipresence of firearms, to name but a few reasons. This difference also manifests itself in the number of people who have succumbed to COVID-19 (more than 345,000 in 2020 and 500,000 in 2021), including numerous police officers. During the first two years of the pandemic, media reported that COVID-19 was the principal cause of line-of-duty-deaths in the United States. As per the *Officer Down Memorial Page*, in 2020, at least 245 American law enforcement officers had died from the disease while in 2021, that number was 301. In both years, this is more than all other causes combined, equaled only by police officer suicides.[73]

Cheap views versus actual news

During my tenure as police chief, I was surprised at the number of times traditional media outlets called our Public Information Officer to ask if there was anything to report, as they were having a slow news day. We were often one of the few consistent sources of news for local media. Police, like many other professions, are now part of the entertainment industry known as traditional media or 'infotainment'. Media often report on police actions as live theatre, whereas police officers work in earnest, frequently providing their last full measure of devotion to their communities. Their intent isn't to provide entertainment.

In 2018, I attended a reception sponsored by the CEO of one of Canada's national news outlets, Torstar Corporation, a media company with significant interests in newspapers and news media. I accepted the invitation partly because I had delivered the company's flagship newspaper, the *Toronto Star*, as a young carrier in the 1970s.

The CEO, an amiable and seemingly pragmatic person, explained some of the challenges facing traditional media in the 21st century, including citizen journalism, the decline in advertising revenue, the 24-hour news cycle and the advancement of online digital platforms. He explained that the 24-hour news cycle only really has enough information for about 60 minutes of actual news reporting. The remaining 23 hours have to be filled with analysis, which often goes beyond objectivity and is purely conjecture and subjective.

This confirmed what I had seen over the years: opinion is cheaper and more plentiful than actual news. That also means that personalities and influencers are slowly replacing news organizations as the internet gradually morphs into the real world.

In some instances, when personal opinion goes beyond objective analysis, it has been defended as "moral clarity," where individual journalists, talk-show hosts, editorialists and bloggers claim to be the purveyors of truth and denounce those who disagree with their positions as flawed. They display a distinctly inquisitional quality in their arguments. This is evident in what some individuals claim to be the "contrarian media" on both sides of the political fence. Self-righteous moralizing risks antagonizing the other side in any debate, thereby entrenching existing ideologies. It doesn't contribute to rational discussions about important subjects. Such 'moral clarity' is possible because it's politically unaccountable.

In her book *The Argument Culture: Stopping America's War of Words* (2012), Deborah Tannen writes:

> The argument culture urges us to approach the world—and the people in it—in an adversarial frame of mind. It rests on the assumption that opposition is the best way to get anything done: The best way to discuss an idea is to set up a debate; the best way to cover news is to find spokespeople who express the most extreme, polarized views and present them as "both sides"; the best way to settle disputes is litigation that pits one party against the other; the best way to begin an essay is to attack someone; and the best way to show you're really thinking is to criticize.

As chief of police, I met with media representatives on three occasions to discuss their concerns about how we presented information to them for their use. I realized the importance of our contributions to their livelihood, as we provided them with the necessary information from which they formed their reporting. I would always tell the individuals assembled (journalists, and the odd news anchor and news director) that my priority and responsibility were to report those items of problem-oriented public interest, not entertainment-oriented public curiosity.

Looking at me quizzically, they replied that the notions were the same for them. For me, the two concepts were very distinct. Public interest supports society's goal of improvement, while public curiosity bolsters news reporting as a means of entertaining people.

I left these meetings with a better sense of their needs and wants, but with the impression that, unlike their take on the relationship, we were doing them a favor and not the opposite.

We all have at least one

We live in nature, which is dynamic, asymmetrical and ever-evolving. We must also deal with human nature, which is interactive and social at its core. So it makes sense to study human nature to understand what drives others, through proper observation and analysis of their character while seeing into our and their depths as people. This means recognizing and gauging our and others' motivations, expectations and emotions. Our goal is to become more self-aware, rational and productive.

Easier said than done, especially when we live in a society subject to life tribulations with others. Nietzsche qualified this state of affairs when he wrote in his book *Beyond Good and Evil* (1886): "Madness is something rare in individuals—but in groups, parties, peoples and ages it is the rule."

One of the most uniquely frustrating aspects of human nature is plain stupidity. We're always left asking ourselves, why did that person (maybe even ourselves) act in such a way? Thus far, our friend Marlo has shone the spotlight on their activities as being, for the most part, stupidity personified, causing pain, suffering and loss while rarely, if ever, gaining or contributing anything in return.

In his superb short essay, *The Basic Laws of Human Stupidity* (2019), Italian economic historian Carlo M. Cipolla provided a formal definition of a stupid person: someone who harms others without procuring any gain for themselves, perhaps even suffering a loss in the process. He wrote:

> Our daily life is mostly made of cases in which we lose money and/or time and/or energy and/or appetite, cheerfulness and good health because of the improbable action of some preposterous creature who has nothing to gain and indeed gains nothing from causing us embarrassment, difficulties or harm. Nobody knows, understands or can possibly explain why that preposterous creature does what he does. In fact there is no explanation— or better, there is only one explanation: the person in question is stupid.

Contrast this with the much more predictable individual who attempts to gain something from harming you, be it to rob you of your money or to attack your dignity to advance their ideological aims. Cipolla labels this latter type of person the *Bandit.* We can also add the qualification *Idiot* to this grouping as someone who does or says something to another to obtain an advantage, usually only an increased sense of self-worth. On the opposite end of the spectrum are those he labels the *Helpless*, individuals whose actions actually benefit another while incurring a loss to themselves. The last type of person is the *Intelligent*, the individual who helps themselves and others they interact with.

Cipolla graphs the actions of these individuals, assigning quadrants to each one while defining their activities.

One of the more intriguing features of Cipolla's short essay (it's written in large font, with only 22 lines a page for a total of 78 pages) is his premise that "stupidity is an indiscriminate privilege of all human groups and is uniformly distributed to a constant proportion." That means that if we were to assign a percentage amount to represent the number of stupid people in society, let's say 20 percent (just to pull a *Pareto* number out of the air), then one would find in any group, large and small, 20 percent of its members as being stupid. That would include police officers, hockey referees, politicians, university professors, economists, entrepreneurs, journalists, snowplow operators, Hollywood movie moguls, lawyers, garbage collectors and judges.

People talk about how important diversity is and how any public service or commercial enterprise should reflect the communities it serves. In regard to stupidity, some public and private entities may actually be over-represented in this area.

Cipolla was not as brazen as I to suggest a percentage; instead, he used the Greek letter 6 (lowercase Sigma) to designate the number of stupid individuals. But he did state that we always tend to underestimate the number of stupid people in circulation.

We should view Cipolla's text as a cautionary tale presenting five constants:

1. Stupid people cause pain to others and themselves.
2. They come in all shapes and sizes.
3. We should never underestimate their numbers in society.
4. A stupid person is the most dangerous type of person there is.
5. Because they are so dangerous, avoid dealing with them.

Cipolla's crucial point is that the numbers or the individuals themselves are not static; a person can be rational one day and stupid the next. Think of the times when you 'lost it,' when you acted in a way that caused pain to others and yourself with no net positive outcome for anyone.

This is what we want to avoid. We want to avoid being a stupid person, a difficult person, an impossible person.

Stupidity can result from many character traits, including overconfidence. One identified cognitive bias is the *Dunning-Kruger Effect.* This occurs when we act quickly, with little knowledge of a subject. We become overconfident and think we know a lot about the subject. This bias was identified through research done on the case of McArthur Wheeler, who had robbed two Pittsburgh banks at gunpoint on the same day in 1995 without any disguise.[74] He had simply applied a coating of lemon juice on his face, reasoning that since lemon juice could be used to make invisible ink, it could also be used to make his face invisible to surveillance cameras. He was quickly and peacefully arrested at his home that evening for the robberies—a perfect recipe of error, hubris and stupidity.

Because of the abundance of TV shows and films that detail crimes that are resolved in ninety minutes or less (including commercials), public opinion about real-life police investigations is subject to what's known as the *CSI Effect,* also known as the *CSI Syndrome.* This is directly related to the *Dunning-Kruger Effect,* as it leads people to believe in investigative simplicity thanks to the presence of some forensic evidence that's sufficient, in their minds, to confirm guilt. Real investigations are complex matters that entail extensive fact-finding and fact-verification processes involving months, if not years, of hard work.

However, if we were to avoid one quality above all others, like the plague, it would be what American professor and author Robert I. Sutton wrote about in his book *The No Asshole Rule.* Sutton advocates active screening, reforming or (if we cannot reform them) getting rid of people who willfully demean and damage others in the workplace. He also writes that having all the right policies and procedures is meaningless unless we treat the person right in front of us, right now, in the right way. This includes individuals who are true victims of such intentional behavior.

Sutton's final words of advice: don't promote them and don't be one yourself.

So, the question becomes: Is Marlo stupid? Or is Sutton's classification more applicable? Using Cipolla's template, the answer depends on whether or not they gain anything from their actions. If they do, then

217

Marlo is just opportunistic, mean, criminal or bandit-like. If they don't, then Marlo is plain old stupid or idiotic. In both instances, Sutton's classification can apply to their behavior as well.

But regardless of what Marlo does, they're most likely manifesting portions of their Shadow Self. Carl Jung further describes the Shadow Self as that unconscious part of our psyche that houses our most base desires, some of which reveal that we might not be as good or virtuous as we think we are. For Jung, it's essential to bring this dark side to the level of conscious awareness, where we can do something about it. Continuing to repress it only brings trouble. As we've seen, in extreme cases, the Shadow Self can become evil personified.

Can a person be intrinsically evil? We have wrestled with that question for centuries. One of the early debates was between two Confucian thinkers, Mencius (380-289 BC), considered to be a qualified optimist, and Xunzi (313-238 BC), considered to be a qualified pessimist. Mencius viewed humans as inherently good and that any evil they manifested was the fault of societal influences. Xunzi took the opposite tack: he viewed humans as fundamentally evil, suffering from grave personality defects resulting in egoism, envy, jealousy, laziness and violence. For Xunzi, the darker side is innate, while the good side is developed through societal pressures.[75]

Such a debate revolves around actions and thoughts that are used as a barometer for evil. The most evident of such examples involves killing another.

David Buss, a psychology professor at the University of Texas, studied such ideas. After finding out that one of his colleagues had murderous thoughts, Buss wondered how many people really have them. He asked the students in his introduction to psychology course whether they had fantasized about murder. Buss found that about three-quarters of them had. Next, he surveyed 5,000 people worldwide and discovered that 91 percent of men and 84 percent of women have thought about killing someone in some way.

Buss's research tells us that we all have "specialized psychological circuits that lead us to contemplate murder as a solution to adaptive problems." We almost all have homicidal fantasies in our lives at one time or another because having them has allowed humans' survival during times of significant threat. It is an evolutionary construct.

Know thyself

The key to dealing effectively with our human nature is to know our character thoroughly so we can break out of our obsessive and irrational habits and better control our actions and life. It also requires displaying and living *mitfreude* while gravitating towards those individuals who do so as well. By acting this way, we can benefit from their abundance of character to further develop ours and contribute to others. But sometimes we can't connect with such individuals, either because they are rare or because of other reasons such as disagreements or hostility, which can rule a workplace.

As part of living with people in society, there are bound to be moments of friction, confrontation and conflict. Rather than shy away from them, we must embrace those moments as opportunities to grow. This is the lesson of conflict.

Calls from the blue line

- Our habits collectively form what's known as human nature. And human nature, as the wellspring of our personality, begets our behavior.
- Unlike mutual funds, with human beings, *past performance is indicative of future performance. We,* rarely do something just once, especially something forbidden.
- We must deal with human nature, which is interactive and social at its core. Study human nature, through proper observation and analysis of people's characters, to understand what drives others, while seeing into our and their depths as persons.
- Watch and understand others, all the while trying not to judge them relative to ourselves, sidestepping our envious urges and delight in their failure, replacing those reactions with visceral empathy and satisfaction in their success. It's better to compare ourselves to who we were yesterday than with who someone else is today.
- People in group settings don't engage in nuanced thinking or in-

depth analysis of issues. The larger the group, the more difficult this becomes. People gravitate towards the emotional and get swept up by the excitement and the promise presented by the group dynamic.

- Envy is another human evolutionary response to scarcity and survival, driving us to attain things, seek power and try to dominate others to allay our fears, often at others' expense.
- Envy can manifest itself in two ways: actively and passively. We deal with our envy by being aware of its presence, admiring and being inspired by others' excellence, comparing ourselves to those with less, demonstrating empathy and regularly exhibiting gratitude.
- The key to dealing effectively with our human nature is to know our character thoroughly. Then we can break from our obsessive and irrational habits to better control our actions and life.
- We can all be stupid at one point or another in our lives. Our overall goal is to avoid being like Marlo: a stupid person, a difficult person, an impossible person all the time. In a word, we want to avoid being an asshole.

8: The lesson of conflict

Create a workplace where time wounds all heels.
-Julius Henry "Groucho" Marx,
American comedian and actor (1890–1977)

Hellish heaven

When I graduated from the RCMP's Training Academy in 1988, my first posting was to a small detachment in the province of Québec. The area was beautiful, situated in a valley just south of Québec City and immediately north of the border with the State of Maine. There were ski hills in the winter, opportunities to canoe, swim and bicycle in the summer. It was a quintessential Canadian rural lifestyle, almost angelic in its splendor.

In all Canadian provinces and hundreds of Canadian municipalities outside of Ontario and Québec, the RCMP acts as the front-line police service. In Ontario and Québec, the RCMP has a discrete, mostly non-uniformed presence, responsible for federal statute investigations involving drugs, customs, immigration, organized crime and national security. In my first role as a police officer, I was a federal investigator.

My detachment was small, comprised of a corporal, the detachment commander and four investigators, all at the constable rank. For most of my time there, the most senior constable was a singular individual who had several personal issues that spilled over into his work life. He was an outgoing individual who enjoyed talking on the phone to anyone who would listen. And he enjoyed the occasional drink. During the detachment commander's absence, be it on training, work or vacation, the senior constable would replace the corporal.

Not being much of a drinker myself, I'd avoid going out to bars on the weekend, partly because many of the individuals we investigated went to the same bars, and partly because I just couldn't afford it as a young police officer. The senior constable would invite the other members and me out for drinks. Some would join him; I wouldn't.

One day at work, he took me aside and told me that he and the others in the detachment had problems with me because I wasn't social enough. The fact that I didn't go out to drink grated him. In his estimation, if I wasn't willing to drink with my workmates, then I couldn't be trusted. He believed that I was fundamentally a good worker but should be placed in a corner to do independent work by myself, separate from everyone else.

As time went by, I started seeing problematic and even unnerving behaviors from the senior constable. Things went missing from my desk. I was advised of important developments in investigations only at the last minute, if ever. When we effected arrests or conducted investigations, the senior constable became unnecessarily aggressive with individuals, leading to yelling matches which could have been avoided. He ignored and treated me and another constable he didn't like with disregard, talking negatively about us behind our backs and, on occasion, directly to our faces. He raised his voice and even kicked a garbage pail in the office when making a point.

When he was acting detachment commander, I was never sent on a single training course. At the time, I attributed it to cutbacks; the reality was that he ensured I never received any training in order to undermine me.

Slowly but surely, the work environment became more difficult and harder to tolerate. His actions and treatment began affecting my morale to the point I prepared to leave not only the RCMP but policing altogether.

In response to the lack of training, I applied to law school. I updated my résumé and sent it out to various organizations, waiting for a job offer before leaving the RCMP. I went to see the senior-most non-commissioned officer in charge of our area, a staff sergeant, to advise him that I would be leaving the Force.

The staff sergeant was an affable man in his 50s who had lost his 11-year-old son to cancer a few years previously. Hung in his office just beside his desk was a pastel portrait of his departed son. Every time I went into his office, I thought about how benign my problems were in comparison.

When I apprised the staff sergeant that I would be leaving the RCMP as soon as I secured another job, he immediately inquired why. I advised him of the difficulties the senior constable caused and my inability to deal with him effectively. I thought that if the experience I was living in my first detachment was indicative of the organization as a whole, I didn't want to continue working for the RCMP.

He asked if I wanted to lay a harassment complaint. I told him I just wanted to work in a place devoid of such constant, overt meanness and disrespect. He asked me to delay any decision, allowing him to intervene.

The following week, he and the sub-division commanding officer visited the detachment. Shortly after that, I was offered a transfer to Québec City to be closer to my studies. I accepted the transfer and ended up staying in the RCMP, working another 20 years.

After I left the detachment, I realized a few things. First, a bit of empathy and compassion, just like that shown by the staff sergeant, went a long way. He listened to my concerns, validated them and then acted on them, all in a prompt manner. It was an approach that I would follow in the years to come as a police leader. Second, I was responsible for my reaction to things that occurred to me. Finally, I knew how to deal with conflict with the general public but not with work colleagues. I recognized my inability to deal effectively with conflict when I was directly involved in it. Growing up, I had shied away from confrontation, avoiding bullies and those who perpetuated conflict.

I'd become a police officer to ward off bullies in society. I just never thought I would be working with one of them.

Finding conflict

The basis of most interpersonal conflict in life is unresolved anger and an excessive concern for self on the part of one or both of the antagonists. For the most part, unresolved anger stems from three sources:

- childhood trauma and abuse
- unmet expectations and disappointment
- grievous loss of love, including the physical absence or death of parents, siblings or a significant other

These sources affect each individual differently. But the one area that I saw that fueled interpersonal conflict the most was childhood trauma and abuse.

When I met individuals who were overtly hostile to police officers, and individual officers who were antagonistic towards supervisors and management as a whole, I saw a consistent bitterness and resentment: they were mad at some authority figure who had hurt them sometime in their past—a coach, a teacher, a church leader or, more likely, a family member or parent, especially their father. Sometimes, a third party had harmed someone else; the individual internalized the harmful actions as if they had happened to them, spawning resentment.

In late July 2013, I was walking in uniform on one of Halifax's main streets on my way to a meeting. I came across a nondescript man who looked at me and said matter-of-factly, "F--king Nazi!"

He kept walking and so did I. As someone whose mother had converted to Judaism while growing up, I was struck by the brutal senselessness of such a display. Nothing in my own past or on that street that day could have justified such a comment.

The best that I could figure out was that the individual was reacting to an individual's shooting death by a Toronto police officer a few days prior. The police officer was eventually charged and convicted of the shooting.

On a Friday in the summer of 2016, I worked an overnight shift in our Prisoner Care Facility. It wasn't a particularly busy night, but it did have its fair share of drunk individuals.

One stood out that evening. He was a local university student who was exceptionally aggressive. As soon as he entered the facility, he became verbally abusive and taunting.

While he was being searched, I provided backup in case he tried anything against the searching officer. At one point, he looked at me and spat out, "Your mother must be embarrassed about what you do!"

I replied that my mother had been dead for some 30 years.

Without pausing, he retorted, "She's probably in hell, giving Satan a blowjob!"

These two incidents were poignant reminders of the abuse that police officers regularly deal with, simply because they are doing their job.

Constant bitterness in the workplace leads to loss of productivity, while resentment leads to loss of relationships. Both can contribute to adverse health outcomes such as depression in individual employees. In turn, this outcome leads to loss of overall health and, in some extreme cases due to existing pathologies and other issues, even premature death.

That bitterness and resentment can become even more acute in a crowd setting. In such an environment, each anonymous person in a sea of many can feel relieved of any personal responsibility, leading to acts of violence that would rarely occur if the person were alone or with their friends and family.

Outside of the home, the most insidious form of violence can happen in the workplace, a space we expect to be devoid of such problems. Most workspaces are free of serious conflicts such as harassment and violence, but, unfortunately, conflict can exist in any place where people converge to work.

Weaponizing the complaint process

Workplace conflict is often the result of three things:

1. Misinterpretation of and disagreement about organizational or unit objectives
2. Poor application and misunderstanding of the processes and methods to reach agreed-upon goals
3. Difficult personalities, personality disorders and poor interpersonal chemistry

Conflict is not limited to employees, but can also occur between employees, clients, stakeholders and partners. The first two sources are responsible for the vast majority of conflicts.

We should welcome healthy friction or intellectual conflict related to an organization's best interests and shouldn't avoid it. This type of conflict manifests itself through robust, respectful dialogue and the competition of ideas, not personalities. It's particularly important to encourage open and honest discussions around controversial topics. If we manage the conversation properly, positive results ensue that propel the organization or work unit forward.

But not all conflict is healthy.

As a senior police executive, for a good part of my career, I dealt with police officer misconduct and misbehavior. This was because of the multiple positions I held and the increasing importance of police accountability in the law and society. Such misconduct would be denounced through internal or external complaints. These complaints often resulted from conflict within work units and conflict between police employees and members of the public.

Unlike many police officers, I didn't work long as a front-line uniformed officer. I spent my early years working as a plain-clothes federal investigator and then a supervisor. I knew many officers who spent entire careers working every day with the public and who faced a barrage of criticism, some justified, most not. Along with that criticism came public complaints. Some complaints were justified, while many others were simple fabulations.

I investigated numerous complaints over the years. I found that many of them were animated by the complainants' desire either for revenge on the police officer or civilian employee with whom they had interacted or to have the legitimate ticket or charge laid against them withdrawn.

I never had a public complaint leveled against me, but I did have three internal complaints: one because I dared to ask someone how they were doing, another because I was honest with a person's performance and yet a third because I had apparently concocted a conspiracy to displace the complainant from a tenured position. All three complaints alleged supervisor harassment on my part. In all the cases, the complaints were eventually deemed to be unfounded.

A word about harassment: it can and does come from those in authority. But it can also come from below. One common thread permeated all the *unsubstantiated* complaints I investigated from subordinates towards their supervisors: these were all individuals who had significant behavioral issues and had decided that they would 'bully from below' by leveling complaints and assigning blame for their failings on others. Bullying from below is a common action by individuals when they're confident that processes protect them and allow them to impose their worldview on others by projecting their flaws and failings elsewhere.

An unfortunate and unexpected result of trying to level the playing field and make things equitable for everyone has been the weaponization of complaints processes to bully and harass subordinates, peers and especially superiors. We've all come across individuals who are rude, arrogant and lack fundamental self-awareness of the impact of their conduct on others. Some even resort to official complaint processes to continue their abusive ways, continually documenting every interaction and in some disturbing cases, surreptitiously recording conversations between them and others.

I saw this happening regularly, to the point where individuals used important legislative processes to vent their grievances, such as through Human Rights Commissions or whistle-blowing legislation. When not satisfied with the results of a supervisor's decision, an internal investigation or probe, or if the union representing them refused to advance a grievance because it had judged the complaint baseless, the individuals turned to a legislated regime such as a provincial Human Rights Commission, claiming some protected right as a means to lay a complaint.[76] They could also use the mainstream media to advance their cause, following up with social media to their extended entourage.

This situation isn't limited to police services.

In a recent court decision that could be qualified as unique, the College of Physicians and Surgeons in Alberta suspended a surgeon for three years for persistently disruptive behavior, such as not following established protocols, openly criticizing colleagues and weaponizing complaints processes against colleagues. The provincial appellate court was tasked with the appeal of the finding of professional misconduct. In dismissing the appeal, the appellate court held that the appellant committed disruptive behavior, including weaponizing the complaints process against colleagues, use of excessive criticism of others and failure to follow through on complaints that had been initiated. This disruptive behavior and related conduct warranted discipline from his professional body.[77]

In investigating various complaints against employees over the years, I realized that I had to learn to become accustomed to interpersonal friction, incivility, conflict and, on occasion, collision. Collision is the most acute form of conflict, in which one or both parties involved employ extreme measures such as violence.

I also noticed that police officers were more inclined to intervene in a bar fight than to deal with a poor performer or toxic employee. I wasn't unlike my work colleagues in this area. But I decided to read and learn as much as I could about dealing with demanding, uncivil and impossible people, and about workplace conflict in general.

I then determined that I needed some hands-on training in dealing with conflict in a controlled arena, so I accepted a work colleague's invitation to become a hockey referee. There I saw conflict almost every time I set foot on the ice, between players and towards officials from players, coaches and fans alike. On several occasions, in addition to separating players engaged in fights, I had to separate parents in the stands who were yelling at one another, coming close to fisticuffs.

Marlo's menagerie on ice: emotional vampires, well-intentioned dragons, clergy killers, and more!

Marlo likes hockey. Marlo played hockey year-round on the ice in an arena during his childhood, on ponds and in driveways, watched his favorite NHL team on TV and dreamed of "going to the Show" as a professional hockey player. When that dream didn't materialize, Marlo decided to coach while his son climbed the minor hockey ranks. Marlo's son played at highly competitive levels and was even drafted by a major junior hockey team, one step below the professional ranks.

Marlo coached a series of competitive hockey teams. So far, it sounds like Marlo had his stuff together.

The only issue was that Marlo had a sour personality and was bitingly critical of the work of his players, fellow coaches and officials. He yelled obscenities at young players during and even after games, never offering a word of encouragement. Referees dreaded having to interact with him as he continually challenged calls, was condescending to younger officials and sarcastic towards older ones, regularly blowing things out of proportion. Perhaps most sad in all this was that, in addition to being an elite hockey player, Marlo's own son was a hockey referee as well.

Marlo became a journeyman coach, as team after team let him go because of his poor behavior and mean attitude. Even off the ice, Marlo had developed a permanently gloomy appearance, pushing people away from him. Whenever confronted about his negative attitude and vitriol towards referees, Marlo would always reply, "Nothing personal."

When one is the aggressor, it never is. Marlo took what was a great game and made it into his personal vendetta. And conflict was his tool.

Marlo came to epitomize those who make life challenging for others—in some cases, a living hell—to advance their own goals. We've all met these people. Many a book has been written about them. They've been qualified as difficult or impossible people, even sociopaths, with such stylish sobriquets as *Emotional Vampires*[78], *Workplace Neanderthals*[79], *Well-Intentioned Dragons*[80], and *Clergy Killers*[81]. Regardless of their appellation, these people make work and general life exceptionally challenging for everyone around them.

Dealing with this type of Marlo requires a particular approach.

- First, we must be able to recognize and identify their behaviors.
- Second, we must come to learn their background to understand

what drives the behavior.
- Finally, armed with that information, we must deal with their be-haviors, directly and indirectly.

It's one thing as a referee to deal with a coach or player's disrespect or other negative actions by warning them, assessing a penalty or ejecting them from the game. It's another thing to deal with individuals who have authority over us or use established processes to continue their abusive ways. In such contexts, we must learn to identify the behavior and influ-ence it to impact the here and now.

But first, we have to understand the why behind their actions.

Communal refereeing

Why are some people more difficult than others? For the most part, peo-ple cooperate and get along with their family members, neighbors, work colleagues and even strangers. This is how our economic and social sys-tems operate: through the goodwill of those involved and those partici-pating. As a police officer, I was always amazed by how little conflict ac-tually occurred in society, especially in large urban centers where people don't know one another. When I read the shift reports detailing the num-ber and types of crime in any given twelve-hour period, I was surprised by the few times there was reported conflict between people that spilled over into the criminal realm and requiring our assistance.

But inasmuch as people can and do cooperate in a collegial, coopera-tive manner, there are always those who choose not to or, more aptly, simply can't. These people do their best to conceal their envy, character flaws and insecurities, projecting those qualities onto others, leaving a trail of victims wherever they go. For the rest of us, this means dealing with personalities that make things complicated and trying to compre-hend how conflict takes hold. Part of that process involves understand-ing how conflict can occur.

In 2000, when I was working in Manitoba with the RCMP as the in-terim commander for Portage la Prairie Detachment (about an hour to the west of Winnipeg), I was fortunate enough to visit a Hutterite colony. Hutterites are one of three major Christian Anabaptist sectarian groups, the others being the Mennonites and the Amish.[82] In Canada, over 34,000 Hutterites live in 370 separate communal farms, each called a colony.

Unlike Mennonites, who tend to be integrated in rural and urban set-tings throughout North America (unlike the Old-Order Mennonites in Central and South America) and the Amish who eschew modern ameni-ties, living apart from mainstream society, the Hutterites embrace mod-ern technology while living communally. On average, each colony con-tains about 13 families with a total population of around 100 members. When a colony's population approaches 125 to 150, the colony divides, creating a new, additional colony. This occurs on average every 16 years.

This limited size allows every colony member to know everyone else, facilitating strong social cohesion, which encourages strict adherence to religious beliefs, family values and exceptionally productive work ethics. Although I can't say there was no crime in the colony I visited, I knew the colony's calls for police service were few and far between and often lim-ited to negative interactions caused by outsiders. The colony members were able to take care of most of the internal friction, pre-empting any interpersonal conflict. This is relatively easy when everyone is busy working, studying or devoting their time to family and religion. And when everyone knows everybody else.

In all my time living and visiting communities throughout Canada, the United States, Haiti, and elsewhere in the Caribbean, I've never seen a more efficient and cohesive social system as in that Hutterite colony. When I asked the local teacher why and at what point the colony subdi-vides into two colonies, she couldn't immediately answer, preferring to say that they "just knew when it was time." Little did I realize that I'd find the genesis of an answer regarding conflict in this Hutterite colony in writings on social structures.

As we've seen, humility is an important quality to have when develop-ing our character and intentionally building relationships. But is humility enough? Are we capable of building and maintaining an infinite number of connections without suffering from task saturation (doing too many things at one time) or hitting the wall of our cognitive abilities? How many times have we run into an old friend whom we've not seen for a long while and been unable to remember their name, despite recognizing their face and even recollecting specific important facts about them? Their name simply escapes us.

Well, there are a couple of things at play here. One of them is what is known as contextual memory. Think of contextual memory as being like brain RAM (random access memory). Our contextual memory can be af-fected by physical and health issues and the effects of drugs and fatigue. It also has its temporal limits. This includes remembering names and events that we may store for a limited time during which we needed that specific bit of information: the name of the host of the party we've never met previously nor will ever meet again, the temporary password we were assigned to log onto a website, or where we parked our car at the mall. This doesn't mean we can't recall these bits of information, but once the need for the information is gone, so usually goes the info. Even if we think we remember the information, we most likely don't. Remember that memory is more reconstruction than it is recollection.

The other thing to keep in mind is that, unlike commercially available computers equipped with dual, quad, 12 or even 24-core processors, we humans are strictly mono-core processors. We can only do one thing at a time and our speed of thinking is limited. Multitasking has been one of society's great myths, perpetuated by each successive generation for the past 50 or more years. Rather than doing several tasks at once, we simply shift our attention between the tasks we're doing at any given time, precisely as a computer does; only a computer can do it considerably faster.

On occasion, we suffer from something known as the *Stroop Effect,* in which processing the information around one task can cause interference with another.[83] We can only do one thing at a time and can't effectively and equally divide our attention between two conscious activities.

To save time, I iron my shirts while I watch football. As soon as the play is whistled down, I get back to ironing. I am sequentially doing two things at the same time: ironing, watching football, ironing, watching football (and occasionally over-ironing my shirts). A quote attributed to Austrian composer Wolfgang Amadeus Mozart (1756-1791) aptly summarizes the best approach to this quandary: "The shorter way to do many things is to do only one thing at a time." Especially when it comes to developing relationships, we're limited in how much we can do.

Finally, our ability to maintain an extensive network of friends is restricted by cognitive limitations. What constitutes friends has become somewhat convoluted in the world of social media, in which people can have thousands of virtual friends, followers and contacts at the touch of a button. For our discussion purposes, let's stick to real people we can meet in person with some degree of regularity or have a meaningful exchange with using technology.

Robin Dunbar is a British anthropologist, evolutionary psychologist and specialist in primate behavior. Through his studies of the correlation between brain size and group size, Dunbar and his colleagues have determined that humans can only manage a network of 150 meaningful relationships at any given time, recognizing the names, particularities and links among those 150 people to know them and influence them. This is known as *Dunbar's Number*.

According to Dunbar, the number 150 has remained constant from early hunter-gather societies to today. It includes a broad assortment of modern groupings such as residential campsites, military units and even Christmas card lists.[84] Dare to exceed 150 individuals in any grouping, and the network is unlikely to last long or maintain its cohesion.

According to what's known as the "social brain hypothesis," humans can effectively maintain an average of six layers of contacts or networks, in which there are:

- Five loved ones
- 15 close friends
- 50 friends
- 150 meaningful contacts
- 500 acquaintances
- 1,500 recognizable people

Extroverts tend towards these networks' outer boundaries, spreading themselves thinly across their numerous friends and acquaintances, while introverts gravitate towards less, more significant relationships. Although there's some criticism of what exact number of meaningful relationships really can exist, one thing is clear: because of our finite time, energy and resources, the number of relationships we can build and maintain is also limited.

From a practical perspective, Dunbar's Number provides us with some guidance regarding group work. If we need a committee to decide on something such as hiring an individual, we should limit the number to five people. If we're looking for ideas through brainstorming, we should expand the group's size to between 12 and a maximum of 15 people.

But what does this have to do with conflict? American geographer and author Jared Diamond explained in his 1997 book *Guns, Germs & Steel— The Fates of Human Societies* that all existing large societies have complex centralized organizations, such as communes, city-states and countries. One of the reasons for this centralization is to deal with the issue of conflict between unrelated strangers. The larger the group, the more difficult it is to have and maintain relationships with people who can mediate potential disputes.

According to Diamond, in a group of 150 people, there's a potential of

11,175 two-person interactions or dyads (150 people times 149 relationships divided by two people in any relationship). This presupposes
that all individuals of a group interact with one another at least once
during any given period. Each dyad represents a potential source of conflict. When strangers in large groups quarrel, no one is present with
enough interest in both parties to mitigate the conflict. Societies of hundreds or more people can exist provided they develop what Diamond describes as a "centralized authority to monopolize force and conflict resolution," such as police and a judicial authority or system. Further, he
maintains that a large society must be structured and centralized to
reach decisions effectively by managing those conflicts.

Diamond acknowledges that when people have no interest in resolving social conflict, they won't participate in the process. By not having a
relationship with one or both pugilists, combatants or litigants, they
have nothing to gain or lose by being involved. Hence, no skin in the
game and no interest in the outcome. Conflict is part of social groupings;
so too, then, is its mitigation.

American-born Canadian author and activist Jane Jacobs (1916-2006)
wrote about public safety, which she coined "public peace," in her seminal work *The Death & Life of Great American Cities* (1961). She wrote
how public peace is kept through an imperceptible network of voluntary
controls and standards among community members and enforced
through social cohesion. The more a neighborhood is closely knit with
strong interpersonal relationships amongst its residents, the higher level
of safety it enjoys. Various community-led mutual aid initiatives promote
individual dignity, self-reliance, and civic pride and engagement. But
when a neighborhood is subject to high population turnover or when little to no social cohesion is present, people don't have the inclination to
know or care about one another. Consequently, this undetectable, casual
community enforcement breaks down, resulting in the need for police.

During my term as police chief, I sat on several volunteer charity
boards. These board appointments afforded me the chance to see the importance of social cohesion, how people vested in the betterment of their
communities could genuinely make a difference, whether it was through
community gardens, late-night downtown safety walks, violence inter-
ruption or soup kitchens. What mattered was that people took the time
to know their neighbors and be involved in their community life instead
of living in separate cocoons. Social cohesion not only wards off crime
but is critical during crises like natural disasters. This social cohesion
was evident in the Hutterite colony I visited.

Although I couldn't find any published research demonstrating the link between Dunbar's Number and the size of a Hutterite colony, I suspect a strong correlation exists between them. What the Hutterite teacher qualified as an instinctive response to subdivision was most likely related to the colony's limited ability to manage conflict and the members' ability to influence one another. Once the colony was no longer able to manage conflict and promote sufficient social cohesion successfully, its members instinctively knew it was time to form another colony.

This was an excellent example of conflict mitigation, which we don't do enough individually or collectively.

Competing and condoning

We all suffer from conflict avoidance at some time in our life, be it at home or work. We may try to avoid conflict, or there may be short periods in our life, depending on where we are and our age, when we attempt to steer clear of it.

In general, we tend towards conflict avoidance because we grew up being encouraged to 'get along'. At times, social pressure promotes avoidance of conflict, as does the desire to appear to be on the side of equity, fairness, peace and cooperation with one and all. Better to look the other way than cause or encourage further friction.

The unfortunate reality is that the only real way to avoid conflict of any type is not to have friends or acquaintances. That way, you rarely have to deal with anyone except those who come looking for you.

Not everyone follows the path of conflict avoidance, however. Fraudsters, hucksters, shills, bullies and abusers all thrive on friction, confrontation and conflict. They know that most people will shy away from it, allowing them to benefit from people's wariness in this area. At a political level, in today's polarized environment, being a centrist is fraught with hazards because of the extreme positions taken on both sides of the political spectrum, left and right. People expect us to have an opinion, and they use this to determine if we're part of their in-group or out-group. This turns off those most likely to be able to contribute while encouraging those most likely to judge. As W.B. Yeats (1865-1939) wrote in his poem "The Second Coming", "The best lack all conviction, while the worst are full of passionate intensity."

The challenge is that life is a constant competition, whether we like it or not. As the opposite of cooperation, intended for collective safety, security and companionship, competition favors individual growth, enhanced status and acquisition. Where there is competition, there is bound to be conflict.

Remember what we learned in English literature class about the three great literary conflicts: person versus nature, person versus person and person versus self. There are two other conflicts that many modern politicized types would add: person versus the state and person versus technology. British authors George Orwell (1903-1950) and Aldous Huxley (1894-1963), both masters of dystopian literature, would have been proud of those last two.

Some have even added a sixth conflict: person versus supernatural, which fits into the comic book and wizardry realms, supplemented by extraterrestrials and superheroes that are so popular today in films and books. The Old Testament story of Jacob wrestling with an angel shows that this is a conflict type with a long history.

Just as literature reflects society and its values, conflict plays an integral part in our culture and values. We're in constant competition with ourselves, others and, to a lesser extent, with nature. As children, we vie for the love of a parent or the favor of a teacher, a position on a sports team or status in a social setting. As adults, we compete for a job, a promotion, a spouse and further acceptance from our peers, all the while dealing with the most obvious biological manifestation of nature in human beings, that being our aging.

In addition to normal life events such as growth spurts, puberty, pregnancy, muscular atrophy, macular degeneration, hormonal changes, weight gain and finally, death, we are also plagued by our fragility, beset by aches, injuries and sickness. As these normal life stages imply constant competition with others and nature, our response to all this competition is determinant of the type of life we live. Ambition, assertiveness and aggression are all parts of the human nature we manifest, as they provide us with the means to compete. And that competition often leads to conflict with others.

But we shouldn't view conflict of any kind as being solely negative. Just as we strive to encourage diversity of thought for better decision-making, we individually require robust dialogue to develop the best ideas and courses of action. That includes having discussions, interactions and negotiations that at times may be forceful, vigorous, and, most assuredly, frustrating. It means encouraging intellectual dissent because it's the competition of ideas that brings about the best decisions, not the competition of personalities. This is the basis of what's known as the dialectic method: arguing back and forth, seeking to understand the contradictory sides of an argument to eventually arrive at the reality or truth from two or more conflicting or opposable ideas through constructive tension. The key to this is assertive inquiry: exploring existing views, including those that run counter to our own.

As we have seen, today's leaders must be more than mere managers because we're not just managing things, we're managing people. Good, responsive leaders are attuned to the views of their clients, stakeholders and especially colleagues as they go about their daily work.

To do this, we need to act like diplomats, deploying the requisite subtlety to deal with the various personalities within our sphere of influence. When we manage people, we also manage their expectations driven by their emotions and motivations. These are at the core of their and our personalities. This becomes even more critical during periods of crisis, large and small, organizational and individual. And nothing makes a crisis more acute than interpersonal conflict.

These past few years have seen a welcome growth in intolerance for most forms of abuse, intimidation and prejudice, including harassment of all types, be it sexual, psychological or physical. At one end of the spectrum are offensive jokes, images and microaggressions morphing into more insidious acts leading to overt aggression: think of the classic pin-up posters in a repair garage work pit or a barbershop, the ridicule and scorn couched as good-natured ribbing, the autocratic exclusion and controlling of work schedules and training, open conflict such as harassment and bullying, and, finally, workplace collisions or violence in which a disgruntled employee injures, maims or kills co-workers. All these examples are comparatively straightforward to categorize and, to a certain extent, deal with. Depending on the situation, that's the role of procedures, strong management and quick reactions in enforcing policies and the law.

The key is not to condone something by saying nothing or by being neutral. Anything you choose to ignore, you tacitly approve of. Condonation (the act of condoning or tolerating something) has three elements:

- being in a position of authority
- knowing what's occurring
- failing to act on what we know

We judge leaders by what they knew, when they learned about it and what they did about it. Leaders cannot afford to be neutral when dealing with problems; they tacitly approve of anything they ignore. And one of the most problematic and neglected areas of human resource management is in the areas of poor performance and interpersonal conflict.

In the workspace, when is the line crossed between being demanding and being harassing? Many a conflict has resulted from a misinterpretation of the two by the individual subject to supervisors' requests. The supervisor crosses the line when actions and words go beyond being directive, demanding and exacting, and become humiliating, demeaning and controlling. Instead of being supportive, actions and words become vindictive.

Everyone agrees that yelling, debasing and humiliating an individual alone or in front of others is a form of harassment. And yet, what do we see on reality TV shows, be it people living together in a big house or a penthouse apartment, on an island or having a restaurant or bar "rescuer" coming in to make changes? They yell, scream and debase others publicly.

These aggressions also play out regularly in the news, on social media, and in online games and movies that delight us in vivid portrayals of conflict of all sorts. And we, the viewing public, just eat this up. Perhaps it's because we secretly wish for an outlet of our Shadow Self through such extreme manifestations.

This isn't a new phenomenon reserved exclusively for today's society. In the past, people attended public executions and punishments, not for their deterrent effect but as a form of entertainment. We're no different. Online platforms add to this as we can participate in heated and hostile debates and character assassination through the cover of anonymity, devoid of in-person contact and responsibility. Technology has simply provided innovative ways for people to express their aggression with little or no social cost associated with such venting.

Unlike reality TV or docudramas, our reality doesn't involve a film crew following us around. The question, then, is what should a reasonable work colleague or manager do to ensure adequate professional results from others? And, more precisely, what should they not do?

Contrary to reality show rescuers and participants, leaders shouldn't scream, yell, curse, kick at things, slam doors, point fingers or bang their fists on a table. These are willful acts of unbridled aggression. If we lose our temper, we lose people's respect. The Hispano-Roman Stoic philosopher Seneca (4 B.C.-65 A.D.) wrote that "Gladiators are protected by skill but left defenseless by anger." This applies to leaders who must control their emotions, including anger, when dealing with their colleagues.

Second, leaders shouldn't belittle anyone in front of others, including openly talking trash about someone behind their back.

During the winter of 2003, as an aide-de-camp, I was assigned to escort Manitoba's Lieutenant-Governor to a community event. I was driving his limousine; the Lieutenant-Governor was with his wife in the back seat.

A portly, successful businessman who thought very highly of himself, the Lieutenant-Governor wasn't happy with the service of one of the other volunteer aides-de-camp, a civilian restaurant owner. During the drive to the evening's event, the Lieutenant-Governor openly spoke of this other volunteer's work performance. The aide-de-camp supposedly wasn't punctual, didn't attend enough functions and was a mediocre driver.

This left a poor taste in my mouth and had me wondering about his opinion of my own work ethic. I didn't have to wait long to find out, as the Lieutenant-Governor eventually contacted my commanding officer, leaving a long-winded voicemail message complaining of the same lack of commitment on my part. I soon resigned from my position as a volunteer.

When trying to determine what the line is between being demanding and being harassing, the question to ask is whether the individual's dignity has been preserved. If the actions, words or intentions of the manager or work colleague are intended to resolve poor performance in a confidential, constructive and respectful manner, there's no fault. But if an individual is openly ridiculed in a way that intimidates them or others, then the line has been crossed and this is harassment.

Critical to this process is maintaining **purpose** for the organization, for others and for ourselves.

Leaving the wire in search of purpose

A few months after retirement, I had a chance meeting in a barbershop (yes, even my chrome dome needs to be professionally sculpted on occasion) with a recently-retired infantry sergeant. Dwayne was 48 years old. He spoke about how he sometimes missed his fellow soldiers and the thrill he received when they "left the wire."

Dwayne had been deployed on five international missions, from ex-

Yugoslavia to Afghanistan, and retired from the Canadian military after 25 years of service. He said that he'd found the integration back into civilian life to be the biggest single challenge for him in his life, what with the monotony of paying bills and taking care of housework and the kids. Dwayne found that what he did in civil society didn't have the same life-or-death importance as in the infantry. He acknowledged missing the intensity of purpose.

I had noticed the same thing during and especially after my deployments in Haiti. It was easier taking care of my basic needs and my security in a land full of threats of criminality, political insurgency, sickness and natural disasters than it was to live a complacent life back home, where others take care of the policing, firefighting, road maintenance and garbage collection. Dwayne was lamenting the absence of purpose in his life that the military had given him. He was still searching for it two years after his retirement.

I asked him what he did to recreate that sense of purpose. He couldn't immediately answer the question.

Dwayne echoed some of the points that front-line journalist Sebastian Junger reported in his book *Tribe* (2016). Junger maintains that hardship and adversity are good for human beings, as we thrive on them. Junger should know. As opposed to merely reporting and commenting on what he read, or witnessing events at a distance, he was a front-line journalist, embedded with US military units in Afghanistan and living the daily challenges the soldiers and marines experienced there.

To Junger, it's not the difficulties, conflict or banalities of life that Dwayne and so many others have dealt with, but the daily meaning we assign to them that counts. When we meet adversity and overcome it, we feel competent, vital and necessary to others.

What humans don't like is *not* feeling necessary to themselves and others; essentially, feeling useless. Junger gave examples of how collective mental health improved during difficult times, such as the London Blitz in 1940, when people confined to institutions left those establishments because they'd finally gained what they didn't have previously: purpose.[85] According to Junger, thanks in part to today's modern conveniences, contemporary society has perfected the art of making people feel not necessary.

After several moments of reflection, Dwayne finally answered my question. He spoke about working out in the gym, and spending time with retired like-minded military and police veterans while remaining on the fringe of mission-centered work through some part-time security job. He asked me what I did to deal with the lack of purpose that policing had previously provided me. I spoke of my regular gym workouts and especially my hockey refereeing. I told him that at times, especially with the older divisions (16 and 17-year-olds), I felt like I was running, or rather, skating, for my life, relishing in the thrill of the game. I spoke of the physical exertion to keep ahead of the play, anticipating puck movements and intervening in scrums and the rare fights while maintaining my composure and avoiding potential injury. For me, this was my way of leaving the wire by having skin in the game.

This discussion confirmed to me the critical importance of having a purpose in one's life. And that that purpose needs to have a physical component as well as a mental one. Be physically, intellectually and socially challenged regularly: officiate a sport, any sport, where you must move and participate in the facilitation of the game; deal with problems that require more than just a passing thought and involve some form of conflict management; commit to a movement greater than oneself that forces you to get out and about while interacting in ways your immediate circumstances would typically not allow; or use your creativity to build something that contributes to the quality of another's life, such as a painting a new home.

The key to growing continually is to provide yourself with frequent challenges and face, on occasion, some adversity and conflict. Adversity comes when you have skin in the game: something to lose or something to gain by your involvement. That's what Dwayne meant when he said he was looking for a purpose beyond the wire.

Remember, we may not choose the challenges and moments of adversity that we face, but we do choose how we react to them.

Good faith isn't always good

One of the best things I ever did from a personal and professional perspective was to go to law school. I went to *Université Laval,* which is in Québec City, one of the most picturesque cities in all of North America.

Founded in 1852 by the Seminary of Québec, an order of diocesan brothers established in 1663, *Université Laval* is the sixth oldest university in Canada. Its law school is one of the oldest in North America and is the oldest French-language law school in Canada. Amongst its faculty's graduates are three Canadian prime ministers, six provincial premiers, eleven Supreme Court of Canada justices and probably more than one police chief.

In the province of Québec, for private law (property, contract, tort and family law), the legal system is civil law and not common law, such as found in all the other Canadian provinces, the United States and elsewhere in the British Commonwealth. Unlike common law, civil law is codified. All the rules related to legal principles, procedure and evidence are found in various legal texts, chief of which is the *Code civil du Québec* ("Civil Code of Québec"). Section 2805 of the *Code* states that "Good faith is always presumed, unless the law expressly requires that it be proved."

For many years, I believed in this principle as it related not only to legal constructs but also to personal interactions with others, thinking that, at a minimum, people were almost always acting in good faith and telling the truth. After all, what about the Golden Rule, which says *Do unto others as you would have them do unto you?*[86]

There are considerable evolutionary pressures on us to assume that others tell the truth, the confirmation bias being one of them. A particular version of the confirmation bias is known as "identity-protective cognition," which states that people process information in a way that protects their self-image and the image they think others have of them.[87] When faced with instructions or direction from a person in authority, we tend to suspend our critical faculties about its legitimacy.

Early in my career, an experienced lawyer I worked with correctly pointed out that this section of the *Code* may be an appropriate legal standard, but it should never be construed as a life principle because we can't assume people will always act in good faith or tell the truth. I slowly learned not to be so naïve around others.

You may live in Edmonton, Houston or Marseilles in a parliamentary, presidential or republican form of government. As such, you live in a liberal democracy. The overarching notions of a liberal democracy can be distilled as follows:

- The actions in pursuit of our interests should not harm others.
- We should allow for the free expression of differences.

These tenets permit the practice of fundamental rights and freedoms while encouraging diversity and inclusion.

However, the challenge is that one person's perception of their rights and freedoms may not necessarily be those of another. This means that there will always be competition and friction between certain rights and liberties. We can qualify these as opposable rights. Examples of this are the competition between individual privacy rights and collective security, religious freedom and state secularism, free speech and gun rights in the United States, and collective health access versus individual paid health access in Canada and other jurisdictions having socialized medicine. These competing rights can only exist when there is respect for their existence.

As mentioned above, the Golden Rule is part of a series of rules, predominantly developed from the Judaeo-Christian tradition, called "The Metallic Rules." They include such notions as:

- The Iron Rule: *Do unto others before they do unto you*
- The Brazen Rule: *Do unto others as they do unto you*
- The Leaden Rule: *Do unto others as others have done unto you*
- The Platinum Rule: *Do unto others as they would want done to them*

and probably the most applicable instruction:

- The Silver Rule: *Do not do unto others as you would not have them do unto you*[88]

The Silver Rule allows members of a liberal democracy to thrive because it instructs us to live and let live and mind our own business, setting aside petty virtue-signaling and finger-pointing. If you want to change, be that change. If you have ideas and are so motivated, work towards the solution by being part of the process instead of merely being a critic.

This includes dealing with others who are different from you, not because of where they're from or their background, but because of a difference in age.

Generational divides

For the first time in recent history, members of up to four different generations congregate, socialize and work together in our workplaces. The diversity between the generations' approaches and cultural mainstays can have consequences in professional environments, leading to tension, friction and misunderstanding. It can also lead to honest and open discussions about social development and progress.

This is because each generation has specific cultural anchors resulting from many factors, not least of which is lived experience. These anchors are that generation's shared tastes, values, whims and trends seen through their fashions, preferences, heroes and even villains. They're less a representation than a manifestation of a generational cohort's inclinations, self-identification and worldview.

As with any in-group, there's inevitable distrust and even envy of out-groups or other generations. We see this in wholesale distinctions between the generations:

- Boomers had all the luck.
- Gen Xers are simply malcontents.
- Generation Y are spoiled and lazy.
- Gen Zers live their lives through their smartphones.

These generational divides also manifest themselves through social media hashtags and memes such as #BoomerRemover, #OKBoomer, #Karen, #echoBoomers and #instaBoomers.

Our cultural anchors influence who we are, what we value, how we act and especially the lens through which we see things. As a member of a particular generation, we each internalize these cultural anchors. As part of the maturation process, each generation wishes to differentiate itself from the previous one, thereby setting a new direction for the world in general and their immediate world in particular. This differentiation results in generational in-group adherence or tribalism.

Islamic scholar and historiographer Ibn Khaldūn (1332-1406) first advanced the notion of intergenerational tribalism across four different generations, each having distinct values that help shape those of the following generation. In his seven-book opus, *Kitāb al-'Ibar*, ("Book of Lessons"), Khaldūn's central concept is that social cohesion (also described as group solidarity or tribalism) results in a pattern of rises and falls of society according to the generation in power. He qualified those four generations as follows:

- The revolutionaries that make a radical break from the past.
- The consolidators who crave order.
- The pragmatists who improve the order.
- The discontents who wish to change the order.

The cycle then repeats itself with a new first generation seeking revolution to overthrow the 'old' order.

This pattern is far from being set in stone. It varies significantly from one society and era to the next, especially with one such as ours today, which is propelled by technology. But that technology isn't evenly distributed and used. Because of their age or lack of available technology, some people are computer illiterate. Although more than 4 billion people have access to the internet, almost half of the world's population doesn't. At least not yet.

Technology through social media, streaming services, television and radio amplify those tribal divisions as each generation lives in a different information universe dictated by their media and platforms of choice. Members of different generations are drawn to various social media platforms that roughly correlate to the type of content they prefer and what they hope to gain from their time online. To gain and retain "eyeshare", applications, social media platforms, streaming services, podcasts, online books, newspapers, magazines and television stations cater to distinct demographic cohorts.

A 2019 survey of generational use of social media[89] queried 627 American social media users in an attempt to understand how social media use varies across generations and what types of content fuel users' social media habits. The finding indicated that 80 percent of every generational cohort use social media once a day. Generation Y or Millennials (born between 1981 and 1996) tend to use more platforms more often. The youngest cohort, Generation Z (born after 1996), tends to spend even more time on fewer platforms.

Image content remains the most popular type of information shared by all generations, with Boomers (born between 1946-1961 or so) posting less of this content than others. As people age, they trend toward using specific platforms, such as Facebook, more than others. There is an inverse relationship for YouTube and Snapchat, with younger generations regularly accessing them while older generations use them less. One thing is clear: all ages use social media to interact with others, with the platform determining how that interaction occurs.

Information and entertainment services such as podcasts, streaming services, newspapers, television and radio stations have developed niches to attract specific cohorts, be it through broad programming intended for younger audiences such as MTV, which targets a more youthful demographic, or VisionTV in Canada, which targets older Generation Xers (1962-1980) and Boomers. Religious programming in radio and television has long been a staple on cable and the airwaves, further using new technologies to broaden its reach, attracting older demographics on average. These diverse platforms shape the discussions around issues according to the particular worldview and anchors of the demographic tribe that adheres to them.

Members of any particular generation share a common view of their history as seen through a lens that allows them to translate how they perceive the present day. Although not static, we can see a particular pattern of sequencing and friction between the generational cohorts. Each cohort has a different worldview based on their cultural anchors. Within each generation, though, some individuals defend existing social constructs and traditions, others advocate for change, while others renounce social structures and practices entirely. The latter group includes individuals who can be qualified as nihilists.

The word nihilism is derived from Latin, meaning "nothing." Nihilism is a philosophical viewpoint that emphasizes the denial or lack of belief towards reputedly meaningful aspects of life, including long-standing values such as community contribution, religious beliefs and positive political involvement. It was born of a diffuse, revolutionary movement in mid-to-late 19th-century Russia that scorned governmental authority, tradition and religion. As the precursor to Marxist-Leninism, nihilism focused on reason, class struggle and radical change in society through extreme measures such as terrorism and assassination.

Today, nihilism manifests itself through two schools of thought. The first school is existential nihilism that proclaims life is without objective meaning, purpose or intrinsic value. The second school of thought is moral nihilism, which asserts that there's no inherent morality in society as today's norms and mores are abstractly contrived through laws and religion.

Nihilists are usually not fond of the many structures, traditions and values that uphold our society, such as giving to charity, donating blood or collective contributions like urban soup kitchens and rural barn raisings. Theirs is a life devoid of commitment to others' betterment, focused on their individual needs and wants. Admittedly, we've all had nihilistic tendencies sometimes in our lives. Individualism, some forms of libertarianism, and narcissism blend to form nihilistic tendencies, putting self-interest, biases and prejudices at the forefront of our thoughts. Amongst nihilists can be found wealthy opportunists and poor anarchists alike, and many others between these two extremes.

Dealing with our nihilistic side requires empathy and the understanding that we can still maintain our individualism within society's confines and constructs, provided we contribute to others. Finding something to believe in beyond ourselves, not based on envy, is crucial to overcoming the self-centeredness that manifests itself in every generation. Individually, we must recognize where our values are anchored generationally, understanding how our generational experience colors our worldview. By resisting or suspending our judgment of other generations, we can see things the way they are, the reality we're currently living. This requires us to maintain a calm historical perspective, recognizing that things will always evolve and always change, not staying in a perpetual status quo.

This approach allows us to avoid the frustration, friction and confrontation inherent when things do change.

No strap here

The lesson of conflict is intrinsically linked to our ability to carry things through despite significant challenges and adversity. By focusing on one thing at a time, we avoid splintering our attention while maintaining our purpose. It also implies being comfortable with being uncomfortable. By stretching our comfort level, we can become better prepared for inevitable change.

The key here is to change, evolve and adapt to the circumstances we face. Just as we develop better fitness through repeatedly pushing ourselves, we must look at our ability to adjust and even profit from disorder, allowing ourselves to move beyond our comfort level. Here our constancy, consistency and persistence of purpose are paramount.

However, this means only concentrating on things within our locus of control. Pushing towards things over which we have no control and out of our sphere of influence becomes frustrating and is ultimately a waste of our valuable time. This is reminiscent of the truncated version of the *Serenity Prayer*, which reads, "God, grant me the serenity to accept the things I cannot change, courage to change the things I can, and wisdom to know the difference."

To deal effectively with conflict, resolving it successfully and equitably, requires superior decision-making skills and advanced empathy. By cultivating diverse views, we can see alternative approaches to problem-solving.

When is the best time to deal with conflict? When the parties are *not* in the throes of emotional disorder. Letting the dust settle and emotions calm down are crucial to resolving any conflict.

Where is the best place? Anywhere that's neutral. When I was chief of police, I would never hear or resolve any grievance or proceed with the termination, disciplining, sanctioning or critiquing of any individual in my office. I would always carry out such vital work in a meeting room. People, even outsiders, viewed a visit to the chief's office as something akin to having to go the school principal's office, minus the strap. So the last thing I wanted to do was to perpetuate such bad memories.

During an early strategic planning session I held as chief of police, one of our staff sergeants spoke of his expectations about me, comparing me to Luke Skywalker in that I was going to challenge the status quo and improve things immediately. As a constant reminder of that discussion and of expectations in general, I placed a light saber on top of my bookshelf. When I would receive visits from dignitaries and community members alike, many would be surprised to see such an item in my office.

I wanted my office to be a place where individuals felt comfortable, safe and welcomed. It wasn't the place to do the challenging face-to-face interpersonal work my position required.

Next up to bat

Once we have a proper handle on those things in our locus of control that we can influence, we can employ the third core competency of leadership: courageous execution. This competency requires decisiveness under uncertainty through the courage of conviction. The key is to go from selfish to selfless in our thinking and actions, to do what's right for the person right in front of us, right now. It implies being accountable to them and us, especially to those values that make up our character. We develop this accountability by embracing conflict, not shying away from it or sloughing it off on someone else. We assume its management and outcomes dispassionately: interested in both the process and the outcome, but not vested in either emotionally.

How we deal with conflict leads us to the next lesson, the lesson of influence. We can now take what we've learned around randomness and complexity, environmental scanning, self-knowledge, and understanding others and apply those lessons to influencing people. There is often no or little difficulty for many people because, for the most part, we deal with collaborative, social beings who want to cooperate and get things done despite their quirks and idiosyncrasies. The challenge is when we deal with people who make things difficult and may seem downright impossible.

This is where the practice of influence becomes trying, and we must be as persuasive as necessary.

Calls from the blue line

- Unresolved anger stems from childhood trauma and abuse, unmet expectations and disappointment, as well as grievous loss of love.
- Workplace conflict results from misinterpretation and disagreement around organizational or unit objectives, poor application and misunderstanding of processes and methods employed to reach agreed-upon goals, and difficult personalities and poor interpersonal chemistry.
- Dealing with difficult people like Marlo requires a tailored approach: identify the behavior, understand the source of the behavior and impact the behavior.
- Multitasking is a myth. Humans aren't like computers; we have mono-core processors, not multi-core processors. Although like a computer, we can only do one thing at a time, we aren't nearly as fast in task sequencing. Stick to one thing at a time.
- Need a committee to make an important decision? Limit the number to five people. Looking to brainstorm ideas? Expand the group's size to between 12 and a maximum of 15 people.
- Encouraging intellectual dissent brings about the best decisions thanks to the competition of ideas, not personalities.
- Never, ever lose your temper. Do so, and you lose your people.
- Trust those who have something to lose if things go wrong. They'll work harder than someone who has nothing to lose. That's the great gift purpose and skin in the game provide us.

- The lesson of conflict is intrinsically linked to our ability to carry things through despite significant challenges and adversity. Maintain our purpose by being comfortable with being uncomfortable. Change, evolve and adapt to the circumstances we face.
- Embrace conflict through the courage of our convictions, not transferring responsibility to another. We assume the management of conflict and outcomes dispassionately: interested in the process and the outcome, but not vested emotionally.

9: The lesson of influence

*There was something terribly enthralling in the exercise of influ-
ence(...)To project one's soul into some gracious form, and let it
carry there for a moment; to hear one's own intellectual views
echoed back to one with all the added music of passion and youth;
to convey one's temperament into another as though it were a
subtle fluid or a strange perfume; there was a real joy in that—
perhaps the most satisfying joy left to us in an age so limited and
vulgar as our own, an age grossly carnal in its pleasures, and
grossly common in its aims.*
-Oscar Wilde, The Picture of Dorian Gray (1890)

Wisdom of the crowd

In the early morning hours of December 27, 1995, I was asleep in a mobile office trailer parked in front of the Haitian National Police station in
Mirebalais, north-east of the Haitian capital, Port-au-Prince. The office's
lock was broken, and since there was some computer and radio equipment inside, I had chosen to sleep there to ensure that the equipment remained undisturbed.

Around 5 am., I awoke to the sounds of a crowd assembling around
the town square next to the grounds of the police station. People were
chanting, dancing and singing. I thought that it was some sort of early-
morning celebration related to the holidays.

Once I had lumbered out of my cot, put my gun belt on and left the
trailer, I encountered a Haitian police officer slowly walking away from
the gathering; he had an empty look on his face, staring into the distance
and mumbling something about a wheelbarrow.

I headed towards the crowd. It was gyrating and moving as one, almost methodically turning in a counterclockwise direction around some-

thing. As I entered the gathering, I saw people pushing an empty, blood-drenched wheelbarrow around a mound of dirt. I presumed that an animal had been slaughtered and transported in the wheelbarrow.

My curiosity quickly turned to horror as a police officer told me that the mound of dirt was a makeshift grave for two cattle thieves whom a group of neighbors had caught in *flagrante delicto* while they were walking off with the cow. The crowd had taken the law into their own hands and summarily macheted to death the two individuals, hacking them into pieces. The group of people, pleased with their work, had placed the body parts in a wheelbarrow and paraded it for the entire town to see.

Minutes before I awoke, the Haitian police officers on duty that morning had investigated the gathering. Upon seeing the various body parts piled in the wheelbarrow, they summoned the local justice of the peace and started to dig a hole to bury the body parts. In Haiti, a justice of the peace is required to declare a person officially dead.

When the local official arrived, he immediately declared the two men dead. He also announced that, since it had been the 'people' who had collectively intercepted and killed the men, no charges could be laid against any individual person. Hence, no investigation would be required. Case closed.

When I arrived on the scene, I saw gleeful participants dancing, singing and laughing around and on the makeshift grave. We had to dig up the remains and relocate them to the local cemetery under the direction of the same justice of the peace. The remainder of the day was noticeably quiet in the town, almost as if nothing had happened.

Later that evening, I went to see the highest justice official in the locality, the *Commissaire du gouvernement*, the Haitian equivalent of a district attorney or crown counsel. He invited me into his home and offered me some tea.

We sat down to discuss what had transpired that day. He was patient and listened attentively to my view that someone had to be held accountable for the murders to respect the rule of law. He had worked previously in the justice system in Canada and understood my perplexity.

After I finished my explanation, he took a deep breath and began to talk. He told me that a cow is often the only asset that a rural family has in Haiti. A cow provides milk to children, can be rented as a beast of burden to others, can be sold outright or can be slaughtered to provide meat to feed a family and to sell.

He then asked me what I would do if everything—absolutely everything—I owned, including my ability to earn a living, were taken away.

This was the predicament that the family, whose cow had been stolen, faced. Their ability to make a living, let alone survive in a country where the average wage was less than two dollars a day, was compromised.

When people don't have food to eat, he told me, we can't expect them to hold to the lofty principles of due process or procedural fairness. Their priorities are much more basic: they need to eat to live. And although principles may feed the soul, they don't nourish the body. Consequently, he agreed with the decision of the justice of the peace not to further the investigation.

Unable to counter his logic, I left the *Commissaire du gouvernement*, humbled and thankful for what I had back home.

Of shields and spears

The biggest challenge we have as leaders in influencing others is that people tend to be stubborn and resistant to our influence by their very nature. This is because their main interests are about themselves and their own needs, based, for the most part, on their self-preservation. The intent of our influence can run counter to their wants and desires, resulting in resistance. This is a natural, evolutionary reaction to potential threats and can manifest itself through reticence, refusal or a lack of co-operation.

This applies to all people, including ourselves. For someone to convince and influence us, we need to see the advantages of following their suggested course of action, sometimes even when receiving a paycheck.

At times, we think of the classic paradox of the unstoppable force meeting an immovable object. It's this contradiction of interests that leaders must overcome to influence others.

The Chinese word for contradiction illustrates this paradox in part. Written as

矛盾

and pronounced *máodùn*, it means: "spear-shield." The term comes from a story found in the *Han Feizi*, an ancient Chinese text attributed to the 3rd century BC philosopher Han Fei. In the story, a man was selling his wares, including a spear and a shield that he touted as both the strongest and best in the land. Asked about the spear, he said that it could penetrate any shield; asked about the shield, he claimed that it could with-stand the attack of any spear. When asked what would happen if he were to take his spear and strike his shield, the seller couldn't answer. This led to the expression "from each-other spear shield," which can be defined as "self-contradictory" in today's terms.

Humans display self-contradiction regularly. We aspire to be the best but eventually learn that we can't be good at all things. We claim to want the best but fail to take the necessary steps to achieve it.

Perhaps the very first lesson I learned in basic police training at the RCMP Training Academy in Regina, Saskatchewan, was that no one is good at everything. The same applies to the teams we belong to, at work, or sports, in our community or our family. Like people, no one team or group is good at everything.

The path to success requires building a personal or team skillset with diverse and complementary talents where the whole is greater than the sum of the parts, as Greek philosopher and polymath Aristotle (384-322 B.C.) is credited to have written some 24 centuries ago.[90]

This provides an important lesson about team composition: build a team of people with diverse talents that complement one another. Your team may look just like you as to gender, ethnicity, college background, religion or area of origin. But ensure that the members have diversity of thought and skills. We usually attain this more easily when people don't look alike and come from a range of backgrounds, but that's not always a guarantee.

Encourage and value the differences in people, as opposed to their commonalities. Those differences can include how they spend their spare time and with whom. Before I became a police officer, the individ-ual who encouraged me to join the RCMP gave me this advice: always cul-tivate relationships outside of policing, starting with my most important relationship, that of my eventual spouse.

I was always surprised to see how police officers, both straight and gay, would marry from within their profession. Then again, this isn't lim-ited to police officers, as all disciplines can have the same situation.

To influence others, we need to lower their resistance to our influ-ence. The key is not to put them on the defensive in the process. They can't feel that they are any less important than us, and we can't act like we're superior to them. To get them to drop their shield of defensive pos-turing, the metaphorical distrust of which we spoke earlier, we must en-courage teamwork while maintaining morale. When collaboration breaks down, hierarchy and distrust become magnified, resulting in a corresponding drop in morale.

A word about morale: as a concept, it's often loosely bandied about and used as an indicator of performance. As chief of police, I had many employees approach me to advance their ideas, repeatedly stating that morale would "go through the roof" if I implemented their idea. Amongst these suggestions were new headwear, such as a toque or baseball cap, a liberal interpretation in leave entitlements, and a policy change around parental leave.

These conversations reminded me of the numerous times when I told myself that if I could have just one thing, be it more money, more hair on my head, bigger muscles or sustained weight loss, my life would be so very different. The reality is that very few individual things can ever change our life unless they delay death or significantly modify our circumstances. Lasting change and increased morale, much like success, as we have seen, results from a concatenation of multiple positive factors and the avoidance of numerous failures. Never view morale as an end state. As it's often an indicator of better performance, use morale as a barometer. Nurture morale with circumspection, knowing that it's always subject to variance.

It's at this point in influencing where empathy becomes so vitally important to the leader. We need to understand what others' emotions are and, in turn, alter *our* moods and *our* attitudes to fit *their* needs. If we're at peace with ourselves, relaxed and genuinely interested in the other person and their needs, we can help them lower their defensive shield and affect them positively. We can then develop trust. And this opens the door to influence.

The lowering of defenses by an individual can sometimes go too far. We've all seen it with shills, frauds and hucksters, who will schmooze us into giving them the shirt off our backs. They manipulate us into thinking they care about our emotions, are mindful of our perceptions and understand our motivations. But they do none of this, swaying us into drinking their metaphorical Kool-Aid so as to drop our defenses.

Once we realize what they've done, it's often too late, and the relationship is irreparably broken, frequently with long-term consequences: they're gone elsewhere, along with our money, our heart or our dignity. We must be careful not to be, and not to be *seen* as being, one of these individuals.

If we enter a relationship or an interaction by setting the right tone with an appropriate attitude, using empathy about the other person's situation in life and demonstrating a work ethic based on superior character, we set the stage for successfully influencing them. To convince them we have their interests at heart, we must be authentic and genuine in our approach.

An essential component of this is our communication. Real communication requires a two-way exchange of information. It must be dialogic, akin to a conversation. This need not be complicated and can take the form of a simple discussion. There is also a 360-degree aspect of communication: we need to read the totality of the information transmitted to us through verbal and non-verbal cues.

Remember that because a large part of communication is non-verbal, people will react more to how we present ourselves through our general behavior, manners, and energy than anything we have to say. This requires establishing the right tone through our attitude, empathy and approach to create the psychological safety critical to influence. It means being alive to the emotions, perceptions and motivations of those we lead and wish to influence. These factors are dynamic and subject to change regularly, often without notice.

It begins with truly listening to the other and seeing what they are communicating. If we're serious about influencing others, we must understand what drives them: their values, beliefs and desires.

Listening deeply involves actively screening for the emotions, perceptions and motivations behind another's words. We must first listen to understand before we can hope to influence them.

Recognizing the critical importance of listening in negotiations and business, a retired British police hostage negotiator, Richard Mullender,[91] established a company called the *Listening Institute*. Its primary mission is to teach people listening skills so they can glean keywords and turn information into actionable intelligence.

But words aren't the only facet of communication. We must also appreciate the emotional aspects of the behavior demonstrated through hand gestures, facial expressions and verbal emphasis. As we do this, we have to be aware that the norms of emotional communication vary significantly amongst different societies, ethnicities and cultural groups. In my culture, emphatic hand-waving may indicate intensity; in another culture it may be part of the baseline of communication.

While we communicate, we need to do three things:

1. Keep our desire to talk at bay.
2. Keep our biases in check.
3. Keep our goals in mind.

Combined, these three actions prevent us from taking anything personally. We maintain a professional approach and use logic to analyze what we're hearing and what we see.

In the specific case of crisis communications, the single, most important thing is message coherence. You may be delivering the message in different languages, using other platforms and different announcers, but the message needs to be coherent to be understood and acted upon. Whenever possible, it must demonstrate empathy and be about those affected, not only about those responding or doing the communicating. It must also explain what's happening: how the agency or company is reacting and proceeding at any given moment.

The challenge in crisis communications is to get ahead of the narrative of rumors and grievances of those who use traditional and social media to advance their worldview and ideology on a particular matter related, even peripherally, to the incident in question. At this juncture, time becomes our most important commodity; as it erodes very quickly, we must seize opportunities to use time wisely.

Because crises tend to develop rapidly, we have trouble telling our story and version of events quickly and efficiently enough to quell public outcry and speculation. In such cases, we need to pre-empt the most pernicious narratives, especially the grievance narrative. We earn trust when we meet broad societal expectations, not individual narratives—including our own.

We want to avoid insensitive comments that focus on ourselves. A case in point occurred in late May 2010 when the CEO of British Petroleum, Tony Hayward, commented on the *Deepwater Horizon* oil spill disaster that claimed 11 lives and spewed 100 million gallons of oil into the Gulf of Mexico. He said, "We're sorry for the massive disruption it's caused their lives. There's no one who wants this over more than I do. I would like my life back."

Following those comments, Hayward faced a backlash as his words were perceived as self-centered and lacking empathy. In July 2010, Hayward resigned from his job, which had paid him a base salary of over $1.5 million US per year.

We want to get the message out as effectively as possible, despite the circumstances. In mid-February 2015, thanks to an anonymous Crime Stoppers tip, Halifax Regional Police and Nova Scotia RCMP were able to foil a plot to commit a mass shooting at Halifax's largest shopping center. Three people, two local men and a woman traveling from the United States, were planning to commit mass murder on Valentine's Day. One local individual was found dead by suicide inside a residence while police arrested the two others at Halifax Stanfield International Airport.

On the evening of Saturday, February 14, I and some 250 HRP personnel, friends and family gathered for our annual police gala to honor excellence in work. We had been planning this event for months, and it was with great pride and relief that we began the evening.

During the meal portion, my smartphone blew up with messages, emails and calls from media outlets (local and national), the mayor, the provincial premier, the municipal Chief Administrative Officer and the chairperson of our Board of Police Commissioners. They were looking for information regarding sudden rumors of a mass shooting occurring at that moment at the same mall.

I wasn't the only one receiving such communications: our deputy chief, director of communications and several other senior officers were also receiving urgent information requests.

I gathered those of our senior management team who were at the gala to determine precisely what was going on. We had units rushing to the mall, and within minutes officers determined that youths at the bus terminus beside the mall had launched rocks at a bus with slingshots. No firearms were involved and no one was injured—false alarm.

I worked with the senior management team to devise a coordinated communications approach on social media and email. We didn't have time to go back to the office and prepare a press release. Within minutes, we had distributed a consistent message on Twitter, Facebook and email to advise the public of the circumstances and that all was well. The message I shared on my Twitter feed was re-tweeted over 100 times in the first ten minutes following its posting.

We did this all from the gala's venue, avoiding public misinformation and panic within 15 minutes of receiving the first requests for information. Just as quickly as the groundswell of worry started, it subsided, thanks to the timely communication of a coherent, collaborative message.

Finally, our goal should always focus on the **clarity** of the messaging. The message should be context-specific, clearly organized and simply written or communicated. We must provide cognitive clarity to the message's recipient by being clear, compelling and brief. Fewer words are usually better.

In communication, sometimes less is more, one of the many contradictions we face as we attempt to influence others. Dialogic communication allows us to influence using narrative persuasion and the effective framing of messaging through appropriate storytelling.

Fortunately and even unfortunately, some stories can't always be encapsulated in 280 characters, another of the contradictions we face.

Self-abnegation

We live in a world where hyperbole and cynicism are rampant, where narcissism and individualism seem to trump all, and where sound bites and false narratives, facilitated and amplified through social media appear to be the norm. At times, we don't know what or who to believe. I regularly talk to professionals in different fields who are always looking for reliable news and sources of in-depth, credible analysis in those areas outside their work domains. Often, the true is hard to find amid the loud.

We also take for granted many of the goods and services we receive, such as policing, firefighting, paramedicine, garbage collection, the immediate and abundant availability of food and other non-emergency services. Described by Sebastian Junger in his book *Tribe* as being both "the beauty and the tragedy of the modern world," such conveniences eliminate situations that would otherwise require people to demonstrate an overt commitment to the collective good in order to receive them. People assume that these essential services should naturally flow to them without their taking any responsibility or making any commitment, simply because they pay taxes or live in a particular jurisdiction.

Think of litter that wouldn't exist if people genuinely cared about the land and sea, and were always mindful of their actions. When was the last time you bent down to pick up someone else's refuse?

Think of any significant humanitarian crisis, even one in your own country, county or city. People's first reaction to major local events such as hurricanes, tornadoes, shootings, and famine is to contribute money. Although helpful and sometimes the only way to contribute, money ends up being a convenient proxy for providing in-kind support and in-person help, which involves having to do and risk something to help others. Consequently, in many areas of our life, we've forgotten the values of teamwork, community contribution and an essential quality called self-abnegation.

Self-abnegation is the contributing to others by denying something to yourself. As an action and lifelong principle, self-denial has played an important role in the teachings of all major religions and belief systems, from Buddhism's renunciation of worldly goods to Christianity, Islam and Judaism; periods of fasting and disavowal during important periods such as Lent, Ramadan and Yom Kippur. Self-abnegation implies self-denial of either worldly possessions or consumable items, but sometimes of one's liberty and even life to aid others. Fortunately, this practice isn't uncommon as some would believe.

During periods of extreme conflict or crisis, history has provided us with incredible stories of self-denial. One of the unique stories of self-abnegation during World War II involved the Polish intelligence officer and resistance organizer Witold Pilecki (1901-1948). Pilecki volunteered to be captured by the Germans so he could infiltrate Auschwitz, the Nazi concentration camp near the town of Oświęcim in southern Poland. Once in Auschwitz, from September 1940 to April 1943, he organized an extensive camp-wide resistance network and documented the mass murder, torture and extreme abuse of the camp's inmates. He endured some of the same abuse as an inmate.

His chronicles were smuggled out of the camp on several occasions. It took six months for his initial report to make its way to the Polish government-in-exile in London and eventually to the Anglo-American Allies. Unfortunately, his reports were not immediately heeded. There was no bombing of the rail lines leading to the camps, nor was there any coordination with the local Polish resistance to harass and impede the camps' principal vocation of human extermination.

Following the war, Pilecki wasn't celebrated, and the Polish authorities did not treat him as a hero. He continued to organize resistance, this time against the new occupiers of his country, the Soviets.

As part of Poland's first Soviet-style show trials in March 1948, the post-war communist regime arrested and tortured him to the point that he described his treatment in Auschwitz as "just a game" in comparison. He was summarily executed on May 25, 1948.

Although his body was never found, his legacy remains as a testament against tyranny from both the extreme right and left sides of the political spectrum.

There are over 20,000 names in the *Righteous Among the Nations* records at the Yad Vashem World Holocaust Remembrance Center database in Jerusalem, Israel. The title is bestowed upon those non-Jews who risked their lives to shelter, rescue or save Jews from the Holocaust. These are people who helped Jews avoid death, putting their own lives at risk. An analysis conducted in 2004 found that, excluding married couples, women slightly outnumbered men in the list of people who risked, and, in some cases, lost their lives to protect Jews against Nazi tyranny. Poland has more names in the database than any other country. Witold Pilecki's name is nowhere to be found in it.

The second example of self-abnegation occurred two generations later in a land far from Poland. Since its creation in 1945, the United Nations has been involved in peacekeeping and peacebuilding missions worldwide. From 1960 to 1990, those missions almost exclusively involved securing peace between states. Since 1990, there has been more focus on conflicts within states, and particularly in supporting development in failed states.

One such example was in East Timor, a small country occupying the eastern half of the island of Timor, situated between Indonesia and Australia. The Portuguese had occupied East Timor for over 400 years, followed by Indonesia in 1975.

In June 1999, the UN established the United Nations Mission in East Timor (UNAMET), whose mandate was to organize and conduct a popular consultation. The referendum's question was to determine if East Timorese wanted to accept a form of special autonomy within the unitary Republic of Indonesia or if they wanted to form a separate nation. The consultation came about due to significant unrest and the killings of an estimated 200,000 people (nearly one-third of the entire indigenous population) by predominantly Indonesian-supported militia groups located in East Timor since its 1975 invasion by Indonesia.

Twenty-nine countries contributed civilian and unarmed military and police personnel to the mission. Canada was one of them. The referendum was held on August 30, 1999. More than 78 percent of East Timorese rejected Indonesia's proposed autonomy package, opting for complete independence.

Enraged by the results, Indonesian militia groups began a systematic slaughter of native East Timorese, killing upwards of 1,400 people through decapitation, disembowelment, shootings and the hacking to death with machetes. Due to the level of violence, the UN began pulling its personnel out of the country.

But some chose to stay including Toronto Police Service Staff Sergeant George Clanfield and RCMP Corporal Magdi Saleh. Together, they were instrumental in providing aid, food and shelter to East Timorese refugees fleeing the violence and the UN personnel who remained in the country. They ensured the safety of the two groups, often at significant personal risk. For ten days following the referendum, Staff Sergeant Clanfield and Corporal Saleh organized and led convoys from the UN compound to the airport to evacuate UN personnel and obtain water and supplies kept at the airport. They also ensured the safety of an estimated 3,000 refugees who had sought shelter in the overcrowded UN compound.

Their convoys were shot at, harassed at roadblocks and threatened by roaming bands of militia. On one occasion, they had to leave the compound to rescue three international police officers trapped at the Indonesian police headquarters.

Both men were tall and looked very official in their UN uniforms. Thanks to their presence, demeanor and interpersonal skills, they were able to defuse many potentially dangerous interactions with Indonesian militiamen, standing their ground and using their acumen to get out of sticky situations while weaving their way through hazardous zones. Danger surrounded them repeatedly as they moved from the UN compound to the airport and back.

Staff Sergeant Clanfield and Corporal Saleh demonstrated the best in what policing offers, willing to sacrifice their personal safety and even lives to keep many others safe and out of harm's way during those ten days in September 1999.

A third example of self-abnegation, this time anonymous and collective, occurred on December 22, 2015, to the east of the Kenyan capital, Nairobi. A group of men belonging to al-Shabab, a Somali-based Islamist militant group with links to al-Qaeda, stopped a bus carrying some 60 people, mostly women. It had become a deadly practice of the group to seek out and massacre Christians and non-Muslims in a terror campaign against the Western-aligned Kenyan government.

While the bus was slowing down, the Muslim female passengers quickly offered their extra headscarves to the non-Muslim women. When an armed intruder ordered the passengers to disembark and divide themselves into two groups, the Muslim women refused to follow the order, encouraging others on the bus to do the same. The flustered gunman left the bus, allowing it to proceed to its intended destination. A non-Muslim man attempted to escape and was killed on the spot.

A final, more recent example of self-abnegation is that of the French gendarme Arnaud Beltrame (1973-2018), who died while serving his community on the Friday preceding Palm Sunday during Lent 2018. Around 11 am. on March 23, near the historic southern fortified French town of Carcassonne, a terrorist claiming allegiance to the Islamic State of Iraq and the Levant (ISIS) entered a supermarket in the town of Trèbes, armed with a handgun, a hunting knife and three homemade explosive devices. He immediately killed two people and took several others hostage. Members of the *Gendarmerie nationale* responded to the scene and began negotiations with the hostage-taker.

Lt.-Colonel Beltrame, the most senior officer present offered himself as a hostage in exchange for one of the supermarket's cashiers, a 40-year-old woman named Julie. When he entered the supermarket, Beltrame surreptitiously placed his open cell phone on a table in the back room where he and the other hostages were kept, allowing police outside to monitor the discussions and activities inside the room.

Just before 2:30 pm., Beltrame attempted to disarm the terrorist, yelling in the process "Assault! Assault!" as an order to his colleagues to storm the supermarket. During the struggle, the terrorist shot Beltrame four times: in the forearm, the hand, and the foot. The tactical assault team heard the shots and immediately stormed the supermarket, shooting the terrorist, but not before he had a chance to stab Beltrame in the throat.

All the hostages were released safely, and Beltrame was immediately taken to the hospital in Carcassonne, where he succumbed to his wounds later that night.

Lt.-Colonel Beltrame was posthumously promoted to the rank of Colonel and was made Commander of the *Légion d'honneur*, the highest honor given by the French Republic. Numerous streets, stadiums, venues and *Gendarmerie* barracks have since been renamed in his honor.

A week before the terrorist attack, Lt.-Colonel Beltrame had buried his father, who had drowned in the Mediterranean the summer prior and whose body had just been recovered in the nets of a fishing boat. Colonel Beltrame was also a devout Catholic, having found his faith later in life in his 30s. His widow, Marielle Beltrame, stated in an interview with the French Christian magazine *La Vie* that:

> [Arnaud] knew how to unite his men, to infuse them with his energy, to get them to give their best. He was driven by very high moral values: values of service, generosity, self-giving, self-abnegation. He had an extraordinary strength of will, always able to recover from his various trials and tribulations (...) His funeral will be held during Holy Week, following his death on Friday, just before Palm Sunday, which is significant to me. It is with great hope that I look forward to celebrating the resurrection of Easter with him.[92]

These are stories of personal sacrifice of individuals who had much to lose but chose to act in others' interests. They all decided to contribute to a higher collective good, to the detriment of their self-interest. They all left a legacy that continues to influence others in pursuit of the good they offered.

Through the examples of their actions and, in some cases, the giving of their lives, these people represent a superior character by intentionally having skin in the game, something they chose to do and especially to be.

Mentors and sponsors

Influence requires specific actions with the expectation that when things go wrong, as they almost inevitably do, others will know where to turn and how to respond. And in times of crisis, in order to influence, a leader must be present.

A crisis isn't just a large-scale event affecting scores of people, but can also be a highly personal occurrence: the unexpected death of a family member, a life-changing medical diagnosis or the leveling of an unjustified accusation of misconduct. Regardless of the crisis' scope, the leader must be present and be seen to be present.

Being seen and visible within the organization, community or family involves being accessible and demonstrating empathy. As a senior police executive and police chief, I visited police employees in the hospital and their homes. I comforted family members as they dealt with the shock of the loss or grievous injury of a loved one. If an overnight incident sent them temporarily to the hospital, I would call, write, email or send a handwritten note to let them know I was thinking of them.

Presence also means being there when people least expect it. When I first became chief of police, I had lunch with the union president. A very outgoing, talkative sort, he was quite open about his evaluation of the senior officer cadre, most of whom he had worked with his entire career.

Using a hockey metaphor, he provided an analysis of each member of the senior management team. He assigned positions to each member, like on a hockey team, stating that a few were first-round draft picks, others were free agent walk-ons, while still others were long past their prime. For him, we had a good goalie, one strong defenceman and a couple of good forwards. The rest were playing beyond their capacity. He said that I was to become the coach of a team that, for the most part, was not very good.

I thanked him for the analysis and then told him that he had forgotten one thing: he forgot that I wasn't just the coach, but I was also a player. My presence on the ice would go beyond simply directing plays and line changes from the bench; I would also be out to score. This meant that I would lead from the front and be present as much as possible. During our municipality's yearly provincial marathon, I would do traffic duty, either static or on a bicycle. During important community events requiring armed police presence, I would be on the ground as one of the assigned officers, not in the command post where highly trained and competent members were already doing their jobs. For me, the key was to be present while contributing to the overall mission of the service in whatever way I could.

The second issue is demonstrating the requisite courage to accept the reality of any given situation in our lives. This involves no sugarcoating or denial either for us or for others. If things are bad, recognize it and get on with dealing with it. Provide updates and tell people when the crisis is finally over.

We accept accountability for things under our purview, command and responsibility. Know that people are adults and will eventually accept the bad news, provided we're doing something about it, being as transparent as we can be and immediate in our communication of accurate information.

Immobilization and self-isolation in times of crisis are destructive actions that prevent us from exercising influence. Don't close your office door and spend the entire day planning in solitude. Bring others into the decision-making process. If you're invited to attend training or a presentation, don't sit apart from the group. Participate fully like everyone else, offering your experiences, impressions and lessons. Enjoy the presence of other people.

Although time and energy-consuming, collective decision-making allows for better decisions, better execution and more buy-in. It also requires continual communication with those most affected by the decisions and actions to be implemented. This applies equally well during normal times when there are no crises to deal with.

When I was a senior police leader, and especially as chief of police, I always kept my door open. My desk was situated so that I was facing outward and could see people as they passed my door.

My open door didn't mean that I had an open-door policy. Instead, it meant that I had a 'screen-door policy', where my executive assistant would screen who could meet with me according to my availability. Whether they wanted to meet with me or not, people saw me through that open door as they passed, and I would recognize their presence with a hand gesture, a smile or a hello.

Nothing would be more disheartening than hearing of a new leader who would keep their door closed, refusing to interact, even minimally, with their work colleagues. Or, perhaps even worse, a senior-most executive who purposely segregated themselves from others by building a glass wall to impede movement in their immediate office area. There were persistent rumors that a former RCMP commissioner even had a button installed under his desk that would allow him to remotely open his office door to signal to a visitor when their meeting was over.

That's the type of miscommunication that breeds distrust.

One of the initiatives I started early in my tenure as chief of police was meeting every new employee in my office to go over the organization's core values before they officially accepted their employment offer. This way, the new police officer or civilian, full-time, part-time or contractual employee would hear about the organization's values and expectations directly from the top. After my short presentation, during which I gave them a one-pager detailing the values, the new employee was required to sign an undertaking stating they understood the organization's core values and would endeavor to advance them in their daily work. They received original copy of the signed document, and a photocopy went into their personnel file. This was all before they signed their official offer of employment.

In addition to explaining our core values, for all police officers and communications center employees (i.e., call takers and dispatchers) I would also discuss mental health and overall well-being. To reinforce the discussion, I would give them a copy of Dr. Kevin Gilmartin's book *Emotional Survival for Law Enforcement*, encouraging them and their loved ones to read the book, preferably sooner rather than later.

Many years earlier, in Manitoba, I had received the same book from an RCMP employee-assistance program referral agent after a particularly difficult ten-month period during which we buried eight police officers and a civilian employee. They'd died because of personal illness, accidents, homicide and suicide. I found Gilmartin's book to be an invaluable resource, helping me to take control of my mental health and general wellness. I wanted others to have the same guidance and encouragement when they started their career with us at HRP.

The next issue is trusting your people by giving them decisional authority. This implies they're free to reach out to whomever they need to get their job done and, most importantly, free to make errors. You must convey that authority to them long before any significant incident and as part of any organization's everyday functioning. That way, when a crisis hits, people know they can act proactively to prevent or mitigate its effects and know they'll be supported in their decision-making after the fact.

Influence can only be exercised if people trust us. An essential skill required to obtain this trust is demonstrating empathy. The requirement for superior empathy by leaders is greater than ever in today's world.

We've seen a gradual increase in self-absorption and narcissism in people since the 1970s, with a spike in recent years coinciding with the advent of the internet and social media. By spending less time in in-person social interactions and more time socializing online, people have slowly lost the interest and ability to develop their social skills, of which empathy is integral.

Part of this results from the decreased quality of our attention to any matter. Unable to properly focus our attention on another because of continual interruptions and distractions from emails, text messages and notifications, we slowly become blind to others' emotions, perceptions and motivations.

We best achieve the goal of influencing others, in particular work colleagues, through a positive and supportive work environment in which people are allowed to fail and to succeed. This environment repels negative emotions and mitigates bitterness and tension.

This is where psychological safety comes in. Much time, effort and resources have been spent in the last few decades promoting physical health and safety in the workplace. What's now required is augmenting psychological safety in the workplace as well.

Psychological safety is paramount in work environments with significant performance pressures, be it constant tight deadlines or high levels of public scrutiny. Psychologically safe work environments allow for a certain level of confidence that promotes a learning, adaptive and inclusive culture. This is particularly important if we expect our organizations to be able to deal effectively with multiple crises.

The key is to shift leadership's emphasis from having the authority, responsibility and accountability for people to understanding and serving their needs as human beings. At the top of those needs is for a leader to facilitate meaningful work for their people.

The key to developing such a culture is hiring the right people, based on their attitude and character. You can't train for either, so you might as well select people who exhibit positive attributes and train them for all the other competencies any job requires.

Such hiring implies weeding out individuals who *do not* display these qualities. This means identifying those qualities in individuals that run counter to psychologically safe workspaces: narcissism, histrionics, lack of empathy and other personality disorders and negative traits. To do this requires developing hiring and selection processes that specifically identify and exclude attitudes that cause the most discord in a work environment.

An interesting example of exclusion in nature can be found through balancing rocks or precarious boulders. Balancing rocks are naturally-occurring geological formations in which a large rock or boulder rests on other rocks, bedrock or glacial till. Although they appear to be balancing precariously, they are rigidly connected to the rock or till base by either a pedestal or stem. Some of the most famous balancing rocks can be found in Zimbabwe, India, Europe and North America. Although solidly fixed to a rock or till base, a balancing rock can be unbalanced, causing it to fall off its stem. A severe seismologic event, such as an earthquake, volcanic eruption or tsunami, could cause such a fall.

The presence of a balancing rock tells us more about what has *not* occurred during the rock's life than what has happened. This becomes important when one is looking to build structures that contain sensitive equipment such as telescopic or radio observatories or nuclear power stations. Knowing what hasn't occurred in the immediate area allows for a certain level of confidence about the area's future.

Like understanding a balancing rock, choosing people based on what they don't display or what hasn't occurred to them is equally important. But we must be careful in this assessment for many reasons, not least of which are exclusions based on legally protected grounds. The evaluation must target behavioral traits that run counter to the culture we're looking to promote, not exclude someone because of a significant life event or a handicap.

One regularly-used tool to screen out candidates is a criminal record check, also known as a "Certificate of Good Conduct." It's often used in hiring practices in business and selection procedures in volunteer positions. Such a document intends to demonstrate that an individual doesn't have a criminal record, implying that they're automatically trustworthy.

There are four problems with such a tool:

1. It's merely a snapshot in time, reflecting official records at the moment of the search. An individual may be charged but not convicted for a crime that wouldn't be reflected in the document, requiring constant renewals of the search.
2. Such a document automatically precludes worthy individuals from applying only because they have a criminal record, often for crimes committed long ago or having nothing to do with the work they'd be tasked with.
3. Such a document is a convenient abdication of the potential employer's or the volunteer organization's due diligence. Rather than relying on a readily-accessible but limited document, potential employers and volunteer groups should do background checks themselves, so they can ascertain the individual's character today instead of focusing on past criminal transgressions. Of course, the latter approach's challenge is the amount of time and effort required to carry out such background checks. Many organizations, particularly volunteer organizations, can rarely afford such extensive checks. But in most cases, the effort is worth the while.
4. Finally, the presence of a criminal record presupposes that people can't be rehabilitated or that they're undeserving of a second or even third chance. This is an error that results in many good individuals desirous of contributing from doing so.

Another part of an exclusionary assessment involves recognizing how people are different and how they interact with others. Introverts operate differently than extroverts, and we shouldn't view their proclivity to a more solitary, taciturn work approach as being anti-team. Women, for the most part, have a different method than men in how they share experiences. In the female system, the center of the universe is the relationship through verbal intimacy and a sense of security. That means that their strengths are predominantly in talking, bonding, intuition, listening to and caring for others, and developing and maintaining friendships. These are all essential qualities that contribute to the requisite empathy leading to the influence of others.

Men, on the other hand, tend to be goal-oriented in their relationships. Once they have achieved what's required, they will let the relationship go but can easily reactivate it later. This can be productive but taxing in the long-term, especially on those people who need constant encouragement.

The key to influence, then, is to forge relationships and express consistent empathy as required. Suppose you are a man not overly accustomed to such an approach. You must facilitate a collaborative work environment, motivating others by appealing to their ability to help the group. Manage group stress through listening, not offering solutions unless asked, but through deep listening and acknowledgment.

Two forms of more advanced workplace influence are mentorship and sponsorship. A mentor can be at any level and attempts to increase the mentee's sense of competence and self-confidence. In contrast, a sponsor must be a senior manager who protects the protégé from negative exposure or damaging contact with senior executives who have poor leadership skills. Mentors provide feedback and emotional support, whereas sponsors give the protégé positive exposure and access to those top executives and others who can contribute to the employee's skillset development. The mentor focuses on professional development while the sponsor attempts to get the protégé recognized by others for their work, contributions and potential. The key to effective mentorship and sponsorship is to be a genuine partner in developing the individual you oversee.

Crucial to being a mentor or sponsor is building and nurturing personal and professional networks with people who are different from ourselves, often at a distance and with whom we have other interests. This is where the diversity of thought, experiences and life is so beneficial.

A final part of mentorship involves recognizing those who helped us when we started out. I have a written list of thirty-two people whom I recognize as having had a significant influence on my life at one point or another. This list includes those who actively assisted and sponsored me, those who provided me with a job, brutally honest feedback or examples to follow. The list also includes those from whom I learned how *not* to do things. I call this my *List of Mentors and Non-Mentors*. I have personally thanked every person on that list for their contributions to my life and career. Some humbly accepted my thanks, while others, notably the non-mentors, just shook their heads in disbelief. But every single one appreciated the feedback, regardless of the content. Gratitude is a strong motivator for some people.

Marlo the Impossible

Marlo always loved playing hockey. He would play any chance he could get—during lunch breaks, immediately before or after work, sometimes during work hours and even when he was off work because of a feigned illness. Marlo also loved to mix it up on the ice, habitually being penalized and getting kicked out of games because of rude behavior or fighting. That same behavior also occurred off the ice, at work, especially during events where alcohol was involved, such as work receptions.

At work parties or social gatherings, Marlo would often target senior members of his organization and goad them into heated discussions and, on occasion, even a fight. Marlo disliked referees and senior managers equally, being very vocal that, in his opinion, they were "all a bunch of idiots."

The only thing Marlo loved more than hockey was complaining about his work. For Marlo, his job was the one thing that had always kept him down in life and was responsible for all of his woes. Marlo's misfortunes included two divorces, alcohol problems and an absence of promotions in his career.

For Marlo, it was always someone else's fault. When asked why he didn't simply quit his job and work elsewhere, Marlo would be very open that he enjoyed the regular paycheck and the chance to play hockey whenever he wanted.

Marlo leveled frequent harassment complaints against people during his career, including supervisors he viewed as having tried to block his progression in the ranks. Marlo also filed grievances against decisions those same supervisors made, openly qualifying in writing the grieved conclusions as being "stupid."

Marlo always sought the same redress for his grievances: a promotion into a position without the requirement to pass any screening process. Before filing his grievances, Marlo had a habit of sending lengthy email messages, withering email flames, directly to various heads of his national organization, outlining his numerous complaints and demanding a promotion as redress.

When people looked into Marlo's claims, Marlo reacted very differently according to the person. After a litany of complaints and grievances during one brief period, Marlo met with the Human Resources Officer (HRO). Marlo was emotional, weeping openly and abundantly while explaining all of his problems and woes to the HRO, hoping for sympathy. It worked, and the HRO tasked me, as the labor relations officer at the time, to deal with his complaints and grievances. From what the HRO had seen, Marlo was a fragile person who simply needed some sympathy and help.

The reality was that Marlo was an emotional chameleon who changed his outward behavior according to the person with whom he was dealing. Marlo was the subject of public and internal complaints detailing rude and abusive behavior.

When I finally met Marlo to discuss his issues, he was far from being a "fragile person." He was highly aggressive, listing off a catalog of complaints and accusations about various individuals, intimating that I was just as bad as those he complained about because I was a senior officer *and* a hockey referee.

Quickly realizing that the discussion was going nowhere, I made the time-out sign (which also doubles in hockey as the signal for unsportsmanlike conduct). This caught Marlo's attention, and he stopped speaking. I then served a written order forbidding him to have any further contact through emails or telephone calls with any senior member of the organization, except for myself, failing which he would face disciplinary action that could result in his dismissal.

In the weeks and months that followed, we investigated all of Marlo's complaints and grievances and adjudicated them: we determined that all were unfounded.

Following that period, Marlo still got himself into trouble, both off and on the ice. He eventually retired at the earliest possible moment after being suspended on several occasions because of misconduct, on the ice and off it.

Dealing with this type of Marlo requires significant resolve and the ability to embrace the conflict that accompanies such interactions. It's crucial to defuse their short fuse. By staying calm, avoiding anger and emotional outbursts, including crying ourselves, we avoid encouraging them in their bad behavior. We can even ignore some of their outbursts, especially of the email kind, where they often only expect to push our buttons. We can be empathetic towards their situations, but in no way should we join them in bashing, blaming or complaining.

Our task in dealing with Marlo, especially if we are their supervisor, is to manage them to limit their damaging effects on us and others.

Deeds, not words

Our overarching leadership goal is to engage others' resolve to have them identify with the direction the organization has set. This identification also means that they want to participate in and contribute to the group's higher aims. This goal requires us to be resilient and flexible when developing those individual and collective relationships necessary for exercising leadership. It also requires being consistent, even relentless, when dealing with those who, by their indecision, defensiveness, intransigence and even hostility, are unwilling to engage in the process. Sometimes their actions amount to passive or active attempts to undermine and derail our initiatives. This often manifests itself in problematic behaviors such as incivility, poor attitude, power-mongering, disgruntlement, base insensitivity and various personality disorder traits. Collectively, we can label such individuals as difficult or even impossible people.

As we've seen, the majority of workplace conflict results from disagreement around objectives and processes. A minority of conflict stems from difficult personalities, personality disorders and poor interpersonal chemistry. This small number is because impossible people, fortunately, are few and far between. But they're present in the work environment as part of the social ecology.

It's essential to understand the difference between an impossible person and a possible person. Most individuals we deal with are collaborative and genuinely wish to work towards a common good.

Although past performance is indicative of future performance, people are dynamic in their moods and react differently to various stressors and unique situations at different times, producing differing results. This applies to us all. Some people simply do not get along with others who also have other, separate, personality attributes. However, we shouldn't consider impossible a person who occasionally reacts negatively to a particular stressor. Impossible is not *having* problems; it's *being* the problem. It's the constancy and frequency with which an individual displays negative personality traits that determine if they're impossible or not.

As impossible people are part of the social ecology, we much acknowledge and understand their presence so we can deal with them effectively. It's simply not enough to say, "Oh, that's just the way Marlo is," and leave it at that. Comprehending what the impossible person is and does is part and parcel of our facing the reality of any work, social or home-environ-ment situation.

From a personal perspective, we should resolve to look at our experi-ences with impossible people as invaluable life lessons. At the very least, they certainly will make us appreciate the *possible* people in our lives.

What do impossible people do that possible people do not? They're often emotional abusers who leave a swath of destruction everywhere they go, affecting productivity, morale and organizational reputation at work, in non-work groups and in families. The smaller the group, the more significant the negative impact an impossible person can have. Im-possible people can make life for others, for lack of a better term, a living hell, resulting in irreparably torn relationships.

Impossible people's toxic attitudes are also contagious. Colleagues of impossible employees can become disengaged through absenteeism and presenteeism because of the toxicity, affecting workplace cohesion. Im-possible people can also give their employers, their in-groups and their families a bad reputation. At worst, impossible people result in others being so disengaged that they, themselves, undertake acts of sabotage at work or vent their frustration on family members and outside friends if they don't leave the work environment.

Experiencing rude behavior can impair short-term memory and cog-nitive ability, most likely because the individuals targeted by incivility are fixated on the 'why' of the other person's actions. Some employees will leave jobs because of the perceived acquiescence and even encour-agement of the employer to such impossible behavior.

When dealing with impossible people, the main objective is to deal with them to solve problems, benefit relationships and ensure a healthy work environment. We do this by identifying their impossible behaviors, understanding their background, dealing appropriately with their behav-iors and leading them to some positive contributions. In three words:

- identify
- influence
- impact

Note that we aren't out to change the individual; we want to impact their behavior positively and productively.

Success may involve holding them accountable under trying circum-stances, addressing those problems and resolving them promptly. A tall order when dealing with behaviors such as incompetence, insubordination, harassment, serial grievances, malcontents and just plain meanness.

But being good at influence is not about us. It's always about the other person and is more beneficial than any moral stance we can ever take. Learning to deal with impossible people is a critical leadership skill. The key is to realize that impossible people, who have conflicting, even dangerous, antisocial ideas and habits, can, indeed, be influenced. Provided we approach them and their behaviors correctly.

Every person brings to their professional and social interactions their unique backgrounds and diverse personal anchors that sculpt their worldview. That worldview is continually evolving and being reinforced or further molded by personal experience and other factors. Included in these factors are inherent biases and overt prejudices, personality type (i.e., introvert versus extrovert), developmental challenges (e.g., ADHD, autism, physical disabilities and other conditions), personal trauma or susceptibility to it (e.g., depression, anxiety and psychological stress reactions), treatable and untreatable physical conditions (e.g., diabetes, hypoglycemia, acute injuries and other illnesses) and treatable psychological disorders (e.g., addictions and bipolar disorder).

The first step in dealing with impossible people is to establish guidelines. That means understanding that we cannot fix people; we can only fix processes. This is directly tied to our dual roles of being a manager and a leader. Remember, management is having authority, responsibility and accountability for systems, structures and processes. Leadership, on the other hand, is having authority, responsibility and accountability for people.

Don't attempt to fix an impossible person. That includes any attempt at amateur psychotherapy. If we attempt psychotherapy on the impossible person, we'll only make them and us sicker. It's better and safer to fix the processes so that impossible people can join us and flourish amongst us than to attempt to fix them as individuals.

Fixing those processes also involves doing so in as neutral and professional a manner as possible. This requires being emotionally detached when dealing with the behaviors of the impossible person. This is more to protect us than anything else. In law enforcement and sports officiating, police officers and referees must be disinterested in the investigation's result (i.e., the final court decision) or game's outcome (i.e., the final score) but genuinely interested in the process that leads to those results. Specific to impossible people, leaders must be steadfast in their fairness and respect towards an impossible person, even if the latter doesn't act the same with us and others. This is part of the tolerant attitude towards all that's required in leadership.

This also means never lying to an impossible person. Truth is the best policy for everyone with whom we deal. Lying to an impossible person will only confirm their suspicions about you, and they will hold the lie against you forever. Don't directly disagree with them either; better to find ways to agree with them without conceding your position.

We must be cautious when identifying and labeling others. It's appealing to label someone an impossible person or suffering from a specific personality disorder or as a problem simply because they annoy us or regularly have a bad hair day. Again, just as we deal with the crush of information, we must avoid dualisms or dyadic distinctions—the tendency to use two-part classifications when describing people or social situations— when dealing with the influx of poor behavior. No person is all or none, but a grouping of nuanced, dynamic character traits. We must learn to recognize and appreciate the nuances and the dynamic nature of the human personality, both theirs and ours.

While we're dealing with impossible people, we must also protect our privacy. While with collaborative people some degree of vulnerability on our part may go a long way, with an impossible person, we can't afford to be vulnerable.

This is very important. Impossible people will use any information they have about us, our family and our larger life to their benefit. They're often specialists in manipulation and are good at making people, including us, talk. This is less from their genuine interest in us and more from a desire to obtain any leverage over us through techniques such as bigoteering and logical fallacies. Such actions intend to thwart our dealing effectively with their impossible behaviors.

The last and most crucial guideline, then, is to be aware of our behavioral blind spots, our actions that could be construed as being hallmark of an impossible person ourselves. If we have limited experience in dealing with impossible people, we must seek outside help, guidance and support, either through a trained consultant, appropriate training, a support group or even some form of therapy or counseling if we are being affected personally.

Dealing with impossible people also requires an interest in such work. Not everyone sees the benefits of this unique leadership (people) and management (process) problem. It can require considerable time, effort and patience. Not everyone is amenable to dealing with the potential conflict, nor do they have the requisite skills to deal with such individuals and their behaviors.

Certain basic skills are essential when dealing with impossible people. They include deep listening and observation skills, the ability to infect people with the right attitude while confirming or acknowledging their worldview, thereby allaying their insecurities, and the determination to use an impossible person's resistance and stubbornness to one's advantage.

As we're dealing with an individual's behaviors, we must pay attention to the whole of who they are: the silences and the language they employ during conversations, their nonverbal cues, the clothes and accouterments they wear and the image they wish to project—in essence, understanding the masks they wear. But perhaps the most important thing we can do when dealing with such individuals is to be aware of our own biases, so we can avoid negating any objective analysis we may form of them. We may be dealing with an individual who reminds us of someone unpleasant or even unfriendly from our past, resulting in a skewed view of who they indeed are today. Never confuse dress, epidermis, sexual orientation, educational credentials, accent, chattiness or our perceptions of these qualities with a person's character. Remember, the only accurate indicator of character is how a person acts.

Once we have established our guidelines and understand the required skill sets we need, the next step to effectively dealing with and eventually influencing impossible people is to understand the factors that shape and influence their particular worldview. Just like investigators, we must look into the individual's past, insomuch as they allow us to do so or it is readily accessible, to determine what they hold as important.

Examine any background or historical factors that may affect their worldview and actions. Included in this are their current home life, their health history and the environment in which they grew up. We're not looking to justify their behavior but to understand it in terms of how they view the world. This will allow us to counter their actions effectively.

Realize that, in the end, it's always about them and never about us. That means that their issues remain theirs and theirs alone. But we must understand the origins of those issues, those insecurities, those character flaws and the potential envy they conceal behind their mask.

An impossible person's distinguishing quality is their ability to define, assign and project blame onto others for all things that go wrong in their own lives. Unlike possible people, who assume responsibility for their actions, impossible people have mastered the art of the blame, especially attributing fault to their immediate supervisor, their colleagues or their hierarchical leaders. Blame is a particularly pernicious quality in that it's a skewed response to the world's uncertainty. Better to believe that someone, somewhere, has some unknown or undefined power and agency over our lives than to recognize the unpredictability in life and our inability to counter it through individual responsibility. That's their take on their situation.

For impossible people, blame is always about others and never about themselves, because the rules apply to others, not to them. Everyone else is impossible; they're the ones who are being reasonable and have been far too long. Impossible people lack insight into themselves and their actions.

This mindset stems from their inability to recognize the error of their self-opinion. Their self-opinion involves some form of superiority over others or some perceived specialness. They may view themselves as being a rebel, disdaining all authority, especially fighting against "the man," whoever that may be. They may view themselves as marginalized, without any privilege, either familial, financial, political or social, feeding the victim mindset, of which the most extreme manifestation is the martyr mentality. Finally, they view themselves as having unique attributes such as beauty, intelligence, charm, athleticism, popularity or saintliness, that others covet. Rather than recognizing a distorted self-opinion, it's easier for them to blame others for the supposedly inaccurate and unfair assessment of them.

Impossible people tend to have excellent memories; that's part of their victim mindset, primarily when they can assign blame to another and hold grudges indefinitely. Impossible people tend to be impulsive, wanting their demands met in the now, failing which they're not afraid to throw a tantrum or display manipulative emotional outbursts. Conversely, when they offer help of any kind, they do so with a hidden or explicit agenda, not in an effort to be altruistic.

Dealing with impossible people requires different assumptions and approaches than what's needed with possible people, who are collaborative for the most part. This means that we need to treat impossible people as children in some circumstances; not in a condescending manner, but with the recognition that their level of social maturity is lower than others'. We can't expect to engage in reasonable conversations with them because of their propensity to assign blame elsewhere. They don't listen to reason, and they can't reason to listen deeply.

Don't call them out by labeling them. Don't show them this or any other document or book on impossible people. Such actions will only frustrate them and put them more on the defensive, entrenching them in their position.

Our goal is to decipher their actions, lower their defensive posturing and defuse their negative traits by staying as calm, emotionless and empathetic as possible. Any emotional reaction towards them, such as anger, crying or pleading, will only encourage more difficult behavior, because they stand ready to use anything we do or say against us in their court of worldview. Empathy does not mean joining them in complaining, bashing or blaming through commiseration. It means understanding where they're coming from. Don't become their martyr. Don't reward someone for abusive behavior; this will only encourage further abuse. Conversely, don't allow them to be a martyr as they attempt to cajole, coerce or control you.

Our objective isn't to win any arguments. Our opinion or view on any topic is inconsequential to the impossible person. We can't convince them of the validity of our views through rational discussion or debate. Part of the recognition that impossible people exist is recognizing that normal relationships with such people, based on mutual respect and equitable exchange, are difficult, if not unattainable. We can't beat them at their own game. We must accept who and what they are, focusing on affecting their behavior.

Our goal is to limit the amount of damage they can create by countering their problematic conduct and even exploiting it, where possible, to mutual benefit. The challenge is to deal with their micro- and macro-aggressions while attempting to build micro- and macro-bridges between them and others to carry on the common good and mitigate their damage.

Eventually, we'll part company with them. If the impossible person is a work colleague, and we are unable to leave them physically, we must leave them mentally and socially. If the impossible person is our boss and in spite of our best efforts we are unable to effect any changes in them and the work relationship, we must leave them and the job. With impossible people we must be as forthright, direct and even relentless as required, but nothing more. The possible people we work with depend on us and deserve no less.

Damage mitigation is our primary goal. That includes protecting us, our personal life and our mental well-being. Directly related to this is our secondary goal of becoming immune to contagious behavior and not being like them; instead, being a possible person. This means being a living example of tolerance, patience, humility and kindness, especially with them.

The identification of an impossible person always begins with their actions as opposed to their words. Here, deeds, not words, matter most. Understand the signature traits of the impossible person, their *modus operandi*, their history of action. Always seek confirmation of what they say from third parties who have dealt with them in the past.

Once their traits have been identified, we need to determine our goals in countering them, picking our words, actions and battles carefully. As we move tactically and strategically to counter their efforts, we must be mindful of their counter-tactics, such as tantrums, emotional outbursts, threats and complaints, that they will employ to get their way.

But we must recognize what they represent in the social ecology.

Who are the (impossible) people in your neighborhood?

Impossible people represent an entire gamut of intricate behavior patterns that are relatively consistent. We can identify them according to certain signature traits. Those signature traits are fluid and subject to change. As such, just as there is a vast diversity of human beings in our world, there is a significant number of difficult traits that cannot be synthesized into one succinct, exhaustive list. Hence, we can only talk in general terms about impossible people according to the types of problematic behaviors they display and their effects on others. In general, then, there are six major groups of difficult behaviors.

The first and most extensive group are what the American clinical psychologist Albert J. Bernstein qualifies as *Emotional Vampires*, individuals who, because of their various behaviors, drain people emotionally dry, affecting others' health and well-being.[93] Their behaviors are characterized by personality disorders, which are fixed and enduring, involving extreme patterns of thought and actions that deviate from social norms and expectations, causing significant interpersonal impairment. Their personality disorders have developed from some hereditary temperamental attributes as well as from environmental and developmental events over their lifetime. The Emotional Vampire's actions are akin to those of a predator, always searching for a new victim.

It's important to remember that just because a person may display some of these traits doesn't mean that they have a particular personality disorder. Individuals may display several features from different personality disorders at the same time. Among these traits are the following personality disorders:[94]

- **Histrionic disorders** – These are the Drama Queens of all gender identifications. They can be the hams, the actors and the passive-aggressives in our lives. They crave attention and approval, doing anything to achieve both, except fulfilling their promises and commitments. Their functional trait is expressiveness, demonstrating a pervasive pattern of excessive emotionality and attention-seeking. They view the world as a stage in which they are a performer searching for admirers through provocation and seduction.
- **Narcissistic disorders** – Legends in their own minds, these are the grandiose egos and tiny consciences who feel they are destined and entitled to greatness, but instead are most often job- and relationship-drifters. Their functional trait is self-aggrandizement, demonstrating a pervasive pattern of grandiosity, a need for admiration and a lack of empathy. They view the world as belonging to them, while others are simply servants in it. They deal with their world exclusively through image management.
- **Antisocial disorders** – Despite the name, these are highly social, even charming individuals who are oblivious to standard social rules. They can be daredevils, bullies and fraudsters, whose functional trait is exploiting others to get what they want. Sociopaths and, on occasion, psychopaths, are people who are often highly intelligent, viewing the world as being cutthroat, a dog-eat-dog place where they're the superior alphas while others are just suckers waiting to be manipulated for their opportunistic and fearless bent.
- **Obsessive-compulsive personality disorders (OCPD)** – Perfectionists in every sense of the word, they can't see the big picture. They are transfixed on the minutiae as puritans, anal retentives, micromanagers and control freaks. Their functional trait is rigidity and tightness, having a pervasive preoccupation with orderliness. They view the world as contaminated, requiring order because others are so sloppy while they're so righteous and pure, forever seeking control. Don't confuse this disorder with obsessive-compulsive disorder (OCD), the mental state in which a person has uncontrollable, recurring obsessions or behaviors that need to be repeated. A person with OCD washes their hands in-

cessantly, while a person with OCPD is forever attempting to get others to wash theirs.

- **Paranoid disorders** – Always suspicious, they view themselves as visionaries who continuously search for the truth, usually being the only ones who see it. They're the conspiracy theorists out in the wilderness, hyper-alert, hyper-focused and hyper-versed on their version of the truth. Their minds are filled with visions of enemies, mostly illusory. Their functional trait is mistrust; they view the world as a dangerous place, with a Hobbesian view that society is a type of war of one against all. They view themselves as being mistreated and misunderstood, and others as being wicked and out to get them.

This list is not exhaustive. There are related personality disorders such as avoidant, dependent, schizoid, borderline and schizotypal. The estimated prevalence of these personality disorders can be upwards of 17 percent of the general population.

The second type of difficult behavior is the *poor or bad attitudes*, those behaviors that make work, neighborhood and family life no fun at all. They include base aggression, anxiety, avoidance, depression, resentment, juvenility and plain stupidity. Anyone can display poor attitudes at any time, as they are often situation-dependent. For the most part, people are consistent in their approaches and have demonstrated many of these poor attitudes since childhood, bringing them permanently into the workplace and their relationships.

The third type of difficult behavior is *power-playing*. For power-players, power and status mean everything. Their self-interest is always their overarching concern, doing anything they feel is required to achieve their aims, centered around obtaining power and recognition. Once they get what they desire, they cavalierly discard any relationship or possession they used to obtain that power. The power-player may or may not exhibit narcissistic, paranoid or antisocial traits, but attempts to hold onto power and increase it for as long as they can, any way they can. This doesn't necessarily mean that they become the group or organizational leader. They're often content with being a quiet second-in-command, anonymously and discretely pulling the boss' strings.

The fourth type of difficult behavior is *bullying*. A first cousin to power-players, bullies routinely belittle others to maintain their own perceived sense of power. Their weapons of choice include humiliation, sarcasm, rudeness, threats, invasion of personal territory and withering email flames. They use these weapons in an attempt to control how they view themselves. The intended victims of these weapons are merely pawns in their game. These are the types who often claim that their actions are "nothing personal."

The fifth type of difficult behavior is *disgruntlement*. Perpetual victims, disgruntled people always have an excuse, procrastinate or minimize their weaknesses, blaming them on some outside issue, factor or person. In the workplace, they're the office gossip, the perpetual pessimist, the know-it-all and the 'frequent flyer' who constantly expresses their discontent through serial grievances, complaints and even lawsuits. They are co-dependent in that they need their job, not just for the money, but also for what the organization they work for embodies: their life's frustrations and failures. In their personal life, they do the same with their spouse and family members.

The sixth and final type of difficult behavior is *incivility and rude behavior*. This can be the most prevalent of all the kinds of bad behavior everyone uses at one time or another. This behavior can range from outright nastiness, the intentional undermining of others' work and contributions, ignoring people's opinions and requests, to discrimination and harassment.[95]

From a corporate perspective, the most effective ways to reduce the costs and effects of basic incivility and rude behavior in the workplace are hiring for character while building a culture that rejects such attitudes. This requires starting from the beginning of an individual's career by ensuring that the person hired is collaborative and empathetic and does not suffer from grandiose narcissism. The person most responsible for ensuring this is the chief executive. This means that they cannot be an impossible person themself.

As a leader, you must recognize the signs related to these negative behaviors in yourself first and root them out. Again, this requires maintaining a constant internal dialogue around your reality to see how your behaviors affect others, making the necessary adjustments to deal with the negative fallout of your actions, and ensuring those behaviors don't surface again.

With the omnipresence of cellular technology, even checking emails and messages on one's smartphone during meetings can be construed as rude or uncivil. American author Simon Sinek refers to the omnipresence of smartphones during work and interpersonal interactions as an addiction.

Towards the end of my tenure as chief of police, at any meeting I presided over, I would not have my smartphone with me so as to dedicate my full attention to the discussion at hand and, specifically, to listen to those talking. Most importantly, I wanted to convey to the people I worked with that they were important to me, because they were.

When I was a simple participant in a meeting, I asked for the chairperson's permission to access my emails before the meeting, indicating what type of situation I was managing at the time. When I wasn't accessing my phone, it would be tucked away not left out on the table in front of me.

Former French president (2012-2017) François Hollande had a well-known practice prohibiting smartphones, tablets or laptop computers in any meeting he presided over. His goal was to have all meeting participants fully engaged in the discussion for the time they were there and to get them out of the meeting again as soon as practicable. One of the requirements I have when I deliver leadership training is for all participants to place their muted smartphones and electronics on tables at the front of the room, in clear view of everyone. I can't compete with the draw of social media and various messages and noise from devices.

On one occasion, while I participated in a hiring panel, the candidate, a lawyer vying for the city solicitor's job, sat down and placed their smartphone on the table in front of them at the interview's outset. They weren't monitoring the time. Those of us on the panel looked at one another, wondering if they were anticipating a phone call or an important message during the interview. They didn't get the job.

The lesson in all this is to turn off the sounds and the notifications from our smartphones. And then put them away. Focus on the person in front of you at that moment. Make them feel that who they are and what they have to say are the most important things you have to deal with right then.

From a personal perspective, the most effective way to deal with incivility is to inoculate or render yourself impervious to such attitudes' adverse effects by thriving in your entire life, not just at work. This implies having a proper work-life balance that gives you something to look forward to after work, not just going home to have a drink or numb your brain from the workday's challenges before the TV or a computer screen. Or, even worse, trying to catch up on the work of the day by spending a few extra hours working online from home.

By thriving, we grow cognitively, being curious and desirous of learning new things. This helps us become physically and mentally healthy, experiencing passion and excitement at work and outside of it. This can be especially challenging for those who identify with their professional personas 24/7 and have limited interests outside of their work.

Once we understand the social ecology, we can then start de-escalation, remediation and even inoculation.

Of containment and contingencies, control and coercion

After identifying the impossible person's traits and actions, we have to formulate a game plan to deal with them. The key is not to approach the impossible person to seek their help, mercy or gratitude, but to appeal to their self-interest. This approach depends on the type of impossible behavior we're dealing with.

Dealing with people with bad attitudes involves understanding what the attitude is and its drivers, and not being sucked into the vortex of their emotions. By maintaining our neutrality and not providing an outlet for their aggression, anxiety, avoidance, depression or resentment, we deny them the emotional fuel they require to continue such behavior. We must be a soothing yet independent influence over their actions.

Nor should we attempt to rescue them from the pit of their despair by lecturing them about how wonderful life can be for them outside the hole. The key is to draw them into positive experiences, reinforcing the personal benefits of avoiding their bad attitudes. As we can't repress their bad attitudes, we must channel their energies into something more positive.

To counter power-seekers, we must be alive to their movements at all times. The saying *Keep your friends close but keep your enemies closer* has its application here. By being aware of their history and movements, we understand their strengths, weaknesses and emotional hot buttons. If we're working for them, we must not outshine them, preferring to make them feel smarter than us if that's what it takes to avoid confrontation. If we can't manage or work for them, it may be best to leave them entirely by finding another job elsewhere.

The most effective way to deal with impossible people, especially those who are bullies, disgruntled and with manifest personality disorders, is through containment and contingencies. But you must stand up to them, especially the bullies, as early, as resolutely, and as calmly as possible, so you don't have to do it more than you should.

When dealing with those prone to histrionics, acting dispassionately is the best course. This way, the impossible person sees that your emotions don't factor into your analysis of the situation and your choice of responses to provide containment and contingency.

Containment means ensuring that the damage these people wreak is limited to a defined area, usually the impossible person's immediate work area, responsibilities and entourage. It can also mean limiting their involvement in a given project to curb their harmful effect. This mitigates their adverse impact on the workplace and the people subject to their destructive actions.

In extreme cases, where an individual is so toxic that their mere presence in any setting is lethal to the productivity and unity of a group, the individual's marginalization may be required. Only take this step if the termination of the employer-employee relationship is seriously being considered. In such cases, the costs associated with a quick dismissal of an individual and eventual lawsuits or settlements may be less than having to deal with their perpetual grievances, time off work, damage and contagion in the workplace over the long haul. Consulting legal counsel is the best course of action before trying this.

Once containment is in place, contingencies must be employed. Contingency is the polite word, incitement is the neutral word, while coercion is the more direct word. Regardless of the semantics, one thing is clear: contingencies are about determining consequences and setting limits for the impossible person. The goal of contingencies is to force the impossible person to have a direct interest in their actions, essentially by putting skin in *their* game, so they have something important to lose should they continue their behavior, and something to gain if they cease it.

This step involves determining a consequence that matters to the impossible person and that is directly linked to their inappropriate behavior, consistent with their worldview. The goal is to ensure that the meaningful consequence will require them to correct, alter or modify their behavior. Practically speaking, the impossible person must understand in no uncertain terms that if they continue to act in a particular way, then a specific consequence will occur: "Marlo, if you do X, then Y will result."

The key here is to demonstrate a clear and convincing connection between their behavior and the proposed consequences. Set and maintain firm, reasonable and conscious limits in terms of behavioral expectations.

Such behavioral correction must focus on the benefits that will accrue from such changes by the impossible person. This is where acknowledging their worldview and the infusion of a proper attitude are critical to allaying their fears. Praise them for their efforts to modify their actions, not for their talents, perceived or otherwise. For individuals who are co-dependent, such as disgruntled employees, the contingency may need to threaten the very existence of their co-dependency, which is most often their job.

Always be prepared to follow through with contingencies. Lack of consistent follow-through is the most common mistake managers make. Once the impossible person sees that the manager's resolve has broken, so, too, is the opportunity to correct the unwanted behavior. The impossible person then interprets their behavior as acceptable, continuing the same with an even greater sense of impunity.

Some final comments related to dealing with impossible people:

- It's always preferable to have the same manager deal with an impossible person. This allows for a consistent approach and continued focus on the problems at hand instead of always having to brief a new manager. The manager must be able to make decisions and carry out the contingencies.
- If you witness bad behaviors, report them. Don't attempt to interpret them to understand, rationalize or mitigate their effects on others, including yourself. When dealing with bullying behaviors, let the bully know that such actions won't be tolerated by reporting them.
- One of the worst things to do is to say, "Marlo is Marlo; that's just the way they are. We can't change them." Indeed, we can't change Marlo, but we can provide consequences to their actions, so they eventually stop their bad behaviors. That's our goal.
- Always keep your objectives in mind when dealing with an impossible person. They'll do their best to hypnotize you into accepting their behavior and not doing anything about it.

Regardless of the techniques you employ, the overall goal of dealing with impossible people and even those merely having a bad hair day is to ensure that our workplaces, play and social spaces, and our family life are devoid of bullying, disrespect and prejudicial behaviors. Only then can we and others live our best lives.

Intentional targeting intentionally

As we attempt to influence others, we must partake in the targeted influencing of people, regardless of who they are. As the fourth and final core competency of an effective leader, this means taking a strategic but personalized approach to dealing with people. This requires a specific emphasis on acknowledging the person's self-opinion. In most cases, it involves learning as much as we can about their interests and what drives them to want to work or partake in a specific activity.

We don't want to challenge any aspect of a person's unique and often immutable self-opinion. In such matters, they're always right. Remember, our intention is not to win any arguments; it's to influence the other person. If we intentionally or inadvertently challenge their self-opinion, we'll activate their defense mechanisms because our approach may be construed as being judgmental.

If we don't address any aspect of their self-opinion, there's no net effect, either negative or positive. But if we acknowledge and confirm their self-opinion, we can still disagree with their appreciation of it without raising their resistance. In that case, we can influence them by bypassing their defensive posture. To allay their insecurities, the key is not only to be, but to *appear* to be as sincere as possible when addressing the concerns they have that their self-opinion fuels. Sometimes it is a tightrope we must walk between our sincerity and their dignity.

This is why we must be careful not to label people. Just as we should avoid labeling an impossible person, we must also be careful how we label a possible person because they'll take on the characteristics of our diagnosis. People mirror expectations. As a leader, if you value and believe in a work colleague's abilities, most times, they'll rise to the occasion and meet, if not exceed, those expectations. If, on the other hand, you don't value or believe in the potential abilities of an individual, they'll meet those low expectations.

In psychology, these mirroring effects are respectively known as the *Pygmalion Effect* (describing how an individual adopts positive traits ascribed to them by another)[96] and the *Golem Effect* (describing how an individual assumes negative traits).[97]

Targeted influence requires us to instill a feeling of inner security in the other person, the psychological safety we examined previously. We must do this before we can even hope to influence them. This applies to every person we deal with: the impossible and the possible alike.

Remember, our goal is to influence people, through trust, towards some higher good. We can only develop that trust when we have confidence in the other's ability to perform and they in ours: trust that we have their best interests in mind, trust that we are not arbitrarily exerting power over them for power's sake, and trust that we will carry out what we said we'd do.

The exercise of influence can be strenuous, requiring significant resources, commitment and patience. To maintain such energy and focus, we need to ensure that we can take care of ourselves in the long-term. We want to be like the pioneers of the 17th and 18th centuries, who built their homes not based on the latest weather, but on the long-term climate.

This is where the lesson of personal sustainability comes in: ensuring that we design and carry out a life that will last us a lifetime.

Calls from the blue line

- We can only exercise influence if people trust us. Obtain this trust is through demonstrating empathy and compassion.
- Show your trust in people by giving them decisional authority. Allow them to learn by succeeding and making mistakes on their own, while at the same time supporting them.
- It can't be said enough: Hire the right people based on their attitude and character. Build a culture that rejects negative and uncivil attitudes.
- Influence isn't about us. It's always about the other person and is more beneficial than any moral stance we can ever take. Learning to deal with impossible people is a critical leadership function.
- Dealing with the impossible Marlo requires significant resolve and the ability to embrace the conflict that accompanies such interactions. Defuse their short fuse: stay calm, avoiding anger and emotional outbursts. Avoid encouraging their bad behavior by repeating it.
- An impossible person's distinguishing quality is their ability to define, assign and project blame onto others for all things that go

wrong in their lives. They're masters of the art of the blame.

- Don't attempt to fix an impossible person. Instead, always opt to fix processes. Don't attempt psychotherapy on the impossible person; it will only make both of you sicker.
- Once we understand the social ecology, we can start de-escalation, remediation and even inoculation of the workplace environment.
- Regardless of the techniques you employ, the overall goal of dealing with impossible people and even those merely having a bad hair day is to ensure that your workplace, play and social spaces, and family life are devoid of bullying, disrespect and prejudicial behaviors. Only then can we all live our best lives.

10: The lesson of personal sustainability

The fundamental core issue for [anyone] is to possess a belief that they run their personal lives. This is the basic separation in orientation between the victim and the survivor. The victim starts to look at personal time as being something to be endured until retirement whereas the survivor has a sense of mastery and empowerment over their day-to-day life.

-Kevin Gilmartin, psychologist, author
and former police officer, in
Emotional Survival for Law Enforcement (2002)

The hardest part (1)

Regardless of their rank, police officers must perform many difficult, out of the ordinary, tasks. These include dealing with families searching for answers about a loved one's death, answering public calls for justice when a particularly unscrupulous crime occurs and coping with a work colleague's injury or death.

In late February 2002, one of the constables working in a detachment I had just been transferred from was shot in the face during a high-speed pursuit on the Trans-Canada Highway near Winnipeg, Manitoba. A stray bullet passed through his cruiser's windshield, ricocheted off the steering column and penetrated his face below the eye, causing significant bleeding which covered both his eyes, severely impeding his vision while driving.

Thanks to a calm and directive dispatcher who managed to talk him down from the high-speed pursuit, he was able to stop his cruiser safely. A paramedical team responded to his report of being shot. In a twist of fate, one of the paramedics was his girlfriend.

As resources were being mobilized to find the two suspects who had fled towards Winnipeg, I met the ambulance carrying the wounded constable in a hospital emergency ward. I secured his equipment and waited as the emergency-room staff desperately tried to save his life. After about 45 minutes of intense work, his condition stabilized. They transferred him to the ICU, where I stood watch over him until a permanent guard could be placed in the unit.

Although the constable's life was no longer in danger, his face was swollen at least three times its normal size, which still constituted a severe threat to his life. I couldn't see his eyes, and he was intubated to allow him to breathe. Alone with him in the ICU, I held his hand.

He was conscious and wanted to communicate. I had him squeeze my fingers while I asked him questions and explained what was going on: one squeeze meant "yes" while two squeezes meant "no." We spent about 20 minutes communicating this way until his parents arrived.

The constable eventually recovered from the shooting, even returning to active duty. Although his physical wounds healed, for the most part, the psychological ones never did. They rarely do in such a situation. But at least he was alive.

I know police officers who had done dozens of what are called 'next of kins' (NOKs) to advise a family of the passing of a loved one. Many of these NOKs resulted from non-criminal incidents, almost becoming painfully routine. They included children who had died from a lightning strike while playing on a sports field, spouses dying in an industrial accident, and whole families dying when their vehicle hit a moose or other large animal on a highway.

Such notifications are an unfortunate and sad part of police work, although the act often has little to do with enforcing the law. But someone must do it.

During my career, I had to advise three families of the death of a loved one, a police officer in each case. The first involved a 28-year-old constable named Peter Magdic, who died in a single-vehicle accident in November 2001 near Portage la Prairie, Manitoba, not far from where the other constable would later be shot on the Trans-Canada Highway. Peter only had 11 months of active service as a police officer when he died.

Peter was the first-ever Manitoban police officer of Croatian heritage. He was able to read, write and speak Croatian fluently. I was his acting detachment commander at the time and had the sorrowful responsibility of advising his parents, with whom he still lived, as he was a recent hire and just starting his career.

When the RCMP chaplain and I knocked on the Magdic family's front door late that evening, his father, who had been asleep, met us. When we advised the man of his son's death, it was as if we'd ripped the heart from his chest. He heaved in agony at the news. Upon hearing his cries of anguish, his wife rushed to his side from their bedroom.

A few days later, at Peter's funeral, I acted as the commander of the honor guard that carried his coffin to his final resting place. Once we folded the Canadian flag that had draped the coffin, I presented it to the divisional commander, Assistant Commissioner Tom Egglestone, for presentation to Peter's parents.

Following the flag presentation, just as Peter's coffin was being lowered into the grave, his mother suddenly threw herself on it, imploring her son in Croatian and English not to leave her. I looked up to see the pallbearers who were lined up facing the grave, all young police officers, men and women, close friends of Peter. They were visibly reacting to the stirring scene unfolding before them, some weeping openly as they so desperately tried to compose themselves. I was no different.

I ended up keeping Peter's handcuffs as a reminder of him until I retired from the RCMP in 2012, when I gave them to one of his pallbearers. Assistant Commissioner Egglestone died of a heart attack less than six months later, at 57. And we had yet another funeral to attend.

The hardest part (2)

My second NOK was for another member under my command, who died by suicide in 2004. He'd killed himself with his service pistol, at his desk, late on a Sunday evening. One of his colleagues found him the next morning, slumped beside a blood-stained note he'd left.

My unit staff-sergeant and I went to see the member's mother at her work, and then his retired father on the golf course, to apprise them of their son's death. Now, just as then, I have questions about what I could have done, if anything, to prevent such a tragedy.

As I mentioned earlier, I learned that, in Canada, potentially more active and recently retired (within the prior five years) police officers kill themselves than individuals die in interactions with police.[98] In the United States, the number of deaths by suicide is comparable per capita, with 239 law enforcement suicide deaths reported in 2019 and 177 in 2020.[99]

The numbers in both countries are under-reported, just as they are elsewhere on the planet. According to the World Health Organization (WHO), close to 800,000 people die every year by suicide. For every adult who die at their own hands, there are more than 20 others who attempt suicide.[100] France and England are among the few countries that actively track the number of law enforcement officers who die by suicide.

Suicide is rarely caused by a single factor. It results from a complex interplay of issues in a person's life. Most people who face adversity and mental health challenges don't die by suicide but are able to find the necessary support, treatment and resources to resolve their issues by themselves or with others' help. For some people, social disconnection and isolation result in thwarted belongingness, further distancing them from the help they need. For others who have healthy family and social circles, they may feel a sense of perceived heaviness that leads them to avoid seeking help, feeling their problems would only burden others. People who attempt suicide or die by it view their death as an acceptable option to the stress, pain and hardship they experience.

For police officers, the risk of death by suicide may be further intensified by repeated exposure to death. Officers have less fear of dying because of their training. They also have limited broader social supports, increased sleep disruptions and access to lethal means.[101] In male police officers especially, the situation can be further worsened by a gender-based reluctance to seek help and the lack of a multidimensional sense of self (as in "I'm more than just a cop"). The high number of suicides in law enforcement can also be attributed to the fact that many police officers are White males in their 40s and 50s, a demographic hit hard in the past forty years by suicide. It has only been in the past ten years or so that the profession has openly talked about the subject.

The March 2016 issue of *Men's Health* featured an article entitled "What's Killing White Middle-Aged Men?" On May 31, 2018, the same magazine published a police-specific article entitled "Cops Are Dying by Suicide—and No One Is Talking About It."[102] The 2016 article detailed that White males between the ages of 45-54 were killing themselves in alarming numbers as a result of four main life stressors:

1. Unmet aspirations.
2. Pain (both physical and psychological from various injuries and trauma).
3. Use of opioids and other drugs.
4. Early-onset dementia.

The men of this cohort accounted for 70 percent of all male suicides in the United States. When men of all races are added to this cohort, the suicide rate is 20 per 100,000 and the highest absolute number of suicides of any age group.

In Canada, approximately 11 people die by suicide each day, resulting in more than 4,000 deaths per year for a population of over 37 million people.[103] The suicide rate in the United States has risen from 10.5 per 100,000 people in 1999 to 14.2 per 100,000 in 2018[104], the year in which more than 40,000 Americans took their own lives. This is greater than the number of deaths resulting from vehicle collisions, and is eclipsed only by the recent spike in deaths due to the opioid epidemic, expected to reach its highest numbers ever during the COVID-19 pandemic.[105]

According to the U.S. Centers for Disease Control and Prevention (CDC), men are 3.7 times more likely to die from suicide than women (22.8 per 100,000 for men versus 6.2 per 100,000 women). However, women make nearly four times as many suicide attempts as men. Per capita, men over the age of 75 have the highest suicide rate, followed by men in the 45-64 age group. By race, the group with the highest death rate by suicide is American Indians, followed by White males. These numbers roughly correspond to the demographic trends seen in Canada with White and First Nations males.

In the January 31, 2015, article entitled "Suicide in America—An awful hole" in *The Economist* stated that White men are nearly three times as likely as African-Americans to kill themselves while the latter group was five times more likely to be murdered with a gun than to kill themselves with one. For White males, the opposite was true: they were five times more likely to kill themselves with a gun than to be murdered by someone with a gun.

Gun violence has killed around 40,000 Americans each year, while injuring another 80,000 over the past few years.[106] Those numbers were expected to be higher in 2021. Most gun deaths are from suicide. According to the CDC, in 2018, 24,432 Americans used firearms to kill themselves, up from 19,392 in 2010, a 25 percent increase. Comparable per capita figures have also been found in Canada, although gun ownership is considerably lower there.[107]

Writing checks that bounce

Today, the three most significant challenges facing police in liberal democracies are

- police legitimacy
- community engagement
- police employee support

A sobering statement I once heard was from a senior police leader, who said, "I've written a check to my family that can never be cashed." He was referring to his sacrifices, and especially those of his family, over the years: all the events missed, and the hardships endured because of his professional obligations. After years of late-night callouts, shift work, sleep-disturbing telephone calls, text messages, stressful situations, weeks, months and even year-long deployments abroad, I echo those sentiments.

For almost the entire 20th century, during the six months or so of basic training at the RCMP Training Academy (also known as Depot Division or just "Depot"), recruits and cadets lived in long, open-air dormitories that housed an entire troop of 32 men or women, with 16 beds on either side of the hall. Each side had eight shared living spaces with two beds, chairs and desks that mirrored one another. For those six months, police RCMP officers-in-training would sleep, study and socialize in that space, commonly known as a "pit." Each pair of members would be known as "pit-partners."

In late 1987 and early 1988, I shared my pit with a gregarious lad by the name of Anthony (Tony) Borovsky. Tony was a jovial fellow from Oshawa, Ontario, who had graduated in outdoor education from Lakehead University in Thunder Bay, Ontario, a few years previously.

A huge outdoorsman who loved the social side of hunting, fishing and canoe tripping, he was as tenacious as he was funny. I eventually nick-named him "Pitbull" because he would snarl about all our physical fitness activities that would cause him repetitive shin splints. At the end of each day, he lay on his bed in our pit, icing his shins and grumbling about all the running, swimming and marching in formation.

We eventually graduated from Depot and went our separate ways, me to Québec and he to Nova Scotia. It was only in 2010 when I was transferred to Halifax that we were reunited.

In early June 2014, in Moncton, New Brunswick, a two-hour drive from Halifax, a lone gunman armed with an assault rifle shot five RCMP members. Three of them died from their wounds.

In the months following their deaths, Pitbull confided in me that he didn't want to die on duty. Within a year, he retired from the RCMP.

As luck would have it, and no surprise to anyone, Pitbull quickly grew restless. Within a month of retiring, he took a job as a provincial compliance officer, doing investigations on bootleggers and smugglers for provincial infractions related to sales tax, illegal tobacco, alcohol and other products. In his new job, Pitbull had peace-officer status, and could effect arrests and conduct investigations. He even had a uniform but was unarmed. He seemed genuinely happy about the change, no longer concerned about the threats he used to face as a police officer.

A few weeks after his 57th birthday, in late February 2018, while he was returning to Halifax from a joint operation with the RCMP in southwestern Nova Scotia, he was involved in a head-on collision. The driver of an oncoming car had crossed the median. Neither survived the crash. Pitbull's greatest worry materialized that night when he died on duty.

His family asked me to be one of the eulogizers at his memorial service. Talking about Pitbull and trying to put some wind into the sails of his grieving wife and three adult sons was one of the most touching moments of my life. I was blessed to have known Pitbull. I also jarringly learned how some checks we write can never be cashed.

One of the most poignant monuments to this sacrifice I have ever come across is in Regina, Saskatchewan, in the regimental cemetery on the RCMP Training Academy's grounds. Buried there are RCMP officers and civilian employees who died on-duty, off-duty or once retired. Some family members of RCMP members are included as well, usually spouses and children.

During a visit in the early 2000s, I came across a tombstone that caught my attention. It was the gray granite marker of former RCMP Commissioner Stuart Zachary Taylor Wood (1889-1966). Commissioner Wood oversaw the RCMP from 1938 to 1951, a tumultuous time that included World War II. He worked for the RCMP and its predecessor, the Royal Northwest Mounted Police, for almost 40 years. Commissioner Wood was the great-great-grandson of U.S. President Zachary Taylor (1784-1850), who held office from 1849 to 1850.

In Canada, the RCMP is known as "The Force," referred to as such in its constitutive piece of legislation, the *Royal Canadian Mounted Police Act*. The lone epitaph engraved on Commissioner Wood's tombstone reads:

The Force was his life.

Many RCMP members and police officers of any service or country can and do make the same claim regarding the commitment to their police service. It's a matter of personal and professional pride that few occupations have.

But what piqued my curiosity was the grave marker immediately to the left of Commissioner Wood's. It was a comparable gray granite monument, albeit slightly older, with the name Constable Hershel Taylor Wood engraved on its face.

Commissioner and Mrs. Wood had two daughters and three sons. Their eldest son, Donald Zachary Taylor Wood, was killed in action in Europe in 1944. The other two sons were members of the RCMP. The middle son, Hershel, died in 1950 while on duty in the United States. Their youngest son, John, retired from the RCMP at the rank of inspector in 1988, the same year I officially started my policing career with the Force.

Commissioner Wood's epitaph sadly summarizes how many police officers and police employees view their entire lives merely as reflections of their professional persona. In Commissioner Wood's case, the RCMP was, indeed, his life. He also lost one of his sons who gave his life for that same Force—a high price to pay, indeed, for one's work. No check could ever cover that cost.

The hardest part (3)

I completed my final NOK via satellite telephone from Haiti with the wife of Superintendent Doug Coates. During the 40 hours preceding the recovery of Doug's body, I'd slipped on a debris pile and fell headfirst into a hole, cutting my left arm from the wrist to the armpit. I had to be unceremoniously pulled out of the hole by my heels by three Chinese police officers.

Constable Julie Dupré, Superintendent Coates' Executive Officer, took me to the onsite Filipino army medical station for treatment. The heat and dust combined with the physical exhaustion, injury, lack of sleep and water resulted in me going partially into shock. It took all my efforts, several bottles of water and Constable Dupré's constant support to steel myself to return to the debris pile to continue our recovery efforts.

Some hours later, as we were scanning the debris field after a sweep

297

of the excavator's bucket, Constable Dupré noticed a boot protruding from the debris, its black sole exposed. It was attached to a body. Upon further inspection, I noticed that the laces were tied around the ankle.

I remembered when I had initially been sent to Haiti in 2008 that Doug, who was then in charge of International Peacekeeping for the RCMP and who was responsible for my posting, had jokingly told me the best way to tie my boots. As a former SWAT-team member, he had his way of tying his boots, which involved wrapping the laces around the ankle, much like military members. He had offered the same advice to Constable Dupré.

The boot was, indeed, Doug's.

It took two more hours of sustained effort by Brazilian and Chinese rescuers before his body was fully uncovered from the rubble. As I took his dog tags and placed him on a stretcher, a Chinese police officer who was assisting me said in broken English: "You. Him. Same uniform."

Indeed, both Doug and I were both wearing the same white officer's shirt and rank insignia. He even had, in his breast pocket, the same bright-orange cell phone I had used during the final months of my mission in 2009. All that was different between the two of us was how I tied my boots. And that I was alive.

We carefully took Doug's body out of the debris field. A Chinese police officer held each corner of the stretcher, and I held onto one side with Constable Dupré following us. While we were transporting Doug's remains from the debris site, Logan Abassi, one of MINUSTAH's two official photographers, captured the moment. He was kind enough to send me the photo a few weeks later.

More than any other souvenir or keepsake from my policing career, that image symbolizes the mortality in everyone, including me. It calls up the Latin maxim, *Vivamus, moriendum est* ("Let us live, since we must die"), reminding us all that death is the inevitable outcome of our life, a life that we must live fully.

The air we breathe

What are the greatest killers in today's world: Homicides? Terrorism? Plane crashes? Natural or nuclear disasters? The answer is none of them. As Hans Rosling reported in his book, *Factfulness*, homicides are responsible for 0.7 percent of all deaths globally. In comparison, terrorism is responsible for 0.05 percent, while plane crashes are responsible for 0.001 percent, and natural disasters for 0.1 percent.[108] The chance of an American dying from an impaired driver's actions is 50 times greater than the actions of a terrorist.

Separately, none of these causes results in the death of more than 1 percent of the world's population, yet they all occupy an important place in the news cycle. Since the April 1986 Chernobyl nuclear disaster, which resulted in at least 31 people dying immediately and countless subsequent deaths from radiation poisoning, there have been no other deaths directly caused by nuclear leaks.

March 11, 2011, the Tôhoku earthquake and tsunami resulting in the Fukushima Dai-ichi nuclear disaster caused three nuclear meltdowns, three hydrogen explosions and radioactive contamination from several reactors. The event, also known as 3/11, forced the evacuation of some 154,000 people who were living within a 20-kilometer radius of the power plant. All 54 of Japan's nuclear reactors were subsequently shut down, immediately increasing the use and cost of fossil fuels, resulting in an 8 percent decrease in country-wide energy production. Upwards of 2000 died because of the evacuations, while another 1,280 people died of cold in their homes because of power outages. Although some 16,000 deaths were caused by the tsunami, no one died because of the actual nuclear fallout.

In order, the top four things that kill people in this world are:

1. Tobacco use
2. Poor or mal-nutrition (obesity and starvation)
3. Hypertension
4. Air pollution (a killer of upwards of six million people per year)

All four killers put significant stress on the human body, resulting not just in the eventual death of individuals but in the simultaneous presence of two or more diseases or medical conditions in people, known as comorbidity. Coupled with COVID-19, comorbidity has led to what some experts have qualified as a "syndemic," or the interaction of several epidemics that exacerbate the disease burden, especially in populations that are already hampered by poverty, lack of education, poor access to quality health care and other marginal social determinants of health.[109] This syndemic accelerates the slow march to death.

Despite the emphasis on climate change today, people are often surprised when they learn that air pollution is one of the top killers of human beings.[110] This is and has been a chronic and acute killer of human beings for decades, if not centuries. Two significant air-pollution events within the last 75 years have become infamous, not only for their deadliness but for their unexpected nature.

From Friday, December 5 to Tuesday, December 9, 1952, an unusual fog in England resulted in the death of at least 4,000 people and illness to over 100,000. The Great Smog of London was an abnormal event precipitated by a period of frigid weather. A stationary windless dome of high pressure caused the collection of airborne pollutants, mostly arising from the burning of coal, the primary fuel used to heat buildings and cook with at the time. Coal, of course, is concentrated carbon.

The combination of windless conditions and particle-laden haze resulted in a thick layer of smog covering the British capital, significantly reducing visibility and even penetrating indoors. London has suffered from low air quality since the 13th century, which progressively got worse in the 17th century. The Great Smog of 1952 is considered the worst air-pollution event in the history of the United Kingdom.

The second event was the Bhopal gas leak of December 2-3, 1984, which exposed over 500,000 people to a leak of methyl isocyanate gas, an intermediate chemical used in the manufacture of pesticides. The official death toll was 2,259 people, but the local state government paid compensation to family members of 3,787 people who had died and to over 570,000 injured victims. Other estimates indicate that upwards of

8,000 people died directly because of the leak, while another 8,000 have since died because of exposure to complications.

These are but two examples of air pollution's ongoing effects on our planet, one of the significant but lesser-recognized planetary and human stressors. Although they weren't caused by, nor were examples of domestic terror, they're human-made examples of domestic horror.

Domestication and domination of the unexpected

We often hear and have probably said to ourselves and others at various times about how "stressed out" we are or how much stress we're going through, at work, at home or in life in general. Much of the stress we have is self-imposed through high, if not unrealistic, expectations. We search for perfection in our work, our home life and our relationships. When we don't meet those expectations, we become disappointed, frustrated and distressed in ways that can result in a mental health issue.

One of the major factors contributing to our stressors and how we react to them is the lack of regular and prolonged opportunities to relax and recharge our batteries. Unable to unwind and rejuvenate, we're incapable of appropriately facing the challenges that pop up and accumulate in our life. Dealing with these challenges involves understanding the various forms of stress we face.

Stress, in and of itself, is neutral. It's an automatic, biological response to physiological, psychological and sociological demands. Without stress, life would have no flavor, no purpose, and indeed no meaning.

What adds to life, creating those favorable conditions, is positive stress, known as *eustress*. It's the good stress that's infrequent, short-lived and associated with positive life experiences that inspire us to action, building us up and leaving us better than we were before. Positive stress lets us meet and overcome life's daily challenges—passing a test, making a presentation or even just getting up in the morning to go to work.

What we try to avoid is the negative form of stress, known as *distress*. Distress may be chronic or repetitive, long-lasting, demotivating, depressing and paralyzing, breaking us down and leaving us worse off than before. Repeated, chronic distress on the body can have long-term, destructive effects we do not counter it appropriately and effectively. These effects are normal reactions to abnormal sources or amounts of distress.

Understanding our stress tolerance threshold is critical to managing stress in our lives.[111]

My son once candidly asked me how many dead people I've seen and how many dead bodies I've handled in my life. I tried counting them all by visualizing their faces. I couldn't. There were just too many. For those I knew by name, I couldn't remember the lives behind all those faces.

Pascal Boyer, an American-French anthropologist, notes that encountering corpses triggers specific mental processes that fall into themes that are part of societal responses to death.[112]

- The first is **predation**. The sight of a dead body provokes a fear that we're potential prey or the prospective victim of some accident.
- The second theme is **contagion**. In the many scenes I worked in and attended where there were multiple corpses, one of the first reactions of rescuers, handlers and bystanders alike was covering their mouths with a mask, a pulled-up shirt or a handkerchief. It was as if the recently deceased could somehow contaminate them, which is a legitimate fear, as we've seen with COVID-19 and Ebola.
- The final theme, according to Boyer, is **violation**. Because we see a human corpse, we see what was once a living being with hopes, dreams and life. Their death contradicts how we viewed and remember them, especially if we knew them personally.

Such triggered responses result in normal stress reactions to abnormal events, 'abnormal' in the sense of rare or unusual.

It has always surprised me the number of people I've spoken to who have never handled or even seen a corpse. Conversely, I've also been surprised by the number of people who regularly see and handle corpses: doctors, nurses, hospital personnel, paramedics, firefighters and police officers. More importantly, I'm surprised how they manage to handle the stressors of such work.

There are two keys to effectively dealing with stress, regardless of the source or type: first, we must learn to balance our various and often-competing life demands, workloads and responsibilities, including those related to exercise, rest and nutritional requirements; and second, we need to view these demands, workloads and duties as achievable and manageable challenges, or at the very least interesting problems to solve, rather than insurmountable obstacles or threats to our well-being.

This approach encourages physiological and psychological responses that improve thinking and decision-making while causing less mental and physical breakdown; in a word, avoiding decline. However, the key is to proactively deal with the situations, conditions and issues that under-lie that distress. And to have the resources, tools and abilities to do so.

In an ideal world, we'd attain a lifestyle in which stress, distress and eustress contribute to our becoming better than before, becoming what Nassim Nicholas Taleb calls *antifragile*: what is fragile breaks, what is re-silient resists and what is antifragile thrives. A succinct representation of this notion follows:

- Distress > Breakage > Fragility
- Stress > Status quo > Resilience
- Eustress > Thriving > Antifragility

The central point is this: do not view resilience as the desired result of our efforts. We want more; we want to grow and be better than before the incident, the event and the stressor that sent us into a tailspin. We want to thrive, to benefit despite and from the disorder we face.

Take as an example a traumatic event in which a person's physical integrity has been rudely tested, even compromised, but not ended through death: a bank teller robbed at gunpoint, the driver of a car involved in a head-on collision, a sailor falling overboard at night into the frigid waters of the North Atlantic, a police officer shot at during a call. As unusual distressful events, they can and do lead individuals to have normal psychological reactions. Depending on many factors, including previous life trauma, personal support during and after the event, and appropriate coping strategies, these individuals may or may not develop a PTSI. But when looked at from an antifragile lens, these individuals can benefit from the disorder they faced by becoming better than before, through what can be termed Post-Traumatic Growth (PTG).

PTG is a person's capacity for growth and positive psychological, cognitive and behavioral changes resulting from challenging events, major life crises, trauma and other distressful events.[113] It requires developing a high level of mental or psychological fitness, including optimism, humor, outside interests, social support, curiosity, personal isolation reduction and mindfulness practices. These factors are complementary to the character strengths identified by Drs. Peterson and Seligman in their work cited previously.

The advantages gained from PTG can be numerous. Thanks to one's antifragility following a significant event, an individual may gain a re-newed appreciation for life, a recognition of new possibilities, a new direction and revived hope and optimism. They may also develop deeper relationships with others, realizing the importance of the people in their life and their importance in those people's lives. They may also cultivate a greater awareness of their strengths and weakness, hence their potential, driving them to make life-altering changes in line with new life priorities. Such an event may also contribute to their overall spiritual development, not limited to religious participation, including mindfulness.

PTG represents psychological adaptability at its best: the ability to adapt to changes in our psychological environment. Such adaptation is a crucial determinant of emotional intelligence (EQ) and working effectively under pressure.

But the unique event need not be so dramatic as to compromise our physical integrity or threaten our life. We can improve our psychological adaptability through mindfulness techniques (e.g., meditation and such activities as *chi kung*, yoga or *tai chi*), acceptance strategies (i.e., Stoicism), physical movement and connectedness with others. But everything comes backs to the attitude we carry when dealing with such events. One thing is sure: we can't grow by playing the victim and blaming others or outside influences. Personal growth does not equate to victimhood. This approach presupposes that we maintain a purpose in our lives, not accept blame which falsely presents itself as purpose.

The daily events in which we adapt to short-term, sometimes self-imposed disorder can also shape and influence us. I saw this situation play out when I officiated higher levels of hockey. When I was 57, my 17-year-old son asked that I referee with him a major bantam game in a regional tournament as part of a four-official system (two referees and two linespersons). Major bantam players are 13 and 14-year-olds who have an honest shot at the elite levels of under-18 hockey, leading to potential NCAA scholarships or playing in one of Canada's major junior hockey leagues, the draft feeders to the National Hockey League. They are fast, agile, big and strong, playing hockey where bodychecking is a refined art intended to displace an opponent from the puck, not a form of punishment.

At the outset of the game, I found myself intimidated and skating for my life. I avoided their slap shots that resembled missile launches from the blue line, their perfectly timed hits and the basic playmaking they were doing every single moment of the game. But as I became more comfortable during the game, especially after having called the first three penalties, including a penalty shot—much to my son's astonishment—I realized that I could deal with the stress of officiating this level.

It was at that moment that my distress morphed into eustress. That's when my view of that hockey game changed radically, and I grew from the stressors I faced at that moment.

At the end of the game, I was on a high, having officiated competently. Best of all, I did it with my son.

Zen and the art of human maintenance

To be an effective leader who influences others through trust towards attaining a common good, you need to take care of yourself, first and foremost. This means paying particular attention to your personal sustainability. Just as with a motorcycle, a car or a home, you need to ensure your regular maintenance. Living results in inevitable wear and tear on the body, mind and soul. The antidote is intentional, effortful maintenance of the self.

If we can't maintain our personal sustainability, we're poorly placed to encourage others to care for themselves. As the pre-flight video or flight attendant demonstrates, we should put on our own oxygen mask first before assisting others with theirs. We want to avoid professional burnout, or, in other words, becoming the depleted leader: someone in a position of influence who has diminished physical, psychological and cognitive functioning. One study identified three distinct symptoms of burnout:

1. Physical or mental exhaustion.
2. Cynical detachment or social disconnect.
3. A reduced sense of personal value.[114]

A leader's psychological well-being matters to their overall leadership and has a cascading effect on those they lead.[115]

Leaders who suffer from repeated cognitive resource depletion are less effective in their leadership role, making mistakes in judgment and even becoming detrimental to themselves and others through risky decision-making and abuse of power. Most important, an unhealthy leader can't 'walk the talk' when driving a wellness agenda.

There are no short-cuts to self-care and personal sustainability.

What's required is an ongoing series of individual choices and initiatives to ensure our well-being. Chief among them is obtaining the requisite knowledge about us through what's known as health literacy. Unfortunately, when we were born or growing up, we never received an owner's manual on how to take care of ourselves. Health literacy is our primary responsibility, and no one else's. And we can only achieve it through self-awareness and constant learning. This empowers us to do the right things and have agency over our health and, ultimately, our life.

Because of the world we live in, we all face challenges and crises, sometimes daily. They can vary from relationship problems to important career decisions, playing in a game or working in a team where the outcome depends on us to guide a business through a difficult time. Such situations require us to be fully engaged, both physically and mentally. An emotional outburst or a response based on intuition, anger, passion or fear won't effectively deal with the situation.

What's required, then, is for us to be fully engaged, both intellectually and cognitively. This also requires an absence of preconceived notions while being aware of our cognitive, inherent and overt biases. Although we take the time to be reflective, we're also urgent in our analysis, seeking out the facts of any matter and weighing others' advice against our convictions and impressions. Developing a habit of appropriate response helps us avoid analysis paralysis. It also lets us marshal the necessary resources that encourage eustress reactions instead of distress reactions because we're in control and aren't overwhelmed.

We all know the critical importance of physical activity, proper nutrition and good hygiene, but are less-well versed in the rational, appropriate use of products and services. This means reaching out to experts and technicians when required, including accessing all manners of health care professionals. This implies having the necessary financial and community resources to do so. Self-care also requires applying the notion of *via negativa*, avoiding those things and activities that cause us to hurt: substances and practices that are toxic and even life-threatening, including inactivity.

Surfeit and abundance: use it or lose it

In their book *Younger Next Year,* authors Chris Crowley and Henry S. Lodge raise a singular premise around aging: either grow or decay. As human biology doesn't recognize retirement or even aging, there's no biological basis for retirement. But our human biology recognizes and reacts to the decisions we make regarding our lifestyle; many of our health outcomes result from those decisions. Fast food, a sedentary routine, modern distress, loneliness, isolation and inactivity have no evolutionary basis in our lives.

We assume that we're purpose-built for life in the 21st century. This is incorrect, as our time's most significant problems are overabundance and idleness, both physically and intellectually. The isolation, quarantines and lack of traveling experienced during the COVID-19 pandemic laid bare one of the realities of having too much unstructured time and idleness: it can become tedious and make us feel aimless. This also applies to us in retirement, when the choice between growth and decay becomes even more pronounced. But that choice exists long before we reach our golden years.

Human evolution didn't involve sitting for extended periods at a desk or a table, pounding away at a keyboard. What this prompts is decay. Humans evolved through physical movement, using their legs to displace themselves and their hands to explore their natural environment. It's this movement that prompts growth. As we age, there is only room for growth or decay, and our bodies look to us to choose between the two.

Idleness is the most powerful signal to the body to accept decay as an inevitable consequence of aging. Inactivity, combined with an excess of food, drink and passive leisure, further accelerates the decay triggered by aging.

However, this isn't limited to older people. Those of us with children who had no school, sports or social activities during portions of the pandemic, saw the negative impact of idleness on them: they became listless and nocturnal, shunning parental contact and losing their natural drive. Although they have youth on their side, which allows them to quickly rebound once their education, sports activities and social lives resume, age impedes those of us who are older from doing the same as promptly, if at all. To stave off this seemingly-inevitable decline, we need to do things: to move, to create, to socialize, to contribute, to learn to be active.

Thinking and managing our feelings around aging are also essential.

Negative feelings towards aging can make us physically age faster. Understand that if we don't continue to grow physically, mentally, socially and spiritually, we'll decay. And yes, we will all eventually die. But in the interim, we can do our best to delay that inevitability, and, more importantly, to ensure the life we lead up to that finality is as fulsome, complete and happy as it can be. We can and must ensure that our life is the best it can be.

Developing an enthusiasm or a passion for doing something can easily occur in our later years. But it's better to start younger to develop habits, activities and social networks that will last a lifetime. Recognize that what we do regularly before we retire, we'll do more of once retired. That means if we watch TV or self-medicate a lot beforehand, we'll do more of the same when we finally have the time. Conversely, if we work out and develop musical or artistic talents, acquiring some new expertise, and have a purpose in life outside of work, we'll be more inclined to expand those activities once retired.

One of the most significant challenges we're collectively facing as a species, regardless of where we live or who we are, is the rise of dementia. Dementia is a combination of symptoms with many different causes, including Alzheimer's disease, vascular changes in the brain, Parkinson's disease, and even treatable and reversible conditions such as vitamin deficiencies and thyroid gland problems. Considered to affect upwards of 50 million people worldwide and increasing every year, dementia is an unexpected and contradictory consequence of one of humanity's most outstanding achievements: our increased lifespans. The World Health Organization (WHO) considers it a pandemic.[116]

There are generally fifteen recognized risk factors that play a part in people developing dementia, in two distinct groups: risk factors we can change and those we cannot. Age is the most prominent risk factor for dementia. For some unknown reason, women have a higher risk than men to develop Alzheimer's specifically, while their risk for developing dementia is the same as that of men. Although genes play a role in dementia, the evidence is still inconclusive regarding its hereditary influence.

We have some control over these risk factors:

- Depression
- Diabetes
- Head injuries in middle age, including concussions and strokes
- Hearing loss

- High alcohol consumption
- High blood pressure
- Prolonged exposure to air pollution
- Smoking
- Low levels of education
- Obesity and lack of exercise
- Poor nutrition
- Social isolation

Reducing our risk factors doesn't mean that we won't suffer one day from dementia. What it means is that we'll at least be able to mitigate some of those risks. The most certain benefit is that we'll also increase the quality of our life by paying attention to these factors. And, as Crowley and Lodge encourage us to do, we'll stave off decay, including possible dementia, by continuing to grow physically, mentally, socially and spiritually.

This isn't a question of continuing to work or do the same things we always have done, but to intentionally do things to avoid the inactivity and excess that trigger decay. Seek out eustress-enhancing opportunities —roller coasters, first dates, skiing a black diamond run, planting a garden, visiting different places, learning a new language, playing a musical instrument, dancing and engaging in other activities and social experiences. Do so at your rhythm and especially your initiative.

And while you encourage eustress in your life, don't shy away from dealing with the distress you face. Remember that we want to retire by design, not by default. And we retire only from a job, not from meaningful projects that must continue in our life irrespective of a commitment to work for pay.

Real-life stats that don't lie

In policing, whatever the country, the county or the community, the three biggest societal challenges are at-risk youth, addictions and mental health issues. Through the two studies I tasked the Halifax Regional Police dispatch center with in 2015 and 2018 around non-criminal calls for service, we determined that a large portion of the calls for service were mental health calls in which family members and individuals living alone were in crisis. We'd regularly receive calls from individuals wanting metal health attention, not knowing where to turn.

During the week-long analysis in 2018, we received 41 calls from people who had attempted to end their lives by suicide. These were often repeat calls or help in dealing with their various mental health issues. Before I arrived at HRP, a new initiative had been implemented whereby four mental health workers were paired with four civilian-clothed police officers to respond to these calls. The result was the creation of the Mobile Mental Health Crisis Team. This unit dealt with those known individuals having a mental health crisis. It was an unmitigated success. Local practitioners now actively recommend contacting 9-1-1 or the Mobile Mental Health Crisis Team if an individual is in crisis.

Calls related to addictions involved individuals who were found unconscious due to an accidental overdose and victims of violent acts perpetrated against them by individuals under the effects of various drugs, including alcohol and cannabis. In Nova Scotia, we've been spared the impact of the opioid epidemic that has affected British Columbia and the U.S. Pacific Northwest and Mid-West. However about 50-60 people a year die in the province of drug overdoses, including fatal medicinal drug combinations and, on occasion, fentanyl. My drug enforcement experience led me to realize a long time ago that drug consumption and abuse, of both illicit and licit drugs, were more a public health issue than a public safety issue. But on many an occasion, those lines became blurred.

In the lead-up to the Canadian government legalizing cannabis in 2018, I was asked to participate in discussions around the subject. People even stopped me in the middle of the street to make their opinion known about cannabis, some against it, some for it. Some people in favor of legalization would claim that, unlike "hard" drugs, nobody ever died from an overdose of marijuana or that consumption of cannabis was the "best thing ever" to deal with all types of pain and ailments, including PTSI, cancer and other conditions. Some even alleged that it could cure many of those ailments.

What I saw, though, was cannabis indirectly being responsible for the deaths of people when individuals, severely impaired by it, ended up killing others: their best friend, their roommate, a member of their family or another driver. Or individuals committing home invasions with extreme violence to steal cannabis caches or plants. Or individuals forsaking their prescribed medicine or treatment in favor of self-medication with cannabis, combining it with other drugs, resulting in their unexpected demise. Cannabis, like any drug, isn't devoid of adverse side effects. And, like any drug, it certainly isn't a panacea.

Drugs are any substance that impairs our cognitive functioning. The most-used drug in the world is alcohol, followed by tobacco. Because it has been available for millennia in some societies, there are rituals, mores, traditions and laws around the consumption and non-consumption of alcohol. In the case of non-medicinal drugs other than alcohol, such as cannabis, that isn't the case.

All drugs are addictive, but they alone aren't responsible for the addiction. There are always other causes of addiction, such as a chaotic home environment, childhood trauma, little or no mutual parental attachment and nurturing, low academic aspirations and parental substance abuse or mental illness.

That being said, there are protective factors that can mitigate those risk factors, providing a measure of defense against addiction: strong family bonds; engaged parenting, including parental expectations and consequences; academic success and strong interpersonal bonds developed in pro-social institutions (school, community settings and places of worship).[117] The issue of well-being from conception on is a critical factor in effectively dealing with addictions and ensuring life-long health and wellness. Hence the importance of strong parental involvement and leadership. These all lead to better individual and community outcomes.

Nowhere else has the issue of collective well-being been underscored more than during the time following the 9-11 attacks and especially during the COVID-19 pandemic. The former affected the victims, their family, friends, and those on the ground with psychological trauma and lasting physical after-effects (e.g., respiratory problems and cancers). The latter affected most of humanity to varying degrees. At one point, more than a third of the planet was in some form of quarantine, lockdown or self-isolation. And almost no country was spared fatalities.

The tale of the tape

Over the years, as I grew older, and especially as I reached higher and higher positions of responsibility, I came to recognize that the currency of life was not money but time.

A simple exercise illustrates this. Take out a measuring tape, the soft, pliable kind our mothers and grandmothers kept in their sewing kits. Or perhaps a plastic tape measure or a self-retracting metal tape measure found commonly in a toolbox. Place it on the floor. It should be in inches

311

and extended no further than 100 inches. Now find the inch that corresponds to your age. For example, if you're 42, mark the 42nd inch with a post-it note or arrow flag. Now step back and look at where you are in your life. The average life expectancy for a North American born in 2020 varies from a low of 76 to a high of 81 years for men and a low of 81 to a high of 84 years for women.[118]

Using a hockey analogy, if you're 27 years old or younger, you're still playing in the first period of your life. If you're between 28 and 54, you're playing in the second period, and the third period of your life if you're between 55 and 81. If you're over 81, you're lucky enough to be playing overtime, sudden-death overtime. Actually, we're all playing a game of sudden death. But not everyone gets a chance to play beyond the third period, which is usually the most exciting part of the game in hockey. Depending on where you are, ask yourself just how well you're playing your game of life?

During the trying, difficult times, we need to have that perspective of where we are in our lives to truly appreciate how far we've come, how much we have today and especially how much time we have left. This is a practical example of what we saw way back in the Lesson of Scanning (Chapter 2) as the grand strategy of elevating our perspective in life. Remember, strategists will always prevail over tacticians.

For an even more poignant exercise, take a slow walk in a local cemetery, reading the individual grave markers and looking at the images engraved on the stones: lifelong hobbies, affiliations, relationships and especially the dates. Some of the buried will have lived long lives while others brutishly short ones. Walking through cemeteries affords us the chance to appreciate that, despite our challenges, we are still alive. Understand that the necessary strategic perspective we require only comes when we appreciate that time is the real currency of life.

Part of trying to play my game well has been to ensure that I kept special times and memorable moments just for myself and my family. I chose these moments as rituals for building and renewing relationships and physical energy. Many of those valuable moments involved officiating hockey with my daughter and son.

When I first became chief, I was asked whether I intended to stop officiating. My answer was a categorical, "No!"

I was lucky to combine my love of officiating with my work on several occasions. I would regularly officiate charity hockey games for the Slain Peace Officer Fund and my son's high school that raised money for Movember and breast cancer research. I even got a chance to meet Canadian broadcasting legend Ron MacLean, himself a former Hockey Canada Level V referee. Before a charity hockey game in which he played and my daughter and I officiated, I presented him with an HRP hockey jersey.

In September 2013, my family and I traveled with a group of HRP and RCMP members to Boston for a series of charity hockey games to raise money for the Sean Collier Memorial Fund and the Officer Donahue Fund. Massachusetts Institute of Technology Patrol Officer Sean Collier was shot and killed during the manhunt following the 2013 Boston Marathon Bombings. Massachusetts Bay Transit Authority Officer Richard Donahue was severely injured by gunfire during the manhunt.

I refereed three games at Boston's Matthews Arena, home of the Northeastern University men's and women's hockey teams, the Huskies. My daughter, an accomplished referee and hockey player in her own right, lined two of those games. Strangely enough, the highlight was giving a penalty to her in the one game she played in for the combined RCMP-HRP woman's team. She has never let me forget that one. Fortunately, I didn't give a penalty to my wife, who played in that same game.

Keeping special moments, especially moments when we share and interact with others we love, is critical to staving off distress and idleness. With our world's constant demands, we need to plan and carry out those moments as often as possible. The fuel for this planning is the attitude we carry in life.

The Dark Night of Marlo

The four most significant challenges to a healthy attitude in life are:

- Escapism
- Denial
- Helplessness
- Blame

To forget our problems, we try to avoid facing the reality of confronting those challenges through procrastination, laziness, forgetfulness or self-medication. We'll also deny the presence of a problem, resigning ourselves to being unable to change the outcome of a situation or issue. Instead of assuming responsibility for our challenges, we'll simply give up, transfer responsibility to others or assign blame to them for our situation. When all four elements are present, we can fall prey to what's known as the Dark Night of the Soul,[119] a period of utter spiritual desolation, disconnection and emptiness in which we grasp for anything to justify our situation.

As a police chief, I would periodically receive threats of all types, mostly when there was a high-profile case that didn't go the way certain members of the public wanted it to. During one highly mediatized file, someone left an overnight voice message in French in which he called me all sorts of names, saying that he'd come from Montréal to Halifax to kill me. He finished his message by leaving his full name and telephone number to call him back. I allowed the Montréal city police to do that. Years later, a person calling from Malaysia also identified himself, leaving a voice message to say that he'd kill me if he ever returned to Canada from abroad. He was wanted on an international arrest warrant and had been on the lam for several years. I didn't expect him to come back anytime soon to make good on his threat.

But one of the strangest threats didn't relate to a criminal case but to an internal staffing matter concerning one of my police officers who was off sick due to a personal illness. Marlo was the sibling of that police officer. Marlo wanted to know what I was personally doing to assist her sibling, whom health care professionals and our human resources manager were attending to. Marlo wrote letters and emails to the mayor, the head of the Board of Police Commissioners and me on several occasions, not satisfied that I could only share information with her if she were designated proxy by their sibling. The employee never gave Marlo that proxy.

Marlo was a well-established businessperson who ended up sending me threatening messages. Marlo intensified her toxic emails to me, stating that her family had contacts "in high places," and she'd do her best to have me fired and pay dearly for the pain I had supposedly inflicted on her sibling and extended family. Marlo even engaged a journalist to advance her complaints. Marlo used expletives on social media to describe her disdain for me, unsuccessfully attempting to rally other employees against me. In one email, Marlo even sent an image of my daughter and me from my locked-down Facebook account.

Meanwhile, Marlo's police officer sibling was off-duty sick, receiving full salary and benefits while physically partaking in the construction of their new home. When Marlo sent me another hated-laced message, I laid a criminal complaint. No charges resulted, but the emails eventually stopped.

I couldn't quite understand why Marlo and her sibling were so fixated on me as the source of their frustration. I saw this occur in other fora, where individuals targeted the head of a company, a department, a political entity or even a place of worship as responsible for their problems in life. These are examples of the victim mindset that doesn't allow individuals to grow in the face of adversity or everyday problems. Incapable of assuming responsibility for their issues, individuals become obsessed, sometimes even pathologically, over others whom they believe responsible for their lot in life, creating a cult of the victim. This is often an example of a dependent personality disorder. Canadian author Mark Milke wrote in his book *The Victim Cult* (2019) that victim cultists should be thought of as "(...) perennial stalkers, roaming to and fro, looking ravenously for someone to blame. Sometimes they are even in charge of nations."

The way to avoid acting like Marlo is to deal with your challenges and adversity through action, not blame. Do whatever you can to improve your lot, your personal life and your work life. By doing so, you continually gravitate towards a purpose and not towards blaming someone else for your problems.

Improving your lot involves assuming responsibility for your choices related to your health and promoting self-care, not self-medication through character assassination.

Filling someone else's cup

In December 2018, I asked Dr. Stan Kutcher, then a psychiatry professor at Dalhousie University in Halifax, to address my senior management team at HRP. In a highly insightful one-hour presentation, Dr. Kutcher laid out his vision of effective workplace wellness and mental health. His basic premise was that individual wellness isn't about feeling good all the time. It meant building upon people's competencies to assist them in creating a meaningful life. Dr. Kutcher, now a Canadian senator representing Nova Scotia in Parliament, also had important things to say about workplace wellness programs.

Over the past decade, there has been an increased awareness of mental health and wellness, especially in the workplace. Unfortunately, there's a lack of data on the efficacy of workplace wellness programs.

One attempt to overcome this paucity of information is through the Illinois Workplace Wellness Study conducted at the University of Illinois at Urbana-Champaign.[120] The goals of the study, which began in 2016, are four-fold:

1. Examine the effects of financial incentives on workplace wellness participation.
2. Investigate who benefits from workplace wellness programs.
3. Estimate workplace wellness's causal effects on employee health care costs, health behaviors, well-being and productivity.
4. Test for peer effects in wellness program participation.

After its inaugural year of study, four initial findings corresponded to these goals:

1. Workplace wellness doesn't significantly change employer health care costs, either favorably or unfavorably.
2. Workplace wellness also doesn't change employees' measured health behaviors.
3. Employees who chose to participate in workplace wellness already had lower health care costs before the program.
4. Employees who chose to participate in workplace wellness were already healthy before the program began.

Initial findings demonstrate that people who use and benefit from wellness programs tend to be in good health already or are willing to change their lifestyle habits. The findings underscored the need for more research in this area.

But what can we do to take care of ourselves and those we care for, including those we work with? There are three components to this.

The first and most crucial component any person can have is a stable, caring relationship with another person from whom they can seek help when needed. This implies trust and empathy, two of the critical components of psychological safety and inclusion in the workplace.

The second component is being able to contribute to and help others, both professionally and personally. An essential element in tailoring such an approach depends on one's lifestyle, including gender adherence. For the most part, men tend to bond through activity, while women tend to connect through discussion and sharing. That being said, there are always exceptions.

My family has a friend, Kerry Maher. Kerry is an astute businessperson, a golf professional, a married mother of three boys and the owner of a fresh-food take-out restaurant located in the downtown core of Halifax. In regular times, she's an exceptionally busy person. She and her immediate family have a long history of being involved in community-based initiatives and fundraising. When the COVID-19 pandemic hit, resulting in the lockdown of businesses and workplaces alike, her commerce withered overnight. As Kerry described it, once she realized she could no longer do business as usual, she cried for about five minutes before picking herself up and deciding to do something, anything, that would keep her engaged while contributing to others.

Kerry started a free Facebook-based workout program for women (and a few daring men), committing to provide a full year of online workouts to anyone and everyone who wanted to get in shape to stave off the 'Quarantine-15,' referring to pandemic-related weight gain. From March 2020, Kerry engaged over 400 women and men to get into better shape while encouraging them to be grateful for what they have. In late 2020, thanks to her workout program's popularity, she started an online business, adding golf and individualized fitness lessons to her repertoire.

Before her early-morning workouts, while she's sipping her coffee, Kerry provides insight and infuses gratitude into the day of people she trains, from all walks of life and from across Canada. She encourages them to "Get Vertical," to get out of bed and work out with her. She's always appreciative of what she has, choosing to fill someone else's cup every day, filling hers along the way. Kerry demonstrates the role of contribution in a leader's life, taking something negative and transforming it into something positive through purpose for others.

A 1986 literature review suggested that those affected by trauma have better long-term mental health outcomes based on "perceived support" rather than actual "received support."[121] People must know that help is available to them. That includes asking someone if they're okay.

When I went back to work following my post-earthquake mission in Haiti in February 2010, only one person asked if I wanted to talk. He was a veteran of several international police missions and had provided me with logistical support before I left. I went to his workplace, and as soon as I saw him, I broke down and started crying aloud on his shoulder. I felt guilty because I didn't bring either Doug or Mark home alive.

He hugged me and listened without judging. No one else reached out to lend an ear. As our work life is composed of our emotions, our motivations and our perceptions, the perceived support we know is available and offered is critical for our response to trauma, both big and small.

Mental health requires having conversations and being open about the challenges that exist. It also requires learning about the various mental health components, including recognizing our status at any given moment. This is where the literacy component of mental health comes in. Encouraging ourselves and others to seek help is paramount when dealing with those problems.

The challenge here is to ensure the availability of that help. For a leader, the management of individual cases is fraught with peril, as some individuals will prefer that we take control and be responsible for their outcomes, good and bad. This runs counter to the overall goal of assisting people to become responsible for their mental health, just like their own physical health.

There must be recognition of the need for strong leadership and management in any wellness program. This includes creating an expectation of recovery and healing following any crisis. These expectations can be facilitated by increasing mental health literacy and lowering the stigma attached to mental health conversations. A critical component is improving existing social supports that allow people to become good peers, but not therapists.

The goal of good peer support should be to assist colleagues and friends in accessing mental health services, not providing those services. This means seeing those who need help, listening to them, and assisting them in seeking additional support, thereby helping them to help themselves.

The third and final component of taking care of oneself and those around us can be summarized as follows: *What's good for the bicep is good for the brain.* Exercise and movement are two critical pillars that enhance and maintain our physical and mental health. Exercise augments cognitive performance, including memory function, attention and concentration. It also staves off anxiety, depression and the condition that some sociologists call 'languishing'.[122] Movement can take any form: walking, swimming, biking, workouts, housework or yard work—anything that gets the body to displace itself.

Dr. Kutcher summarized the most important determinants of mental health, all equally important, as:

- Exercise
- Sufficient sleep
- Proper nutrition
- Helping others
- Seeking help for yourself

For him, the key is to look at this list as being a buffet, not separate entrées. Ask the right questions around what you can do to encourage every one of these determinants in yourself and in those you work with and love. It means developing self-awareness of your overall health and wellness while demonstrating agency over them through small, daily steps that eventually become lifelong habits.

Dr. Kutcher's presentation was instrumental in informing HRP's approach to good workplace mental health and physical wellness. It also brought to the forefront the notion that good mental health, like good physical health, isn't something we *have* but something we *do*. This requires judging our contributions and role in society by reasonable, rather than unrealistic, socially-driven standards.

The power of quiet reflection

Avoiding personal depletion means developing an interest in life's broader pleasures, never being satisfied with what we know. As American science-fiction author Robert Heinlein wrote, "Specialization is for insects." Humans require a wide-ranging set of experiences and abilities to be fulfilled in life.

This requires tenacity, perseverance and the willingness to push the boundaries of our comfort zones, visibly changing who we are and the circumstances we live in while driving for a deeper congruence between our inner and outer lives. As leaders, especially as we become responsible for large numbers of people, we must avoid specialization. Leave that to the experts. Our objective is to demonstrate a clear preference toward generalization, listening to the specialists' expertise while not being intimidated by it. Leadership also requires learning diverse skills and how to combine them in creative ways.

The most celebrated samurai swordsman of all time was Shinmen Musashi-no-Kami Fujiwara Harunobu (1582-1645), also known as Miyamoto Musashi. Musashi left behind a series of written works, of which the most notable was the *Gorin-no-sho* ("Book of Five Rings"), in which he exposed the reader to the model warrior way of life through a series of books, or rings. It's arguably one of the most influential and widely read martial art treatises in Japan, if not the world. But it also has applications to areas of your life outside of the martial arts.

In the first ring, "The Earth Scroll," Musashi provides nine rules or principles of "combat strategy", the code by which warriors must live. Amongst the rules, Musashi directs his reader to acquaint themselves with all arts and vocations, to become knowledgeable in various disciplines while attempting to see the reality in life, uncolored by biases, and paying attention to important things both large and small. He also encourages the reader to be mindful by living in the moment and eschewing superfluous, useless or damaging activities.

One of the most underrated things in life is a quiet moment of reflection, taking time to contemplate where we've been and especially where we're going in our lives. The goal is to seek some perspective when our world goes out of equilibrium, as it tends to do. We don't have to engage in such reflection every day, but we should do it regularly, for example, once a week as we prepare for the upcoming week. That reflection shouldn't be done during times of difficulty or distress but during times of relaxation and tranquility. Find a place where you can unwind to process your thoughts. Ensure that you can capture digitally or on paper essential thoughts or ideas you want to act upon. Such reflection allows for appreciation in ways that develop an upbeat mood and further encourage harmony and direction. I always preferred early Saturday evenings as the week's events had transpired by then, and there were usually no pressing concerns at that moment.

Mindfulness encourages psychological flexibility: the ability to adapt to change through focused thinking. Mindfulness involves shifting your attention to processing situations more slowly and thoughtfully, thereby responding with greater reflection and clarity on the most pressing issues facing you. In today's society, that means developing advanced decision-making skills and the requisite willpower to deal with moments of stress and uncertainty. The challenge is that the biology of stress and the biology of willpower are incompatible. Stress depletes willpower.

Willpower is the ability to resist short-term temptations to achieve long-term goals. Willpower is complementary to but different from will, which is the inner drive that propels a person forward in the presence of adversity. Willpower is like a muscle, and we can support its development through practice, stress management and sufficient sleep. Research has shown that when college students have tasks that require self-control, such as tracking what they eat or using their weaker hands on the computer mouse, they can develop greater willpower overall after only a few weeks. Mindfulness practices also help develop willpower because they focus on training the mind toward self-control and self-discipline.

The problem with self-control is that we have limited quantities of willpower to work with, and every time we use our self-control, we draw from those reserves. When willpower is reduced through a simple distraction test—such as avoiding the temptation of fresh cookies, trying not to cry at a sad movie or trying not to laugh at a funny joke—people are more likely to do things they would otherwise resist doing. Limited or depleted quantities of willpower result in negative behaviors such as overt expressions of anger and prejudice, infidelity, substance abuse and overeating, as our self-control becomes diminished in those areas.

One psychologist has opined that this limitation of our willpower reserves may make marriage more challenging for dual-working couples. They further posit that if you use all of your willpower and energy to behave well at work, you may be out of willpower by the end of the day and find yourself angry and irritated at your spouse for every little thing you find offensive.

We develop mindfulness through encouraging conscious, effortful regulation of the self. It means thinking intentionally instead of acting impulsively, and overriding unwanted thoughts, feelings or impulses. It leads to a calmness of mind, what British philosophical writer James Allen (1864-1912) described in his book *As a man thinketh* (1903) as being "one of the beautiful jewels of wisdom."

We can achieve this state by emphasizing physical mastery and intentional movements through such activities as yoga, *tai chi*, meditation or any movement that requires sustained concentration on the activity. Exposure to unusual or alternative approaches allows us to relax, recharge and refocus on what's truly important in our lives.

You don't have to be a Samurai master. All you need to facilitate this regeneration is to carry the right attitude in life.

Don't worry, *charhdi kala*

The attitude we habitually demonstrate is a characteristic that transcends our effective leadership and complexity management abilities. It permeates our entire existence and affects everyone we encounter.

All cultures have social norms that drive behavior, dictating how we're supposed to behave in society. Cultural norms allow members of a particular group to behave similarly, often acting as a beacon for in-group dynamics and personal conduct.

In Sikhism, the term *charhdi kala*, "positive attitude" or "ascending energy", refers to the aspiration to maintain a mental state of eternal optimism and joy, even in the face of adversity, acting as a clarion call to maintain a higher state of mind through happiness. *Charhdi kala* is the tacit recognition that our overall health and success in life are mostly dependent on our attitude.

Grounded, lucid optimism is an essential attribute for any leader. It presupposes that the leader is confident that they can get the job done. The key to such an attitude is to develop mastery over and satisfaction with one's life by accomplishing actions that propel us forward in our life's purpose. It also implies that we fervently love life and live it passionately, while taking our success in it very seriously. We must sculpt our attitude to be the single most important creation in our life, being forever responsible for its development.

Never equate success with perfection. As we've seen, humans tend towards satisficing more than optimization and perfection. That's not necessarily a bad thing. We can measure and appreciate success in many ways, but perfection shouldn't be part of that assessment. Such an approach only creates more stress and frustration as we can rarely, if ever, achieve it.

Not all situations and aspects in life can and should be taken seriously, though. We require moments of levity, lightheartedness and unbridled joy. That's where humor comes in. Humor can be beneficial in different settings, providing a source of comfort and community. Victor Hugo identified the tangible benefit of humor: "To make people laugh is to make people forget. What a benefactor on earth, a distributor of forgetting!"

Some of the downsides of working from home during this pandemic have been the absence of a physical break between work and personal life, the social aspects of work, where outside traditions like Halloween, Christmas and birthdays are celebrated communally, and moments of shared in-person humor in the workspace. Humor produces laughter, which is the outward expression of joy and enthusiasm. This fuel encourages people to momentarily forget their trials and tribulations, allowing them to move forward in the face of adversity. Sometimes humor is the only healthy reaction to setbacks, failures and distress at home and work, especially when that work deals with deadly situations.

During my repatriation mission in Haiti in January 2010, the French gendarmes who had recovered Mark Gallagher's remains also salvaged a barrack box belonging to Doug Coates' executive officer, Constable Julie Dupré. She had resided in the same building as Mark, and all her possessions were destroyed in the collapse. Or so she had thought. In the box were some personal documents, clothes and a bottle of wine that was still intact. It was intended for a celebratory supper she, Doug and another member of their team were to have held in the days to come. During a time of great sorrow, the bottle's finding was a small source of comfort to Julie.

That evening, several of us gathered to dine in what was known as "Canada House," a two-story home where we were all staying in cramped temporary housing. For many, it was the first time we could enjoy a regular meal and reflect on the days prior. Included in the meal was Julie's bottle of wine, among several others.

With the wine flowing freely and the events of the day behind us, we began to talk about what we had gone through since the earthquake. The day had started with a significant aftershock prompting all of us to evacuate the home precipitously in various stages of undress. My temporary roommate, a senior officer from the Québec provincial police, had been taking a shower when the aftershock began. I yelled at him to get out while I started running down the stairs of the home. Within seconds, we were all outside. I was dressed in my boxers and a white undershirt while my roommate was buck naked, with only a timid smile on his face. Recounting that event led to great hilarity around the dinner table.

We then started talking about how soldiers of a certain country's contingent had transferred bodies from one five-ton military truck to another. The soldiers threw the body bags from the truck onto the roadway, then lobbed them up into the second truck's bed. We could hear the bodies inside the bags slamming to the ground, in some cases crunching bones. For whatever reason, most likely fueled in part by the wine, we started laughing at the bizarre and incongruous scene we were recounting. We all partook in a long, hearty belly laugh until, individually, we realized the absurdity of our gallows humor. One by one, we stopped laughing, and some, including me, started to tear-up. Without speaking another word, we all silently put our dishes away and went our way to bed with our respective demons.

An overdose of contentment

If you take only one thing from this book, make sure it is this: always be more than the confines of your job. Be more than just a cop. Be more than just a referee. Be more than just a lawyer, academic, entrepreneur, journalist or civil servant. Be the person you were before your chosen profession(s) and be the best you can be after it (or them): the sibling, the parent, the neighbor, the athlete, the cousin, the reader, the doer, the person you have always aspired to be. I found it unfortunate that some people would retire from one job to avoid the constant distress it gave, only to start another comparable position with the same stressors, because they identified too much with the same work persona.

Our identity does not depend on the role we play or the work functions we perform, even if that work lasts several decades. Remember, we don't have a separate work life, home life or family life. We only have a *single life.*

Keeping this in mind will help you maintain agency over that life, the things that happen to you and especially your responses to them. It also helps you effectively answer the critical question about what type of legacy you'll leave when you're gone. Remember the singular, limited inscription on Commissioner Wood's tombstone. What would you want on yours? How would you want people to understand what your life was about and what was important to you?

Be like the Spanish artist Salvador Dali (1904-1989), who said, "There are some days when I think I'm going to die from an overdose of satisfaction." Without explicitly mentioning it, Dali touched upon the essential aspects of mental health.

The three recognized elements of good psychological health are:

- A sense of control, even mastery, over one's life.
- A sense of connection to something larger than oneself (a movement, family, service, community, faith)
- The constant pursuit of challenges, both large and small.

These elements, when combined, lead to an abundance of satisfaction in one's life.

Good mental health also means thriving cognitively and affectively (yes, with an 'a'). By thriving cognitively, we build new memories and neural pathways to new skills. Taking courses, learning to play a musical instrument and practicing a new hobby or activity allows for new skill development, especially if we use our creativity and produce something. The key is to master a skill or item, anything that's outside the traditional realm of work. It also requires dealing with those automatic drives that cause us pain: the allure of alcohol, drugs, sex, power or food. Many of us are driven by automatic responses to stressors, leading us to act in ways contrary to how we need to lead a good life.

Thriving affectively implies a whole-person approach. Proper sleep, nutrition, exercise and mindfulness training allow us to be at our physical and mental best to deal with the challenges and opportunities that a work and personal day bring. Physical health includes good dental health and hygiene, as they have an important effect on our overall well-being.

Having positive work relationships is also critical to help you avoid falling into the trap of thinking that all work colleagues demonstrate incivility and rudeness. Look for and develop strong relationships with people who have a healthy sense of humor and who lift others' spirits through common decency, and who share your sense of connection to the betterment of their and others' lives.

Reading abundantly

Like many people, I enjoy reading. During my career, I had a twenty-year period when I would only read non-fiction works: mainly management, self-help and personal health books. Also, like many people, I underlined important passages. But I went one step further and copied those passages into a Word file that facilitated research for future presentations and speeches, thereby embedding the essential lessons of the books I read in my memory.

I abundantly shared my files with others to encourage them to read what I thought were the books' salient points, with the hope they would purchase the books to read them more completely on their own. Such compilations were time-consuming but worthwhile. Over the twenty years I have been doing this, I've made 91 compilations.

Reading a book critically to retain as much content as possible takes time and energy. One thing many leaders have little of in today's world is leisure time. So, when I saw a headline in *Inc.* magazine stating that most CEOs read a book a week,[123] I knew that to be physically and cognitively impossible. Physically, most people don't have the time to read a book a week consistently; cognitively, people don't have the cerebral resources to retain what they read, at that reading rate. After all, CEOs are human like the rest of us.

In the article, which appears to be more of an infomercial, the author quotes a speed-reading guru with a uniquely apt name who states that the "average person" reads two or three books a year while the "average CEO" reads four or five books *a month*. No research to back up the claim, of course.

When I was police chief, if I had the time and they were of high quality, I read around four books *a year*. I knew voracious and non-recreational readers alike. The avid readers often read fiction, while the non-recreational readers told me that they read enough during the day at work; the last thing they wanted to do at home was read.

One of the books I found worthy of summarizing and sharing is by Israeli-American psychologist Daniel Kahneman. In *Thinking Fast and Slow* (2011), Kahneman presents his understanding of judgment and decision-making shaped by various recent psychological discoveries. In 2016, when Halifax Regional Police Deputy Chief Bill Moore first began his Master of Studies in Applied Criminology and Police Management at the University of Cambridge, England, he had to read Kahneman's book as the primer for his learning experience. With his encouragement, we bought copies of the book for the entire management team, and for over a whole year, we held "Book Club" in which, for about 20 minutes at the end of every senior management team meeting, we discussed a chapter.

I remember the initial reaction of my senior management team—senior-ranking police officers, civilians (including a lawyer, a strategic communications manager, a dispatch center manager and a chief information security officer), all educated and knowledgeable men and women—when they were handed the 418-page book. Some looked genuinely intimidated by the prospect of reading it. One even quipped that we should have a *Nancy Drew Mystery* novel for the Book Club's next read.

Deputy Chief Moore guided us through the first few study sessions. Then we hired a research coordinator with a Ph. D who led us through the remainder of the book's chapters. Any new member of the senior management team had individual sessions with the research coordinator to bring them up to speed on the book's teachings.

One goal was to embed in the thinking processes and decision-making dynamics of the senior management team an awareness of cognitive biases, behavioral economics, prospect theory and loss aversion that affect us all. The other goal was to develop a culture of reflection and character development amongst the senior management team and, eventually, all levels of our organization.

One of the things I learned was the importance of a leader's impartiality during important discussions, eschewing pronounced preferences and expectations from the outset. Instead, through listening and developing the willingness to do so, I let others talk and provide their opinions before I spoke and provided mine, so as not to influence or sway their initial view.

Reading is an essential activity to attaining success as a leader. Read a book, a research study, an article or a blog. Reading staves off mediocrity by allowing for an overall increase in knowledge while facilitating our attention-building focus. This is part of continuous learning, a lifelong curiosity to continually expand what we know, what we experience and how to learn. With audio books becoming more popular, along with digitally available texts, reading and learning are more accessible than ever.

The goal is to expose us to useful input. Of course, reading is not the only source of helpful information. There are countless YouTube videos and podcasts available to resolve immediate problems and develop a quick skill. YouTube is the second most popular search engine in the world after Google, and for good reason. Spending a few minutes watching, listening to and using the skills demonstrated in a video or discussed during a podcast can help you deal with immediate and limited problems. Such videos or podcasts frequently provide a quick introduction to important subjects and learning matter that you can explore further later.

Regardless of the medium you use, the goal should be to develop an independently acquired understanding of the areas you oversee and are responsible for.

With constraints on our time, our cognitive resources, and the thousands of books, blogs and podcasts available, what should we read? The answer varies wildly, according to our interests and our needs. One thing is true, though: read books that have stood the test of time, such as the classics, including fictional accounts that tend to better reflect the truth in our lives and are often more relatable. The classics are not just those books that come from centuries past, but those recently written and recognized for their timeless lessons. A classic is a book that we shouldn't do without because it can contribute to something in our lives.

Good books expose us to sound thinking, intellectual thinkers and expansive ideas. Following my twenty-year period of reading non-fiction exclusively, I realized that I was missing out on the lessons present in fiction, particularly the classics of literature, old and new.

The advantage of reading the older classics is that they provide lessons that for decades, centuries and even millennia, readers have found invaluable. In 2003, I took a unique course on leadership taught through the literary lens of four books: Herman Melville's *Billy Budd*

327

(1924), Leo Tolstoy's *The Death of Ivan Ilyich* (1886), and William Faulkner's *The Unvanquished* (1938) and *An Odor of Verbena* (1957).

The course, which at first resembled more a grade 12 English literature class than a study in leadership, focused on how the books' protagonists influenced others and how they, in turn, were influenced, providing compelling examples of leadership. The course was a true study in leadership.

Alfonso X (1221-1284) was the king of Castile, León and Galicia (much of modern-day Spain) from 1252 until his death in 1284, long before the Spanish Inquisition (1478-1834). He fostered a cosmopolitan, diverse court of Jews, Muslims and Christians alike, focused on higher learning. Nicknamed *'el Sabio'* or 'The Wise,' Alfonso X had a maxim: *Quemad viejos leños, leed viejos libros, bebed viejos vinos, tened viejos amigos* ("Burn old logs. Drink old wine. Read old books, Keep old friends.") His was a positive, lasting example of the power of books and diversity.

Reading is essential, but we must read critically, not blindly accepting all that we read. That includes the contents of this book. The next step is to apply the knowledge we glean from a read. Studying leadership in textbooks won't make us a leader any more than drinking a protein shake will make us a bodybuilder. Without the required intentional application of lessons learned and the necessary experimentation that goes along with it, we can't succeed.

In his book *Outliers: The Story of Success* (2008), Canadian author Malcolm Gladwell popularized the notion that 10,000 hours of concentrated practice is required to develop a world-class skill in areas such as medicine, chess and sports. Gladwell based his 10,000-hour rule on the research done by Swedish psychologist K. Anders Ericsson, internationally recognized as a researcher in the psychological nature of expertise and human performance. As subsequently detailed in his own book *Peak* (2016), Ericsson focused on extensive, deliberate practice instead of a skill's rote repetition.

In essence, what's required is highly focused skill development, which continually goes beyond one's comfort zone, frequently a tedious and challenging practice. Ten thousand hours roughly translates into seven years of sustained and intentional effort.

Even if we aren't setting out to develop a world-class skill, we still need to spend time and effort to create a new talent or aptitude. Fortunately, many of the skills out there that we need or want don't require 10,000 hours. But they do require the purposeful investment of our time and energy. Part of that intentional effort is having a good coach to teach the correct technique, thereby minimizing the risk of wasted time and frustration. The other part is being open to and capable of making the effort.

To sleep, perchance to dream

The most underrated and often-sacrificed human activity is sleeping. Contrary to Bon Jovi's 1992 song's premise, *I'll sleep when I'm dead*, human beings require sleep to be at our best, especially to make the best decisions. This is a critical feature of our cerebral demands, the recharging of our cognitive batteries. An old French expression sums up the importance of sleep; *Qui dort dîne* ("They who sleep, dines"), stating the primacy of sleep even over food.

On average, we spend six hours a day on emails at work. At home, we may spend a few hours more online or in front of a television screen. During our off time, we may even respond to work emails to get ahead, resulting in a feeling of being stalked by our jobs while at home. When we turn off our devices or forget them, we may be beset with a nagging anxiety that we are missing out on important business. When we go on vacation without our electronic devices, we're punished for not checking our emails and messages with even more emails and messages upon our return. Electronic devices spewing forth sounds and notifications, information, demands and entertainment continually seize our attention. The unfortunate victim in this competition for our focus and finite attentional resources is often our sleep.

So how do we turn off a world that doesn't even have an off switch?

Certain jurisdictions have responded to this particular problem. In France, government workers can set their email program to delete all new incoming messages during their vacations. They must provide an automatic return message advising the sender that because of their absence from work, the sender's initial email message will be deleted. Should the sender still need assistance, they can contact another person at an indicated telephone number or email address. However, not all countries or work cultures accept this approach.

To allow for proper sleep in this world of attention competition, we need to turn off our electronics, smartphones, computers, laptops, tablets and TVs long before we go to bed. And only open them long after we've gotten up. During the day, we must limit how much of our attention our electronics monopolize.

My smartphone was always on silent mode as chief of police—not vibration mode, but silent mode. I would check it when I had the time, not when I felt I needed to or when it rang or vibrated. I tried to do the same with my email messages, allotting certain times of the day to respond to them. I didn't always succeed.

A considerable amount of energy through public-service messaging and law enforcement is spent on convincing people not to drive under the influence of drugs or alcohol. A comparable amount is also spent on traffic-calming measures, roadway design and traffic enforcement focused on seat belt use and distracted driving. But from what I've seen as a police officer attending accident scenes, working evening and overnight shifts as well as extended work periods (24 or more consecutive hours), and having driven extended distances myself, is that one of the most overlooked killers of people isn't speed, drug impairment, animals on the roadway or distracted driving. It's driver fatigue.

Many, if not all of us who drive regularly have been in situations where fatigue impaired our driving. This appears to be an unfortunate consequence of the demands in life today, resulting in many of us driving to and from work, social events and even shopping in less-than-optimal cognitive shape. Lack of sleep can affect how we drive just as it affects how we decide.

Decision-making suffers significantly as a result of fatigue. When we drive, we make near-simultaneous and sequential decisions regularly from departure to arrival. In life, we're doing the same, continually making decisions that determine what we do, how we do it, and where we go. The key is to make those decisions whenever possible when we're rested and at our cognitive best. Quality sleep, including napping, is key to this, but we can do some other things to ensure that we and those we work with are at our cognitive best.

When I was with the United Nations in 2008, the mission leader would almost always schedule a late Friday afternoon meeting of his senior staff as a way of ending the week, usually around 5 pm. I saw the meeting attendees' tired faces, including my own, after a long week of dealing with numerous challenges. I also noted that discussions during these meetings were either subdued or agitated, reflecting the participants' late-week temperament and impatience to start their weekend. Either way, these meetings were rarely conducive to good decision-making, as people just wanted to get them over with.

From that experience, I learned only to hold meetings when we needed a group decision. Having a meeting to simply convey information was a waste of people's precious time. I also learned to attend only those meetings where I could contribute something to the decision-making process.

I further learned to avoid holding Monday and Friday group meetings, especially to seek critical collective decisions. I reserved such discussions for meetings between Tuesday afternoons and Thursday mornings, when people were at the height of their cognitive abilities. I determined that the best time to hold meetings requiring robust, intelligent dialogue amongst many individuals was on Wednesday mornings, preferably from 10 am. to noon. After-lunch sessions were always challenging because of the participants' spikes in blood sugar, so I avoided them as much as possible.

I reserved Mondays for low-demand administrative meetings and Friday morning meetings for short brainstorming sessions where imagination was required. I also limited the time spent in meetings to a single hour, if possible. Adults learn and function best in 50-minute increments, so I always encouraged meeting for a single hour, or having a break every hour during a multi-hour meeting. For one-on-one or small group meetings, I preferred mornings, when everyone was most awake. I also held some of my one-on-one discussions while walking outside if my interlocutor was amenable and interested in doing so.

The whole issue around fatigue and meeting length and times underscores the importance of leaders developing the essential skill of conducting efficient and effective meetings. This knowledge includes encouraging optimal meeting conditions that contribute to superior decision-making, including the level of participant alertness, which can only be ensured through individual proper rest and sleep.

Other factors such as room temperature, availability of water and healthy snacks, and proper seating also play a role in creating optimal meeting conditions. When I met people in my office, I got up from my desk and greeted them as they entered the room, then guided them over to a chair or couch to sit on. I didn't have an individual sit opposite me at my desk unless we were going over a document or I was receiving a quick briefing. Whenever possible, for any meeting over ten minutes, I had some tea and/or "dainties" brought in. Never underestimate the power of breaking bread with another.

It doesn't always have to be food. I always invited guests, especially community members, to have tea in my office. I was never a big tea drinker, but I recognized the calming effect of sharing a drink and/or food with another.

Holding an effective meeting isn't just related to proper time management. Ensuring that people's cognitive and physiological needs are met as much as possible during that time together is key.

End it all, thankfully

Today's leading causes of death are heart and circulatory disorders, followed by cancers, respiratory diseases, nervous system disorders and digestive disorders. Infections, non-transport accidents, suicide, transport accidents, mental health disorders, homicide, medical complications, war and terrorism round out in order this non-exhaustive list.

Regardless of the cause, one thing is certain: we'll all die one day. This means that life is short. Because of our envious urges, we tend to waste our time in fruitless searches, pursuing effortless change and entertaining ourselves with no real benefit beyond the immediate chuckle. We avoid uncertainty, looking for constancy in our world and feelings. Instead, we should embrace the uncertainty that confronts us, not waiting for something better to turn up, but by gravitating towards and provoking change as we realize how little time we have left in this life.

I prefaced this book indicating my gratitude for the people, experiences and lessons I have known, lived and acquired. I end it by reiterating my appreciation for all that I have lived thus far. Whether I'm in the gym pushing out reps, writing an article, walking the dogs, enjoying a family meal or calling a tripping penalty, I try to be mindful of the moment I'm in, relishing what I'm doing, knowing full well that one day, someday, I will be no more.

Perhaps the most critical element of personal sustainability is for us to fill our days with the appreciation that we are but travelers in this life on a one-way trip that will eventually end at the same destination. This means loving life while taking it very seriously, embracing the conflict, adversity and ensuing challenges and benefits that we invariably encounter.

In a unique survey out of Britain in May 2018, 30,000 people responded to questions around death.[124] The study's authors found that a quarter of those surveyed don't even talk about death, claiming they didn't want loved ones to worry.

The reality is that most people don't want to think about death. One of the questions asked in the survey was, "What makes us consider our mortality?": 28 percent of respondents mentioned the passing of a family member; 22 percent answered reaching a milestone age; 16 percent stated a news report of a death; and 13 percent said being aware of terrorism. As expected, the older the respondents, the more comfortable they were talking about death. Finally, 24 percent of survey respondents dealt with bereavement by keeping themselves as busy as possible, while 16 percent held the news to themselves, and 13 percent chose to do something to distract themselves from thinking about their loss.

In his book *The Denial of Death* (1973), American anthropologist Ernest Becker wrote:

> (...) the idea of death, the fear of it, haunts the human animal like nothing else; it is the mainspring of human activity—activity designed largely to avoid the fatality of death, to overcome it by denying in some way that it is the final destiny for men.

Becker was awarded the Pulitzer Prize for General Non-Fiction in 1974 for his book, a year after his death to colon cancer at age 50. In his various works, Becker recognized that mental illness, especially depression, results when we don't have direction in our lives. Specific to death, he recognized a striking irony in human beings: we bury our fear of death by engaging in busywork. Or, as he put it, we mindlessly engage in "heroic activities" almost as if we hope that we can live beyond our earthly limits and be immortal, thus giving our lives meaning through contribution and belief.

Some even suffer from what could be called the 'pharaonic effect': they think that by accumulating things, they can take them into the afterlife or at the very least delay their departure to it. The Ancients displayed similar approaches on even grander scales, such as the first emperor of China and founder of the Qin dynasty, Shi Huangdi (259-210 BC), buried with a Terracotta Army as guardians of the tomb and servants in the afterlife. Egyptian pharaohs were consistently buried with their worldly possessions and miniature carved figurines called *shabti*, representing future servants and guiding possessions in the hereafter. Their lessons from beyond the tomb teach us that life can't be hoarded but must be lived.

Perched in front of my computer keyboard around the neck of a duck figurine I use for hanging my eyeglasses is a miniature hand-made glass Klein bottle, which I loosely consider to be a modern *shabti*.

A standard bottle has two obvious sides to it, the inside and the outside. This allows us to fill the bottle with liquids easily. A Klein bottle is unique in that it only has a single side. It's a very precise mathematical construct resulting in a closed surface with only one side formed by passing one end of a tube through the tube's side and joining it with the other end. If you were to pour a liquid into the bottle, you would have to continually inverse and righten the bottle to fill it because it only has the one side.

Clifford Stoll, an American astronomer, author, and teacher, gave me the half-inch high Klein bottle. He's best known for his investigation into a German national who was a notorious hacker in the 1980s, long before people understood what hacking was and what damage hackers could do. He's also a renowned maker of Klein bottles, both large and small.

I met Cliff during a conference in 2019 and was fortunate enough to present on the same stage right after him. He's known for his more unorthodox old-school methods of presenting, such as using acetate slides with an overhead projector and a slide rule to make on-the-spot calculations. Part scientist and part philosopher, Cliff once wrote, "It is the voice of life that calls us to come and learn."

This is not the voice of our ego, which craves attention and quick gratification. Instead, it's the voice of living fully that inspires us to learn, grow, create, love and influence others. It's the same voice that drives us to understand that life is short and that we must live it with a certain degree of urgency, zest and ownership. Whether we live our life with gratitude, humility, appreciation, love, temerity, verve or curiosity, only we can choose how to live because it's our responsibility and our destiny to shape it.

But we must first own that destiny and have agency over it. This means that we must recognize that there's no such thing as a perfect life. We can strive as much as possible for perfection in some areas of our lives, but we must start by owning it all; owning both those aspects that are perfect and those that are less than ideal.

What we can strive for and attain is our best life possible. Success is facing and dealing with the constant, complex demands of the reality we experience, provided through events and people. We do this by focusing on those things that allow us to challenge our skills to grow and fulfill our potential.

We derive our best life by developing a sense of satisfaction that only comes from focused accomplishment. Contentment and happiness then become the byproducts of those accomplishments, which Hungarian-American psychologist Mihály Csikszentmihályi describes in his book *Finding Flow* (1997). We attain serenity when our skill level approaches, matches or surpasses the complexity of the challenges we face.

After our focused accomplishment, we can then concentrate our energies on recognition and gratitude. By being appreciative and thankful for what we have and what we've become, we become content. This leads to our best life possible.

It's easy to show our gratitude by saying, "Thank you." Better than saying a rote thank you is to mean it honestly. And even better than meaning a thank you is to live that gratitude. And we live our gratitude through reciprocation: by giving back, contributing to others and serving them.

One of the first initiatives I undertook as chief of police was the creation of a departmental thank-you card. It had the HRP shield on the front with the words 'Thank you' in dark blue and the same words expressed in no less than ten different languages in the background in light blue. Senior managers and employees could use the card and a handwritten note to express appreciation for anyone's contributions.

To reach out to the growing Muslim population in Halifax, as chief of police I attended several local mosques to talk to the community during Friday prayers. After each visit, I would send a hand-written thank you card to the Imam to thank him for allowing me to attend his service and address his congregation. One of the languages in which "Thank you." was written on the card was Arabic. I was struck by the number of individuals who commented to me afterwards how pleased they were that we would acknowledge their culture through the inclusion of their word for gratitude on official police stationery.

Whether we donate our money, our time, our expertise, our sweat, our blood or even our life, we live our gratitude by influencing others to attain a greater good. In doing so, we become better people, contributing to a better society and eventually becoming better ancestors when we leave this world.

The fab four

As we have seen, the four key competencies you must develop to become an effective leader are:

- Advanced thinking skills and superior decision-making
- Intentional relationship building
- Targeted influencing
- Courageous execution

Without executing courageously on our decisions, we can't hope to benefit from the first three competencies.

Courageous execution means making a commitment to carry something out and then doing it. Just like our family friend Kerry, by contributing to others in a hands-on manner where we risk something in the process, we demonstrate courage: the courage to care about someone, the courage to influence them, the courage to effect change and the courage to risk something in the process. The key is to live like French philosopher Henri-Louis Bergson described when he wrote: "Think like a [person] of action—act like a [person] of thought."

In his work *Unto This Last*, British art critic and social commentator John Ruskin wrote of his obsessive interest in wealth and abundance. By wealth, he meant striving for virtue through kindness, curiosity, sensitivity, humility, godliness and intelligence. To Ruskin, that collection of virtues represented what he defined as the entity of "Life." He wrote:

> There is no Wealth but Life. Life, including all its powers of love, of joy, and of admiration. That country is the richest which nourishes the greatest number of noble and happy human beings; that man is richest who, having perfected the functions of his own life to the utmost, has also the widest helpful influence, both personal, and by means of his possessions, over the lives of others.

Dynamic, helpful influence in the lives of others is what leadership is all about. Despite all the trials and complexity the world hurls in our direction, having the courage to see and face the reality, the challenges and the benefits of living a meaningful life of influence is the single, most important quality we can hope to achieve. It allows us to help others succeed while we fashion a life that will last a lifetime.

The success resulting from that lifetime then affords us clarity and a singular pride, letting us look back and say that ours was a life well-lived. It is our defining work of art.

For if we must wait until the evening to see how splendid the day was, then we cannot judge our life until we reach its twilight.

Last calls from the blue line

- To be an effective leader, one who influences others through trust towards attaining a common good, we need to take care of ourselves first and foremost. If we can't maintain our personal sustainability, we're poorly placed to encourage others to do the same. This starts with health literacy.
- Our time's most significant problems are overabundance and idleness, both physically and intellectually. As we age, there's only room for growth or decay, and our bodies look to us to choose between them. Overabundance and idleness promote decay.
- Remember, the currency of life is time, not money.
- The four most significant challenges to a healthy attitude in life are escapism, denial, helplessness and blame.
- Deal with your challenges and adversity through action, not blame. Do whatever you can to improve your lot in life by gravitating towards a purpose and not blaming someone else for your problems. Assume responsibility for the choices related to your health, promote self-care, avoid self-medication through blame.
- In an ideal world, we would strive to attain a lifestyle whereby stress, distress and eustress contribute to our becoming better than before, becoming *antifragile*: remember that what is fragile breaks, what is resilient resists and what is antifragile thrives.
- Do the tale of the tape: What period are you in your life? How are you playing your game? Is your game going according to your strategic plan?
- Individual wellness isn't about feeling good all the time. It means

building upon your and others' competencies so you and they can create a meaningful life.

- The most crucial component of wellness that any person can have is a stable, caring relationship with another from whom they can seek help when they need it. The second component is being able to contribute to and help others. Finally, don't forget physical movement, because what's good for the bicep is good for the brain.
- The most important determinants of mental health are exercise, sufficient sleep, proper nutrition, helping others and seeking help for yourself. Good mental health, like good physical health, isn't something we *have* but something we *do*.
- Unlike Marlo, assume responsibility for your choices related to your health by promoting self-care, not apparent self-medication through blaming others or character assassination.
- Grounded, lucid optimism is an essential attribute for any leader. We need to sculpt our attitude to be the single most important creation in our life, being forever responsible for its development.
- Always, always be more than the confines of your job. Remember, you don't have a separate work life, home life or family life; you only have a *life*.
- The whole issue around meeting fatigue and meeting length underscores the importance of leaders knowing the essential skill of conducting efficient and effective meetings. Only hold meetings if decisions need to be made. Only join meetings if you can contribute something to the decision-making process. The best times for group meetings are from Tuesday afternoon to Thursday noon. Make them short, to the point and devoid of electronic distractions.
- We derive our best life and a sense of satisfaction from focused accomplishment.
- Be grateful, all the way to the very end.

Select bibliography

Amabile, Teresa & Kramer, Steven, *The Progress Principle*, Boston: Harvard Business Review Press, 2011.

Banerjee, Abhijit, and Duflo, Esther, *Good Economics for Hard Times: Better Answers to Our Biggest Problems*, New York: PublicAffairs, 2019.

de Botton, Alain, *Status Anxiety*, Toronto: Penguin Books, 2005.

Bernstein, Albert J., *Emotional Vampires—Dealing with People Who Drain You Dry*, New York: McGraw-Hill, 2012.

Brafman, Ori and Brafman, Rom, *Sway—The Irresistible Pull of Irrational Thinking*, New York: Doubleday, 2009.

Buckingham, Markus & Coffman, Curt, *First, Break All the Rules*, New York: Simon & Schuster, 1999.

Canetti, Elias, *Crowds and Power* (*Masse und Macht*) translated by Carol Stewart, London, Macmillan, (first published in 1960).

Cloud, Dr. Henry, *Integrity—The Courage to Meet the Demands of Reality*, New York: HarperCollins, 2009.

Cipolla, Carlo M., *The Basic Laws of Human Stupidity*, London: WH Allen, 2019.

Covey, Stephen, *The 8th Habit*, New York: Free Press, 2004.

Crowley, Chris & Lodge, Henry S., *Younger Next Year*, New York: Workman Publishing Company, 2004.

Csikszentmihályi, Mihály, *Finding Flow*, New York: Basic Books, 1997.

Diamond, Jared, *Guns, Germs and Steel—The Fates of Human Societies*, New York: W.W. Norton & Co., 1997.

Edmondson, Amy, *The Fearless Organization*, Hoboken, NJ: Wiley, 2018.

Gilmartin, Kevin M., *Emotional Survival for Law Enforcement*, Tucson, Arizona: E-S Press, 2002.

Gladwell, *Outliers: The Story of Success*, New York: Little, Brown & Company, 2008.

Goleman, Daniel, with Boyatzis, Richard and McKee, Annie, *Primal Leadership*, Brighton, Mass: Harvard Business Review Press, 2001.

Greene, Robert, *The Laws of Human Nature*, New York: Penguin Random

House LLC, 2018.

Greene, Robert, *The 48 Laws of Power*, New York: Penguin Random House LLC, 2000.

Fairweather, Jack, *The Volunteer*, London: Custom House, 2019.

Halliday, Ryan, *Stillness is the Key*, New York: Penguin Group, 2019.

Hallinan, Joseph T., *Why We Make Mistakes*, New York: Broadway Books, 2010.

Hasselbein, Frances & Shinseki, Eric K., *Be, Know, Do—Leadership the Army Way*, San Francisco: Jossey-Bass, 2004.

Homer-Dixon, Thomas, *The Ingenuity Gap*, Toronto: Random House, 2000.

Junger, Sebastian, *Tribe*, New York: Hachette Book Group, 2016.

Kahneman, Daniel, *Thinking Fast and Slow*, New York: Random House, 2011.

Kaplan, Robert D., *Warrior Politics: Why Leadership Demands a Pagan Ethos*, New York: Vintage Books, 2003.

Kluger, Jeffrey, *The Narcissist Next Door*, New York: Riverhead Books, 2014.

Lawrence, Paul R., and Nohria, Nitin, *Driven—How Human Nature Shapes Our Choices*, Hoboken, NJ: Wiley, 2002.

Martin, Roger, *The Opposable Mind*, Boston: Harvard Business School Press, 2007.

Maure, Ben J.S., *Leading at the Edge: True Tales from Canadian Police in Peacebuilding and Peacekeeping Missions around the World*, Vancouver: self-published. https://www.benmaure.com/book

Milke, Mark, *The Victim Cult*, Toronto: Thomas & Black, 2019.

Musashi, Miyamoto, *The Book of the Five Rings and Other Works*, Translated by Alexander Bennett, Tokyo: Tuttle Publishing, 2018.

Palmer, Parker J., *Let your Life Speak: Listening for the Voice of Vocation*, San Francisco: Jossey-Bass, 1999.

Peterson, Christopher & Seligman, Martin P., *Character Strengths and Virtues*, New York: Oxford University Press, 2004

Rosling, Hans, *Factfulness*, New York: Flatiron Books, 2018

Ruskin, John, *Unto This Last,* New York: E.P. Hutton and Company, 1862.

Sagan, Carl, *The Demon-Haunted World—Science as a Candle in the Dark*, New York: Ballantine Books, 1996.

Sanderson, Catherine A., *Why We Act—Turning Bystanders into Moral Rebels*, Cambridge, Massachusetts: The Belknap Press of Harvard University Press, 2020.

Sutton, Robert, *The No Asshole Rule*, New York: Business Plus, 2007.

Taleb, Nassim Nicholas, *Antifragile*, New York: Random House, 2014.

Taleb, Nassim Nicholas, *The Black Swan*, New York: Random House, 2007.

Weick, Karl E. & Sutcliffe, Kathleen M., *Managing the Unexpected: Resilient Performance in an Age of Uncertainty*, San Francisco: Jossey-Bass, 2001.

Wilkinson, Richard & Pickett, Kate, *The Spirit Level: Why More Equal Societies Almost Always Do Better*, London: Penguin Group, 2011.

JM Blais

Acknowledgements

I want to thank four groups of people for their support in writing this book.

First, those who accepted the daunting challenge to read and correct the initial manuscript: David Peter of Winnipeg, Manitoba, Theresa Rath of Nova Scotia/Costa Rica and Mike Murray of Dartmouth, Nova Scotia. They each offered a critical and constructive eye to detail that would have gone unnoticed had they not taken the time and care for this project. Each one also brought to the book perspectives and enhancements that made the text more reader-friendly and pertinent. You folks absolutely rock!

Second, I want to thank all those who offered their testimonials within a relatively short time frame. Not only did they read the advanced manu-script with a critical eye to detail and offer glowing endorsements, but many also offered further suggestions for improvement that I was able to incorporate before publication.

Third, I thank those who allowed me to chronicle their lives and con-tributions, many of whom live locally in Nova Scotia, but still others who are 'from away' in other parts of Canada, the United States, Haiti, France and Africa. Included in this group are those who are part of my *List of Mentors and Non-mentors* who, during a lifetime of human observation, have provided me with some of the best lessons in how to do things and how *not* to do things. Included in that would be all the Marlos out there who also provided, on occasion, a certain degree of dreary entertain-ment.

Finally, I wish to thank my editor, Andrew Wetmore of Moose House Publications, who immediately saw the value of this project and engaged me in some unique discussions on writing, including correcting a lifetime of 'cop speak' in a few short months. He also impressed me by being only the second person I have ever met who mows his grass with a scythe.

This book is dedicated to my children. It is intended as a way for them to understand who I am and why I act the way I do, and to help them in a certain measure understand the origin of my bad dad jokes. Of course, their presence in my life would not have been possible without the endless support of my wife, Marianne, who encouraged me throughout the majority of the most challenging and rewarding times in my life, sometimes on and most times off the ice.

Thank you, one and all.

JM

About the author

Jean-Michel "JM" Blais spent 31 years in policing as a senior executive with the Royal Canadian Mounted Police and the United Nations, and as chief of Halifax Regional Police. He has worked throughout Canada and was posted in four different provinces. He spent almost two years in Haiti, working as a frontline police officer and senior executive.

Of Franco-Ontarian background, from Sudbury, JM grew up in Montréal and Toronto. He obtained his undergraduate degree from McGill University in Montréal and his law degree from Université Laval in Québec City.

Since 2005, JM has officiated minor hockey as a Hockey Canada Level III official. He initiated both his youngest daughter and son into the world of officiating; both have since surpassed their father in the levels they have officiated. He still regularly officiates out of Halifax, Nova Scotia, where he resides with his wife and two dogs.

JM has published several works on international and national police-related topics and lectured extensively on leadership and modern police management, including mental health and wellness. He has a TEDx talk to his credit. *Working the Blue Lines: Lessons in Leadership from Hockey and Policing* is his first published book. He is also one of the co-authors of a novel, *Less Than Innocent*, which Moose House will publish in the fall of 2022.

JM Blais

Notes

1   Jerry Ratcliffe, *Reducing Crime, A Companion for Police Leaders*, Routledge: London and New York, 2018.

2   See Eli Sopow, *Corporate Personality Disorder*, iUniverse Inc. 2007.

3   Ayiti cherie or Haïti Chérie ("Haiti Dear") is a traditional patriotic song of Haiti adapted from a poem written by Othello Bayard who initially called it Souvenir d'Haïti ("Memory of Haiti"). The poem was composed to music in 1920 and is widely considered a second national anthem as well as one of Haiti's most famous méringues.

4   Promoted posthumously to the rank of Chief Superintendent.

5   The United Nations lost 102 of its staff in the earthquake. Their names and biographies can be found at un.org/en/memorial/haiti/

6   To see the photos taken of that meeting, see *Haiti – One Year Memorial Film* at youtube.com/watch?v=dtf84d5kZ0c.

7   See news.un.org/en/story/2010/01/327552-after-five-days-buried-alive-haiti-un-worker-recalls-moment-rescue

8   Nassim Nicholas Taleb, *Skin in the Game—Hidden Asymmetries in Daily Life*, Random House, New York, 2018, page 125.

9   In his 2005 book, *Fooled by Randomness*, Taleb gives the origins of the notion of the Black Swan: "In his Treatise on Human Nature, the Scots philosopher David Hume posed the issue in the following way (as paraphrased in the now famous black swan problem by John Stuart Mill): No amount of observations of white swans can allow the inference that all swans are white, but the observation of a single black swan is sufficient to refute that conclusion."

10   Numbers varying from an estimated 300,000 HIV-related deaths in 1991 to a high of 1.7 million deaths from 2003 to 2005. On November 30, 2021, *Le Monde* reported that over 680,000 people had died worldwide in 2020 with 10 million infections.

11   And not without its share of intrigue. In the early morning hours of August 31, 1959, 75,000 doses of the polio vaccine, the province's entire supply, were stolen from the Institute of Microbiology and Hygiene of Université de Montréal. Rumors swirled around who could have committed the theft. The chief of the Québec Provincial Police at the time personally led the investigation and speculated that it could have been the new Communist leader of Cuba, Fidel Castro, who ordered the theft or possibly some Arab agents. The stolen vaccine was eventually found on September 3, 1959, in an apartment in downtown Montréal. Two local men were arrested, one of which was convicted of the theft. The trial ended up detailing not only the actions of the men, who had neither sympathies nor links to Cuba or the Middle East, but the chaos surrounding the development of the vaccine, the lack of quality control, the unorganized vaccination campaign, the black-market resale of serum and the many pockets lined in the entire process.

[12] Cyber Crime Assessment 2016, National Crime Agency, at nationalcrimeagency.gov.uk

[13] Five-year cybersecurity study carried out by the UK internet service provider 'Beaming'.

[14] The term is associated to the work of American mathematician and meteorologist Edward Norton Lorenz (1917-2008) who developed the metaphorical example of a tornado being influenced by minor perturbations such as the flapping of the wings of a distant butterfly several weeks previously.

[15] See theguardian.com/business/2008/feb/10/businesscomment1

[16] Strathern was generalizing in her paper "'Improving ratings': audit in the British University System," *European Review*, John Wiley and Sons, 5(3): 305-321, what is known as Goodhart's Law which reads: "Any observed statistical regularity will tend to collapse once pressure is placed upon it for control purposes." Goodhart's Law is named after British economist Charles Goodhart.

[17] Likely misattributed to Albert Einstein, the quote was first documented in William Bruce Cameron's 1963 book *Informal Sociology*, p. 13.

[18] First presented in his book *Out of the Crisis*, published in 1982.

[19] Paragraph 27 of his speech found at mi5.gov.uk/news/the-enduring-terrorist-threat-and-accelerating-technological-change

[20] See 1st NAEF (2021) "Whitepaper: How a Full-Spectrum Approach Will Address Critical Gaps in Countering and Preventing Extremist and Terrorist Threats", available at 1naef.org/media

[21] Sable Island, a small land mass off the east coast of Nova Scotia, is home to a herd of 500 feral, or wild, horses left from numerous shipwrecks in the 18th century. Locals have dubbed the area surrounding the island the "Graveyard of the Atlantic."

[22] The 'Theseus paradox' was first developed by the Greek historian and philosopher Plutarch (46-119 AD) who questioned whether a ship that has been restored by replacing all its parts remains the same vessel. A literal example of a Ship of Theseus is the DSV Alvin, a submersible that has retained its identity despite all of its components being replaced at least once.

[23] On September 10, 2020, a ransomware attack, initially intended to target the computer system at Heinrich Heine University in Dusseldorf, Germany, struck instead the adjoining Dusseldorf University Clinic, preventing the timely treatment of a woman. This resulted in her death.

[24] See Carl Benedikt Frey and Michael A. Osborne, "The Future of Employment: How Susceptible are Jobs to Computerisation"", September 17, 2013, University of Oxford, found at oxfordmartin.ox.ac.uk/downloads/academic/The_Future_of_Employment.pdf.

[25] See ca.news.yahoo.com/blogs/dailybrew/halifax-police-tactical-gear-criticized-at-201514858.html

[26] Cynefin, pronounced "ku-nev-in", is a Welsh word that signifies the factors in our environment and our experience that influence us in ways we can never understand. Dave Snowden of Cognitive Edge developed this approach. For a concise, overview of the Cynefin Framework, see David J. Snowden and Mary E. Boone, "A Leader's Framework for Decision Making", in *Harvard Business Review*, November 2007, pages 69-76. One notable resource using Cynefin is the European Commission's field guide for decision makers, entitled "Managing complexity (and chaos) in times of crisis" and available through the European Union's website at publications.jrc.ec.europa.eu/repository/handle/JRC123629.

[27] Rozenblit, Leonid & Keil, Frank, *Cognitive Science*, "The misunderstood limits of folk science: an illusion of explanatory depth", May 2002, Volume 26, pp. 521-562.

[28] *The Economist*, Obituary – Andrew Marshall, Ask the right question, April 13, 2019 print edition.

[29] See the video entitled "The Invisible Gorilla" at youtube.com/watch?v=UtKt8YF7dgQ. Notice the random presence of the gorilla during the beginning of the video as the psychologist walks into the building.

[30] See deepskyeye.com for more information.

[31] Irving L. Janis, *Groupthink: Psychological Studies of Policy Decisions and Fiascoes*, Boston, Houghton Mifflin, 1972.

[32] See Gary Klein, "Social spatial cognition", *Harvard Business Review*, 85(9): 18-19.

[33] A notion developed by Amy Edmondson in her book, *The Fearless Organization*, John Wiley & Sons, Hoboken, 2018.

[34] In his book *Nuclear Folly* (2021), Russian author Serhii Plokhy documents a slightly different dénouement to the incident, writing that, when the B-59 surfaced, it was harassed by American warplanes firing tracer bullets and flares. This convinced Captain Savitsky that war had broken out. He ordered the B-59 to dive and prepare the T-5 torpedo. At the last moment, the B-59's signals officer noticed a message being flashed by the destroyer USS Cony, apologizing for the aggressive behavior of the planes. According to Plokhy, this action led Captain Arkhipov to countermand the order.

[35] Recognizing that "Media coverage is a flawed gauge of importance," *The Economist* conducted a keyword count analysis of their archives as well as those of *The New York Times*, reporting its results in their of December 19, 2020 to January 1st, 2021 issue of the historical domination of COVID-19 in news coverage.

[36] In March 2019, Lady Gaga appeared on Jimmy Kimmel Live, where she vehemently dismissed social media rumors concerning a possible romance with her co-star in the film *A Star is Born*., stating that "Social

media is the toilet of the internet." In November 2020 during a series of interviews with the BBC, former U.S. President Barack Obama spoke of his concerns about the "erosion of truth", blaming social media for the dissemination of false information and conspiracy theories.

37 See Alex Dorfman *et al*, "Social spatial cognition" in *Neuroscience & Biobehavioral Reviews*, Volume 121, February 2021, pp. 277-290.

38 Geir Jordet *et al*, "Scanning, Contextual Factors, and Association With Performance in English Premier League Footballers: An Investigation Across a Season", *Frontiers in Psychology*, October 2020, Volume 11, Article 553813.

39 An interesting side note to the Haitian riots occurred immediately afterwards on April 21, 2008, 1900 miles to the north of Port-au-Prince in Montréal, Québec. That night, the Montréal Canadiens beat the Boston Bruins to advance to the second round of the Stanley Cup finals. Following the game, a huge victory mob congregated on Montréal's iconic Ste-Catherine Street, and developed into a violent riot causing $500,000 in damage, the burning or smashing of 16 police vehicles and the arrest of as many people. Unfortunately, Montréal has a sad history of such moments, having had a total of five riots related to the NHL franchise (1955, 1986, 1993, 2008 and 2010). Most Haitians I knew and associated with were very embarrassed about their own April riots, but when they learned of what had occurred in Montréal and especially the very short time it took (only two hours) to create so much damage, they were rightly smug to think that even a first-world country like Canada could behave worse than they—and all because of a victory in some game. They were correct in their assessment. It was a humbling experience.

40 Nassim Nicholas Taleb, *Skin in the Game—Hidden Asymmetries in Daily Life,* p. 241.

41 Researcher Rodney J. Korba reported that the extended word count of subvocal activity represented an equivalent rate of speech in excess of 4,000 words per minute. See journals.sagepub.com/doi/10.2466/pms.1990.71.3.1043

42 See the article in the *Journal of Abnormal Psychology*, 44, pp.118-121.

43 One of Barnum's competitors, Syracuse, New York banker David Hannum, coined the famous saying.

44 See Bruce A. Macfarlane, *Wrongful Convictions*, p. 20. Available at attorneygeneral.jus.gov.on.ca/inquiries/goudge/policy_research/pdf/ Macfarlane_Wrongful-Convictions.pdf

45 While writing this book I communicated with Warrant Officer Dumarski, telling him my version of the story. He wrote that, when he saw Julie and me looking so dejected on that street corner, he couldn't help but offer us some assistance. In his words, he offered "a bit of humanity in the chaotic world that surrounded us at that moment."

46 See burnfundmb.ca

[47] See naso.org/survey

[48] Corliss Bean *et al*, *Negative Parental Behavior in Canadian Minor Hockey*, PHEnex Journal, Volume 7, number 3, 2016.

[49] As detailed in *First, Break All the Rules* by Markus Buckingham and Curt Coffman, Simon & Schuster, New York, 1999.

[50] Created by John Manoogian III for Buster Benson.

[51] Interesting examples of such illusions are: the *Müller-Lyer Illusion*, in which three lines having different ends are all the same length although they appear to be different; the *Rubin Vase*, which is an ambiguous or reversing two-dimensional form; and the *Ponzo Illusion*, in which where two identical lines drawn across a pair of converging lines, similar to railway tracks, appear to be of different sizes although they are in fact identical in size.

[52] Although the phenomenon of "flashbulb memories" had been recognized by psychologists for decades, it was only in 1977 that American psychologists Roger Brown (1925-1997) and James Kulik coined the term in their paper of the same name in *Cognition*, 5(1), pp. 73-99.

[53] Initially described by Brazilian lyricist and novelist Paulo Coelho de Souza in his book *Maktub* and reprised by Argentinean psychotherapist Jorge Bucay in *Let Me Tell You a Story* (2013).

[54] Per Wikipedia, "The Fifth Estate is a socio-cultural reference to groupings of outlier viewpoints in contemporary society, and is most associated with bloggers, journalists publishing in non-mainstream media outlets, and the social media or 'social license'. The 'Fifth' Estate extends the sequence of the three classi-cal *Estates of the Realm* of French political structure and the preceding *Fourth Estate*, essentially the mainstream press. Use of "fifth estate" dates to 1960s counterculture, and in particular the influential *The Fifth Estate*, an underground newspaper first published in Detroit in 1965. Web-based technologies have enhanced the scope and power of the Fifth Estate far beyond the modest and boutique conditions of its beginnings."

[55] "Halifax police force more diverse than community it serves", CBC News, July 14, 2016: cbc.ca/news/canada/nova-scotia/halifax-police-force-community-diversity-ethnicity-race-1.3679001. In Halifax, 12,1 percent of police officers are either indigenous or visible, non-white minorities. According to the 2016 census, 11.6 percent of the population of Halifax was non-white.

[56] See cbc.ca/news/canada/nova-scotia/halifax-regional-police-spending-merchandise-1.4995659

[57] See cacpglobal.ca/index.php/cohorts/cohort-2018.

[58] Roger Martin, *The Opposable Mind*, Harvard Business School Press, Boston, 2007.

[59] See npr.org/2020/09/10/909380525/nypd-study-implicit-bias-training-changes-minds-not-necessarily-behavior

[60] In a January 6, 2021 article, the *New York Times* reported that from a high of 1.7 million in 1991, car thefts in the US dropped by more than 50 percent in subsequent years. A major uptick was noted during the pandemic in 2020 as people were leaving their key fobs in their cup holders and elsewhere in their vehicles. Or they would take their key fob with them when they left their unlocked and still-running car to run an errand, allowing the vehicle to be driven away – though not restarted later. In a few cases, criminals have also used technology to reprogram keyless cars. See wwwnytimes.com/2021/01/06/nyregion/car-thefts-nyc.html.

[61] *Does the Relative Income of Peers Cause Financial Distress? Evidence from Lottery Winners and Neighboring Bankruptcies* by Sumit Agarwal, Vyacheslav Mikhed and Barry Scholnick.

[62] *Keeping up with the Joneses* was an American daily newspaper comic strip drawn by Arthur R. "Pop" Momand (1887-1987) from 1913 to 1938. The strip depicted the four members of the McGinis family as they struggled to "keep up" with the lifestyle of their neighbors. Although the comic is long gone, the phrase remains as a reference to people's tendency to judge their own social standing according to that of those around them.

[63] T.J. Scheff, "Shame as the Master Emotion in Modern Societies," *Journal of General Practice,* 04(01), 2016, in which he qualifies shame or its anticipation as being "virtually ubiquitous, yet, at the same time, usually invisible."

[64] See newsweek.com/sociopaths-more-likely-refuse-wear-masks-1526985

[65] Believing firmly that some people deserve to suffer the ignominy of consigning their crimes to silence, I didn't refer to Constable Czapnik's murderer by name.

[66] Several high-profile police officer deaths have also occurred recently in Canada: a lone gunman shot and killed two Fredericton, New Brunswick, police officers and two citizens on August 10, 2018; five RCMP officers were shot, three fatally, on June 4, 2014 in Moncton, New Brunswick; three RCMP officers were shot, two fatally, in Spiritwood, Saskatchewan, on July 7, 2006; and four RCMP officers were shot and killed in Mayerthorpe, Alberta on March 3, 2005. Canada's worst mass shooting occurred in rural Nova Scotia on April 18-19, 2020, at the onset of the COVID-19 pandemic, when an individual went on a 12-hour shooting rampage, killing 22 people, including one RCMP officer.

[67] https://www.washingtonpost.com/graphics/investigations/police-shootings-database/. In the five years since *The Post* has been compiling the statistics, the number of shooting deaths has remained steady at nearly 1,000 per year.

[68] newsinteractives.cbc.ca/fatalpoliceencounters/

[69] See the Police Executive Research Forum (PERF) guide "Suicide by Cop: Protocol and Training Guide" at policeforum.org/suicidebycop

[70] In 2018, a graduate student in criminology at the University of Toronto wrote a paper entitled "The CBC Police Deadly Force Database is Misleading." Erick Laming wrote of the importance of a such a database, but that it must be official, accurate, consistent and complete, qualities that the CBC database didn't demonstrate. He examined several of the cases reported and determined that, although officers may have been present, their actions in no way resulted in the deaths of the individuals. In his estimation, "the database exaggerates the number of people killed by police and this is an unfair and deceitful representation of police 'deadly force' in Canada."

[71] Research Note, "Work-Related Deaths in Canada", by Steven Bittle, Ashley Chen and Jasmine Hébert, available on the Workers Health & Safety Centre (Ontario) website.

[72] "While our hospitals save lives every day, they're also the third leading cause of avoidable deaths every day. In Canada, medical errors and hospital-acquired infections claim between 30,000 and 60,000 lives annually. Thousands more are injured," wrote Kathleen Finlay, CEO of The Center for Patient Protection, in her 2015 blog post, "Preventable Medical Error is Canadian Healthcare's Silent Killer".

[73] See odmp.org/search/year?year=2020. The "2020 Law Enforcement Officers Fatalities Report" and the "2021 End-Of-Year Preliminary Law Enforcement Officers Fatalities Report" published by the National Law Enforcement Memorial and Museum.

[74] See J. Kruger & David Dunning, "Unskilled and unaware of it: How difficulties in recognizing one's own incompetence lead to inflated self-assessments" in *Journal of Personality and Social Psychology,* 1(6): pp. 30-46, January 2009.

[75] Daniel Breyer, Illinois State University, *Understanding the Dark Side of Human Nature,* Chantilly, Virginia, The Great Courses, 2019.

[76] A recent case of such abuse in Canada was that of Jessica Yaniv, a transgendered woman who laid numerous complaints against various waxing salons in British Columbia that refused to wax Yaniv's existing male genitalia. All of the women complained of were young immigrants, a group of people the complainant had openly been hostile to in prior social media posts. The complaints were either found to not be established or brought for improper motives. The complainant was subsequently ordered to pay $2000 to three of the alleged defendants because of the improper conduct.

[77] See the decision *Al-Ghamdi v College of Physicians and Surgeons of Alberta,* 2020 ABCA 71, at http://canlii.ca/t/j59f9

[78] See Albert J. Bernstein, *Emotional Vampires* , McGraw-Hill, New York, 2012.

79 See Albert J. Bernstein and Sydney Craft Rozen, *Neanderthals at Work*, Ballantine Books, 1996.

80 See Marshall Shelley, *Well-Intentioned Dragons*, Bethany House, Minneapolis, MN, 1994.

81 See G. Lloyd Rediger, *Clergy Killers – Guidance for Pastors and Congregations Under Attack*, Westminster John Knox Press, Louisville, KY, 1997.

82 thecanadianencyclopedia.ca/en/article/hutterites

83 Named after American psychologist J. Ridley Stroop (1897-1973), it's the delay in reaction time between congruent and incongruent stimuli. A common example of a *Stroop test* is when participants are asked to state the color of the font in a series of words that depict colors, none of which correspond to the actual color stated by the word.

84 See the BBC article "Dunbar's number: Why we can only maintain 150 relationships" at bbc.com/future/article/20191001-dunbars-number-why-we-can-only-maintain-150-relationships.

85 Numerous studies and works detailing the unexpected 'positive' effects of war on mental health outcomes such as suicide include French sociologist Émile Durkheim's *Suicide: A Study in Sociology* (1897), Canadian psychologist John Thompson MacCurdy's *The Structure of Morale* (1943), and Irish psychologist H.A. Lyons' *Civil Violence: The Psychological Aspects*, published in the *Journal of Psychosomatic Research 23* (1979): 373-93. They all observed that rates of suicide are higher in peacetime than during wars, leading them to postulate that people who have purpose have corresponding improvements in mental health, even during periods of war and extreme violence.

86 Matthew 7:12.

87 Per Dan Kahan *et al* in the paper "Culture and Identity-Protective Cognition: Explaining the White Male Effect in Risk Perception", found at papers.ssrn.com/sol3/papers.cfm?abstract_id=995634

88 Used by the Greek rhetorician Isocrates (436-338 BC), Rabbi Hillel Hazaken (Hillel the Elder, 110-8 BCE) and also found in one of the two major Sanskrit epics of ancient India, the *Mahabharata*, which at 13.114.8 states: "One should never do something to others that one would regard as an injury to one's own self. In brief, this is dharma. Anything else is succumbing to desire."

89 Conducted for *The Manifest*, a website based in Washington, D.C. See the article by Toby Fox, "How Different Generations Use Social Media", at www.manifest.com.

90 What Aristotle actually wrote was: "In the case of all things which have several parts and in which **the totality is not, as it were, a mere heap, but the whole something besides the parts**, there is a cause." 980a, *Metaphysics*. As well, "... **that the whole is not the same as the sum of its parts** are useful in meeting the type just described; for a man who defines in this way seems to assert that the parts are the

same as the whole." 100a, *Topics*, both translated by W.D. Ross.

[91]   See listeninginstitute.com

[92]   Translated from the original French. See her comments during the interview at lavie.fr/actualite/france/arnaud-beltrame-mon-mari-26-03-2018-88964_4.php

[93]   See albernstern.com/checklist.php for helpful descriptions, check-lists and protective measures pertaining to *Emotional Vampires*.

[94]   Some of the information detailed here comes from the "Personality Disorders in Social Work & Health Care" course materials workbook, Third Edition, by Gregory W. Lester, Cross Country Education, 2004.

[95]   See "An Antidote to Incivility", by Christine Porath, in the April 2016 issue of the *Harvard Business Review*.

[96]   The effect is related to the Greek myth of Pygmalion, a legendary sculptor who fell in love with one of his sculptures. Also known as the *Rosenthal Effect*, named after the German-born American psychologist Robert Rosenthal, who, along with his research associate Lenore Jacobsen, developed the idea that a teacher's expectations help shape students' performance. Subsequent research has questioned this view.

[97]   Essentially a form of self-fulfilling prophecy whereby lower expectations placed on individuals either by supervisors or the individual themself result in poor performance. The effect is named after the golem, an animated human-like creature made from clay or some other inanimate matter found in Jewish folklore, long before J.R.R. Tolkien wrote his epic fantasy, *Lord of the Rings*, in which the character's name was spelled Gollum.

[98]   See Chapter 7. Per research conducted by the CBC, since 2000 27 people on average die every year in Canada through interactions with police. Between 20 and 30 police officers die by suicide in Canada every year. If we include recent retirees, those figures are considerably higher.

[99]   Per the website *BLUE H.E.L.P.* whose home page reads: "All officers, regardless of method of death, deserve thanks; all families deserve your support." See bluehelp.org.

[100]   See who.int/mental_health/prevention/suicide/suicideprevent/en/

[101]   "Suicidal Ideation, Plans, and Attempts Among Public Safety personnel in Canada," in *Canadian Psychology/ Psychologie canadienne*, 2018, Vol. 59, No. 3, pp. 220-231.

[102]   By Jack Crosbie. See menshealth.com/health/a20944664/police-officer-suicide-rate-mental-health/

[103]   As reported by Statistics Canada at canada.ca/en/public-health/services/suicide-prevention/suicide-canada.html.

[104]   As reported by the US Centers for Disease Control (CDC). See nimh.nih.gov/health/statistics/suicide.shtml.

[105] As reported by the Centers for Disease Control and Prevention (CDC) National Center for Health Statistics, there were more than 90,000 overdose deaths from all types of drugs in the United States for the 12-month period that ended in October 2020, up more than 20 percent from the same period a year earlier. The Police Assisted Addiction and Recovery Initiative (PAARI) expects the 2020 numbers related to fatal and nonfatal overdoses to be even higher.

[106] "A Public Health Crisis Decades in the Making—A Review of 2019 CDC Gun Mortality Data (February 2021)", jointly issued by The Education Fund to Stop Gun Violence and The Coalition to Stop Gun Violence, reported that 39,707 people, 86 percent of whom were male, died in 2019 of gun violence. One in ten gun violence victims were children or teens. In 2019, firearms were the leading cause of death for American children, teens and young adults aged under 25. The report detailed how young Black children and men die from gun violence at a rate twenty times higher than their White male counterparts. See efsgv.org/2019cdcdata.

[107] See the report in the *Canadian Medical Association Journal* at cmaj.ca/content/192/42/E1253. According to the June 2018 *Briefing Paper* prepared by Aaron Karp for the Geneva-based research group *Small Arms Survey* (smallarmssurvey.com), there are 120.5 firearms per 100 Americans and 34.7 firearms per 100 Canadians. It is estimated that Americans possess 46% of the world's 860 million civilian-held legal and illicit firearms.

[108] On January 22, 2021, the NGO *Germanwatch* reported that in the twenty-year period from 2000-2019, nearly 480,000 people died as a result of more than 11,000 extreme weather events. See germanwatch.org/en/19802

[109] As reported in the article "Five insights from the Global Burden of Disease Study 2019," *The Lancet*, October 17, 2020, "The interaction of COVID-19 with the continued rise in chronic illness and risk factors, including obesity, high blood sugar, and outdoor air pollution, over the past 30 years has created a perfect storm, fueling COVID-19 deaths." See healthdata.org/news-release/lancet-latest-global-disease-estimates-reveal-perfect-storm-rising-chronic-diseases-and

[110] A February 2021 study published in the scientific journal *Environmental Research* detailed how the World Health Organization estimated that in 2016 there were 4.2 million deaths worldwide caused by air pollution. The study, "Global mortality from outdoor fine particle pollution generated by 2 fossil fuel combustion: Results from GEOS-Chem", determined that, for 2018, there were 8.7 million deaths attributable to air pollution, or one death in every five across the planet. China had the most victims with 2.4 million deaths, followed by India with 2 million. In November 2021, India ordered a four-day closing of schools and construction sites to deal with a spike of deadly

particulate matter in the air because of increased pollution resulting from the burning of crop residues in neighboring states that coincided with cooler temperatures that trapped the deadly smoke.

[111] One of the best overviews of stress and its potential benefits can be found in the TEDx talk *How to make stress your friend* by the American psychologist Kelly McGonigal at ted.com/talks/kelly_mcgonigal_how_to_make_stress_your_friend

[112] In *Religion Explained: The Evolutionary Origins of Religious Thought*, New York, Basic Books, 2001.

[113] See the article by Joyce Mikal-Flynn *et al*, "Mental Fitness and Post-traumatic Stress Growth" in *Police Chief Magazine*, November 2018.

[114] Heng, Yu Tse and Schabram, Kira, "Your Burnout is Unique. Your Recovery Will Be, Too", *Harvard Business Review*, April 12, 2021.

[115] "The influence of leaders' diminished psychological resources of leadership behaviors," Alyson Byrne *et al*, *The Leadership Quarterly*, Volume 25, Issue 2, April 2014, pages 344-357. See also "Minds Turned to Ash," *1843 Magazine*, August/September 2016 issues, pp. 82-87.

[116] See *The Epidemiology and Impact of Dementia – Current State and Future Trends,* World Health Organization, 2015, at who.int/mental_health/neurology/dementia/dementia_thematicbrief_epidemiology.pdf

[117] US Department of Health and Human Services, national Institutes of Health, National Institute on Drug Abuse, (1997) *Preventing drug use among children and adolescents: A research-based guide,* NIH Publication No. 97-4212.

[118] Per the *Population Reference Bureau*, see prb.org.

[119] From the poem of the same name, *La noche oscura del alma*, by the 16th-century Spanish mystic and poet St. John of the Cross.

[120] See nber.org/workplacewellness/

[121] Elain Wethington & Ronald C. Kessler, "Perceived Support, Received Support, and Adjustment to Stressful Life Events", in *Journal of Health and Social Behavior 1986*, Vo. 27 (March): 78-89.

[122] Described by the *New York Times* columnist Adam Grant as "a sense of stagnation and emptiness" in his April 19, 2021 article *There's a Name for the Blah You're Feeling: It's Called Languishing*, citing the work of Corey L.M. Keyes *et al* in the research paper "Change in Level of Positive Mental Health as a Predictor of Future Risk of Mental Illness" in *American Journal of Public Health 100*, pages 2366-2371, December 2010.

[123] Book review by Brian D. Evans in *Inc.com*, June 27, 2017.

[124] *Making peace with death: National attitudes to death, dying and bereavement*, Co-op Funeralcare Media Report, May 2018. See secure.co-operativefuneralcare.co.uk/news/making-peace-with-death/